CAT MAN

at the

HORN OF AFRICA

To: Anthony & family
Feb.18/22

Abas

ABAS HASANTU

ISBN 978-1-64349-202-5 (paperback)
ISBN 978-1-64349-203-2 (digital)

Christian Faith Publishing, Inc.
832 Park Avenue
Meadville, PA 16335
www.christianfaithpublishing.com

Printed in the United States of America

CHAPTER ONE

Part 1
The Cat Birth

I recall I was a tiny, naked African baby who would suck on my mother's bosom's disrobed body. I had no idea what was happening to my family and surrounding area. All I knew was to be bumped on the head like a cow in a slaughterhouse by my mother. I could hear her harsh voice and see her tiger face of anger whenever I might have bitten her breast. It was as if she wanted to swallow my head alive from the pain that I had to put her through. No matter what the consequence had been to my skull, hands, or buttocks, it became my hobby and everyday chore for which I could not give up.

One day, my mother took me to a far sheer village on crest of a mountain about eight miles away on bare feet. For I could not walk yet, still strapped on her back, I tried gazing everywhere beyond our path just to take in as much as I could. I didn't know why she took me there, but for some reason, I enjoyed the trip on her back, with her song for me, *daadde borruu gallaa,*[1] I didn't completely understand it, but with time, I began to learn her language. A narrow pathway leading us to some settlement surrounded by a farm densely covered with sorghum and corn trees. The bushes were about to swallow us up for dinner as we passed by. My heart began to beat faster and harder than a drum, threatening to pop out of my chest. There was something stuck in my throat that I had no clue what so ever to

---

[1] Even if we crawl, we will be home tomorrow for sure.

3

what it was. Then, I felt as if my lung was about to explode on her back when I heard a noise that deafened my ears. As we kept going, we reached a lake that was joined by a river, and we had to cross the small, wooden bridge that was shaking with gaps in it, to get to the other side. Again I was frightened by the bridge's state, but I enjoyed the view of the blue water that was like the sky, flowing under it to another lake. I was happy seeing a big sapphire lake full of different huge white birds like swans as big as boats and many kinds of ducks I had never seen before.

As my mother was climbing a high mountain, I felt as if I was about to fall off her back, down to the bottom of the mountain into the lake full of those swans and ducks. Instantly, I filled with more fear as I gazed down from her back. But this time, my mother came to my aid, patting my bottom gently, and it was so cozy that I wanted to fall asleep despite the spooky mountain. There were birds as bigger than any I had ever seen before running in front of us from one bush to the other. I was amazed how big the birds were, and I thought they were going to peck us. My mom was reassuring me that they were only bush birds and not harmful to us. She was breathing as if she had asthma because of the height of the mountain. About half an hour after, we arrived to a village full of strange people. My mother was talking and saying hello to them and they seemed to praise me for being one of her children. Some of them came to caress my head. Some even pulled my nose in a funny way, and others also pulled my Mohawk style hair cut with their filthy, mucky hands. I did not like the way they welcomed me, but I had no choice than to bear every-thing that they did to me. I was dealing with these people until we finally arrived to the beautiful, nice old lady's house that didn't smell like a farting zone.

As we were entering her house, she greeted my mother warmly and grabbed me from her back into her arms and embraced me. When I got a closer look at her, I stared at black spots on her face, wondering what it could be while she looked in my eyes. Her kind-ness and beauty engulfed my curiosity from the black marks. After our greetings, she ran to her *dera*[2] and brought freshly-made *injera*[3] and wood-scented milk that I had never seen and smelled before. As I munched on injera and sifted milk, I began to float in space like a balloon with my bulky stomach. I said to myself this must be a heaven people talk about and brooded to stay with her forever and wished not to leave at all. Unfortunately, she forced me to leave even though I cried and argued to stay as much as I could. When she took me back home, day after day, I wanted to go back with her so that I learn the way how to go there by myself.

I started gazing surrounding area and villages where I was born, especially to that direction where I discovered that delicious injera and milk. Many beautiful mountains, two big lakes and blue sky made me think how crazy and tough they were for God to create all these things that spread in front of me about fifteen kilometers away from our house. It astonished me how the sun could appear every day behind mountain of our house in the morning and travelled all day long on top of us and then setting behind the mountain of that old lady's house. It made me overjoyed any time it came out, for I could see all kinds of creatures running around. All different types of birds, some noisy and scary, and some had a beautiful sounds of songs they made. Farmers were going to their lands to dig with spades on their shoulders as cows moo, goats and sheep cry along them with whatever they got. There were also many shepherd kids going with their animals to grazing land by those lakes, which made me jealous. Everything happening as the sun came up made me excited to see them all.

At about age six, my job as shepherd was to watch our only cow and my mom would give me *dumucho*[4] circled like a ball, sometimes filled with hot chilli powder poured in the middle, which was my favourite food to eat for lunch. I would go with crazy villagers boys and girls who were almost adults and mostly bigger than me to grazing fields. About noon, everyone brought out their different lunches

---

[2]   Little storage room made of mud like bigger fridge very dark inside, or spooky.
[3]   Wide, flat bread made from Teff.
[4]   Cone-shaped grain bread filled with various fillings.

and some shared and some ate alone. We played different kind of games at or after start of lunch time. While we were going to eat, adults would say "Let's play a game. Younger ones to look up to a blue sky and make a hissing sounds like bees while we look down and make funny munching sounds." After a while, they would order us, "All right you can look down, game is over." When we looked down, there nothing was left on the sheet, all lunches were gone to make us cry and go home hungry.

Sometimes our cow ran like crazy, and I didn't know what was happening to it. I ran and ran to catch it, becoming unsuccessful to stop it and it would disappear from my sight. I cried every time this happened because I was afraid that my father or mom would kill me for losing our only cow. Later, I found out that there was a type of vampire fly that bit the animals to suck on their blood and hurt them very seriously. They had to run for their life to escape it, and it was very hard to catch or stop them. I ran to catch our cow, but she got lost and I got very tired anytime this happened. I returned home without it and told my mom and she would tell my dad. Then he would go around the village to find it. If he found it with a bunch of cows, he would leave it there until next day and came back home without it since our area was infected with hungry and dangerous hyenas roaming around villages and streets as the sun went down. Sometimes they stayed in the fields or nearby bushes by road. As soon as animal passed by them, they would jump on it and ate them to the bone, the reason why my dad was scared to bring it home. Even young children and some adults were at risk in the evening because some of these hyenas were very daring and strong wild animals that stayed in the farms. If a farmer chased from his field, it just went to another farm, refusing to go to their home in the mountains.

One day, my mom told me that she was going to the nice old lady's house, and I asked, "Can I go with you to her house?"

"Yes, you can come with me," she assured. I was so happy to hear this news.

"Wait! Who is going to take care of our crazy cow?" I wondered.

She replied, "Your dad will tie her to a tree in the farm and then give it weeds, grass, and corn leaves from the farm." I was relieved hearing that it was going to be taken care of by him. I was so anxious to go with my mom; I woke up several times from my bed to wake her up. When I couldn't be patient anymore, I went to her bed many times to wake her up, but she kept saying that I should go to bed and wait until the sun rises. I tried to fall asleep again and again, but I couldn't stop thinking about it. I kept saying, "When will this sun come out?"

I felt like almost cursing her why she didn't come out as quickly as usual. Suddenly, I heard the birds chirping, singing, and some calling my mother's name, saying, "*Gu gu, gu gu gu.*[5] *Faten laga kutee*[6]," which I heard from people that interpret a song of pigeon especially for my mom. Every time these birds came close by me and opened their mouths and sang for my mother, these people, young or adult, would sing along, looking at me and mocked me. They would keep going and going at it until I cried and drained my tears. I felt like beating the hell out of them if I could and swallowed them alive like anaconda with these birds every time this happened. I found all of them being rude to insult my mom like this on purpose as I believed. However, this day, these birds became very special, singing and chirping her name to alert me that it was morning time so that we got ready to go to that old lady's house. I gave them special thanks only for this day so that I ate that delicious food of my dream and hoped they would not sing this song again to piss me off.

I ran to my mother's bed and woke her up saying, "Mom! Mom! Listen! Birds calling your name, get up, get up, and tugged her hand."

She said, "All right, son," she got up and went to fetch water to cook for us as usual and to give me shower with it. I waited for her eagerly outside our house till she appeared with it from far away. When I saw her entering the village, I ran as fast as I could to help her and brought her home quickly. She warned me not to drop a gourd full of water on a ground, and I promised not to do it. I also helped her cutting onion and potato so that she could cook lunch rapidly since we ate our lunch early morning as our tradition. After we ate,

---

[5]   Song melody.

[6]   "Your mother, Fate, went to fetch water from valley river."

she washed my body, and we were getting ready to leave. Then my best friend of all, Muste, showed up as usual for us to go to our shepherd's duty. I told Muste, "I am going with my mother far away and not able to go with you." After Muste had gone very sadly, my father had also left with his spade and crazy cow to our farm. This time since I got bigger, I had to walk behind her, for she could not carry me anymore.

I faced bushy, narrow roads with prickles, not easy to walk about as different thorns began tugging, cutting, and boring my skins. Blood began to flow from it and some leaves even irritated and swollen my hands and legs. Some of the black feathered thorns of weeds glued to my pants and began biting my legs. I tried to be patient until I reached that milk and injera that would soothe my cuts and skin. I found this day to be very difficult and tiring, for I was running after my mom with pain because she was very tall and her strides were like an ostrich. I had to constantly sprint and catch up to her so that I save my life from being pecked by ducks, geese, snakes, ostriches, and hyenas that were scaring me. I was also feared those cannibals I heard snatch kids from street and murder them if not staying with the family. These fears to save my life and those delicious treats made me run harder after my mom. At the same time, I tried to learn the way if some day I had to go there alone to get these delicious foods. I asked my mom to teach me the way too, but she murmured, "You should know the way by now to your grandma's place." I came to know she was my grandmother after all, and she was the best master chef in making soft white injera and wooden, smoked milk better than anyone in the country, which I could eat and drink all day long if I had a belly the size of an elephant. Knowing this, I tried my best to remember the route as much as I could and realized that it was very far away. I asked my mother how much farther we had to go to get there. She assured me that it wasn't too far. Once she realized that I got tired and unable to keep up with her, she sometimes tugged me like boat onto the shore.

After a while, we then saw some villagers from grandma who were going to draw water from that blue lake full of ducks, swans, and goose. Then I was happy feeling we might be getting closer to grandma's place now. Villagers greeted us, "How are you fate, kid?"

I replied to them in a shy manner, "I am fine." After we went on that difficult narrow road filled with bushes and thorns, we again encountered that scary, heavy big birds ran in front of us and my heart started drumming. I ran to hug my mom and hid between her legs and *sadeta*.[7] She assured me again that they were not dangerous birds, but *gogari*.[8] I was surprised to hear this and asked if there were more scaring animals from past people that left to scare me. She giggled a little bit to my question and curiosity. She explained, "Those foxes howling every morning and trying to snatch chicken from our village are ancient people, dogs, rabbits are their cats and so on." Finally, I understood that all these wild animals that were scaring me and running in the bushes were ancient people's domestic animals. I had no idea why some were scaring me and some were very dangerous to us while some of them were scared from us. I did not see any wild humans who owned them yet, but wondered what they looked like and if they also came out to attack me. Everything about the past life began to hunt me down as I wobbled along my mom.

By the time we had to climb that very high hill again, at one point, I was unable to move anymore. I cried when I was almost slid down the hill and she caught me from point of falling to death. As my heart was beating, we finally reached grandma's place; I could not wait until she greeted me with that delicious food and milk; I was hoping to pass them on my lips. Her house was so beautiful the way she designed it, putting lamp on, a few ornaments made of gourd, mud shelving, and curved short walls. The house smelt very good as if God lent her one of those houses from heaven. A dry cow's skin carpet she furnished on ground was so soft, not stained with pee like ours. I wanted to roll on it back and forth like donkey in the ashes. I wished we had all these things in our house. While I was talking to some of my aunts whom I had never seen before, my grandma went in dera and came up with a cup of her signature milk and that white

---

[7]   Long and loose skirt like traditional dress.

[8]   Ancient People's domesticated chickens looked like turkey

injera made of corn flour and white sorghum, looking like white wings of angels.

Seeing these things on her hands, I wanted to fly like a bird and grabbed them from her hands quickly and shoved them in my mouth. Anyway I waited patiently and at last she gave them to me to drink the milk and chewed that soft injera. My stomach that was boiling and burning like a volcano soothed right away. I felt them healing those cuts and pains all the way to my feet. I forgotten all that had happened to me. I found myself in different world, like floating in space with happiness. I told her how I loved her food and mentioned to her that my mom could not make food like her at all. They then all laughed at me. Grandma seemed very rich with many cows that she milked, and she had a variety of grains to make nice injera. Her hands were neater and more beautiful than my mom's, as if she borrowed them from caucasian people, and God gave them for free. I thought her beautiful hands had to do with baking this nice food and smoked milk so neat and fresh. I wished my mom had an exact copy of her hands and wondered why God didn't give her, too, for being her daughter.

After indulging myself with these delicious foods, I thanked and blessed her for everything. While they were talking about me, I began thinking how I was tired getting here and eager to eat the food and brooded about staying with her forever if it was possible. I hated my mom's injera and the rare milk I got from her which didn't taste like grandma at all. Going back home started to bother me. I went outside to look around what the village might have looked like and the view from grandma's house. It was very scary to be on this hilly village with a lot of bushes and looking down the hill I felt as if I was going to tumble down from there. I also feared there might be so many wild beasts there coming to snatch me. It might not worth to stay here just for food and milk, I thought. Besides, the hill above me had huge bulldozers, which I had never seen before. I was scared they might roll down on the house and flatten me there in it. The mountain view was breathtaking and it frozen me like statue to see down to bottom of mountain at that blue lake and surrounding irrigated land full of vegetables around it. There were hundreds of farmers working in the farm, bare skin digging with spade. Many birds in the lake swimming and boats made of grass pulled by long stick with hand like motors by their captains. I was excited to see all these besides its scary hill, rocks, and bushes.

After studying and understanding everything in the area, I jumped like a little goat and went back inside. I sat by the side of my mom full of happiness swallowing me. Every second, I wondered and thought about staying there, and feared when my mom would say, "Let us go back home." Then as a day became short, I saw a big, red sun closer like I had never seen before. Its long legs stretched over the mountains to the west where it usually set from where I used to see it, but now, she was so close to me. I felt like I could jump and touch its face while she was setting. After a couple of jumps like a kangaroo, it looked it could set.

My mom seemed on her last words with grandma for us to leave. Then at last she asked me to get ready to leave and my heart shocked to leave grandma and her delicious food. She said, "Get up, we have to go."

"No, no, I don't want to go," I reiterated.

"Do you want to stay here?" she asked.

I replied, "Yes."

"Get up, get up," she stressed. She wanted to know, "Why do you say I do not want to go?"

I replied, "Beautiful grandma's house, injera, and milk will not allow me to leave! I have no chance to come back here soon so I like to stay here for good. Grandma's house very comfortable for me." I tried to convince her.

Seeing that I was very serious to stay, she suddenly bombed me, "Your older brother was also adopted by grandma. You didn't know him yet, if you remain here who will take care of your crazy cow." She added, "Besides, if I leave you here your dad would kill me. He was still crying and regretting for your brother who we gave to your grandma every single day. He was mostly accusing me as my fault to pressure him for your brother to be given away." She further filled me in, "When your brother was about two years old, he got very sick and we have exhausted all medicine and doctors who could not cure him, and on the verge of his dying, grandma asked us to give him in case he survived for her. I mostly agreed to give him up and he miraculously got better and survived after he came here. It looks as if grandma made him sick on purpose to get him with her evil eyes as some aged people do in our area, or God had listened to her prayer to have one boy which she did not have at all. Ever since then he stayed here as her son." She went on, "I have eight sisters altogether and most of them are married." No wonder grandma adopted my older brother, and I got jealous for he was the lucky one to stay in the house full of milk and good eats every day these delicious foods. I felt he might be cured by grandma's food, but got sick with my mom's diet.

I wanted to know where he was and she told me he was in a far away farm, with a big tree in it. I could see from grandma's house a farm and this big tree where they usually sat under to eat food, smoke, and chew kat^9 as they took break. I wondered how big he could be and what he might look like. What he might say if he saw me or what he might say if he knew I wanted to stay here with him. It was our culture for boys to stay home to end their life at house they were born at and took care of elders while girls got married and bred kids for other families. Son meant their welfare till they died and a way of only survival since there was no pension or help from the government. My mom assured me that my brother was forever grandma and granddad's welfare. He had no chance to come our house, and I was shocked to see my mom cried that they were going to miss me and I was their only son. She said that my grandfather was very old and he needed my brother to help him in the farm and also to shepherd their cows that gave me nice milk. She begged, grabbed, and pulled my hand to go with her.

I said, "I will go with you if you only give me injera and milk like grandma."

She then said, "All right, I will give you like her." I agreed, doubting that to be true. My grandma saw I was about to cry to leave her, and she assured me that my mom would again bring me to her.

---

9   Green, chewy leaf with the same effect as caffeine makes you high.

She stressed my mom to bring me next time she came, and I was happy to hear this comment.

Grandma said, "All right, goodbye now," and she encouraged us to go fast home for it was going to be dark soon. Then I got scared, if we could make home safely, for the way was far. The road was full of those dangerous animals, especially the hyena, which I feared my mom wouldn't be able to defend it, dragging me from her side.

The sun was going down, and we had to go in a dark street that had no light and very scary even in a broad daylight. The fear of facing that scavenger hyenas began to worry me. Down the bad hill, we began and I had almost slipped and fell on the challenging hill for I didn't have proper brake for it. Again, my mom helped me to go down as my knees bent down like dinosaur's front legs. Once I almost smashed my face in cactus thorns if I didn't get help from her. After sometimes, we managed to finish dangerous hills, and I began running in front of her as if I was saving my life from animals might go behind me. When I was tired, sometimes I ran after her, scanning both sides of the bushes for any giggling hyenas and its movement. I was also on the lookout for knee ramming skunk that people talking about that usually roamed road ways in the dark. When I burped that delicious food of grandma, I was excited and tried to forget these fears that bothering me to rest. My running around also made me feeling like I was going to throw up. I was happy; at last, we reached home safely. In the evening, my dad came home, I told him with excitement how I ate nice food at grandma, heard about my brother, and all things I had seen and learnt there. I saw my father got very proud of me for things I learnt.

When morning came, I woke up very happy to tell my friend Muste about that milk and injera that I had and things I learnt, but I was sad for him, for he didn't get a chance to enjoy like me. I promised him to take him there very soon so that he ate that injera and drank that smoked milk, and showed him all amazing things I saw for being my best friend. He agreed to go with me someday. I could not wait until I took him with me. We continued our shepherd duties, and after two weeks, I started thinking to go with my friend to grandma's place as promised without telling our family. I didn't expect bad things to happen. I had never thought what the consequence would be to go alone without telling them.

One day, we had a fight with one kid out of the blue. He was bigger than me, and someone I would not able to defeat and dared to fight. When he began chasing me, I tried to escape by running as much as I could in a flat grazing land and all the kids ran after us to see the fight. After a kilometer chase, he finally caught to me and we held each other's arms and shoulder and started to wrestle who would drop on the ground first like a ball and sit on the belly. All kids purposely wanted to see who could defeat who and there was no way they wanted to separate us or come between us to stop the fighting. Muste and my dad were little far away from us, but they might think we were playing as usual and they had never thought I was in a fight at all. If my dad knew that I was in a fight with that kid, he could have come to cut his head off with *mancha*.[10] After many struggle of pushing and shoving, I was able to drop him on a ground, and sat on his tummy like horse and tried to keep him down to give up a fight and respect me as strong and tough boy. All fight watchers were applauded me and I didn't want to get off him. He then tried hard to tumble me off his stomach on the ground and on his last hard attempt; he let one big fart went off like huge grenade. Every one there cracked like old wood. He also made me laugh as birds left their nest without their chicks because of his explosion.

I was proud to defeat him in a shameful way as farting in public was very bad thing in our culture. He would be known and insulted as *Abba Dhufu*.[11] No one dared to do it even by accident. After he sprayed me like skunk, he began to scratch my hands like crazy. Then I got short sorghum's shaft and was able to hit his forehead several times and heavy blood started gushing down and washed his face. I was really shocked by seeing heavy blood, what I had done and jumped of him. His villager's shepherds started crying loudly, "U, u, u." Blood running and crying of everyone there made me dizzy and

---

[10] Sharp, crescent shaped iron weapon fixed on long stick used for cutting plants or for self-defense.
[11] Father of the gas.

vomit. I was scared and began running as much as I could toward my home about three kilometer away. Bloody kid also got up and ran after me. Before he got me, I grabbed sorghum cane and tried to stop him by swinging side to side. When he did not stop, I hit his waist three times and he fell down. Then after a while, I realised that kid's father and relative with many farmers ran toward us as crying escalated around us. As his father and uncle followed and got closer to me, I grasped I might not be able to escape them. Then I headed to close by Taro village and decided to enter a house closer to me to hide myself. After a few seconds, I thought I might not be safe in it, and decided to run again. As I reached a thicket nearby Taro village, I hid myself in it while thorns pricking and cutting my skin. I was lucky they didn't find me there.

After they left, I began running to my mom and told her about bloody fight, and she was very sad for me and encouraged me to defend myself against anyone who attacked me. She said, "I am willing to pay for any damages as necessary." She supported me not to be afraid when I thought she was going to punish me for it. I was glad to hear she was by my side at all times and my worry was lessened, but I was only worried for my dad. The father of the kid complained to my dad and they both took him to doctor to fix him. I was afraid that my dad was going to punish me at night. I begged my mom to tell my dad not to beat me, and if she could not stop him, I would go and hide at my friend's place. My mom said, "I will talk to him when he comes home."

As soon as he walked in he said, "Where is the kid?" Then I hid under the bed and listened to their conversation. My mom advised, "Don't hurt him. He has to stand up for himself when someone fights him, otherwise he would be like chicken."

Knowing that he was not going to hit me, I came out from under the bed and saw him washing his muddy legs from the farm. Then I said, "Dad, did you just come home?"

"Yes! My son," Father said.

"Today, I spilt Ahmed Baker's head in fight," I explained.

"My son, from today on, you stay close to me near our arrogated land and watch our cow," he advised. "You do not need to stay with other kids, you and Muste can play near us. If you stay with older kids, they will beat you," he added. After our talk, I was so happy that I was going to go with him in the morning and I felt asleep. The next morning, I woke up, Muste and I, left with our fathers to our farm with cattle. We stayed close to them as my dad said. We spent all day helping and staying near them feeding weeds to our cows. We were so happy doing this ever day, and soon it became our regular routine.

Part 2
Dare Escape to Grandma

One day in the afternoon, I decided to remind my friend Muste about that promise land of injera and milk. He was willing to go with me anytime I wanted. I said, "Yes! Today is the day, let us go." I advised him if we asked our dads, they would not let us go. So I suggested to him we should pretend to go to the well to swim. We then slowly crawled like cats toward the well. There were a lot of children and animals about the well; we sat by it as if we were going to take a bath and then glimpsed at our dads. They seemed busy to pay attention to us, so we continued to crawl over a wooden bridge, out of their sight.

After we crossed it, we held hands and ran as much as we could. As we continued this journey, I began to worry if I was leading him in the right direction. While guessing the way I had travelled before with my mom, I didn't want to scare Muste, but I kept urging him to follow me while looking back to see if our fathers were following us. My heart drummed in fear of those creatures if they attacked us, or our fathers running after us, with a chance of getting lost. I kept praying to God to take us there peacefully. Thinking about those foods, every step toward grandma's house became like a year and I began drooling and craving until we reached there. With guessing and heart stopping ran, somehow we reached my grandma's village and climbed those tough hills to her house. Unfortunately, grandma was not home except my aunt. She was astonished to see me with my friend. She asked, "How did you get here?"

I replied, "We just run from grazing land and luckily came here." Being very shy of her, but I didn't tell the secret of why we came. She was surprised and concerned for our safety and advised us not to do this again. After she got sad with our action, she placed a blanket on the ground for us and told us to sit down. Then she gave us that smoked milk with injera we were waiting for and came all the way for them. Muste was indeed amazed by them and said he had never seen such injera and milk before. He began to cry just like me, having them and kept saying these were from heaven and would like to come with me every time.

As we were eating, grandma came home, and I ran and greeted her by kissing the front and back of her palm. She was surprised to see us, but said to me to sit down and eat the food since she knew that even angel *Israfil*[12] would not troublesome one to take his/her life while she/ he was eating something, at least until you finished whatever on your plate. I was so scared about this saying as if I was going to die with my friend after finishing this meal. I ran back quickly to finish plate with Muste. We were so happy to eat all that injera and milk. Grandma and aunt wanted to know more how we came. I answered, "We ran away together from our dads, and came here."

"So your parents didn't know you are here?" she asked.

In a very shy manner I replied, "Yes!"

She was also shocked and advised us, "Please do not do this again. Thank God you didn't get lost, or harmed by something." After this was over, we went outside to look around area and listened to bird's songs we had never heard before like radio. Some of them seemed to cry in a funny way and made us laugh, and we mocked them as much as we could. While we were walking around and enjoying the view we got a bit tired.

As we were having fun, the sun started to say her goodbyes, and some farmers already coming back home from farm with their cattle. As we came back to grandma's yard, I saw a kid and older man com-

---

12   Angel of death that extracts soul when dying.

ing. I stared at a kid who looked like my brother and the older man as my grandpa. Then grandma said, "This is your brother, and this is your grandpa." And she introduced us. Then I ran to grandpa and I kissed his hand and he was surprised that I was getting bigger and he blessed me. I greeted my strange brother and he was surprised that I was his brother too and he met my friend Muste. My friend Muste had also saluted grandpa and my brother same. We talked for a while about everything, how we came and grandpa was also surprised we came by ourselves. Then after a while dinner came and we began eating that delicious food. It was the happiest day of my life; I could not believe the paradise I came in with my friend. I had wondered what would happen if I stayed, or went, and the consequence of coming here without family's permission, but I said this could be a dream came true. Then for Muste and I cheated our family to come here, I doubted, we might not spend the night and saw any milk to drink in the morning.

While I was in this fantasy factory, there before dinner was over grandma's house yard was shaken like earthquake. I feared the village and mountain to slide down the hill with amount of vibration that began to shake us. Suddenly there were over hundred people flooded my grandma's house and yard. The entire area was illuminated as if the sun came to visit us on earth. I was surprised to see a flood of flashlights, burning wood, and many *mashos*[13] I had never seen before. I could even see ants and insects crawling in the grass at night. I thought there must be a serious wedding, or matter happening in the area. Then there was no place to hide seeing my dad entering grandma's house breathing hard like a mad gorilla. He shot his word like bullet, "Are the kids here?" he wanted to make sure we were here. Abas…Muste…and began yelling our names million times per second. I had no choice but answered with small, tiny voice like kitten, "Yes, Dad, yes, Dad," confirming we both there. He seemed to swallow me alive and I wanted to run and hide behind my grandma. I saw his eyes were red like dragon and breathing flame from his mouth. His face's blood vessels stretched as pen while his hands and

---

[13]   A big lantern.

fingers turned like tiger. He seemed ready to hang me like meat, or roasted me alive. His shirt was soaked with sweat in agony and fear that we were lost for good or died somewhere in the lake, or some cannibals had taken us like a lot of people. Animals were taken and disappeared without trace in our area before. My mother was also came crying and so Muste's father and mother were no better than my parent. Everyone was terribly shaken and they could not believe we were alive.

Seeing all these commotions, villagers from grandma were also descended from everywhere; the ground began to shake on a Richter scale of nine and a half. My dad announced louder, "These kids are thieves. They didn't tell us anything, they escaped from us. Right now there were many villagers looking for them in rivers and wells. They were also searching around grazing land where they ran off. Some were looking in the bushes. We were afraid they were drowned and might be died." Muste and I were really scared this night we might not survive the consequence of running away. The milk and injera we were enjoying became so sour and poisonous like snake's spit. We faced the reality that we tried to get them illegally without telling our family. Now so many people might be hurt or die looking for us in the river and everywhere. We predicted the end of our live once they got us home.

My dad said, "Get up," and held my hand, and Muste's dad did same. They dragged us outside of grandma's house like chicken to take us home while uttering threatening words, for all the troubles we created for them. As we went down the hill from grandma's place, accompanied by hundreds of search people and lights and they murmured, "These is not forgivable." Anxiety fell over me to what to happen as soon as we reached home. I thought of the night when the universe ended for us. I knew there would be no tomorrow to walk around. It was as if my dad had already dug a grave to bury me in alive, I feared. Muste's dad was very dangerous father; he felt it too, for his dad had beaten him almost every day for being one of the worst kids to walk around on earth that I knew. I heard Muste was saying to young and older women, "Please give me vagina," same as he used to ask for orange and mango. When they complained to

19

his dad, he was tortured for it. He had stolen eggs from his family and sold it for his smoking habit, at this young age. He tied grass on the ground like rope and made everyone fell down and hurt them specially elders who could not see, just to laugh at them. That was why for him, this night was just another night of pleasure while for me it was going to be one of the worst hell I had ever seen. I was not beat badly like him even though he tried to make me rude like him. Thanks to ladies and people who didn't complain to my dad, but today it looked no one would stop him at all.

After going little far from grandma's village, we suddenly saw many people running around with lights to find us in wells, rivers, and dams just like my dad said. I confirmed that there were more troubles than I imagined we brought to people looking for us. There were many other groups I saw running around and each group calling each other to see if they found us. As soon as we approached the first group they called on my dad's group and they told them they found us. One group after the other they got information that we were found including my uncle's group. Other villager's group that heard the news we were lost also heard and went to their respective villages. We were finally surrounded by hundreds and hundreds of lights and people and reached our village. I realized no one left in our villages except few older and younger people. At last, everyone went home, relieved that we were found, but a few came with us and entered our home. After a little talk with my dad, the rest left for their home. Then my dad tied me to bed with strong rope and wires both my hands and legs. I could see smoke continued to come from his noses and his flamed red eyes like tomato. Our house was little remote from village and he waited until everyone had gone to bed and he started beating me with rope of cow's skin like mad dog. He slashed and slashed my back and buttocks area relentlessly and the pain was totally unbearable. I cried like a fox, and my mom could not take the cruelty of him beating and she came to help. She was slashed many times as well with the same cow's rope. She had to run away backward, and he told her not to stop him, or she would be beaten, too, and she halted and cried for me. My sisters also began crying hard and begged my dad to stop killing me. He yelled to them to stop crying. At last he slowed down on beating seeing many sisters crying for me. As tradition of our society no one seemed to help me for being beaten by head of house. No government's soldiers or officers could stop the punishment and no law at all to help me.

After the beating had stopped, my dad decided not to let me go, or untie me for the night to show that it was needed for this run away crime. I had to cry for few hours for rope and wire kept cutting my skin. After some begging of my mom and crying I had made, he came and untied me by warning not to run again. I assured him not to run again and went to sleep with pain. In the morning, it was hard for me to wake up for I was in pain. I hardly woke up and unable to walk at all. My dad warned me not to go anywhere, not to move even few meters from the house. Muste had been beaten same like me and ordered not to go anywhere as it seemed to me his dad and mine had agreed to leave us at home, might be for good. It looked no more shepherd's job for us as if they had taken action to stop us from getting lost again. Days passed since I was grounded at home and my job became playing with other younger kids all day long.

After some time, my dad seemed had enough life being a farmer and decided to leave for town's work. I had no idea that he was the only person from our village who could do carpentry work, could build tall buildings, made table and chairs, etc., as if he was little educated person, but he didn't seem someone who became a student at all, no idea how he learnt these skills. I wondered how he was able to write numbers and alphabets of our country's language I had never seen before. He looked like one of our villager's Albert Aniston. News of his departure somehow made me happy that the monster who beat me like that no longer around. I wondered what kind of town around us for I had never been to one of it, and tried to look and understand around our village and mountains, the whole area. Once I heard there were small town and huge university behind the hill of our village I was born at, I wanted to see it, but I was not allowed to move at all for I was grounded for ever it seemed.

Part 3
Heading to Elementary School

One day, my dad came home from his carpentry job and told me that he wanted me to go to school with my sisters to the town I fervently wanted to see. I was excited for him to say I would be a student even though I did not know what it benefited me by going there. Hearing the news, my mom jumped through the roof over my dad. She opposed we should not go to school at all. Hearing this from my mom, I was afraid and felt something must be wrong about it and we might face bad thing. Our going to school was not the right choice for us. She said, "It is against our tradition and religion; this would change them to feared Amhara's[14] character and bad tradition of town's people." She wanted me to grow up and become farmer like her people and everyone in the country side being sheltered in grass igloos, which its wall was made of cow dung, not the life of the devil town's people which looked crooked and drinking *taji.*[15] For my sisters they should stay home and helped her with house chores and later get married like her. My dad refused to listen to my mom's concerns and idea and decided to take us to school, for he was the lion and king of kings as in our tradition. It was naturally declared that no wife could stop a husband from doing what he wanted to do as the main leader of the house. I was really afraid what might happen to us, but in the morning my sisters and I began marching toward town with him. We climbed a mountain of our village and when we reached on top of it, we looked down and saw a small beautiful town next to many villages. He informed us that the big buildings on the right of town to be one of the biggest agricultural university in the country. The trees and flowers in university were breathtaking with many different sizes of tall buildings by big lake full of birds. I was excited to see these things for the first time in my life.

---

[14] Ethnic group believed to come to power in our land with the help of European after Berlin conference of 1818.

[15] Smelly, alcoholic drink made by town people, especially Amharas.

This beautiful town was only about fifteen minutes walk from our village it looked, but it could not be seen from my village as if we were sitting by paradise. As we closer to town, I saw many people going to town, and coming out of it. Once I reached its center, I saw two big things like bus with four wheels and a lot of windows around them and swallowing many people. The only car I saw before that was running on the ground and amazed me was a little car looked like turtle with smoke coming out of it from back side and driven by two caucasian people; we used to run after it in the country side by my house. When I saw these two huge things standing under the tree full of people in it, I thought they might be the mother of that beetle. It was amazing to me to see that these things not only swallow many people, but a *Kulli*[16] was loading many heavy sacks of tomatoes, potatoes, and vegetables coming from country side and transport to another bigger town about five kilometers away. People seemed to speak some weird language I had never heard before as if I came to another country. Some of them also spoke the language I knew, but I heard that there were other different races I had never seen before. Then we reached to a gate entrance of school, surrounded by wire fencing, and many students were flooding in it. I saw them forming a line up of their own like ants according to their classes. It seemed the teachers of every classes standing and directing them to make perfect line up.

We stood and watched what they were doing. After they sang something like national anthem, in that weird language and raised flag up on a pole in front of them, every one began running toward their classes. My dad then held our hands and took us to a person who looked really old, balding school's director that had small ratty long hair left near both sides of his ears. I wondered how he attached his tiny hair passed from one side of ear to another using his saliva like cream from time to time. When wind came to scrap off his scalp that little hair, he kept spitting on his hand and attached it back on his head. I was amazed by it as my dad greeted him with that weird language he knew little and asked him if we could be registered.

---

[16]   Men working for less Money like Donkey.

Then I was instructed to pass my hand over my ear. I was little scared why, but dad told me not to be afraid, this was checking to be registered. Then they took us into a class full of kids with another dangerous-looking old man who had a cow-skin rope on his hand, slashing kids with it. It was very scary for me to see this merciless-looking old man wanting to slice any students he wanted to. I was really scared about learning at all. I felt like going back home with my dad, but they told me to sit down on a long chair next to other four kids. Then my dad left us by saying that we had to come home for lunch.

First day of school was like horror for us, any time we made a mistake saying an alphabet wrong, the teacher would ask us to remove pant down to be slashed several times as a punishment. Sometimes we had to stretch and show inside palm to a teacher and he would slash us several time until we cried hard and begged for mercy to stop it. After a while, a bell rang and I was appalled by the noise coming from it, for I didn't know what it was at first. Then students were happy to hear and run out of class for break. We were relieved at least we got break from old man. As we went outside, the kids began to play, but my sisters and I were watching them like guest for we were new. We watched how all students were playing and I was happy with break in general knowing that we could play after beating was over. After a few minutes, the bell cried again and all students ran to their classes. We also followed them to class for learning, and there came an old man with his cow's skin. The noisy kids like chicken were suddenly silent right away as Pacific Ocean. My heart began drumming again. I didn't understand his language, but tried to say what students were saying as loudly as I could along them. He pointed his stick to weird alphabets and said its sounds and if we didn't say like him, or look somewhere else, he would slash us. When we said alphabets together with kids, it made me happy, but any time he asked us individually, it was not pleasant at all. This beating and cruel old man worried me a lot to be in school. Thank God, we had to go home with my sisters for lunch. I was so happy to go to school as a student, but the memory of the teacher's cow's skin worried me from time to time. It seemed as if he'd never put down the cow's skin and prepared to hit us any time he desired.

After we had lunch, I told my mom I was going back to school with my sisters. She didn't like us to leave for school, but she had no choice fearing my dad would not let us stay home. She warned us to watch out for dangers and we finally left for school again. Then, we went back to class with the dangerous teacher, began to learn the language we didn't know. Some of the strange kids were rude and pushed us around. At last, I fought back and the teacher slashed all of us with his cow's skin. I found that school wasn't as great a place as I thought, and became scared of it. Since we didn't understand his language, the beatings got worse, and worse, I wasn't able to learn as fear over took my brain. I couldn't pay attention at all in class, and everything I was taught seemed like a dream. I began to hate having to attend school, so I told my mom what the teacher was doing and how bad it was. She was able to stop my sisters from going to school, fighting him that town's alien's school was not for girls, and he at last gave up on them. She said, "Girls aren't allowed to go to school." They should stay home just like her, to get married and spend their life as mother of children for someone else and my dad was ruining their life, and she won her case, for my sisters to stay home for good. Then she said this was your entire dad's fault that I was being beaten. After she stopped my sisters from going to school, she advised me to hide in the bushes of farm behind our house, from morning to lunch time, and then come home like I just came from school for lunch. After I finished my lunch, I would go back to the bush. At end of the day came home pretending that my day was done at school. She couldn't convince my dad for me, to stay home for good, and my only solution was to hide as my mom planned for me until my dad gave up and I continued hiding in the dense farm.

After two weeks of hiding, one day my dad asked me to show him what I learned at school. I didn't know what to show him, and then he got mad at me and smashed my head saying I was a lazy boy. Then, he would write a letter of the alphabet and asked me to say it. I felt that my dad turned in to be the brother of the teacher, with the cow's skin, who lived in my house. One morning, my sisters came and saw me hiding in the bushes. They told my dad that I was hiding there, instead of going to school. That evening, my dad had beaten me for not going to school. Then my dad asked a few kids from another village to take me with them to school every morning. When I went back to school, the bad teacher asked me where I had been all this time and kicked me out of school. I returned home crying. Then I told my dad that the teacher kicked me out of school. He came with me to school to beg the teacher for me to come back, for he didn't know I was skipping school. And then the teacher agreed to let me come back to school, for the usual learning and beating. From that day on, my dad asked me what I learned at school each day, I felt like I was being beaten from both sides at school and at home. I was able to complete a year of schooling in this difficult situation and my dad continued with his construction job as a carpenter at the university next to my elementary school.

Part 4
Moving to Bate Town

After dad saved some money from his construction job, he opened a small grocery store near my school, which moved me to town converting half of my body to town's boy. I was so happy to live in town, for school was only a few steps from our store. Only when I missed my mom and smell of the country side, I headed out of town to visit them. After a year in town and schooling, I came to understand this strange Amharic language and its subject being taught and school became little easier. I was not the best student in school, but I was happy with my progress, helping me pass from class to class. I was delighted to learn different subjects and the whole town's life in general and it made me felt like more of a city's boy. It was the happiest time of my life. There I came to understand a little truth about our country that we had two major different languages and religions, but not understood deeply the magnitude of division between cultures and politics that had been going on and what about to happen. It seemed to me that the people ruling the country were the powerful

Amharic speakers, and had a king and some changes were on the horizon. After a few happy years, university students all over country appeared not happy with the king's rule or the government, and those who knew about politics were making riots by throwing stones at the schools and began damaging them. I didn't understand what the university students were doing, but one day, I followed elementary students to see what was going on.

It was now clearer that the students all over the country weren't happy about the feudalism government ruled by king of Ethiopia, and they wanted to overthrow him. I heard this king owned all Ethiopian lands, money, people, and everything in it like God and being worshipped in the country. Rumors said that he had agents that kill people, drain their blood, and he would then take a shower with it for his dignity and purification of his body. I heard people in town always sworn by his name like God. One day there was serious riots in our town by students and heavy military came to the university. They began shooting in the university to stop the riots, and everyone had to run away scared of the shooting we had never heard before. I tried to escape through the opening of small barbedwired fence by pushing apart, but seemed to catch my pants after I got out. I quickly untangled my pants from it, and continued running as much as I could run, about five kilometers from school to the countryside. Once I stopped and looked behind to find that no one was chasing us. Then I felt that there was something wet in my pants and it seemed to stick to my right leg. I doubted that I peed on my leg or run in water, but I checked and found that blood was the culprit. The more I checked, it was indeed my blood gushing out of my thigh. I had no idea if I was shot, or something else did it, but at last I discovered that barbed wire gored my skin with my pant. I looked down from top of a mountain toward town and there were some unusual smoke over town, but shooting had stopped, and after we returned to a calmed town. There were no more shooting, but the trouble of uprising of students didn't stop.

We continued our school after what it seemed the military itself defeated the king and took over the country. Again it looked as if some people and students opposed a military government that in power. Some students had formed their own political parties and their fight had begun and some killing was reported around country. I was too small to involve, or care for anything, but continued my school as usual, but little scared that I could be affected, or killed as a result of other student's troubles if a military came again. After a while, it seemed to me the country was little stable with the rule of military government. I was then happy to be elected as a leader of the minor's soccer team, or group B. I was assigned number nine position as special player for the team and tried to organize it very well. I was responsible to raise some funds for our team to buy our uniforms with a help from my dad's grocery store. After school hours, I made my team mates *Jeblo*[17] by giving them items from my store so that the profit went toward our uniform. Once we had enough funds, we bought uniforms and started to compete with other town kids like us. I was happier than ever in this way and managed to reach grade five. Life was good and tasty like honey. I felt I was one of the richest kids in our town as my dad shop got bigger and bigger. Most of the time, I would only eat pasta and rice at one of our town's best restaurant, for I had a lot of money. I was popular and some girls liked me in town at about the age of ten and sometimes I went out to have a fun without telling my dad.

One day, I told my friend Muste to stay back after school, so he would enjoy like me in town with one older girl that came from another city to work as maid. He agreed and stayed back from going back home to his village. When sun set and little dark, I told him to wait for me in a little dark place so that I came back and showed him sign of my hot dog being wet if she came out. Luckily she came out and I lured her at the back of our grocery store and climbed her legs up like small monkey going up a big tree. After some difficulty as a camel, she held my bottom and pushed me up toward her waist. I attempted to find that juicy and heavenly hot channel, but I was shocked touching the hairy samosa. After a few exhausting attempt on bushy pub, somehow I was lucky to touch that juicy edge of it with my tiny hot dog for a few seconds. I was excited and told her

---

[17] A person going back and forth in town, or street selling small items.

to wait there for me. Then I rushed and showed Muste proof of this virgin oil and he was so excited to get his share like me. I quickly dragged him to her and requested that she did the same thing for him. As soon as he tried to untie his pants, his dad came out of nowhere with a flashlight looking for us. He called our names Muste, Abas…getting shocked for what we were doing with this older girl, catching us redhanded. He shouted, "*Balagee*!"[18] He tried to grab us like mouse and we were shocked and ran away. I couldn't believe he chased and caught both of us right away, in a few minutes like a lion hunted two mountain goats with a flash light, for we could not out run him in a dark. After he dragged us to our store, he explained to my dad how he found us. Right away my dad tied one of my hands at store's ware house and Muste was dragged to his village for usual treatment.

After the store was closed for business, my dad tied both of my hands around butt like barbecued duck and began slashing me like never before with gas hose that he found in the barrel. Once I couldn't bear the pain, I had to twist my hand backward and it got one of my middle left fingers' main blood vessels. The blood squirted from it as if a cow was urinating on the ground. I thought I was dying and felt dizzy seeing so much blood I had never seen come from me. When he saw this, he even cried with me like baby and got very sad for what he had done. I understood he didn't mean to do this the way he acted. He then rushed me to the town's clinic to repair the cut. Learning my lesson this night, and I had never again attempted to dip my Pennine like that anywhere. I tried to be a good son by help-ing my dad after school right away. I only went out to play with my soccer team. Focusing on my studies, I became very good at school and enjoyed everything town had to offer me, but I didn't expect bad thing to come soon.

---

[18]   Very rude.

Part 5
War of 1977

Not so long, I heard that some trouble was brewing over horizon, east of us. Rumor was not confirmed to me, but looked as if war was to start. Everyone seemed to worry, what to happen to them as if a sun to set and never to appear again. This was strange and bad news than what we experienced with military take over, and strange war to come as it was rumored. I didn't know what kind of war, or with whom, or which country, but heard on its way to us. After a while it was confirmed on the radio as people heard it, a Somali army infiltrated our border to fight our country. *Suta-dema*[19] who dressed ugly with long Rastaman hair, smelt funny when he passed by us, and always begged for food and had no real address who believed to be possessed by Jinn,[20] begun warning people in our area that they should run toward north if they wanted to survive at all from this war coming from east. He stressed that trying to escape south, east and west would be deadly to everyone. From his lunatic dirty looks and characters no one should believe what he said, but news on the radio confirmed that there was war coming and he might be right. Everyone at our area really worried for their life to be in danger and began praying to God day and night to be alive.

As anxiety overpowered me, after a few weeks, we heard some gun fires at a faraway mountains and the rumor started to be true. Fear increased, and a few nights later, a town next to us experienced some gun shots. We didn't know how long it would last, but gun shots increased more at night at another far city. Everyone felt on the brink of running north, but gun shots coming from this direction besides south concerned us that Suta dema might be wrong. We were not in serious danger at moment, but hearing these guns going off like pop corn, my dad chickened out and began to move our store's merchandise little by little to country side to be sold from there for a while

---

[19] Slow-goers.
[20] Unseen beings like human race.

until war was over. After a while there was a rumor that some people saw Somali army passing by far away villages at night, but no one confirmed seeing them face-to-face. I wondered what kind of beast they might look like for I had never seen them before. No Ethiopian army to fight this Somalis in our area and I wondered who they came to fight. Their gun shots seemed to increase after sun set, but no one hurt or died so far as we heard it. It was real war, it looked like, and our heart now jumping up and down and bothered me so much I was afraid that my education was going to be halted. Somehow I was at the end of my grade five levels. Corns and sorghums vegetations were almost grown to my waist side and I could hide in them in case I had to run in them. A season was great for cultivation and farms were full of farmers. Now our store had only about one quarter of grocery left in it and my dad had completely abandoned coming to the store at all. He was enjoying selling few items from village and worked most often in the farm. I was the only person left to run grocery store refusing to give up during the day. I went home to village at night even though my dad was not happy with my decision. I was very disappointed to what was happening, but seemed less chicken than my dad to run the store with little items in it.

One day, I invited my friend Muste to come to our store to help me with customers. We were very busy in the afternoon when we heard two MIGs[21] we had never seen before flew low above the town about five kilometers from us. Their noises were almost ear deafening to hear and the trees, houses vibrated like earth quake and they almost wanted to fly after them. We ran outside and saw these two jets flying toward west then shoot straight up in the sky at ninety degrees and came down. After a few nerve wrecking noise, they disappeared in the horizon. I was so surprised seeing such thing for the first time ever. While I was stunned by this noise and kept looking in the direction jets had gone and expected them to return, there I saw heavy dust arising from the road that leads to another town. I thought there were heavy tornados running around and covering trees like cloud. It was very unusual dusts that I had ever seen so I

---

[21] Fighter jet.

was astonished and kept watching it. The more I watched, it seemed the dusts were rushing toward us. Then I saw many strange cars I had never seen before dashing toward us from inside the dusts. I thought there were many people running back and forth in town and these cars were rushing to help them carry loads to another town. When they were getting closer, it seemed abnormal to see hundreds of vehicles like that in line. I feared something might be wrong. What they could be, I was astonished because the sky was clear and there were only few clouds. I was sure not dreaming in the broad day light. About a half kilometer from us suddenly a gunshot erupted one by one. "Is this war?" I asked myself. I was shocked already this might be war and felt like running, but wanted to make sure if I had to run from it. Some bullets passed by my ears whistling and buzzing like bees and I thought regular bees passing by my ears as usual and listened to it. Shooting cars were coming toward me very fast and noise of shooting increased by seconds, and some bullets landed next to me. Gun noise increased badly and made me uncomfortable as they were closing to me. I was appalled than ever. Muste and I realized that this was war and we were going to die. I declared to myself time to run and we ran toward our store to escape from it.

When we reached our store, we tried to close door behind us, and did not see two ladies from countryside was running behind us to enter our store. They begged me to let them in before I closed a door. I commanded them to enter fast behind me and as they entered shooting was increased more and more. It got worse and worse I tried to hide in boxes and grocery like mouse. Muste did the same. We were scared where to escape. Whole town became noisy and hell zone. I feared we could not survive in the tin roof of our store as bullets rained like hell. Muste and I didn't know where to hide our soul, with two ladies. They were begging for their life to be spared by God, their mouths were rattling with fear and my heart moved in my throat to come out. I tried to swallow back like heavy tablet toward my stomach.

Shooting got worse and worse, and I kept crawling like small baby from boxes to boxes to save my life. My mouth was closer than a skunk sniffing the ground and swung side to side hundred times per second just to hide from noise and bullets showering on the roof. Muste and ladies did same like me, and I didn't know how many times we collided head to head in a dark. Heavy shooting died a little down and my heart got better to be still alive. Thank God, so far I was not bleeding, when I checked my body: face, buttocks, stomach and legs. My companions also made it out with no scratch it looked, we were safe. I was happy, but a few minutes later, again shooting had increased, and seemed even closer, ear-deafening than before. I expected to die this time, as if a soldiers were shooting at us from outside store. I said, "May be time to open door and run for life, as this may be for sure last time to be alive." I had increased hiding and running around store, but it was not helpful. Then I said, "I may not make it safe now for bullets raining hard around us and if shooting dies down one more time and still alive, I will open the door and run." For a second time, the shooting died down and the two ladies opened door and ran out. Muste also ran after them when he saw the ladies ran. Before I ran away with my soul, I wanted to close the door and locked it, fearing we might get robbed, and I couldn't find the key right away while in panic. After a few glance, I found it and went outside and tried to close door as my hands were trembling crazy. Shooting began again and my hands were extremely shivering like someone killed a cat, for my thought of gun shots and bullets raining toward me.

Finally, I was able to lock it and almost lost direction to run in a confusion state. Hanging a key on my hand, I ran behind our house where long and dense bushes were full of dangerous thorns. Gun noise was shattering my ears and became worse so I had no choice I must enter and ran in dangerous thorns with only sandals on my feet. My skins were caught and pierced by many of them. I felt them ripping off my skin and this time it looked like nothing at all, compared to bullets wanted to take my life. I kept going like hyena in this difficult bushes while losing some skin and suffered pain rather than dying by bullets. Suddenly I felt something held me not to move at all after I thought I got away from it. It dragged me back wards with such a force and I was afraid, this was it, I was stuck and they got me. "Someone caught and drag me back," I said. I looked back quickly realised that the key chain in my hand was hooked to the wire fence. As I jumped over the fence, I fell in dense bushes and I tried to find it, but shooting noise and bullets rained near my sides and ears, scaring me to look for it. I advised myself that my life was more important than the key and I shouldn't die looking for it. I decided to run with bullets advice. I ran as much as I could toward one village with head down like monkey on four limbs from bullets chasing me. No one was running in front of me as it looked to me. Corn and sorghum leaves were denser and I could not run fast, for its leaves cut my bare skin, and I had to stumble or kick its stems as I tried to run blindly.

After a while, I found a narrow road in a middle of farm and ran a little, but found this was more dangerous way to escape from them, for soldiers were shooting my direction. I realised I might be a target on the open road of my side and tried to run to a big tree in the farm. Then I fell down behind water terrace and kept my body flat like small lizard behind a stone, trying to hide from flying bullets. People hiding there told me not to run, and stay down with them. Bullets were shredding leaves on our body like rain; we laid in a dangerous spot and direction. I expected bullets to riddle us any time there. I tried to cover my both ears from noise of guns and was unable to stop it and I felt I was going to die. I wanted to run quickly by getting up and the owner encouraged me to stay down to save my life. After a while I thought, I was not going to make alive as a farmer advised me. I did not find his advice to be sufficient and satisfying, so my instinct forced me to run again. I didn't know where my friend Muste had gone, I was afraid and thought he might had already died, or lost somewhere since I had not seen his trace so far. No signs of those ladies too. I continued my running in the farms and seen some people running in front of me. Some of them rolled their pants like rolled oats up to their knees to escape fast. Some of a farmers removed their skirts over their shoulder ran showing their under wear only. Those who hadn't under wear swung their little men side to side like horse smashing corn leave as fast as they could. Ladies ran, bouncing their oranges and rubbing mangos with each other to escape bullets. Some of them had running river down their legs, but no time to laugh; it was time to look just amazed by it. I ran as much as I could to ward north as it was said by *Suta dema*, remembering his advice. I couldn't run like them, but tried to keep up with them, and finally after a little ran, gun shots had stopped when we reached over top of a mountain. I unloaded the gas that inflated my stomach like party balloon to make myself lighter, fearing still this shooting might start. I prayed hard for the shooting to go away and there at last it was calmed down.

How many people were dead or wounded, I had no idea. I did not know the reason why they rained bullets on us. No one knew. Are they Ethiopian army or Somali? No idea either. Now, I could walk slowly, still heart not resting, but alive and breathing. I looked down toward town from mountain of my village and everything was very quiet, not even bird's cry. No cars or humans, made any sounds, or moving at all. I found it amazing. All roads to town and villages around it were empty as if bullets licked them off. I slowly walked up to side of mountain, to main road that leads to my village and saw one guy I knew, and I greeted him. I wanted to know where he came from. He told me, he ran from town up here and he was happy to be alive up to now! And I said me too! We walked a little and saw that a road had many abandoned eggs, fruits, tomatoes, and different types of vegetables, with gourds full of milk. It looked that some brokers who usually sat and bought these things at side of roads from farmers had left them, and ran away. Those who marched to town with their goods had also dropped them and ran backward to where they came from. I felt everything was a disaster today and astonished by how the roads looked. Another guy I saw, suggested we took home some of these items scattered on the streets since there were no owners. I refused him to forget about it. We needed to save our life first, and these items not worth our life, or trouble to come from it. He didn't agree with me, but he took a load of potatoes and many eggs. Then he put on his head like ladies, which he was not supposed to do as men would not do it. After we walked a while, I got jealous of him and grabbed about six kilograms of potatoes and strode toward our village. As we got closer, I thought my dad might question me for bringing potato from the road and I got scared that he might punish me for stealing from someone. I thought about leaving it on the road and advised the guy with me. He then replied that it was my choice to take it or leave it. I was ashamed for my family what villagers might say to them for bringing potatoes home from road, and left it to the side of road and then went to our village.

We reached our village and saw no one in it. My heart began beating and wondering what would happen to me if my family not found, gone, or died. The area was really quieter than ever. I shouted the names of my dad and mom, sisters one by one to see if they were around and no one replied. Tears poured down my face like river for separating from them and afraid that I lost them. They might had also scared and ran away as shooting began. I did not know where to find them. It seemed I would be by myself from now on. I went to check a potato taker and he was also sitting and crying, for he didn't find any of his family members. We cried together and talked what we should do if we didn't find any one. I suggested to him if we didn't find them, we could go to search for them at another relatives villages far away, knowing that he could protect me from hyena since he was bigger than me. He agreed we should go, but we wanted to wait until dark in case they returned in the evening since no more gunshots were coming. I invited him to come to my house to eat injera with me for we were very hungry. We found big injera and ate with green hot pepper since there was no sauce for it. Suddenly I heard a voice and I went outside to check it. I was not sure where it came from, but I raised my ears like rabbit to find its direction by holding my breath in a quiet manner. It looked a bit like my dad's voice. I wanted to make it sure, but my eyes already filled with tears that I might see him. Tears began rolling my cheeks like golf balls. As the voice got closer, I felt he was calling my name hundred times and he was saying I lost my son, I lost my son…Then I knew that my dad was crazily looking for me like he would never see me again. My hair stood like porcupine, I began crying heavily, knowing that he was looking for me hard. I tried to call him as hard as I could, but he couldn't hear me saying dad, dad, dad…and our call to each other was intensified. I began running toward where he was calling me from, repeating his name. His cry made me very sad, but seeing each other at last made me happy like someone came back from a grave yard after a long time. It didn't seem reality to lose my dad whom I loved more than anything in this world, I told myself. We ran toward each other very fast until we crashed on each other's face. He didn't look like my real father, his face was red as morning sun, feature of a mad man, I had never seen before. He was totally looked someone else. He might be running around all day, looking for me as a mad dog from his appearance. At last he was so glad to see me, cried tear of happiness and I did the same.

We hugged with excitement as much as we could, and he wiped tears from my face, but his shirt was soaked with tears as wet mouse in water, then we went to our home. He sighed, and sighed "thanks God" in relief that we were together again. He asked, "Where is Muste?"

"I had no idea where he went. He sprinted out of store ahead of me with ladies and I had never seen him since. He might be lost," I explained. He told me to stay put and run out of our house to find him. I went out, and looked where my dad was running to, and he was already gone off my sight. Tears ran down my cheeks again and sadly returned to the yard and looked far away little mountain north of our house. There I saw many people were flocking to our villages. I dreamed to see the rest of my family coming back, waited eagerly, in the mean while thinking what happened to me and Muste. I confirmed that all villagers were coming close to me and I ran toward them to look for my family. There I saw my mom in happiness, not so worn out like my dad, and we were all reunited after all, in happiness with all relatives. Muste came swinging like a drunk person after running all day from getting shot, and I was happy to see him again. Muste's dad was also running around to find him, and finally they came back to find that we were all all right. Not any one of us got killed today, besides running around like chickens going to be caught for slaughter. The damages were only getting tired and panicked by everyone. They were all astonished about this new event and began talking about it. We expected shooting to continue at night, but nothing had happened, we were unable to sleep very much in case we had to run again. Our area looked as if nothing had happened at all. In the morning, we discovered that the shooting was from Ethiopian soldiers who came to settle in our town, to protect us from Somalian army.

Their shooting seemed to scare the Somalians in the area to flush them out if possible. We were then concerned for we didn't know what to happen next since they settled around town and inside the university. We also learnt that they did make a fortress around town and heavy machine guns were set around town and on top of tall buildings mainly all guns directed toward our village. They looked as if they were waiting for Somalis to show up from our side. Now this scared me to go back to our shop in case shooting was to start again even though it seemed peaceful. My dad was scared so much and warned me not to go to town anymore.

After three days of peace, the main town, about six kilometers south from us had a few gun shots at night. It rumored to be that Somali soldiers were the one firing on purpose to terrorise the area. Everyone in the vicinity of ten kilometers from shooting town fell in anxiety to what to happen next and if they survived, for war seemed in inexorable. We prayed day and night to God to save us from wrath of war, and spared our life this time. Then after few days while we were listening and watching that far places for gun shots not to come to us, there in the evening, gun shots started to come from north of us toward our town. We went out of house to check it where they were shooting from and we confirmed they were shooting toward our town and village. The Ethiopian soldiers who directed their guns and mortars toward us not responding back to them for they might be thinking that the area Somalis shooting from was little far from them. We were now extremely concerned and worried to what to happen soon and began staring toward Somali shooting. In fear our stomach began roaring like lion that the Ethiopian army would respond any time. As we expected, there firing began to come from south of us, from Ethiopian soldiers toward us. We ran inside our house like goose, and I tried to hide between our cow and goat, holding my ears from loud gun noises. Some of my family put rags over their ears and ran under the bed to escape bullets. We couldn't tolerate the noise of guns, for they looked so close to us. We had to move from spot to another spot in the house to hide from it when we were unable to open door and ran away in the dark. We could hear bullets raining over our tin roof like grains of sand. We prayed and prayed to God to spare us, suddenly the shooting had stopped to give us some relief and breathing room. Lucky we were still alive and made sure that no one was so far bleeding and dying. From now on, it seemed to us that there would be no more peace we used to taste like orange. The sky began bleeding from raining bullets. We couldn't sleep all night long worrying what to happen next. My father began preaching us that we must start moving north if we wanted to make it alive becoming another *Suta dema*. I was not sure if this was going to be the best thing to do for we must be heading to Somalis' direction.

Part 6
Running from Mother's Village

My dad stressed again and again we could not stay at this bad location, in the middle of these two angry bullets that were whistling over our village. Then again suddenly shooting had stopped and relaxed us for a while. We didn't know where Somalis had gone and shooting was halted for a while and we didn't see them face-to-face either. I kept wondering if these intruders were white, red, blue or black and they were here to eat, help, or kill us all. We had no clue why they came to our country at all and expected them to be somewhere around us. I was afraid they would again be back the next night to open fire. We stopped doing any work for the day to see what would happen very soon, but we feared it would happen again. We decided it was time to save our life if this happened again. Evening time gun shots from Somali were back just like previous day, but this time stronger and stronger accompanied with very nasty bad, loud boom that shook my stomach, was added to it. We had to run around the house including animals. This heavy boom sounded from *RBG-7*, which I didn't know at the time. Its sound was so loud that even underground hogs would drop their belly in there and jumped out. This time; it demolished many things including the trees lost their leaves. It was so scary for us to stay in the house and village. So we ran from the village in the dark toward the west in the direction of grandma as fast as we could. We saw everyone in the village was running except the farm animals to save their life. Even the birds were scared and took flight from their trees into the sky. We found out that war was not good, for humans and animals, and it forced us from our place to flee beyond the lake. We had no choice, my family and I went to my grandmother's place to save our life since there was no other way to run.

When we got there, I got the chance to eat that nice white injera with milk, but I swallowed it with fear, and it tasted bitter. My grandmother's house was little far from shooting zone for bullets to reach us, but we could still hear the battle going around our area. We stayed with grandma for three weeks, and we felt safe there, but we hoped Grandma was not mad to us for crowding her house as Oromo said, "*Keysuman ayama boda nihadoyti.*"[22] While we stayed there, some people sneaked, one by one, back to the village, to get their belongings, as much as they could carry. My dad also brought our cow and a few items left over from store for our provisions to help us. After a while, no one seemed to move about our village and it became like ghost zone. We heard that Ethiopian soldiers sitting on top of university's tall buildings were betting to kill anyone they saw moving around villagers for a piece of cigarette. One would say to the other if you shot and killed that person, I would give you a piece of cigarette and the other bets he could do it. They did not care if you were enemy, or innocent residents, as long as they saw something moving, and they took you out like chicken. We heard that many people were killed like this and the news appalled us not to go to our villages anymore since they had a view of at least four kilometers in all directions. Those who had no relatives like us to stay with, they had to sleep around houses of safe villages like a mad dogs and trees of farms with children. Our villages and farms became perfect hiding grounds for Somali army, and they seemed to move closer and closer

---

22 A guest bitters after a week.

to escalate attacks on Ethiopian army mostly at night. Ethiopian army also began to move forward during the day from their nests robbing our villages and burning them to the ground as they went along and returned to their barracks at night. This new campaign of Ethiopian going out of town from time to time to attack the area was not good news for us. We were afraid that they might head to my grandma's village next. We began to raise our ears like satellite dish toward town from top of grandma's village. There one day shooting came closer to us. My dad panicked us, "We must go north to save our life now." We agreed to move again leaving grandma and her villages behind toward that north direction as our best option. As we heard it from there, Somali soldiers were already contaminated all north side of the country where we were heading. Then we began our journey to the place named *Dhandhama*[23]. When we reached there, my dad took us to the house of someone he knew. They welcomed us and we were happy a little bit to find a place to sleep. There we saw some Somali soldiers looked dark like us carrying guns. I was scared of them. Some of them accompanied by our own language speakers who probably joined them after being preached that they were Somali too or forced to fight with them. Then I heard that the Somali calling my people, we were Somali *Abbo*,[24] speakers of "*Abbo*" and they were Somali *Wariyya*[25] same as "*Abbo*" in their language. I felt little happy thinking that might be we were same people and they came to help us liberate from Amharic people as rumored. My worrying decreased a little, they might not kill us after all and we might be safe from them except this Amharic people whom they believed came to our country as colonizers about 1818 when European tried to share Africa at Berlin conference. I had no idea why we were related to Somalis, but not to the Ethiopian even though we all were black people with different languages and cultures.

The prediction of *Suta dema* that said we had to go north if we were going to survive was getting to be true as we felt that we were

---

[23]   In Oromo, it means to taste.

[24]   You.

[25]   You.

also some kind of Somali. This *Dhandhama* was only about ten kilometers from my village and Ethiopian army had not reached here yet, but it seemed that Somalis go from here to attack them at night and come back here to rest and rob people of their food, or animals for meat. They escalated their encouragement for everyone to join their army, and some villagers had already joined them willingly to fight with them. Everything surprised me specially knowing that we could be Somalis as rumored. We stayed almost two weeks around *Dhandhama* while watching the fight toward our villages then fighting was getting closer to us. We had to march north again to the places I had never seen before that excited and astonished me seeing different valleys, mountains and many other new villages. I thought the sky was attached to the mountains around my villages wondering how God was able to create such a huge land and rivers, but now seeing more mountains and valley full of other villagers began to surprise me even more. I found myself to be wrong perception of the world around me. I began fearing new places, people, and war, but gaining new knowledge of my country made me little happier. The further I went from my birth place, the more I worried if I would ever seen it again. I had no idea where my adopted brother, grandma, any of my uncles, and villagers disappeared to except Muste and his family. My dad decided to take us and run as much as he could to save us without worrying for any other relatives, or my adopted brother. I was afraid that he was a little chickened person more than any one in our area if not the whole country, for I didn't see any of them running like us. I believed others moved a little around, but not seemed to run like my dad dropping tail like frozen dog.

The further we went, the more Somalia army we began to see settling and moving around villages even camping in the bushes. They encouraged us moving north to save our lives. I became restless seeing so many soldiers in the area. We walked almost the whole day helping each other as much as we could carrying things, but became really tired, thirsty and hungry. Then we reached a place which had two small mountains shaped like cones, or similarly arranged side by side like young breasts. We saw more than two thousands Somalia army covered these breasts like bee hive. It looked as if we stepped in their head quarters. This place was very far from our area and we felt a little safe here to stop by village on one of the breasts, but we had no relative house to move in. We didn't know anybody so we had to stay outside in an open area. For the first time, we began counting stars at night, in cold weather, but we were lucky there was no rain, or mud. My dad begged a villager to help us with room to stay and one of them let us stay in his yard where there was a little hut not in use by them. I felt much better for having a place to sleep for the rest of the night, but we felt like strangers staying there. My dad sold some soap and tobacco in order for us to eat a few things in the area. After about twenty-five days, one morning we woke up to gun shots before we ate our lunch. Then that loud noise from *RBG-7* fell next to us to kick our butts like never seen before. My dad grabbed us quickly with bouncing heart, we ran north. It seemed the Ethiopian army was getting stronger and came there to kick us out with Somali. We had to jump up and down across many boulders with hunger and thirst like handicap person. I had never walked sluggish like that before. A mountain looked standing firm for a purpose as if it guarded down from jumping over to our land. There were many people running out of the breasts.

This time fighting was different because we heard heavy guns and explosion that rushed toward us very quickly. We had no time to take our belongings just to escape with our life. We ran and ran until we came to very strange big mountain I had never seen before. Its unique roads had heavy rocks as big as cars which surprised me to see it. Some of them were round stones tripping me while others were as sharp as a knife trying to slice my feet as I stepped on them. I could not believe the grinding noise coming from our feet. The trees were different: big, small, dense and some leaves smooth as silk. Some of them felt good to the touch, and others smell different than the other trees. I wished to stand there to look, hug, caress, and kiss, and spend some time with them, but we had no choice, we must go on until we were safe. We hardly made to the top and unable to move anymore. I thought we were safe on top of this huge hill and we sat down to take a break under those beautiful trees. After we relaxed of heavy fatigue and fear that shocked us from *RBG-7*, I asked my mom and dad the names of these beautiful trees. They told me that they had never seen them before themselves. I said to them you were ignorant like me. I asked some other people with us, and they told me their names. I was very surprised.

We stayed there for three hours and found that the Ethiopians army settled back to *Dhandhama*, the place we saw Somalis first. We decided to go back to get our stuff from breast hills if we could stay a while, or at least get our stuff for we had nothing on us. It looked to us we were going to be safe to do so, and we began our difficult journey back again with hunger and thirst. After we went down the mountain and passed few villages, some of the houses were already smoking cigarettes. We thought ours might be already burnt, and the bad feeling was true to see that breast hills were smoking as we got closer to it. We saw only few soldiers of Somalis walking around and their camps were not there anymore. Then we came to our new small muddy grass house given to us and we saw it smouldering. The only thing left was dough half burnt, smoked badly in a wooden container, which was not fit to eat. Some soap was almost melted and some where intact as it was. We had nothing to eat and nowhere to sleep and all clothing and bed sheets were gone. The villagers were crying to see their cattles all burned in a fire alive, only cooked and sizzling in ashes, a very gruesome situation for me to see. We saw only aluminium foils and baking clay that left intact with some items not fit to use. I didn't seem to understand its purpose why villages were scorched with everything in it. What a disaster for us to see and face! I had no idea, what we were going to eat! I was surprised to see that the villagers also dug the ground about two meters deep like wart hog as we did to sleep in it. After hole to sleep in was dug, they were forced to open ground wells of grains and gave us some to boil and eat for dinner. We felt much better and slept in this torched village on a muddy ground without any clothing for the night as cold weather beat as alive. I was unable to sleep well, thinking and fearing what to happen next.

When the sun born red, strange and very noisy guns we had never heard before laughed toward our direction. Its loud booming sound made us fart that we got up and ran so fast like never before. It seemed they were flying from faraway places and exploded very loudly near us. The *RBG-7* explosions we heard before became chicken cry compared to these things. We ran and ran so hard toward that difficult mountain again to get away from this appalling noise, convincing us that this war had gotten worse than before. This time, we were hardly able to reach other side of this mountain, becoming the first walking challenge we had ever taken on. It had denser bushes and narrow paths that were very hard to stride on, but we kept going to escape this noise as it seemed to follow us.

The more we ran, we began to slow down by hunger and thirst and I was scared to fall down and get caught by these explosions. As we finished this desert mountain with difficulty, there I saw never-ending milky chains of desert mountains, ahead of us as far as my eyes could see. They bothered and gave me a headache how far we had to go through them. My believing of the sky was attached to the mountain behind my birth place was getting false now. One sky after another sky behind the mountain was popping up with desert mountains looked endless. I was unable to see many villages like our area. I was really freaked out this time being very tired, hungry, and thirsty with noise increasing behind us. I had to carry my young brother to help my dad and mom, for they had to carry my other sisters on their back and shoulder who couldn't walk at all. With my brother's weight holding me down, cannon explosion shook my body like lizard dancing on the rock. My heart appeared to fall down to my stomach like ball. My skull was torched with heat as if my brain was melting in a pot. I felt like falling down, but shelling of cannon kept me moving, jerking and swaying side to side like finished old man and disabled cow. We cried to God, "Why did you forsake us? Are we paying for our fore fathers' sins, or for the sins we committed?" We murmured and groaned as much as we could as human beings did. We didn't know what to do than keep going these difficult terrains up and down with many rocky mountains. Thirst and fatigue took tall on us. My face changed its colour like old liver, darker than before. I thought dying was better than these sufferings while feeling that the soul was already travelling from my feet, or toes to my neck, but cannon explosion and my dad encouragement kept me moving even though it already seemed as if I was dead in my cloth.

Part 7
Arrival in Rocky Desert

As we came to a very rocky mountains, we saw the first villages of the desert I had never seen before. I was astonished our country was divided in two: where I was born to be very fertile land with lakes of swans and fishes, vegetables, corns, sorghums, etc., and now this desert with different type of houses and rocks. I couldn't believe my eyes to see them with many peach trees that had fruits like mermaids' chest dangling from them. I was excited to see something new, and I showed to my family. I wanted to sink my teeth into them since they told me to eat them alive. My dad asked the owner to sale to us so that we had something to eat for the first time after we left burned breast.

We also begged the villagers for water seeing they were very sad for us. As a lady trying to hand me a cup of water, she hesitated a little bit and began staring in my face to verify as if she knew me from somewhere. I was not happy that she did not hand me water very fast as I wanted. Then her face began to shrink in anger like ginger root for recognising me who I was. I had no idea what she felt about me because I had never seen her before or remembered her at all. Suddenly her tiger face looked as if she was ready to suck blood from my neck. The only reason I thought was I might be very ugly to her, or I acted rude in her village, or I might had said something offensive when asking for water. While I was trying to answer a few questions in my brain: where did I saw her? What did I do to her family or village?

She suddenly said, "You are that kid! You insulted me one day and kicked me out of your grocery store when I was badly thirsty and begged you for water to drink!"

My jaw dropped like donkey that was going to die. I tried to rewind my video clip of that incident in my potato brain to recall. Right away, I saw a flash of her picture that I was nasty to her or someone like her. I was not sure, but very shocked by this news, and I wanted to verify, "Really? Are you the one?"

"Yes!" she replied.

I didn't know what to say, I neither flew to sky like bird to get away or the ground opened to hide me from her. I was extremely tired, and I couldn't get up and run, but my head shrunk backward like turtle which saw a vulture above with no shell to hide in. I regretted my action now, and insulted myself as a rude person, but unable to say I was sorry at all. I lost any word to describe the situation and apologized to her. I felt like dead person in my shirt. Then she continued, "I cannot be like you!" She handed me the water. I felt little better that she was not going to kill me or kick me out of her village. My dad and mom were very shy for what I did to her and warned me not to repeat such rude thing again, for God might take me to such unknown places in my life. I agreed with them, I learned my lesson and tasted the seed I had planted for myself long time ago. I promised not to do it again to anyone.

After we quenched our thirst and relaxed a little bit, there they brought that mermaid peaches that ripped my heart from underneath my ribs and I felt in love with. I quickly filled both of my pockets and hands and began to sink my teeth in it one by one while hardly chewing it, for it was as smooth as a Greek yogurt. I pushed them down quickly my swollen tight throat. They smelt so good that my taste buds were tingled and danced my brain nerve cells. I wanted to shout in happiness and roar like cat, but this could wait until next time, for I had no energy left to do it today. I wished we had such peaches in our farm. The peach tree in my uncle's farm, just forty meters down from my house that I used to pick and eat was insulted by this desert beauty. They even laughed at its taste and texture. I could have argued with these peaches for my area vegetables which they did not have, but all that matter now was to find these peaches which had no comparison at all and saved my life.

After we rested for a while, there again the Ethiopian army came from two sides of the peaches. We had no choice than to dash east direction of the desert. We could run north, but its mountains were tall and sharp as a knife, wanting to slice our body and we decided not to attempt it. So we tried to get up and go east, but a heavy rock, we sat on didn't want us to move at all, for we were extremely tired and wounded for the journey. I wanted to stay and sleep on it for days or so, but when we heard heavy engine noises and tanks accelerating toward us, as guns began to sing. We got up fast and began jerking to the east direction of another big mountain.

On our way, we saw a few Somalian soldiers passing us, but looked peaceful journey without seeing any villages for a while. It didn't look any human soul lived in these areas at all for miles and miles that we kept going and going to the unknown and it was getting darker. We felt safe again, besides fear of these big mountains, thinking of when to get a chance to rest again. Resting seemed not safe because the mountains not invited us to stay at all for thousands of us flocking over it with animals. We kept going up and down all types of amazing mountain ranges and valleys while we were so tired to move at all as it got darker and darker.

I thought, by now we must be out of our country since we crossed many mountains and valleys. Again we were tired, hungry, and thirsty, but the area had no lights of villages in sight, and I was worried. I thought these scary mountains were only the homes of wild life like lions, monkeys, elephants which could endanger our life, and might not see any villagers to help us. I had imagined some dangerous animal jump and snatch me from behind my family and kept watching the bushes for any of them to make a move toward me for its dinner. The hunger and thirst got worse, and our body seemed to be worn out like fifty-year-old rugs. I thought of eating desert tree like Kat to make us survive until we got some help. We had no energy to walk any more, but fear told us to keep moving, the only source of power we had. After we passed two mountains in a dark, we saw one light far ahead of us and I asked my dad, "Is that a village light?"

Then my dad commented, "It might be a village or something else, we do not know for sure, let us go quickly to check it out, and we pray to be a village so we can get some help and rest." As we got closer to that light, we heard a donkey singing from it. It was truly a nice beautiful small village surrounded by couple of mountains and breathtaking desert trees around it that astonished me how it looked and to be found in such a location, and how it was built with nice designed houses. It was miracle and unconceivable to see this here for me.

When we entered the village, residents and Somalis soldiers in the area were shocked by our arrival, for they feared that we were something dangerous came to them. As they ran toward us, they found that we were only innocent fugitives people came to save our life. We expected the worst from them, but nothing happened and the Somali army was gone somewhere I did not know. We knew we were safe and asked a person for water to drink. The water looked dirty to us, unpleasant and undrinkable, comparing to our water we used to drink. We were convinced that it was not a time for us to choose good and bad water, and we drank it right away to survive. My dad then begged a villager to help us to sleep at his place since these rocky stones in village were not fit to lay on. We also suspected that we couldn't be safe to sleep outside, and a person called Adam took us to his house. Adam was short old man with milky hair and something was peculiar about him and his family. I doubted he could be Amharic speaker from his texture, the same ethnic people the Somali army came to eradicate from our land, or remove from power in Ethiopia. I didn't try to find out that they were, but found him to be very nice and kind person to give us water, food and allow us to spend the night with him. If he was Amhara, what was he doing here? How come he survived the Somali's soldiers? While I was brooding about many questions, my family and Adam kept talking with Oromo language, which was also doubted me that he might not be Amhara at all.

After we ate dinner, I was unable to keep my head above ground and my eyes were shutting down many times. His house was also different than all others. Its roof was made of tin and walls were made of special marble as if Adam was desert's Bill Gate while all other houses made of mud on all sides looking as if residents were living in a ground like squirrel. I was swallowed with conditions of Adam's family, but I was tired and needed to sleep, for I couldn't sit any more. They spread a soft cow skin on a ground for us to sleep on, and I felt asleep in few seconds. I had no idea where I was for the night until morning. When they tried to wake me up for lunch at 7:00 AM, I was really mad at them. I refused to get up, for my body was totally disabled from traveling there, and they somehow forced me to get up. Now I realized that we were far away in the desert as I went out to see true pictures of a place I slept overnight. I looked around trying to confirm if the Ethiopian soldiers were coming, and only saw Somali army going about with heavy guns. I was freaked to see many dangerous-looking soldiers as if they might hurt me. Where about of Ethiopians I could not guess, but they seemed not close in sight. I was not feeling any guns smell; I was able to leave my fear to the side for the time being. I went in a farm to perform my urine business just like my birth place. As soon as I pulled down my pant and sat down, there a lot of monkeys I had never seen before terrified me with very fierce and cruel looking as Somalis fighters that every one feared. I heard they were somewhere around us, but when I saw them face-to-face, I was scared to look at them in their eyes as human flesh eaters. I hated to face them feeling they were going to finish us soon.

We ate our lunch while in fear of them, and dared to go out with my friend Muste to visit the surrounding like children born there. We saw hundreds of people settling around village, some under the trees and bushes. Some made home just behind someone's house cooking something to eat. The whole mountain and villages looked as if it was covered by displaced people like blanket on a bed. No place to put our feet as if bees were covering its hive sitting on top of each other. The smokes arising from their fires for cooking had covered the entire area like fog and hard for us to see everything with heavy cloud and rain over side of a mountain that made the whole area very dark. Even though the whole area was very scary to see, we kept going to explore it. Muste's younger brother Malik followed us, and we told him to go back home, for we didn't want him to come. We told him not to follow us and urged him to go back home with anger toward him. He refused to go back home and kept following us. We finally let him to come, but never to cry in case something happens to us. He said all right, and came with us. We all three went to see the dense mountain together. It was scary, bushy mountain, hard to walk in it, and I went in front and Muste followed me with his brother.

I started to have a bad feeling about this trip. The more I went, the more bumping stomach I got. I told Muste, "Something might be happening, for my stomach getting disturbed again and again. My eyes were rattling like snake tail and something bad was about to happen to me."

And Muste criticized, "You are a chicken and wrong on your eyes, nothing will happen."

I warned them any way to run for their life if something happened. As hyena was my scary friend, Muste was not even afraid of it when back home, for he was travelling alone in dark where infected by it. I kept scanning the bush for something to happen while walking, and there I saw something very big and hairy dashing toward us. My heart felt like it was gored out with knife. I asked Muste what was running toward us. He said, "He didn't see anything coming."

Then I urged him to bend down quickly and look the hairy beast coming toward us. When he saw it, he thought the creature might look like baboon. I verified, "Baboon! Baboon!" surprised, for I didn't see such thing before so big and scary, covered with a lot of hair.

He said, "Yes, Baboon, like big monkey," and I was surprised by it and felt little better that was not a lion, for its hair was so long and had big front like lion. What we didn't know was this baboon being the head of a group, for we didn't see what was behind it.

When we saw more following behind it like beads, hundreds of them, we wanted to run or climb a tree so that they did not hurt us like I heard horror story of monkeys: a group of them like these want to hurt kids and females only. First they beat you hard with anything they could find around like rock to bleed you badly, or smash your head. After they beat you with branch of trees as much as they could, they pricked your eyes out with heavy thorns they could find so that you remained blind for the rest of your life if not dead. Malik hearing us saying baboon, he had run like crazy, crying hard toward the village. Muste ran and climbed a tree. I ran like crazy and forced myself to hide in dense bush that was hard to enter to safe my life, for running didn't seem a safe option since I was not good at climbing a tree. My heart was pounding and I almost peed on myself, fearing if they found me. My body was hurting and bleeding from entering this dense bush which was impossible to enter. For I was seriously scared of them, I watched them in pain, while praying to God to save me from these extremely big animals that could toss me around like coin and shred me to pieces. I gazed them coming toward me, I prayed and prayed, "Oh, God! Do not let them see me, save me today, these beasts are fierce and cruel to children and females, put cloud on their eyes, and pass them around me safely." The first one came about eight meters from my bush and stood looking back to others. It said something I guessed and it didn't see me and continued walking in pride and passed by me followed by others. I was relieved a little, but still kept watching what they did and amazed to see, some talking to each other in their way, and some got beaten by strong males while being caught cheating over girls and wives. I saw many amazing actions in their society. I was scared seeing their fierce aggression toward each other, but their dazzling funny action and living made me laugh in my heart. I learned many things about them which I didn't know before that made me happy.

What a relief that they all passed me, and I sighed and thanked God for it, for I was still alive. Fearing they might return or others might come, I came out of bush while it scratching my body; and began to look for my friend in pain. I was afraid to shout his name, for the beast might hear and come back, I slowly said his name, and saw him on a tall tree. I was glad to see him alive and encouraged him to come down. Still shaking, we laughed by our action and agreed not to return again and headed home. We found Malik made it safe home, but our families were laughing at him when he told them about the monkey that scared him. We also told them how we escaped and they laughed at us. They warned us never ever again to go to the mountains, for there were many dangerous beasts in them.

We agreed not to go again, for baboons already scared us and became our first lesson. They added, "You came very close to main Somali army camp in the area where there were many extremely dangerous soldiers settled. They could have shot you by saying you are spies for Ethiopian army." They scared us not to leave the village again. We thanked God to spare us from these close calls today. They were right, many soldiers dressed in very different uniforms like green leaves and heavy boots. They carried a variety of guns with chains of bullets wrapped around their body. Some guns were short and heavy it looked with circle pan like case under it.

Really scary guns and soldiers began roaming the area like ants. Like I thought; I found that this small village had twenty-seven total residents and twenty two of them were the Amharic Ethnic people, and only five of them were Oromo. I realised that these Somali soldiers came to visit these Amharic people they never saw before as a zoo from time to time and surprised why they didn't kill them. I also found that they all had Muslim names, the same as Mr. Adam who was kind to us to stay in his yard the next day. I wondered if they had these names changed before, or after to save their life, or they had them before Somalis came. It was a mystery what happened here, but amazing to see all these things especially how these Amharic got to live in the desert far away from their usual town's life. My dad had left some money in his pocket to buy us potato from residents and their potatoes were too small, not tasty like our area. I found it amazing they grew them there in their desert farms when I visited Mr. Adam's farm. A sorghum stems were very small, shorter than me while our area were twice as tall as me. I wondered and amazed at all these things.

I saw some coffee trees I had never seen before. Their main income came from contraband items like cigarettes and clothing from the surrounding area. Things were different, how to survive and live here. It looked as if we finally found a place to live free of danger and war, for we were now far away from Ethiopian army protected by heavy mountains I thought. I also felt that Ethiopian army could not reach here to these rocky mountains, which had no roads for tanks and army vehicles, assuming that crushing all these heavily armed Somali army was not possible. I began comparing our area of birth with these places, fearing that we might be trapped here for a long time in the desert with small potatoes and weird living style.

Part 8
Settling with Baboon

It looked we had no chance to go anywhere or return back so we had to get used to this life of desert jumping from rock to rock like baboon giving up thinking about going back home. After a while we ran out of money and in order to survive my dad begged for dates from Somali army's camp for us to survive the whole week. On the first day, I was shocked to see my anus dropped a waste similar to gory liver like baboon that ate red cactus fruit. I thought I was going to die from bleeding at the bottom, eroding my stomach and intestines. I wondered why these armies didn't die eating this bloody food every day. Several weeks later of eating this dates, we heard some shelling behind big mountain sounding like music to the ear from a place called *Iftawa*.[26] We heard that heavy Ethiopian army came there to fight. This news of first heavy fighting in the area suddenly made us to move again, this time toward south west side of big mountain which my family thought safe to go rather than north predicted. It was like going back to the direction we came from toward danger. My heart began beating again to what to happen, now that we were going toward disaster. We had to walk like turtle the whole day while smearing trees and bushes with red diarrhea on the way to reach a very big mountain.

Once we made to the top, I saw a fecund land behind it, similar to where I used to live. This place was said to be *eggu*.[27] From Eggu mountain when I looked down the hill, we saw a flat land as far as

---

[26]   Bright and very shiny.
[27]   To wait.

almost eyes could see covered by corn and sorghum plants. It was really nice green land that took my breath away. It made me very happy to see this, for I thought I would never see such a place again.

My eyes that had dried in a desert now became wet green and its current rushed through my body as electricity. I had an amazing feeling of hope to stay in this place and enjoy it if we could survive this war. I was surprised to see many villages in this green land and there was only a few heavy red rock on top of this *Eggu* mountain that made it little different than my birth place. I found the whole area to be very beautiful. I asked my dad the name of this flat place and he said, "*Raree Eggu*"[28] and I was curious to know why they called it *Raree Eggu* since *raree* meant "flat, green land" and *eggu* meant "waiting."

He said, "The place where our ancient army of forefather's used to wait for each other during war time, most names of places and towns you hear in our country were given like this and became our history. Our town, *Bate*,[29] was given after the soldiers spent the night walking, and the sun came out on them." He then taught me many other places names how it happened and I was excited to learn new things. We could have attempted to reach a village my dad wanted us to go, but it was getting darker so we decided to spend the night at one village of *Eggu*, just down the hill since we were tired walking all day. Somehow we survived the night and the sun said hello to us, and my dad told us to go to the far place of my mother's relative village located at top of Eggu mountain just little down its hill we saw from here. I was surprised to hear that we had relative of my mom this afar place which now getting there was not going to be easy at all as I felt it.

My dad encouraging us to go faster and I kept going like lame person for the road had difficult terrain and stones as big as huge beetle. Somehow we hardly reached its first village of verdant land for the first time. There was heavy rain in the area and a cold air at *Raree* seemed to cut my hand and leg to throw it away. My face and

---

[28] Flat, wet and grassy land.
[29] Rise (of Sun).

body was frozen, with fatigue of travelling and put us in dangerous situation. We were unable to reach our intended place so we begged from villagers some wood and fire to keep us warm for the night and laid down next to it and I felt asleep for it felt good.

In the morning, draft of cold weather woke us up, without our permission. Since we didn't have fire left and nothing to eat, we could be freezing to death sitting there. Then we chose to go toward our *Eggu* relative village, for we were going south at this moment. I was worried that we were getting close to war now than ever. We kept going in the cold morning weather where the roads were narrow and full of long grasses that were wet with morning dew. I didn't have the right shoes for weather like this and walking in it made my feet wet and frozen more. When I jumped to the farm from grass, not to make me wet, then the corn and sorghum leaves dumped water on my dress, and made me like wet rat. It was hard for me to move because I was badly bitten by cold and empty stomach which made my intestine hardened like cold chain. My spinal cord bent down like hundred years old lady adding difficulty to my steps. My cloth was frozen with water icicles like my skeleton that it felt to break like glass. I feared for my life, for there was no road to escape these dew and wind co-operation that shrunken my body like old rug. Children were also crying from it and put me in more anxiety. I kept going in this state and feeling so terrible nothing could be done. "Nothing, nothing, and nothing," I whispered. I repeated while kept going with my family, "It was beautiful and good to see everything of this nature and world life!"

When we reached the flat lands' halfway, I asked myself, "Where is our beloved sun? Why didn't she come out to warm us up from this cold beast?" There she was suddenly appeared a little from her house, and I wanted her warm hand right away, but she was far and walked slowly toward me and I was toward her. A few minutes later, she began to chase that freezing wind and wetting dew.

"Oh, benefits of the sun, who really understood its blessings carefully, if she was not there to help, I was dead, we were all dead," I flattered her in my heart. I was not fully warm yet, but gave my thanks to both God and the sun to help me like this. After a while, she did warm me up good, but not enough, and sometimes I hated the shadow from corn leaves that covered my body, for the sun was not high enough in the sky to wipe it. A few kilometers after, I was very warm besides annoying clouds that came to pass over my head. I felt like cursing it for not caring for me and urged it to move on quickly, but nothing I could do. This was nature, beyond my control and order. When the cold friend was gone, only two friends, hunger and tiredness left to go with me to *Eggu* village. At last when we all arrived at *Eggu*, I told them to sit down with me and they all gladly did after refusing for a few hours, not to sit alone. My relative and villagers were happy to see us, and welcomed us all. Then the villagers and relatives felt sorry to see our situation and spread in front of us injeras that were not better than my mom. This was not a time to judge food, no other choice left and I ate very fast to fill my peanut bag to defeat hunger that was bothering to kill me. I chased and buried thirst by sipping, once water, once milk, and hot tea until they were out of my body without any ransom money, but my body was so tired that I didn't have any weapon to show them way out of me very fast.

Knowing that this tiredness was stronger and smarter than me, I left it alone predicting it would go away by itself sooner or later by hating my body. I thought I had a child body, and it might not like to stay in me too long and I ignored it, but gave it some change I had in my pocket and identification card to leave me alone quickly. It was happy about getting these two things and began its journey away from me, but not willing to go away completely. I tried to sleep more to screw it up even though I gave it something to make it happy. It knew what I was doing to it, and said, "You will see I am going to avenge it when you try to go outside."

I replied, "All right let see, I will not back down from you, what you are going to do to me? For now just stop bragging toward me." Then it begged me, "Please forgive me, the reason I said all these was for you made me mad, now you can sit and chew Kat, or if you want go to bed, just do." And it gave me its good advice. Right away, I wanted to make it my friend for it was always around me as my partner, for I realised it was inevitable to see each other again. For hunger and thirst, I made them understood that they would not able to hurt me as long as these villagers around me.

After I asked tiredness to promise me, not to hurt me anymore, and then it sworn, "If I hurt you again, let God kill my mother and make me fly than walk on foot!"

Then I was surprised to hear these, "This is not swearing, you just blessed yourself, this is not swearing," I opposed.

Then it replied, "I cannot say more than these swears, God kill my mother is not easy thing to say."

I replied, "You are unique English person, I had never encountered before, now I want to go out to pee so don't be an obstacle."

Then it said, "All right," before I got up then it pulled my leg down as if something stabbed my thigh.

"Go now! I will free you slowly assisting your body, all you have to do is be patient and keep going," it added, "I don't like someone that gets angry and worry. My worst enemy is this person, who ever got angry to me, will hurt itself." After I stood and paid attention to its softly voice advice that took my breath away, like it said to me, I made it to the farm to relief my bladder from hell liquid.

"Yes, you are right, I had nothing to say to you, you spoke the truth," I clarified. We could see a town of *kombolcha*,[30] far down the hill of *Eggu* that was annihilated by war, became a ghost town. Anxiety abducted my brain to hear from villagers that this town was dangerous fighting place from time to time. I was very scared to be closer than ever to the nose of war we were running from, and prayed to God to keep me safe. I kept watching the Somali army going by and resident's action to understand what was happening. On one hand, the Somali army said we came to liberate you from oppression and we were Somali like them, and on the other hand, they robbed villagers for their needs using excessive force and tactics. I said to myself, "The reason of this war from both sides was to dismantle us from place to place and make us hungry to beg for food and kill us." I didn't see any benefit at all and it looked I would never see in my lifetime as I doubted. I was swallowed by thought of this war, human

---

[30] Overthrow.

THE CAT MAN AT THE HORN OF AFRICA

suffering, and the shape and condition of the country. I prayed to God to keep us alive. Like devil, my soul began to jump from mountain to mountain, valley to valley, land to sky, desert to fertile land and I was perplexed by it. Everyone got worried and became unhappy like dark clouds hovering over them. They began praying to God like me to spare their life feeling something coming.

When afternoon arrived, there we saw smoke arising from a village south of Kombolcha, and then we heard a few gun shots there. We felt the Ethiopian army moving toward us, shaking ground like elephants, and started burning everything on their way from coast to coast as far as eyes could see. All mountains and villages covered by smoke and made a heavy cloud moving on the ground toward us. We feared this was going to be a very big and dangerous army toward us. I wondered why the trees and bushes didn't run for their life toward us. Everyone at *Eggu* went out to watch this action like squirrels came out of holes, on lookout for foxes. Some astonished by it while some were ready to run. There was no doubt; I had to run again with my single pant and shirt on my body. I had no other possession to take with me as I used to it, but watched amazing blaze like mountain goat saw a lion while standing my ears like rabbit for action. It was late afternoon; everyone and I guessed that they were little far away to get to us tonight. We assumed that they might stay overnight around burning sight. Besides, like it was rumored, the Ethiopian army had a chicken heart to move forward in the dark which gave me some hope that running from them right away might be a foolish thing to do. If needed, I was ready to step on the fart pedal with my foot. I wondered where we would go next to escape them. The sun was set as I was watching the smoke and shooting also died down with burning. I felt little better. It was true, they didn't move and burn anything at all after sun set, but Somalis were running around like bat about mid night by saying the word I didn't know "*Habash*,[31] *Habash*" repeatedly. They seemed to get ready for a fight without sleeping. We, too, sat on our behind like dog and watched toward Ethiopian side in case they moved early morning. The Somalia army seemed to be very

---

[31] Arabian and Somlian way to say Abyssinian.

happy to go and fight the Ethiopians and kill all of them right away. I could see they were unable to wait and engage them. I began to question them why not scared to fight and die, or kill as much as they could. Was this what they did for a living? I didn't get it.

As the morning sun was rising, there Somalis were rushing like river toward Ethiopians for a fight. Shortly after there, guns began to laugh harder and harder. It sounded that both sides were opening fire. Then we heard heavy gun noises we had never heard before that began to shake my nerves. Many crackling guns sounded like music that I never heard before, sounded good to hear from very far. If they guaranteed not to come close to me, I could fall asleep to it. We watched them fight, standing on the top of the hill like thousands chicken singing at the same time. Then, suddenly there was heavy explosion in it that raised my hair like grass and even shooting was halted right away. It also spoiled my music like moulded bread. Once again, this boom sound had begun charging my battery to run like Hawaiian's lizard. I was surprised why they halted shooting for many seconds any time loud hooting go off from *RBG-7* and cannon. "How come they were able to stand the noise of them? May be they scared, too like me any time this happen, and stop the shooting," I guessed. These bombs had shaken my lips and the foundation of my body. The sound I didn't want to hear at all. The Somali fighters became water running down the hill in front of Ethiopians. Then the crackling of guns, and smoke started to get closer to us. When Somali soldiers were pulling backward, it indicated that we had to put our leg in gear eighteen with them.

Part 9
Raising Tail North

We raised our tail high like camel, we called each other from where we were, and some children began crying. Cows already began mooing and donkeys braying. It was unbelievable so many people on the move with us, and I wondered where we could go, or ended today. We continued toward north as much as we could and came close to that impossible mountain to cross. My brain was burdened again, how we could go over it fearing we might not make it safe. My dad and mom were helping to carry younger ones as my friend; the tiring began to climb my legs. When I looked at some old people moving with no help and the blind ones made their stride to escape; I was really saddened by it and encouraged myself to go more, but unable to help them. My complaint of being tired was unfair and it seemed like joke comparing with them. Pregnant women were whining to move with family for those had no donkey, or horse to carry them. Some women had their baby on the way trying to escape while moaning and bleeding. I was overwhelmed by so much suffering. A woman having a baby must stay in the house for forty days helped by her family and friends, or villagers: not to move, not to cook for her safety and health, but this war didn't care of them at all. I was sad everyone had to try to get away however they could, crawling, running, walking and it motivated me to go on, but some weak and disabled ones lost their life.

On the way to mountain, bombs, and bullets seemed to stretch their hands to pull our legs, but we kept going to escape them. Then we realized that climbing this big mountain very fast was not easy and safe, so we changed our direction to the two little mountains and valleys, east south of the big mountain. This direction even forced us a little bit closer to a fighting than we wanted and it began to twist my intestine like snake in motion. Forming huge animal chains, we increased our speed as hot fighting rushed behind us. We saw thousands of fresh Somali army rushing by us toward Ethiopians as if to stop them advancing toward us. Heavy gun and bombardment increased making echo ahead of us, so loud that we thought we were in the middle of two guns. I was very appalled by it as if I was already dying. Burning houses, smokes of weapons, donkey's asses mixed with human farts were not very pleasant, and started to damage my nerves accompanied by headaches. I tried to cover my nose and mouth to minimize them, but these new smells, upset my stomach, I didn't know how to stop it.

After we passed second small hill, there I saw another huge mountain, a mother of all the mountains that might be blocking another desert I feared. There were two huge villages on the bottom and side of it. My heart muttered, "There we go again to desert, may be these are last villages to see," but my father said my grandmother was born there at a big village on the right. My heart was delighted as if another beautiful injera was waiting for me since this place was where my grandmother might have been trained to make that delicious bread. I imagined good things on my way, besides bombs if we really went there. We kept going on to the road that lead to that village when suddenly two extremely noisy, ear deafening big birds made awful noises and flew over our head. They were trying to poop on us something by turning their noses straight in the sky, and I could see their dark round hole on the bottom flashing something toward us.

Then a flash turned into loud *boom* that a whole ground and mountain danced with us. We were baffled with merciless, balloon-sized bombs and afraid that we would never make to that village. It had also loud deafening shooting gun rounds that my liver hit a bladder. I thought this was the end and ran to hide in bushes behind trees any time these noisy birds kept running over us, shitting and shooting terrifying things that even the ground begged them to stop. Many got killed in horror state, we were so close to die and lucky to still breathe and move. No place to go, or hide from heavenly bombs and machine guns raining from the sky with tanks, RBG-7 noises on the ground that furnished and garnished us with bad smell that became nightmare to handle. I cried and cried to be saved by God at least for the day. I wished to enter a ground like armadillo or jinn. We found no way out, seemed stuck there for more danger. I tried to call my dad crying, "Father, Father," while shivering, lowering my voice down for the planes not to hear me. He cried, "Hide your fingers nails and cover your eyes, a plane could easily see them and bomb us." He also asked us never to look up. I tried to bury my head down and wrap my hand around my body becoming human ball to save my life. Any time they threw bomb, I was expecting to hit me and frowned my face like lobster shell. Finally, they came close to the ground as if scratching the bushes over our head and made earth shattering sounds, deafening our ears on purpose it seemed; and ran to the west probably running out of weapons. I doubted they had gone, but I was still in one piece with my family, and no one was taken away, or hurt. We began our journey on a dark street, praying for eagles not to come back. That big mountain was covered by smoke as if it wanted to be dressed white and I feared not to be the same place where we were going.

Finally, we arrived at the village my dad said belonged to grand-mom. The ground looked strange which I had never seen before as if someone painted with blood and vegetations were beautiful. I asked my mother about strange red colour and she told me that the place and village was named *ella dema*,[32] for there were many unexplained red holes. Indeed, its colour was very beautiful and took my breath away; I was surprised by its nature how it came to exist close to this huge mountain. When we arrived at my grandmother's brother house, they were also on a verge of dashing to a mountain, but welcomed us to their house. There were infinite numbers of Somali soldiers in the village and the mountain. They didn't seem to care much for fighting going on far down the hill even though their body and language showed a little concern. It seemed they were just enjoying the meat of robbed animals from villagers. They settled around many villages that we passed through and I had no idea why my heart was crippling with fear every time I saw them; they might hurt me soon or later. I heard that the Somalian army around *Ella Dema* and *Fellana*[33] were so strong and dangerous that several times they managed to disarray the merciless advancing Ethiopian lions. Only a few of them escaped on bare feet to where they came from and this shade light on good news and guaranteed they would defend us there. I didn't mind to stay at beautiful red holes even though the area was contaminated with heavy intruder fighters.

We came to learn that *Fellana* was like *Kombolcha* to be the most dangerous fighting place where Ethiopians managed to come from

---

[32]   Red hole.
[33]   Spoon.

time to time. There were thousands of unburied corpses laid around with burned tanks and army vehicles. We could see vultures hovering above *Fellana*, to feast on the dead and some of them flew with soldier eyes, skins and muscles in their beaks. I was more appalled by cruelty of this fighting and I thought I could be one of those bodies to be ripped apart by surgeon scavengers. I tried to find what name and city might lay behind a mountain of *Ella Dema* if it would be dangerous, or not, and they informed me that *Hama*[34] laid behind it. I was even more breathless to hear word *Hama*, for we could be mow down by something like its meaning, and pondered if we went there might be end of my life. However, it was exciting to learn new places, its impressing names and trees in the mountain, and my relative names I never knew before. I accompanied my relative and villagers kids to that big mountain for shepherding duties. I wanted to go to the top of this mountain to see what laid beyond, but going there didn't seem good and reality by myself. I could see in front of us toward *Fellana* and *Kombolcha* as far as eyes could see. All the little mountains and villages toward that big town of Harrar where all the Ethiopian army were pouring toward us like rain. The place I was born could not be seen from here, but it seemed I could smell its air. Certainly I could have seen it if I made to west side of *Eggu* mountain from *Ella Dema's* mountain. At least I had enjoyed peaceful life and spectacular view of the surrounding area for one week without any gun shots. Again I thought the Ethiopian army wouldn't dare to pass Fellana where they lost several times.

When second week started, shame on my thought, there I was wrong; we heard that a heavy Ethiopian army was on the move from Harrar cleaning Somalis toward us. We saw this to be serious offences and threatening to us as the Somalis were shaken and ran around like fox with tail down its legs from *Kombolcha* toward us. When Ethiopians reached a place called *Chefe Annani*[35] the neighbor of Fellana which was very close to us, we were able to see smoke rising with heavy bombardment. I felt this was dangerous and my heart

---

[34] Mow down.
[35] Milky grass.

64

began to hammer my ribs. We watched them fighting there all day long and they seemed to stay for the night even though it looked like they had a power to come forward. There were not many houses to burn this time, but some smokes were coming to heaven from a few houses. Only villages close to *Ella Dema* were not burned on previous fights since Ethiopians were unable to come this far. People from these areas were able to watch fighting peacefully whatever was going down far side of *Fellana, Chefe Annani*, and *Kombolcha*. This time as a rumor from Somali fighters and some villagers confirming there were over ten thousand Ethiopian soldiers at *Chefe Annani*. This number of Ethiopians told me about our move might happen somewhere evening time as I was standing next to Somali fighters who were watching toward *Chefe Annani* with something like binoculars turn by turn.

The way they handed these binoculars to each other and talked, shading light on something extraordinary never seen before was coming toward us. I was even more appalled hearing that they saw Ethiopian soldiers who were very dark, tall, large noses, which their feast could fit in their noses and had the eyes as big as a cow and their skins looked like dark hippo. It looked Somalis were peeing on themselves like goat to face these soldiers and I found this was bad news Mengistu[36] brought them from a far province of the country as a dangerous army with no mercy for anything. I was afraid we could be eaten alive if we got caught by these soldiers whom I might not understand their language even if I wanted to beg them not to hurt me. With their fear and suspicion they might move, I sat and stayed all night on the big stone next to a village while looking toward them without eating my dinner. I thought of journey to a desert again, and I prayed for the fighters' plane not to show up in case we had to move since I comprehended that they were the most terrorising things ever from the sky. I cursed the person who ever created this thing to throw up on human beings from above especially the innocent people who had nothing to do with this war and no benefit out of it. My brain

---

[36] Name of Ethiopian military leader took power by force after King Haile Selasse.

was swollen as balloon in fear where to escape it if they appeared with their bad ass to fart on us and thinking about them kept me awake all night long.

At dawn, I was really tired and then felt sleepy. I just napped while sitting by the stone and there someone was trying to wake me. It was my dad, and I refused to give up my sleep, and he repeated many times, "Get up, get up, shooting began, can't you hear it?" Suddenly my sleep was erased from my body and my heart, stomach, and intestines formed a sad orchestra. He added, "Let's get ready in case they come." It was too early morning that looked still little dark to see clearly. Shooting was not strong enough, but only heard as a giggling hyena.

Somalis began knocking their guns with bullets on their sides and began to flock toward shooting area. I gazed their actions with worried eyes. Fighting intensified by minutes as the Ethiopian came down to *Fellana*, and the direction we came to *Ella Dema*. Now those virgin villages never toasted before began to smoke from fire. The sun couldn't kick out some fog from the entire area and they settled on the ground and mixed with burning. *RBG-7* and few bombs started to go off to make things worse and they were moving little by little toward us while fighting in those fogs and clouds.

Part 10
Flight to Laga Hama

When shooting got closer, we got scared and began moving with animals to the mountain through a narrow road toward *Laga Hama*[37] direction. Somalis were backing up like truck with their noises and their commotion indicated that they couldn't stand Ethiopian force to make us climb this big mountain, which even the cattles were unable to move properly. Some owners began to pinch them while

---

[37] Place to mowing grass.

others beat so that they moved quickly, and animals were groaning as if they were cursing their owners and the fighting. While laboring, we were able to make it to the top of the mountain of *Rabo*[38]. We stood there and looked down to the foggy war zone. As soon as they came to my grandmother's village and we were shocked and decided to go down to *Laga Hama* a very steep mountain that scared me to death as if I was about to fall off to the bottom. The view from the top was breathtaking for the eyes could see many milky mountains as far as to the end of the world. It almost made me forgot the war itself. We kept going until we reached *Hama* a very exhausting journey where I faced desert again.

I could see some thorny trees I had never seen before that greeted me with a lot of camels moving in them. Their farms had strange sorghums and corns stem as heavy as a leg of a Mosquito and they were very short. I was very astonished by these, and we reached a village called *Huwe*[39] *Hama*.[40] The heavy fighting now reached *Rabo* mountain above us where corpses were rolling down its sides; I was relieved there was no way we could be hit by any bullet from there. I looked up and enjoyed this intense sound of fighting like a pop corns. Sometimes the gun looked as if they fired toward us to scare me, but we surely felt safe. We were so tired and hungry; we began boiling a whole grain and beans that we brought under the tree like our house.

After we exhaled fear and tiredness air, we continued our journey more in the valley; deep in *Hama* mountains, leaving behind my grandma's relatives from *Ella Dema* who didn't want to follow us. For the first time, I saw a beautiful never ending sand to play on as soft as a silk, in the valley of *Hama*. I was bruised from a journey, but I began rolling in it like a donkey playing in the ash. These sands made me so happy that I thought I was on carpet of heaven people talking about that made me forget everything about a war. With other kids and friends, we raced in it as fast as we could, just trying to beat each

---

[38] Huge and steep mountain named after Rabo.
[39] Name of Place probably named after kind of grass.
[40] Cutting plant or long grasses with sickle.

other. We were so excited to see such a beautiful creation in *Hama* that I had never seen before. The fighting had died down, and we didn't know where the Ethiopian army gone, for they didn't follow us down to *Hama*, but it got darker after a while in our journey in the sand. We had to stop when we reached center of great *Hama*. There we saw only two houses near to the mountain, which made of wood and mud on top as a roof. We asked owner permission to stay the night. Knowing we were running from war, they allowed us to stay, but told us their rule of men and older boys must sleep out-side, in the open yard with camel while only small babies and ladies allowed sleeping inside muddy house. Then I wished I was a baby, regretting to become a ten-year-old boy. I asked them if the area had any hyenas, and they told me there was one here and there, coming from time to time which made my heart shrank by 10 percent. I was concerned and feared that it might visit me there since this animal had no mercy at all. I was not happy with this rule and told them I was afraid to sleep outside.

Then they began treating me like female. "Even ladies here wouldn't afraid of hyenas like you." The comment to call me a lady made me angry and I tried to defend myself, "This hyena is stronger than me, having forty horse power and very foolish in doing things when it wanted to. It might come to tear open my belly as I sleep."

They informed me, "Even little camels and goats sleep outside. How come you are afraid like this?" They pushed me to stay outside with them. As it was getting little darker, there I saw hundreds of camels and goats lead to a compound outside house surrounded by fence made of little thorny bushes, and no one watched them during the night. I tried to sleep while my heart was wondering about my safety. There I heard a loud cry that appalled me from a crazy camel. It became so aggressive and began spewing foam of saliva like laundry machine from its mouth. They had to lash both front legs together from dashing around and harming someone. This chilling noise I had never heard before added to the dread of hyena and I was con-cerned so much for my safety. Smell of manures in the area was also unbearable to fall asleep in it. I spent the night in this condition and I found *Hama* to be eccentric place to stay, the vicinity untouched by war where everyone lived a normal life. We were forced to stay in thorny *Hama* for one month with peace, but we were suffering of hunger and learned that *Iftawa* was also safe and very close to us. I could not bear drinking yellow and watery camel milk with its disgusting meat which I had rarely forced my soul to try, having no other choice. When I got skinny with my family, my dad worried and decided to move us to *Iftawa*.

After two hours journey, we managed to reach the mountain of *Iftawa*, which seemed not too high, but very long on the ground. We had to rest several times to be able to arrive *Iftawa* village. This time, we went to a side of small house, at the end of village and decided to build our own leafy house made of soft tree branches we collected from nearby bushes. It was funny leafy house not possible to put mud on it like *Iftawa's* people. It could not stop the sun rays, rain, and wind at all. My dad then bought two donkeys to help run villagers of *Iftawa* to transport Kat to *Arbukale*[41] and *Jaldeysa*[42] about one day journey from *Iftawa* so that we could have earned some money to buy food. As I heard, *Arbukale* was like town with so many houses made of tin roof built by Ethiopian army, but now under control of Somalian army. At night, it was flooded with many vehicles to bring supplies to them including *Jaldeysa* where trees naturally looked like grass house with little man made town. My dad liked his rising business of dealing Kat that mainly sent to Somalia, and began as independent dealer. He was happy doing this, and I was surprised by it. His business motivated me to do *Jeblo*[43] to the locals if my dad bought it for me. When I asked him about it, he said good idea and bought a carton of cigarette to try. I was happy and began to learn the area little by little while selling it.

One day, I was able to go to a Somali camp while my heart was shaking. I was glad nothing happened to me even though I didn't sell much of the cigarette to them. I was not robbed by them either like I feared they would do, but little Somali's soldiers carrying guns

---

[41]   Name of place after some one.
[42]   Name of place named monkey.
[43]   Small movable business of selling cigarette or roasted and unroasted peanuts.

bigger than them, began insulting me by their language that I didn't know what they were saying. I couldn't say anything to them, for fear they could hurt me with their guns and accepted their blessings without any question. Their insult didn't matter when I saw how tiny they were and the big gun they carried around. I was swallowed by thought of how courageous they were to come to fight that big-nosed Ethiopian who could swallow them alive. "Are they afraid at all? Are they going to fight for sure, or just joking and pretending," many questions bothered me about them, which I didn't have any answers about it, but the guns they carried made me respect them. I blamed on war and time to be harassed by them. All I could do was insult them back in my silence. I saw some youth running away from danger being caught by Somalis and brought to camp as a spy for Ethiopians. They tied their faces and legs to the trees, and poked them with bayonet their behind to make them accept spying; then riddled their body with bullets and dumped it in the nearby bush, next to their camp for the vultures to feast on them. My sadness was covered with fear, and saw that human soul became little as lice. It became my routine work to go to their camp every day; lucky I was safe because they thought I was a local business boy. It seemed no war in sight for the time being; I became cigarette broker. I wanted to go farther place to sell cigarette, but little scared something would happen to me on the road. One day when I was at the camp, they decided to leave, and they made me carry, their two heavy cooking bails, to set up a new camp at far mountain of *Rabo*. I was little wondered why they changed the camp and scared that something might be happening. I doubted that this might be a sign of trouble to come. This *Rabo* mountain was connected to *Mucha*,[44] but not as big as *Mucha*. It had a lot of big trees close to river which made perfect camping ground and hiding out place from an airplane. In case of shelling by Ethiopian army, it looked perfect hiding place.

After I had seen this new place, I went home. My mother was sick, and I was unable to run my business as usual to help her to fetch wood for cooking from bushes. I was scared to travel far in a

---

[44] Breast (of cow).

thicket. I would collect quickly dry soft branches, and walked back fast, looking behind me for any beast that ran after me. We started to hear some shelling at far place of *kombolcha*[45], and other side of *Rabo* mountain hit by shelling from time to time. This concerned me, but as shelling increased many residents behind *Rabo* fled toward us. Some of them arrived on the back of donkeys with no limbs and while others suffered many wounds. Some also were grieving the loss of their immediate family members. This appalled me, but so far we were happy to be safe in *Iftawa*. Shelling was unable to pass *Rabo*. We saw planes bombarding behind the *Rabo* mountain. We rarely saw planes fly over *Rabo*, far away. We looked safe from them. Now we felt librated by Somalis since nothing was happened in this area and we began to treat ourselves like residents of the stones.

Part 11
Traveling to Arbukale

I had a desire to explore more land with my dad who became a dealer of Kat in the area. The day I wanted to go with my dad, I sat all night long organizing and tying the bundles of Kat without sleeping. Early morning before birds singing, I asked permission, "Dad! Can I go with you this morning?"

My dad replied angrily, "Shut up! You're rude! You can't go with me, the place I am going is too far, it takes me the whole day to go there, and probably I will reach there about evening, and I know, you are too weak to go there." "You can't keep up the pace with me all day long and if you are tired, I can't carry you, so shut up and sit," he warned me again!

Then I was mad at him for saying these, and tears filled my eyes. I was choked to say anything in anger. I broke my silence after a serious thinking, with strong voice. "Dad, I will go today! And I will

---

[45] Over turn.

not stay home," in threatening manner as if I wanted to swallow him alive. After he looked at me with his fierce eyes as hot as red pepper.

He warned me again, "Stop it, son! You cannot make it." Then again, I was mad at him for saying these, and tears filled my eyes, and I couldn't speak at all.

After a while, I repeated, "Dad, I will go today and I will not stay home." Then he warned me again, "If you said, I am tired in a trip at any time and give me troubles, I will grind you like a grain."

I assured him, "I will not complain if you allowed me to go today."

At last, he said, "Yes, you can go!" I was filled with joy tears in my eyes, and it rolled down my face like ball. I wiped it with my hand, then my mother gave us something to eat, and we loaded the donkeys and began our trip. The donkeys began moving fast and fast, farting nonstop, *dat, dat*…and I smelled their grassy gas blowing my face like wind. I was surprised how fast they went, and I must run to keep up with them jumping from stone to stone to keep my word. After short trip, I had realized, what my dad had said. This trip needed fast moving and speeding than I thought and it invaded my head. I was not sure if I could complete it at this pace. Running became my only choice to keep up with them, and I increased it recalling the promise I made to him without saying any word. We began going up and down of many mountains and he wanted to know how I was doing. I lied to him that I was still strong, not to show him my weakness and he praised me to be strong so far that I didn't fall, or complain about it.

He added, "You are strong and brave to keep up the pace with us." He praised and encouraged me to go faster, and faster. Once I went in front, once I went behind and once to his side, gazing east, west all mountains as tourist so not to upset my dad at all. The mountains were very scary, and they had little thorny trees. Its boulders were bigger than the house. After short trip, I was glad to see, nice gorges with a lot of sands and stones. I was afraid they might erode my feet. I asked my dad, "Are we going to see those nice sands like carpet at all until we reach our destination?"

He said, "Yes, we will be walking on those sands."

"You will like this part!" he added. I was happy to say, "Yes, indeed I like this kind of road." "Don't say you are tired, but this is the kind of road we travel from now on," he assured me. I didn't say anything about being tired, but shortly I began watching my feet sinking in the sand, and it dragged me behind. I couldn't step forward as I wanted with my ability. My strides were the same, but I seemed to walk in the same spot again and again as mouse in the science lab as if the sand said, "Don't leave me behind, stay here with me as my beloved friend." Sometimes it looked kicking my feet to dump me on the ground. I found the sand was good to walk on, but it tired my knees, and it entered my shoes to cause another nightmare. The thought of not making, got worse and worse, and I talked to myself like lunatic about diving into it, seeing never ending sand and my falling was eminent.

Now, I regretted my decision to come with him. "I should have listened to him in the first place," I brooded. The food and water, I gassed up from home, no longer existed in me, and my stomach became empty and filled with air. Water was evaporated from my skin in the heat. Hunger and thirst were beating me, and I was listening to problems of travelling. Fearing my dad, I told him I was thirsty. He said, "Thirsty!"

"Yes, I am very thirsty," I repeated.

Then he said, "Until we reached a village ahead of us, there is no water, and you have to be patient until we go there."

The sun was burning my body, I was thirsty, my knees were weak as old man, and I wished to see the village sooner rather than later. I couldn't keep up with my dad's stride. I hated myself, and I thought about going back, but it looked too late now. I was afraid, if I tried to go back, I could be a toy to baboon, and might be dinner to hyenas, so I took off my shirt and covered my head from sun, and continued my jerking journey without making him angry. The donkeys were also slowed their pace and intensity, they were tired, thirsty, and hungry as I did. My dad said, "*Hich*,[46] *hich*. He began beating them so they moved quickly. Was the place too far away or my dad

---

[46] Sound to move the donkey faster.

just wanted to go fast? He didn't seem to feel and care to what I was going through, and he began annoying me. He didn't seem to slow down, and his body was wet with sweat, raining down his face. A load on one donkey tilted to fall, and he urged me to run and hold with him to fix it; and I was happy to do it, for this gave me a chance to stop for a while taking break. I thanked the donkeys in my heart and begged them to do this for me more often.

After we fixed a load, my body accumulated some energy and I was glad to stop and getting some power to go on, but my dad started to push the donkeys aggressively as if to make up for the time lost fixing weight. Instead of walking faster, I chose to do small running in the sand to keep up with them. I liked this and able to do a few kilometers. The more I ran, the more I was tired, and for the second time a donkey's load tilted. My prayer seemed to be answered to rest again. We began our journey in the tiring desert; the sun looked closer to our skull than any other place on earth I had ever seen. After a few hours difficult journey, we reached a small village. We tied our donkeys to a tree and I was happy to march with him to a village. A villager gave water to my dad and I snatched from his hand quickly, and began gulping very fast as much as I could without breathing a minute like a donkey that never drank a water in a year. Then I stopped to take a breath, and my dad grabbed it from my hand and said, "Stop!" before I started on it again.

I was mad at him to take it back. I said, "Why did you take it, I didn't satisfy yet?"

And he advised, "Son you are young and don't know the consequence of drinking a lot of water especially when you travel. You drink less so you able to walk. You don't have any idea how far we have to go; and what you already drank may be too much, adding more would be more disaster for you to walk." Yes, he was right, I had already bulging tummy like basketball and my belly buttons overstretched as pregnant lady. I could take only a small step I realized, and then I walked like a ninety-years-old lady with my two hands down to a ground, unable to straighten my body. "Father, Father, my belly stabbed me and I was unable to take any step forward," I complained. I asked him, "Now what to do, I couldn't walk?" He assured,

"There is no remedy now, but you could walk slowly until you get better." I added, "Can't you see water is pouring from my nose and mouth, I am going to die." My dad understood a serious trouble I was in and told me to sleep a little bit under a big shade of a tree by side of sand. A shade was really cool with nice soft sand, and I was able to roll in it like donkey in ash with my back, and this excited me very much.

My dad forced me to sleep on my back for a while and I couldn't do it, for water began to push me. He asked, "How are you doing?"

"I got a little better," I answered.

He commanded, "Then get up and try to walk!" I didn't want to leave that cool place, but I held my knees with two hands and I got up slowly walking like a baby even though he wanted to stride very fast right away. My tummy didn't prick me badly this time, but my legs were unable to move forward; and I felt tides were clashing inside my tank as I took steps. I just realised I was committing suicide with my own hands. I whispered, "If I am thirsty, I will not drink like it again." The more I walked slowly, I got better and better. My dad noticed my progress and asked me about it, and I confirmed to him that I got better. Then he said, "Let's go quickly." Even though I wasn't perfect, I tried my best to make up to him so that I would not be an obstacle. I did my best strides and runs to help him move faster. My belly pain got worse with running, but I kept my words because slowing would be shame on me. I continued with the same pace while tolerating ache. We kept going like bullet with agony and rarely stopped to arrange a donkey's load.

After a while, we came to an Isa person sitting under a big tree, making tea for sale. I was terrified seeing him face-to-face for the first time ever. Since there was rumor back home said that travelling in Isa's territory was very dangerous because if one of them wanted to get married he must chop off penis of stranger passing in their territory to show how powerful he was to the girl and her family, and then she could only marry him. Besides this chopping, one might kill for sport and fun. I began staring at his long machete blade as tall as him and the way he looked, made me to fear that I was about to lose my little third leg, or get killed there.

My heart began pounding and pounding like never before as I got closer with my dad. Then I asked, "Dad, is he going to cut our bed snakes and kill us as people say in our area?"

He confirmed, "He will not do it, I always pass by him and he is respectful person. People might be wrong about it."

He made my heart less pounding my chest, but I still did not trust him as fear hovered over my head. I sat behind my dad staring at his texture and huge blade in case he decided to cut us so that he would rip my dad first. As he gave us water and tea, I imagined that he might draw his sword at anytime. After we drank his tea, and rested for a while, my dad ordered me to get up and I quickly got up and moved ahead of him so that I would not be attacked first if he wanted to do it. As we had gone little further, my heart cooled down from fear and I asked, "Are these people occupy the entire travelling area?"

He answered, "Right! They are the only people live all over this area. You are going to see their houses, women and children very soon." I was surprised; we were in their territory and began scanning for the sign of them and their houses. After a while, there I saw a lot of camels drinking water and people walking by and my heart began melting in fear like magma down the hill. We slowly passed them as they looked on us and I was glad they did not run toward me and my hot dog was still in place.

I was astonished to see that their women carrying something very big, soft, and shiny like seal, dancing on their back as if they were breathing creatures. I asked my dad, "What are those animals on their back?" He said, "They were carrying water in those shaved goat skin." I was breathless of their technology and invention I had never seen before, and I was curious to know if water was safe to drink from these skins I expected to be stinky. He assured to me that water wouldn't smell at all. I was even astonished by it when he said that the water would be as tasty as our areas buckets and gourds we used. "I wouldn't trust to drink from it even if I am thirsty," I was disgusted by it. I had seen many animals I had never seen before. When my dad told me their names, I was surprised and we kept going in the soft sand which joined with different sandy water. Then my dad informed me that we would be travelling in this river from now on. I got a chance to roll in it, wet my whole clothes and cool my body from the heat. After a short walk, I was surprised to find that my clothes already crispy dried to the knees. When I asked my dad what happened to all that water-soaked clothes and skin, he explained that the extreme heat caused your skin to swallow them. I found this to be fun and kept rolling in the water to cool myself, and to see if it dried up again, and the results were the same. About the evening we reached a town called *Jeldeysa*, where I saw so many cars head lights coming in and out like a bead to be Somalis' army vehicles. When we arrived, its houses were amazingly different than houses I ever seen. Strange trees were planted, or naturally grown in circles like houses and tied at top, making perfect house and they had a door opening to get in, and I was surprised to see many of them. There was no single tin roofs, grass, or mudhouses around. I had to guess that they might be crazy, primitive, or poorly creative people to call it a town with condition like these. We tied the donkeys to one of these tree houses, and unloaded their weights and entered inside. There was no bulb, or lantern lights besides burning wood on the corner. I was so tired to stay up, but I laid down where I sat to watch my dad selling the Kat, and suddenly went asleep very fast. A few hours later, my dad tried to wake me up for dinner and I hardly knew where I was. I managed to swallow food a couple of times and went back to sleep for my head became extremely heavy and unstable. My dad tried to force me to stay up and eat, but it didn't work. I went back to sleep again by telling him that I had enough food. In the morning, he woke me up to tell me that we were returning home, for he sold out all Kat. I hardly managed to wake up and then confirmed that I was in a strange tree house and shocked about it. I sat up and looked around inside of it and I went outside to see more. Then I saw thousands of Somali army and heavy tanks under the tree with other strange fighting vehicles, I had never seen before.

While shocked and amazed by these many dangerous equipments and army, I washed my hand and face with sandy river water and went back inside. My dad bought very big red tomatoes for us and said, "Take it, this is your breakfast!"

I joked, "Is this for breakfast, or for sauce?"

Then he commanded, "My goodness! This is your only breakfast, eat it now!"

"This is unbelievable! How could one eat this alone for a meal, only tomato by itself without some thing? We learned in school that tomato and salad could cause amoeba, and this big one especially more risky to take," I stressed like MD. "Forget about science and eat it, a long journey awaiting you soon, and you need energy for it," he warned me. I nodded, "Yes, you are right!" I grabbed three large tomatoes and sank my teeth in them, and its juices washed my chins and they filled my stomach up to the throat. We started our long and difficult journey back to Iftawa again, and my legs were swollen like an angry cobra's neck. Then my dad was curious to know if I wanted to go back with him second time. "Not again, ever again! You were the one suffering, and you continue to suffer; I thought you were enjoining the trip here, but I didn't know all these troubles. I never again dare to go with you," I stressed to him. He bragged, "I was doing this for you people so that you have something to eat, I am not doing for fun!" He bluffed and I was shocked to his comment that he was almost dying for us. I survived the trip back home learning my lessons. I stayed at the village and finished the cigarette I was selling.

Part 12
Becoming Blind Cat

After one month, I got strangely sick, and my both eyes would not open for one week. I was as if in a grave, I didn't know what was happening to me, there were no doctors to see me in the area. My family was unable to do anything to open my eyes. They tried traditional pills from the village attempting to open it, and it didn't work even more dirt was accumulated on it. It had swollen like golf ball and seemed heavily wounded, and I was unable to touch it, or wash my face for a week. It was sealed like baby mouse eyes just born, and I was afraid it was their turn to laugh at me, calling me smooth potato face. My mother and sisters helped me to the nearest forest for shooting my poo when I needed it. I had severe headaches from the pain of my eyes. I couldn't sleep night and day, the world become totally darker for me. I officially became blind cat from there on wondering if I ever saw again. My dad had halted his Kat business and every one sat by my side, and kept crying, for this was unusual thing ever happened to me and strange sickness ever known to them. They had no idea what it was and no solution, or treatment to fix it.

On the second week, I attempted to open them, but still failed to do so. There was no hospital to go to in the desert, unless it was baboon clinic in the bushes closer to the villages to help open my eyes. My family cried and commented that I became blind even more appalled me. On the third week, in the afternoon about 2:00 pm, we heard shelling approached to the mountain of *Rabo* and *Fellana*. One of them suddenly fell about two kilometers and everyone beside me shocked and ran out side to check it. My heart clicked and I sat up to listen to what they said, "It fell on that place near mountain, can you see its smoke rising from that place?"

Everyone was talking to each other and there was no shell came for about three minutes. Then another one fell closer to previous one, and they said, "Oh, God! It looked little closer to where we were." My heart began extreme beating and I shook. I was sure a person who stood ten meters from me, could hear my heart beat. I tried to open my eyes for emergency if I had to run, and I couldn't open it. I heard my mom grumbling that if we had to run, how could they able to take me along, and she began crying with my dad. My sisters also cheeped like little birds after them. Their cry had worried me more for my life, and I was sad for them. "Please don't cry for me, I will accept whatever God brings to me; and you try to save your life rather than we all die here," shouted and encouraged them to run without me.

While I was saying these words, suddenly one shell whistled above our hut like a sound I had never heard before and exploded about hundred meters from me. My body rattled like snake tail, and the noise deafened my ears while a big lightening flashed and torn my eyes lids like mushroom from the ground in less than a second. My visions had never been so perfect before, I could see even bacteria flying in the sky. I got up and ran outside, jumped so quickly down the hill like kangaroo about twenty terraces with a force of twenty horse power. Another whistled toward my direction I was running, and I lowered my head from being hit. I said, "This is it, I am hit this time. It is over for me!" I had almost defecated on myself feeling its heat warming my body. It then exploded in the village above me, and I flied and bounced like ball on a ground. I groaned of some pain and searched for traces of blood and checked if my body was intact. I dug for my soul, which was in the body and still breathing. I tried to find spots of wounds caused by it, and my eyes were still in business. I got up and looked toward the village and some were running toward me. Residents were running around in the village of smoke raised above it. "It was not a time to gaze the smoke, and commotion but to make it alive. I must be running," I said to myself. I ran on the road toward nearest mountain with heavy pain, putting my leg in thirteenth gear like never before. There another one hissing again, and I prayed not to hit me, and then exploded behind me to seal my hearing. Then, I heard a piece of it flying toward me, and I bent down to escape from it and it dug out a big stone ahead of me. I had stumbled on and grazed dirt with my chin. My teeth seemed sprang out, and blood was heavily poured from my mouth. Seeing heavy blood made me dizzy and I felt like throwing up. I was still alive and my heart rhythm still there and I got up and ran more with the blood flowing of my mouth.

After I ran a while, I felt a voice was calling me. I didn't know whose voice it was, but I saw some humans in front of me like hands waving probably Adam and his family under a huge rock. It looked they were waving for me, and I couldn't talk, but my heart was saying to them the F words and screw you, for calling me to stop running. I felt the insult in my heart for sure for my lips moved I believed. I had said to myself why they sat here, and called me to wait for danger. All I wanted was to get away from cannon sight before it got me. I ran to the direction of east rather than south west where shell coming from. I entered a farm with thorn and I felt they were stinging my feet as

I ran. I entered more dense forest where there were more dangerous thorny bushes pricked and chopped my skin badly. I reached denser bush, which I couldn't run in it, but I managed to crawl in it like snake for a few minutes. I was afraid it would come back again and crawled like four-month baby pushing stones by hand in front of me, and sometimes passed over them to reach a deep cliff. I realised that I couldn't jump over the cliff, but held a big tree root and dangled myself from it, for I couldn't go backward for fear that shell might come back to slap me. It was very deep cliff to try and I decided to stick my body between tree roots and became one of them. I felt that a tree was happy to have me in it and protect me from cannon. I spent there some time and felt safe and a shelling seemed to have died down. I tried to use my finger to scrap off a chunk of dried blood from my mouth that stuck together like crazy glue with my torn lips and I was unable to remove any of it. I just realized that I was unable to touch my lips and a pain was excruciating me. When looked down at my sore feet, I saw my shoes torn as rugs by thorns and gravel. No one was there to help me; I tried to call my dad, mom, and all family members one by one, none of them replied. I felt alone and lonely in the thick bush and scared that it was getting darker. I stood with pain to look for my family.

I couldn't able to stand at all as if my knees were broken, and its caps were shattered. My mouth was swollen and protruded like a pig. I could not see without looking down and I felt I was stunt pig. My body was tired, bruised and broken, I needed someone to move me, but there was no one. The sun was leaving and losing my family also concerned me.

It was the worst time of my life. Since I couldn't walk with many thorns in my feet, I cut the biggest of all thorns to dig out from my feet the others broken in the skin. I managed to remove about 40 percent and unable to see the rest in dark. A beast warned me to leave and I began to limp as much as I could while biting my fat lips. Somehow I could reach a farm and saw a person sitting under the tree. When I approached him, he got shock by the way I looked and he wanted to know what happened. I explained everything to him and he felt sorry. I begged him to take me to the village. He was scared of shell to come back and he was cautious for us to wait a little longer before going back to it. We waited in the farm for a few minutes, and I was restless about my family where about. I tried to convince him that there would be no more shell to come. At last, he agreed to hold my hand to the village. As we approached to it, we heard loud crying of people, indicating that there was life lost in the village; and I feared bad news to come of my family. I was in a panic state, my heart was pounding. If my family perished, I feared what was going to happen to me, how was I to survive? Who was going to help me? Who would be like my family? And many thoughts conquered my mind. Taking my soul to join them was the only solution, I saw. I asked my body to forgive me if I had to do it. Then, we arrived at the village to see huge commotion about a house where it looked as if someone kicked ant's building making terrifying noise. It was hard for me to go up, or jump the terrace quickly like I did before. I asked him to assist me to our hut and it looked no one there. Then we headed to noisy area where I saw my dad and mom to be alive.

I was glad they were alive, but my dad shocked to see me in that condition and hugged me. I felt little better that they were alive, and my dad was in tears like a baby and took me to our hut. I confirmed my siblings were alive, and I told them all that happened to me. We were glad that we all were all right. I asked him how many people died in the village. He replied, "No one had died, but a lady lost one leg and a lot of bits sifted her body. Some fragments hit her child's face and neck looked like tiger and zebra body with blood came out." I was sad to hear what happened to them. I was depressed to hear that a lady lost her limp was the sister of the person who allowed us to erect our bush hut in a yard. My dad was amazed and excited that I could see again as a miracle. A story of shell becoming my doctor was everyone's mockery including my family, but they were relieved that I could see like them. They thanked surgeon Cannon to cure the incurable sealed eye. Shelling had stopped as if it came to restore my eyes for free. I learned that some bad was also good. I had to make a little celebration and laughter to thank Mr. Cannon of Ethiopia to bring sight, once more to my face and happiness to my family. The blood on my lips, damaged skin, and knee pains were the only payment Mr. Shell needed.

My dad said, "You will be fine for the wounds." He helped me to remove remaining thorns from my feet, and he encouraged that I should move around to help them heal. I limped to the house of the lady lost her limp. I saw she was tied on wooden borrow like coffin and taken to *Hama* Somali's army camp to treat her. I sat in her house with remaining people of the village with sadness, crying and wiping their tears. About midnight, they returned her to village while crying, and some of people in the house were afraid she died hearing a cry nearing the village. Then my hair began to crawl one by one. My heart began jumping, my skin trembled, and my eyes spun. Some ran toward them and began to cry and noise increased. Little ones also began crying like tiny mice. They moved me to cry with them. Then her dead body arrived, and every one cried the whole night.

Morning arrived, and they took mother to grave and her child returned to her brother's place. We grieved her death for two days, and on the third day, about eight in the evening, there came whistling shell again. I had to put down the unsalted bitter porridge for dinner back to the bowl and ran to hide toward five goats and three cows in the barren. As the shell went off, they freaked and began to kick and step on me. I had to bear severe pain and smell of their waste, for running out side was not possible. One fell above our house and one down the village and one far-off village and it had stopped without hurting anyone, but it made me flow warm urine on my thigh. We were relieved that its attack contract was over for the night in our village, but shelling continued to roar like lion on *Rabo* mountain across us. We were afraid the whole night it might come again and we were unable to sleep very well. We knew that this explosion came from very far city of Harrar as we heard it before. We didn't want to run. We were not sure if they got our address to bomb it on purpose, or by mere chance. We were astonished and kept on blabbering about it. We were tired of running and we had no choice than to stay and depend on God to keep it away from us. We took our chances to stay while listening to the drumming shell across mountain from us. We felt that war was getting more muscles than before as shelling was continued on a regular basis across the mountain. It seemed as if the Ethiopian army strengthening its attack toward us to get back control of what they had lost.

After one week of shelling, as we suspected, Ethiopian army commenced its heavy attack north toward us. Frequent hovering of fighter planes over the sky and its bombs raining at far mountains trembled us. Those mountains were also covered with heavy clouds as if to swallow us and their fogs settled on the trees, dressing white and milky state scared us. While we were in this alert mode, fearing bad war to come or start we heard strange loud explosion coming from west side of mountain, which we had never heard before. Explosions of shells that opened my eyes looked a baby to this one. If my anus was clogged with garbage and ears were deafened, these ones definitely would open them right away guaranteed. I was shocked even the mountains would run from it if they had limps to dash with. Its nonstop explosions were unbearable even to the trees and I lost my breath. I did not know why we didn't run right away. As these terror of automatic sounds increased toward us, we decided to move toward Rabo mountain close to previous shelling place; for we had no choice now that west side was very dangerous. It made us walk very fast to this mountain to escape these loud automatic noises; our safety was started to be ruined. We wanted to reach to the mountain as our saviour. We couldn't wait until we reached it safely, but it looked too far from reality, for the approaching noise and shelling seemed too close than before. Somehow we reached one mountain with great fear. I heard another name of this mountain to be *Keira Siraj*,[47] which we would only find and face on judgment day that would take one thousand years to climb up and another thousand years to reach its bottom. I wondered how it was able to descend in front of us. I feared that we had reached the end of our earth where the sun usually would set. I was surprised to see this mountain while I was still ten-years-old child, long before I died. Climbing this mountain became scarier than this new automatic explosion that began to grind my

---

[47]   Super big hill to climb on resurrection day.

stomach. I didn't know what to do and had no other choice than to climb with people.

Part 13
Judgment Day on Mountain Siraj

We began to climb *Siraj* as if we were in judgement day. As expected truly this mountain was steep high and difficult to walk straight up ward. I walked just like old man while my mouth was colliding with my knees and almost grazing the soil any time I tried to take a step. I found it to be strange and miraculous thing to face at this age. Mostly my brooding became about this mountain and the shelling didn't matter as much. No one was walking straight just like me becoming grazing animals on four legs while groaning up the hill. Somehow, we managed to reach small flat part of it after long suffering and tiredness.

The fog was kicked out by sun from this part of the mountain, for we could see a little further ahead, but the rest was covered with more fog and unable to see the top of it. It might take many days if not a month, or year to climb on top, it looked. Here we saw a lot of Somali fighters and they seemed not ready and willing to fight. They might be cornered like us and scared of this earth shattering automatic noises they had never heard before. This thing so appalling that even trees and mountains could have run from it if they had wheels, let alone the Somali soldiers who only had spider legs to fight as I felt it. They too, began their journey to the direction of Mucha mountain, for there was no other way to go from this point to escape these terrorizing explosions. We also followed them, running out of any other option to escape them. Those soldiers closer to us were saying, "We are going home." I was not sure if they were scared of what was coming toward them from Ethiopian side, or they might have enough of this fighting and wanted to go home. We were confused to know the truth, but heard some of them said a word like *Amri,*

Amri,[48] which also related to my language as fate. We also thought their president; Ziad Barre might have ordered them to return to Somalia. We were astonished and scared what would happen after all these troubles we faced in the mountain. Shortly we felt most of them were running for their life while some left to slow down fast advancing Ethiopians.

As we walked on this mountain, we looked down toward north where we moved from, and fighting seemed to be heavily escalated and lucky we moved from there. We kept going very fast, and reached about mid day the mountain of *Mucha* with Somali fighters. Grandma's village was already burnt down after we separated. We learned that they managed to return to live in it peacefully since we left them. We were persuaded to stay with them in these toasted and grilled houses. We learned that it was safe there for a long time, and Ethiopian army was unable to go back there to attack them. This news delighted us that we felt we were safe again, but we could see the war still alive and groaning at far mountains. After one day and half at peace, we saw Somali cannons in *Fellana* were fired toward *Kombolcha* and *Harrar* towns. The Ethiopian also firing toward them. Now seeing these firing, we believed Somalis were not running at all. We stood on the boulders at *Mucha* village to watch both side to exchange fire and what was happening.

Almost at about sunset, we could see the shell from Somali side landing *Kombolcha* area and making some smoke and fires there. As doubted and expected, there shelling from Ethiopian side also began landing toward Somali and our direction in retaliation. One shell from Ethiopian side suddenly came whistling and exploded on the east side of *Mucha* village, just little above where we were watching from, barely missing us. I looked and saw flash of light sparkled between stones as it wacked it. Once more terror of explosion rocked my stomach. I didn't know how I jumped many boulders in a few seconds and found myself in the center of toasted grandma's brother's house. I ran around the house to find hiding spot fearing another one would come right away. There it was as if it found where we

---

[48]   Fate, or order in Somali.

were, another one pounded a few meters from village and gave us one louder shake. I was so terrified and lost were to hide from it, but then found a bed where I jumped and laid flat under it like cat waiting for mouse as my heart dribbled my chest in fear. I began counting them one by one and counted a total of nine of them close to us. I couldn't believe that I was alive and my head still attached to my neck and shoulders, not losing any limbs when it had stopped. The vibration rained a black powder of smoke from the ceiling on our head and some houses with tin roof looked like sifter of grain. I could see the sky. Even shelling had stopped, my head still was echoing to explosion and I was unable to rest.

As the sun went down, the villagers began to hit me with heavy rumors and grumbling that Somalis were leaving. Again this news scared me; we might be in serious trouble. When it got little darker, Somalis in the area looked preparing to retreat from the area. We also heard that the Ethiopian army moved from *Iftawa* to *Hama* valley which was just behind us to north of the *Mucha* mountain. We could not run toward North as *Suta dema* had predicted, but the only way to run and survive looked running north on the mountain. The Somalis also looked trapped with us in the middle since Ethiopians were down the mountain behind us and they also seemed to come from south and west. Hearing Ethiopians coming from all these directions began to trouble us. It was confirmed that heavy fighting and attacks were brewing from all sides toward us. While we were worrying of all these, there at night we heard heavy gun battles in the distance. After a while we heard *Kombolcha* was already under control of Ethiopian army. We couldn't sleep at night knowing that the Ethiopians would push toward us in the morning. Somalis were already on the brink to get away as we were only seeing their shadows in the village. As I tried to nap a little bit at down, there shelling and guns eruption told me not to sleep anymore. There also those bad bomb shitting birds began to hover above our head. I predicted today was the last day for us to breathe air when more Somalis fighters were backing away toward *Mucha* village. It seemed a few of them were fighting at front, and we began to move with those leaving *Mucha* mountains while hiding from planes like snake in the trees and bushes. I saw everyone was doing their best to save their life by going different directions over the mountain. It looked we were so lucky to walk in the thick forest of *Mucha* where the planes might have not able to see us face-to-face. We kept going while praying to God and reached a top part of this mountain and able to see down toward *Hama* and *Fellana* valley where fighting was escalated on both sides of this mountain.

Now we realized that our only way to save our life was just to go east on this mountain. The other three directions were full of heavy Ethiopian army sweeping Somalian fighters toward us. It looked no one was safe from them how they swept trees and rocks, and came toward us not leaving small stones unturned. Hundreds of villagers kept going with the Somalis as if they were heading to Somalia with them. I was surprised that my parents decided not to enter these floods and took a chance to stay on the mountain whether we escaped alive, or not in our own country.

As we kept going, we came across one of the widest and flattest stone I had never seen in my life with small opening. It was as if the mountain had its own hat to protect its treasure from rain, or animals. As villagers waking in front of us disappeared one by one under its cap opening, we had no choice than to follow them. I was very impressed to see that this was what people called cave and how God or nature did this.

At least I thanked God and this mountain to be here while praying for planes not to see us and throw its faeces on us and buried us alive. I lost my breath seeing that this opening was as big as football stadium, swallowing hundreds of us to hide in it from soldiers and planes. In the middle of all these actions, I felt that I could play even soccer in this cave and this gave me a hope that we would survive somehow if the Ethiopians didn't see us on foot. I was sure everyone entered except cows, goats, sheep, and donkeys that no people left in the bush. The more we stayed alive in there, I was lost by nature's creativity and chance of survival, but mostly sorry to see animals were the only running around creatures in the bush when planes zoomed by fast with loud noise, and hit it with rockets from time to time. After a while, it looked very safe for many people and some of the villagers began to cook their meal like they were in a village. I checked around its ceiling how the stone was made flat like that and every part of it from inside. I felt I was in another world and its house, but I feared that if it cracked on us, or earthquake came, we did not need any other grave to cover our body. I didn't feel all right to be buried in it until judgement day and this feeling rattled my stomach. I thought about being killed fast by shell and bullets were much better than to be crashed alive by this stone. I had never thought I could even come out of this rock that judgment day prophesized about.

As I was afraid, there a plane pooped on top of us and its vibration rained small dirt and mud on my hair. I was scared; this was the end a stone might come down on us anytime. I ran and hid between my dad's legs to be saved, or die there. My dad asked, "Would you stop this foolishness thinking and running around? I am sure this stone would never come down on us by anything. We are safe unless soldiers come here to find us." He tried to make me feel better, but I was almost leaked on myself whenever bombs fell, and mountain began to shake and dance in fear. Every time these bombs fell, I could hear the mountain sang toward others. About two o'clock in the afternoon, we heard no more bombs and gun shots. Everything in the land calmed down and even birds were silent. There was a rare small fire down *Hama* valley far from us, and we could smell fresh air of peace as shots in *Hama* Valley was losing its final sounds. My stomach seemed to calm down as if heart was smeared and marinated in fresh oxygenated peace, it began to rest. Something looked different; I guessed that we might be safe after all, very little fear left in my body, hanging by thread, unwilling to trust this fresh air. Later, we heard Ethiopian soldiers were in control of our area. Some senior and wise men of village advised us to stay in the cave until they confirmed that peace was for real and war was over. Fear of Ethiopian soldiers, what they might do to us began to wonder me. Were they going to kill us, or show mercy? When seniors left to find it out, we scared they would be killed, or led Ethiopian to us.

At this moment, I was really scared what to happen to us and my belly began shaking. Anxiety filled my soul, expecting the worst to happen to them as they approached the army in the village. I had a day dream about Ethiopians jumping up and down in celebration in the area, after chasing Somalis like fox stolen a rooster in the bushes. "What do we want?" I asked myself.

"We want peace, and this war gone," I said with doubt we might not out of the woods yet. I couldn't believe that those strong Somali fighters, having all the mothers of weapons I saw, just left like that, or beaten like wet rats out of the country. Or this was a miracle, nothing was believable. What I saw of Somalis didn't add up together. I had no answers to many thoughts and questions that I had. Then, suddenly we heard a big bang on the mountain, and I said there it had begun again, and the war was not over yet. Everyone in the cave felt same and shocked by it. They buzzed like bees about it, and I envisioned the seniors might be killed when they walked toward Ethiopians. Ladies feared the seniors were in the center of fighting and might be attacked or dead by now. They lamented and dreaded, "We told them not to go." And we began fearing the worst for them. We heard no more explosions and began to wonder if seniors were dead, or that was a greeting to elders' arrival toward Ethiopians.

After one hour of wondering about them, seniors arrived to our cave safely, and we were relieved that they were alive and they did not bring along the Ethiopians army. They said, "As we went down the side of the mountain, the army sent one shot of RBG-7 toward us, thinking that we were Somali army. When we raised white towel and our hand and told them that we are village people, they stopped shooting, and welcomed us. We also informed them that many of you are in the cave, and we came to get you down from the mountain."

We were delighted to hear the news that the Somalis were gone, and we could return to the village safely. Every one began kissing and shaking seniors hands in happiness and thanking them, for their effort and sacrifice they made for us. I could not believe that my body which was filled with soft muscles and nerves grew green leaves while all fatigues, shocks, and suffering were dropped on the ground like a pumpkin.

We inhaled fresh air for the first time, shell and gun smoke had disappeared from our lungs and land by the news. Then we began our move like ants by lining up the hill feeling excited and little worried if this was for real. We somehow made up on top of the mountain to see down the valley again. The land seemed calm as far as the eyes could see with some smoke still rising. My heart pounded a little like rabbit thinking that the soldiers might tricked us and then kill us. This might be their tactics and plan to get us, for it was not easy for me to trust a snake in the bed. Farm's vegetations like sorghum and corn were dry, and I was brooding about our country being safe and war being really over. After we went down the hill for a while, there another *RBG-7* shot toward us, hitting trees close by, with loud boom so close that my hair and green leaves dried and fell beneath my feet. My doubt of them to trick us became reality and my heart cracked again. I feared we were doomed. I blamed the old men who let us come face-to-face with *RBG-7* fire, to get us killed. They forgot to swing a white towel as they were being told. Once, they began swinging a white towel, and instructed us not to run, but to walk in straight line, the fire had stopped. We were still afraid of soldiers what they were going to do, or say to us and once we meet them, or entered grandma's village. While my stomach was grumbling with fear, facing those big nose and mouth soldiers, somehow we made it alive down to the village. As we met them and greeted, they welcomed us like respected citizens. They weren't as beasty as I expected, but some were really people I had never seen before, the binoculars of Somali didn't lie. They told us to rebuild our burned and demolished homes and they assured the war was over. I could not believe we were still alive and welcomed by them and the war was gone for good.

After we thanked the soldiers while my stomach still shaking, we went to grandma's relative house with happiness knowing that we were safe. The war that made us running around for almost one year, at last quenched like thirst. We, all the surviving humans, animals, birds, and insects breathed peaceful air for the first time. The smell of all heavy guns and cannons were gone, and we all surprised how clean the air had become in short while. There were many lives lost and corpse scattered and bones laughing to the sky, houses burnt and demolished, and lands and farms were toasted and trees were uprooted. Many people were robbed of their belongings, the rich became poor, and the poor became depraved of their survival. But we thanked, and thanked our God, for he made this war, at last to go away. We stayed at grandma's brother's house for one week, as a caution and to breath out all hell and guns' smoke. I often visited *Mucha* mountain with peace every day to thank it, for saving our lives.

I wished we had such a big mountain in our area that smelt very good with beautiful trees and that had many flat stones to jump from one to the other like monkey. Still I was worried if the war would return back one more time, but tried to advice my soul that this war was over and it would be no such a thing would come, I assured myself. At last my dad wanted us to go back to *Haro*,[49] for everyone was gone to their respective village. I didn't like to leave this beautiful mountain and red ground that a war showed me, even though I missed my village. I suggested to my dad to stay grandma's village for a month, or so, to play with the kids and later join them. My dad, then somehow convinced me to go with them promising me, I would return someday with him.

Part 14
Journey to Haro Village

When the dawn arrived, we began our journey back home, and I looked back at *Mucha* from time to time to make it my provision. "*Chiao, chiao,* and *chiao*! My friend *Mucha* you made me happy, saved my life, concealed me from danger, goodbye until I see you again, fare well my dear friend," I blessed it to stay in peace forever.

"I wouldn't be able to repay what you had done for me, *chiao, chiao,*" I exclaimed. I also showered with my blessings every time; I took step forward looking behind me and praised it, for God created it in a unique way than any other kind of mountain. I showered, "I love you forever. You are my heart and eyes. I learned many of the

---

[49]   Lake (where I was born).

truths about a good friend like you in this life. I also realized that sometimes not a good idea to know each other and fall in love, for it would end this way. I promised you, not to forget your cow's breast forever." Little by little, step by step, it had slowly disappeared from my sight. We reached that cursed *Rabo* mountain which made me graze the ground like a cow, groaned me as a lion, and caused me to fart like old man. I threw my word to its face, "You should be ashamed of yourself to hold me in front of bullets and shells, you are cruel, son of a gun. You wanted to kill me like those bastard soldiers. *Mucha* is lovely and saved my life by hiding me in its belly like kangaroo baby."

I made it very jealous until it cried mud and stones down its belly. I pointed my finger at it saying, "*Rabo*, you are bad, bad… the worst mountain I had ever met in my life." I insulted it "*Maja Majut*"[50] I even cursed it to have stomach pain on a regular basis, for no other mountain had done what this mountain had done to me. I added, "I was surprised why some people live on you! Don't they have another place to go? Are they stupid to make house on you? How did they become patient with you? They would be better to get off of you!"

It made me so furious that I even became very rude at it, "You never feel sorry for any one, the sick, the old, the young, the disable. You have never helped anyone in your life, you want people to die, you are the enemy, and I will not live on you even you gave me a billion US dollars. I will never walk on you again. You can see war was over, eat your own stone and trees, not my flesh again. I am going to my home where there are friendly little mountains and hills. You will never see me again; I am so disgusted to see you again. Goodbye, *Rabo*." I made it, more and more to weep its stone and trees as it did to me.

I kept going recalling all the good and bad mountains and everything happened to me, for almost a year. As soon as we passed

---

50   The biggest mountain on our planet that have never been seen before and protecting us from being attacked by those beings that have ears as big as a blanket they use one for sheet and other for carpet.

a little mountain to the other one, I looked behind, and there, I saw my best friend Mucha, from afar the second time. Oh! Oh! *Mucha*, my cow breast with milk! I stood and watched it like I had never seen it for twenty years while my family was walking away from me. Then my dad yelled, "What are you looking at? Move on!"

I answered, "I am watching *Mucha*, you told me to go from it, and I suppose to stay with it." Then he answered, "*Mucha* never go away, it will be there for good, you will be back to visit some day, now move!" he urged me.

I replied, "Maybe this is the last time I put my eyes on it, so let me watch it for the last time." Then he said, "All right stand there and watch! Later you will be lost to find your way and there are so many hyenas here, might come to eat you."

He scared me with my nightmare's scavenger to make me move. My heart wiggled and put my leg in high gear, halted watching *Mucha*, and followed them. Once a while, I still glimpsed and we reached very flat land. Now Mucha had gone from my sight, I kept studying these new roads that I did not recall travelling on before. The damages from war were so catastrophe that the land and its people were in worst condition. "War, War!" I cursed for all it did to me, people and land. "You made me climb rocks and mountains, you toasted me in the sun, made me suffer with hunger and thirst, you weakened my heart, you drove me crazy with your explosion, you made me coward you forbade my peace, you kicked me out of my school and deny me to gain knowledge, you were an asshole to me, you made me worthless all this time, you tried to destroy my soul, you killed many people and animals, you war! You war! You kicked many animals from their home, you burned the fertile land, you made a mess in the air, many left their home land, many became poor losing their wealth, oh war oh! War! What did you hear and come at this age of mine.

I never forget what you had done to me and our people, if I had some kind of power, I could stop you behind a big mountain, you silly war, you never brought any good to anyone, you were in vain, you were cursed by our people and land, you brought no good to yourself, but now gone without any ransom and benefit to you.

They called this war! They called this war, like good thing…you were hated truly by mankind, you were disgust! You were disgust! You never come again, you never come again, and you perished many." I said while I counted one by one, all corpse and craters on the way. I saw many debris around holes, learned that what killed and made big holes. I shoved as much as my pant pockets hold, and filled my palms, to take them home. They got heavy on my legs and began piercing my thighs, forcing me not to take steps as if they did not want to come with me. Then I decided to abandon them on the side of street one pieces at a time after I could not bear its assault. We were able to reach *Eggu* village of my mom's relative about evening.

Their house's roof looked a very big sifter, with many holes in it, and they asked my dad to repair it for them since we stayed at this village for three days. I was lucky enough to watch *Mucha* from here for three days in a row sitting under the tree shade like shepherd, but all I saw was a very milky big mountain far away erected high in the sky. I said to myself, "Oh, *Mucha*! Oh, *Mucha*!" For three days and on the fourth day we began our trip toward our house. I started thinking of our house and that big lake sitting down our village if I ever saw them as we left them. I also wondered if our atmosphere was the same, and Every one was still alive! Everything I knew hovered in my brain and I was filled with doubts if I found them same again since it seemed we crossed many mountains and countries. My heart began beating as hard as a person walking to unaccustomed land when approaching *Negus*[51] mountain, but seeing it with my naked eyes became like insurance to see my birth village and lake. It was miracle to see these surroundings again, and I begged my dad if we could pass by *Negus*, but my dad missed the way leading to it.

Shortly after wards, we found our self on top of *Dhandhama*[52] hill, which gave me a chance to see those two breast hills where we first stayed fleeing north. My heart began pumping hard to climb *Dhandhama* because I could not wait to see my village and lake from top of it. I had to run, and run like mad cow with happiness leaving

[51]   King (might be named after Ethiopian king of the past).
[52]   Tasting (a mountain where Ancient Oromo might have tasted dish).

behind my family, just to take one quick peek at it for the first time after a long time. When I reached top of taste, there I saw *Tinike*[53] Lake to fill me with joy to my neck that it was still there and not disappeared. I hopped and hopped like grasshopper that won foot ball cup just gazing that pumpkin mount of our house. I was restless until my family reached me to see it like me. I slowed like turtle to tell them this good news and also found that there were many complicated roads, which I did not know which one to take anyway. I decided to sit and wait for them while breathing fresh air at the junction of these roads. They irritated my nerves for walking like sloth and I grumped. If I knew the way, I could have been sitting in our home by now. Once they reached, the top of a mountain, I asked them, "Were you lame? Were you paralysed by flea? Couldn't you see our hill and Lake? Now, hurry up! Go faster!" I ordered them with excitement. They defended, "I was crazy and need to slow down, we are soon going to reach there." Eagerly and quickly I wanted to reach our village and lay my eyes on my pigeons and house if they were still alive and intact. My heart began to be shimmering, murmuring, and disturbing with happiness. I was restless to reach there, while screening the mountain of *Dhandhama* vegetations for the time being. We continued our journey. It was a soothing sight to watch such vegetation and fertile place which I believed like nowhere in the world.

Finally, my eyes were divorced from arid rocks, huge mountains, and nomadic land after almost a year. Now seeing all these beautiful land and passing many villages in our area, and breathing fresh oxygen of green veggies became my first doctor to treat my body from torturing and dressing my eyes green. The cool air sank in my body cells and I could see they were laughing in happiness, they were saying, "What a paradise on earth." The sun I used to see setting behind grandma's mountain to the west was doing the same as I saw a year ago. This view brought back all the memories I used to have had, and I felt home again. I realized that nothing was compared to this place, besides lacking *Mucha's* hill. I was full of joy like I had been given another chance in life to come back to it, not sure if I had the

---

53   Squirting.

same life, or better from here on. We entered our village in darkness and found that the way lead to it covered with tall grasses like jungle and very spooky and ghostly way. I saw the first house of my friend *Muste*, my class mate. I felt better to see his house door was opened and it had a lit lantern in it. My parents wouldn't let me to check them out, for we were tired. They told me to visit in the morning. They didn't see us coming to village either.

When we reached center of the village, someone saw us and shouted, "The Mummies[54] had come!" Hearing this cry, many poured out of their doors to greet us, and we hugged and hugged and went our home together crying in happiness. I was not able to satisfy myself with their hugs like never before. As noises of joy increased in our house, my uncles and aunt with their children thought villagers were fighting and ran toward our house and found us. They were surprised to see us alive and we cried some more again. It was an amazing feeling and greatest night of our lives we had ever had before because they thought we were dead, or the Somalis had taken us away with them. Our house was shredded with bullets, its tin roof had many holes, even Jupiter and Moon said, "Hello" at night. I had counted many stars in the galaxies; I usually used to count them from the outside. We found that our *Ferenji*[55] chickens were dead and their carcass were scattered in the house. My pigeons were dried in the attic like rock, and the smell from the house was terrible to bear. I was deeply sad and tears ran down my face, but being alive and seeing our relatives and villagers had overwhelmed the desolation. We sat and chatted until mid night, and my eyes were exhausted to sit anymore and shut down for the night.

I woke up in the morning like a lame chicken. I went outside to say hello to everything I missed. Grass and tall weeds growing to my waist and became like a jungle threatening to timid me in broad day light. My war ravaged heart began to tingle, for the beast and snakes might be hiding in it and I felt they were ready to jump on me. Then I steered my body to our farm to visit and walk in it, but I was una-

---

[54]   Another twisted name of my dad, equivalent to Mohammed.

[55]   Caucasian, or they meant French in many Ethiopian languages.

ble to step in, for the weeds and vegetations were so thick, tight, and longer than my height. Some bad weeds' thorns cut my skin while some others stuck to my body like glue and turned me back irritating and suffering me with pain. I was also sad, there were no more fresh corns to cut and eat like every year because its season was passed when we were on a run. Thanks to the war that ruined everything for us and I went home empty-handed to wait one more year until I saw fresh corn again, but I was happy to see my dear friend Muste, which I lost in a desert war, to be alive.

Part 15
Being Cat Farmer

I was glad to be back to our village in peace as before, not knowing what laid ahead of me because everything that I had known was not the same anymore. At least, I was happy to learn that kids from my village were attending school. After taking some break from the trip and breathed enough fresh air of peace, I wanted to go back to school with villagers kids where I thought I would belong. For two weeks, I stayed home playing with my sisters while thinking of my school, but I was not sure how to do this after one year of absence. I doubted if I would be accepted by school, or if my family would allow me to go back to town at all. Then I heard rumor from my friends about my soccer team mates who were looking for me to give them back team jerseys which we had before war. I heard they wanted to come and get them from me, but feared that I might have weapons from the war to stop them. After a while, I heard that they carried loaded guns to defend themselves and came almost halfway toward my village and returned back scaring of my machine gun and grenades which I didn't have. Hearing this rumor of my team mates, carrying loaded guns toward my house for a soccer ball and team jersey scared me to go back to school. I looked around my house for any traces of team jerseys and soccer balls that I left there, but I had no idea what happened to them, they just disappeared with the war. I had no idea why they even bothered to get such things lost in a war. Let alone team jerseys and soccer balls, even our house's door was not there when we arrived to it. Now I panicked they might kill me, or take me to jail soon or later. I was happy at least they were afraid of my machine gun and grenade, which I didn't bring with me besides a few long bullets left behind without their mothers by Somalis. Their loaded guns story began to terrify me even to go to town, let alone going back to school where they were attending. Every time I heard, they attempted to come, but returned back made me proud that I was a very powerful cat boy they should not mess around with anymore and dared to visit at all. Hearing these rumors, my dad warned me not to think about going back to school, for I might be killed for these materials. He stressed that my grade five classes I attended were already more than enough for me. I must help our cow and little ox feeding them weeds from our farms. I could also work in the farms doing light duties such as cutting small weeds cleaning in the farm until I grew up to be an adult farmer like our villagers. He then recommended me to study Quran[56] in the morning at village located down the hill from our house with those villager kids who probably never allowed, or cared to go to regular school. I could not believe my dad saying I should not go to town's regular school, or Amharic school as it was known by countryside. He was the one who didn't want me to be a farmer in the first place and took me to school before the war as my mom opposed it, but now his suggestion to stop me from education shattered my dreams of being doctor or engineer forever.

All dad now wanted me to do was learn to read Quran, which we didn't understand its Arabic meaning and get married like him and country side people becoming a farmer. He warned me not to attempt about going to Amharic school, for the last time as my life could be in danger. From here on, he shaded light on my life becoming a true farmer in the country side altogether. We heard that our

---

[56]   Book came from God, or Allah's Own Words as Muslims believe it revealed to his Prophet Mohammed (PBS).

little shop in town was taken by my dad's best friend whom he helped in the first place to start his own grocery store in his far village. When he didn't give it back to my dad, he went to a towns' administration office to claim back his shop from him, but officials warned my dad that he shouldn't seek it anymore being his fault for running during war. Officers were also threatened him not to come back again as it was a clear sign that his friend bribed them to kick him out for good. This made him scared and he decided not to seek the shop anymore. I was sad losing our shop, but we were happy being still alive, surviving the war. My dad decided to let it go, and stayed in the village. As a result, I hated the town itself and I guessed I was going to be a real cat farmer. As my dad recommended, I began going to the Quran reading place down from our village with those kids left in the village some my age and others smaller than me. When those friends of Amharic school called each other door to door like I used to do with them and made me jealous, I began going with my Quran boys to *Taro* village for couple of hours under a big tree in the middle of a village. This style of one tree class, seemed to me strange, but the same throughout many villages, and I was afraid it might lead me to become a sheikh if I went all the way. Even though Ibru was the only older kid of us, I acted to be a leader to call them every morning to *Taro* village. I couldn't wait until I grew big to be peasant and get married someday like my dad in the country side if not started another life as some sheikhs did sit around to treat people who got sick or other opportunity of it. Mr. Osman, our Quran teacher, began slashing me with his teaching stick, and I found it hard to be under the tree learning Quran this way, but no choice and no place to escape it as my dad would not allow me to drop out of it.

After a while, I became used to learning Quran this way, but more envy began to creep on me of my friends going to regular school holding many books on one hand, and a ball on the other hand. Every day, they went happy to town to learn while kicking a ball on the way and its' memory invaded my head, singing national anthem and sitting in front of black boards and teacher. I felt they were luckier than me and I smelled their learning while I was struggling every morning to study Quran with cruel teacher. Day by day, my soul was unable to stop thinking about my friends' life as student, and all the things they did in town and out of school and my chance halted to finish regular school to become an engineer, or doctor which was burnt alive in front of my eyes. I was haunted by dreaming every day to see myself being a cat farmer as our forefathers, but when I checked the reality of dying in town in vain, I could finish the whole Quran and go little further studying some more of it. I could be a great sheikh who could treat people of sickness and many other things come from it like being respected Mullah. I thought this would be a cool thing, which might be good in the afterlife as people believed it rather than going to demonic school as some said about regular school.

"If I couldn't be a useful sheik, I might help my family being a farmer boy inheriting dad's farm to be their welfare and get married and have a kids," I thought to myself. This also gave me some hope and a dream for my life.

Every morning when I went to my friend's house to gather their young siblings, every one of them began mocking and insulting me. They scrutinized, "How come you study Arabic Quran after finishing grade five and going to be sheikh[57] who sits in village and probably harm people by some Sorcery actions violating God's Law that says you shouldn't study magic and perform actions that hurts people." Every time they saw me, they would attack me as if I became useless person studying Quran. I couldn't totally avoid seeing them even though I didn't want to face them at all. All I could do was just blame the useless war for this to happen. Adding insults to injury, my sisters were beaten and insulted every time they went to town by those soccer team members who accusing them I took their soccer ball and team jersey. As the beating increased on my sisters, they also blamed me that it was my fault losing these items, which they urged me to give back, but as far as I knew, some of the uniforms were perished in our house and some I left in our shop that was given to my dad's friend. Then I recalled the ball was given to repair person who happened to be one of our team member. I had no idea where to find him whether he was dead or alive. There was no chance and hope to

---

[57] Title of someone advanced in Quran study or wise man.

go to town and find any team jersey and ball. All I could do was just watch and grieve the suffering of my sisters on the regular basis. Our farm had nothing to survive on besides weeds hugging each other, so my dad decided to go to afar town of Harrar to seek carpentry work for us to survive. He was hardly coming home once a month to visit and give us money to buy grains for our food. There was no one to defend us from troubles which caused a great concern for me with my sisters. At least, I thought about going back to Satanic school to face the music of my team mates and protect my sisters from death. Since my dad was not home to take me go back to school, and for sure I knew he wouldn't let me do it, I asked one of my uncles to take me to school who didn't know the whole story. He was afraid my dad wouldn't be happy and I would be in danger since he heard kids were looking for me in the past. He advised me to get permission from my mom at least, but I begged and encouraged him to take me there, without my mom's input. At last, he somewhat agreed to take me after I begged him from heaven to his feet. With this exciting news, I was not sure if I would be accepted after long time out of school, and running inside country side along the enemy. Even if I was accepted, I worried about being alive facing that soccer team who might beat me to death, or call police to arrest me. The whole night I did not sleep, and morning came. My heart then began to pound as I was unable to go to *Madrasa*[58] under the tree. Like a student, I grabbed some shrunken note books I could find that covered in dust and spider web from our *Dera,*[59] which mice chewed most of them its center and cover. I cursed the mouse and war, and told my mom the news of going back to school. She was freaked out hearing this news and begged me to stay away from it. As I left door, not listening to her, she came out of house and stood by door, begging me to return back so that I wouldn't be hurt. I ignored her and went to my uncle's house.

He asked me, "Are you ready?"

---

[58] Quran school.
[59] Attic.

And I replied to him, "Yes! I am more than ready." My heart jumped like small rabbit.

I began wondering to what would happen and seeing all those kids for the first time, and from time to time, my fear shot down my legs leaving his house every minute I was closer to town like I was going to unknown land expecting the worst to occur. It didn't seem reality to seeing school kids again in my life, and when I came to a road led to town full of many students rushing to school, it became more, a more reality my being going to school and face everyone. My heart beat increased worse than war shelling time, and I was mad at her, why she always did this to me. I wanted to hit it with my feast and realized I could hurt myself instead, and let her go on beating, but tried to suppress down on her with my hand on top of the chest area. Pressing on it didn't help me at all. I began to listen to its desire and shock, rather made me walk like lame person with shivering legs under my waist, my legs kept colliding like rocks rushing down a hill. I was surely troubled like never before if this came to pass, or not. My uncle was not slowing down and he seemed to me, walking faster and faster while my legs were slowing down in fear. I got mad at him why he went fast, not caring to take me slowly to danger.

I said to myself, "I shouldn't get mad at my uncle, for I was the one who wanted to go to school and face my demons." I started walking faster and faster after my uncle. I was afraid that the kids on the way might recognize who I was and said something, even they saw me what they were going to do I said to myself, and I was filled with shyness in me like I had done something wrong and believed they wouldn't eat me alive at all. We entered a very busy road, full of people flocking to town for business carrying vegetables and Kat on their donkey, their back, and some on their head as usual including many students from surrounding area. Seeing all these my heart felt a little better and it seemed I was invisible for a while hiding in a crowd if no one recognized my head and face. After walking a while, there, I saw the town laughing at me in distance like it had seen me coming like stranger. My blood veins on my face stretched like hose with fluid as if it was going to burst. At this moment, I was even appalled to go further, and a danger my dad had warned me about to come face-to face. I expected something drastic to befallen me, and regretting my trip to town, contemplating to go back before it was too late. I was seriously troubled marching forward. I felt someone big standing inside me, urging me to run back home quickly, and I walked like blind cat, not knowing where I was going, but still faced toward town taking very shy steps.

At last, there I saw kids that knew me, and we greeted each other and hugged, and we went chatting together feeling a little better and happy toward school. I asked the students if I was allowed to register at all, and enter school with them. They said, "We started two months ago, and you could try your chance." My fear became little better with their chat and advice. We then entered and passed the first three houses. I saw our shop and I said, "Hello!" And looked at it for the first time and like last time, knowing that no longer belong to us. I recalled all that happened in the past at this shop including the last day, I almost peed on myself. Then, we reached a bus stop, its town center and saw many cars and buses with tons of people. I was wondering if the town was the same, or different than before, and I didn't greet those who knew me fearing what they going to say. My heart was drumming harder and harder, fearing to see those soccer team mates who were beating my sisters and what about to happen to me. We entered the school yard by fenced gate, there I heard school bell rang for students to line up in front of flag to sing national anthem before going to classes. I was excited to see this in a long time, and not seemed reality that I would come back like new student and a guest to school. My uncle and I sat under the tree, and watched students line up and singing the national anthem. After all students rushed to their classes, we got up and headed to school director's office. He was sitting and relaxing like lizard in the sun warming up his body, giving it vitamin D.

After we greeted him, my uncle asked him to register me. He asked, "Were where you all this time?"

And I replied, "My family and I were fled to save our life because of war, and now we were back since it was over!" He wanted to know if I was involved in the Somali army (intruders), and I said, "No, no, I was never became one of them, but we had to run to save our life."

Then he wanted to know what grade I was in before the war, and I told him I completed grade five, and I was supposed to be grade six classes. Then he laughed and checked the record he had and found my name. Then he confirmed to be in grade six, and asked me to catch up with the kids by copying every single page of notes from my class mates and study hard, to catch up to them. He took me to grade six class teachers to let me sit in. The kids were very surprised to see me in the class, and made some noises calling my name again and again and teacher commended them to keep quiet with harsh anger voice. They all shut their lips up right away. There were some of my soccer team mates who saw me and began to threaten me with their angry face to wait and see what they were going to do to me afterward. Fearing they were going to beat me up during break time, or take me to the police station, I was unable to focus and listen to the teacher. As my lips began trembling and eyes ringing, I felt this was going to be bad. I tried to prepare my body for pain and bleeding in case they just decided to rock my world like my sisters. Then there the bell rang for break time and my heart jumped and stuck in my throat for what to happen. Every kid was happy to hear the bell rang and ran out to enjoy, and mine was thrown around like ball with fear. I began shaking and shaking, hesitating to get up and go outside to play. I wished our teacher didn't let us go out of class or ask me to stay with him. There the inevitable came and I tried to put myself together and pushed myself out the door, knowing soon, or later I must go outside to play. There I saw five of my team mates waiting for me to get out of the class. I gathered myself together and tried to leave by them.

There one of them, the most aggressive boy of all who were beating my sisters as they told me strangled my neck with my shirt and asked me for uniforms to bring them right away. I rewound my brain cells and viewed all those beatings and cries of my sisters by this kid and it pumped my heart as I was praying to face him one day anyway. Those stories of my sisters and the way he strangled me forced my fist and punched him hard in the face. He was confused and let go my neck and right away I kicked him in the stomach with my knee and put him down. Others pulled my both legs and I was down with him like camel on the ground. They began dragging me like a toy while some kicked me in the stomach. Suddenly I twisted and kicked one by accident in his groin, and he fell down too. I was glad; some older kids came and stopped our fight. Then a teacher who came to find out what was happening took us to the school principal. He asked, "Who had started this fight and why?"

I told him, "They fought me for the soccer team jersey and ball that was destroyed in the war." I explained to him how they were lost and destroyed. Then the director punished three of them and warned them not to bother me again about those items lost. He said, "If they ask you again inform me about it." My past fear of them looked over in about fifteen minutes except I felt little shaking and bruised, and I was still alive. I sat in the class to face teachers like everyone at last, guessing it was over. I tried to listen to the teacher completely, but still the fight memory had invaded my brain, and I began to rewind and watch as I sat in the class. I was afraid that team jersey quarrel might come up again, but I decided to fight if any of them wanted to beat me, and I began to solace myself. I was happy of my actions, once more going back to school, standing firm to the demon of war that suffered my sisters and threatened me to lose my regular school.

I planned to work in the farm after school and also fed our only cow and ox which my dad wanted me to take care as a farmer so that he would not upset about my going back to school. I wanted to compete with my two uncles, to do what they did all day in the farm to make my dad happy. At last the school bell rung to go home, I was happy to kick myself, at the back end like baby goat while mixing with other villager's kids that mocked me before. I had crushed an insult of my villages' students who were picking on me every morning ever since I came back to the village from war.

After all, my dear mother that was worried for me earlier going back to school was happy to see me come home alive since she wanted me to be a farmer. I assured her not to be worried about it because I would be farmer and student at the same time. I requested her to be happy just like my friend's mothers who let their kids to go to town to be a student. She seemed to agree with me. Then she gave me injera, stuffed in the wooden bowl with watery soup. I washed my hand and started rolling in my palm like little golf balls, shoot them down my throat barrel to the belly very fast as many as I could with joy. Then I ran quickly to our farm to pick some weeds for our cow and little ox that born during a war at my grandmom's house. After I snatched my books, and ran to my friends house to go back to school for the afternoon class. We kicked the ball as usual before the war to school, and I was excited to go back to my normal life, besides living in the country side, and no one seemed to be exhilarated like me.

One day in the evening, as I spread my note books in front of me by the side of lantern trying to do my home work, there my dad showed up from carpentry work to visit us. As soon as he entered the house with greetings, my heart cracked in fear and I jumped like a kangaroo from the cow skin carpet toward him. I hugged him being unaware that I had thrown my school books further away. I wrapped my hands around his waist overwhelmingly, happy to see him. He was also excited to see me unaware that I was trying to solace him from being not to get mad as he eventually might come to know soon the reality of my going back to school. After he buttered me with words of affection by saying my son, my son, we sat together on the skin of cow. Then he saw the magic pile of devilish books by the gas lamp and he asked, "Whose books are these?"

Then suddenly my happiness of him coming home had been evaporated like water in the sun. The shock had shot me in the foot like bullet, and I lost what to say to him. I began to scratch my hair like it was eaten by fat lice. He repeated a few times, "I am talking to you, can you answer me?" and I was unable to say anything in fear of him. My words and answers were stuck like golf ball in my throat. Then my little turtle sister talked unauthorized. "Dad, Dad, he is going to school, these are his books," she blubbered.

Then he wanted to know, "Son! How do you able to go there, and when did you do this?"

The turtle spoke again, "His uncle was the one!"

Then he splashed, "Didn't I warn you not go there?"

Then in a few seconds, my eyes became flooded with tears, and began bombarding my note books. He saw these drops and began to solace me by saying, "I was just curious to know how you did it." I hardly mentioned to him all that insult my villagers kids gave me after we had returned back from war, and my sisters trashing in town which forced me to school. He wondered, "What happened to jersey and ball that kids were threatening you about?" I explained everything about fight and director's warning to kid and he hailed me to stand for myself and sisters. His praise totally pumped my heart with happiness and the yolk of my nightmare and fear of him were taken away in split seconds. I was excited to be student again and back to my past life. I assured him of my plan to learn and be a farmer at the same time, and he became proud of me, but not to kill myself as a farmer.

I began to study with bigger Muste, best of school classmate in the village. We made one of their little huts our studying place from many distractions of our families and neighbors which excited me even more after I completed farm duties. In this way, I had completed grade six after a few months, and then I got two months of break time to focus on our farm and feed cattle. After two months of farms' muddy hard work, a new class of grade seven started with every subject changed to English language except Amharic language which was strange to me by itself, limping from one weird language to the weirdest of all. I found it to be hard and strange, for not understanding it completely. I struggled to learn and understand them all, and after a while we became like friends, and I began to study hard. Then farm seeding season was born, and my dad had returned from town to cultivate the land, and prepare it for seeding. My dad formed a team with another farmer, pairing our ox, and they began ploughing our farm for two days, and then other one vice versa while I had gone to school. I couldn't wait until my class was over every day to go to help, learn and practice being a good farmer. During lunch, I quickly went to observe them, and gone to class, but I spent more time after school to learn and help in the farm as much as I could like taking oxen to river to drink water, and collecting *Burranas*,[60] which were very crunchy favourite eat for them. I couldn't wait until

---

[60]   Grasses root look like white spaghettis

weekend arrived, the two days I could help in the farm whole day, but studied and did home work in the evening.

After seeding season was over, my dad went back to town to his carpentry, then I was worried who would maintain our farms which was many kilometers long. I was too young to take care for all of it, and my dad was concerned it might break my spinal cord as such a task not to be performed by young person like me. My dad recommended to my mother the use of *Kullis*,[61] but they were mostly useless personals, not productive at all like they were known very well in the area. My desire to work in the farm to help my family, at this age was unstoppable and also wanted to continue my school at the same time. I began a competition with my uncles just like them, to do what they did as the seed pop out of the ground grown to the size of a pen. *Chinki*[62] needed to be separated from the good ones including unwanted weeds. I decided to take on this daunting task after school by myself just like my uncles did. I was able to do, in two to three hours after school till the sun set whatever my two uncles did all day long. First, I looked at the work of my uncle, how much they did, and I tried to match, or exceed their dams, or lines. Everyone who saw me dropped their jaws and some hailed my ability to be good farmer while too young and going to school all day long. Their talk gave me so much encouragement I was able not to miss both school and farm duties. I saw jealousy in the faces of my uncles, I was afraid they might want to kill me, or swallow me alive for it.

My dad was shocked to see what I did every time he came home. I was a good farmer better than my uncles, and himself, being full time student which was impossible to do at this age especially with my tough many Ferenji[63] subjects, which I supposed to focus on day and night. After all, my palms became like original farmers, bruised and hardened like dark granite, hard to cut with knife. I could easily dent a face of my enemy if I slapped with it in a fighting. I could only hold a pen as if I was a leprous cat with no nerves. My hand writings

---

[61]   Cheap laborers
[62]   Plants overcrowding
[63]   English, or foreign language subjects

were mocked by my teachers as if I was writing with chicken fingers, for they did not know that I had a serious farmer's hand.

I wanted my dad not to worry about our farm anymore, but just to focus completely on his carpentry. I was determined to take responsibility for my family while dreaming to be a doctor, or an engineer. My friends were free to play soccer after school and focusing on their study, and their farms were also small like flea compared to us. Their dads had never gone to town to work like my dad so they just focused on their school. When farm vegetations reached to my waist, I began adding natural fertilizers by loading on the donkey, and plants were very excited and become very green. I was more proud of myself because sorghum, maize, potato, onion, sweet potato, tomato, garlic, and cucumbers, all of them thanked me and greeted me with salutation by swinging and dancing in the air with happiness. I had never seen such excitement of plants in our farm before as they gave me a massage to my face and hands; I also hugged them from time to time as much as I could every time I walked among them. Sometimes, I had to run coast to coast inside them stretching my both arms like plane wings with happiness while caring for them and breathing fresh oxygen they gave me as a reward, which I also thanked them for. I was little sad for town people who had never experienced such love and blessing from vegetations in their life, but give insult to farmers as ignorant people lived in the country side. They also felt that they were better human beings than farmers while they were being fed by them all along working so hard day and night. When I harvested everything, I produced grains and vegetables as much as my uncles who weren't going to full time school like me. I was able to complete my grade seven class with even good marks like never before better than my colleagues who also never worked in the farms. No wonder, many people said that if a student had learnt some Quran in the past life, he, or she could become very smart in school and achieve better learning and marks, which I suspected might have beaten my friends and classmates. I had said and believed that the Somalian war might have done good thing in this case by making me a better student. Even though war was bad for human and everything, I was glad it made me learn some Quran that helped me achieve good grades which might not possible as I felt it. I could see my brain could absorb more notes from school books and understanding just like Quran verses which I must record in my brains page by page and line by line not knowing its meanings. There was a rumor told in our area that some top students were excelled in regular school after studying Quran and my friends and class mates amazed by my cleverness and needed my help sometimes which flattered me that I was the best in my class.

When new seeding season approached, school was closed for two months, and my dad seemed too busy to return from town. He could have helped me how to start farming from scratch, but I had to dare by myself the whole things I had never done before. Now that our ox could be paired with another ox, I decided to ask Mamad Musa to bring his ox with mine so that we started ploughing together like we were pro-farmers. When we brought them together, instead of collaborating like us they started to fight each other, but after a while of begging them not to fight and many tries, we were able to bring them together under the yolk. We ran them plough from corner to corner in my farm first just like those pro-farmers. I was sorry to see the oxen got tired doing hard work as their necks began to bleed from hard work. Since this was our first experience, I lost my voice saying, "*Korrow*[64]" and "*Dhoq*! *Dhoq*[65]" all day long as those farmers did in their farms. Sweats ran down my body in the hot sun as if I was taking shower in the rain. It was tiring and difficult job to do, but my dream and desire to feed my family with cane of sorghum and fresh corn encouraged me not to stop at all.

After several days, I almost became expert in ploughing with oxen and seeding which made me happy to help my family in the absence of my father. I liked everything of being a farmer, but found out that it was not easy profession that causes a lot of pain. When the school opened, I didn't want to leave my farm friend whom I enjoyed working with him very much as a team, but had no choice than to go back to school, for my school friends surely insult me becoming

---

[64] Sounds to encourage Oxus turn around
[65] Sounds to stop

111

a farmer again. I went back to school having no other choice to start grade eight. Then teachers warned us that grade eight was a turning point in elementary school and it was harder than other classes since this was where we were going to be examined to transit to high school by the government exams. We needed to study very hard day and night in order to pass these examinations. We were also being advised to stop playing around and be very serious in our learning and studying. I was shocked to hear this news and afraid if I could still work in our farm and pass this class at all. I was troubled by this new development; it was as if a donkey bone was stuck in my throat. I deeply thought about both sides, my brain orbited close to the sun, and I began sweating blood. I found no alternative, besides taking on both challenges and decided to do my best. I didn't want to fail my school so that my friends would laugh and mock me as a farmer who lost school. I determined not to abandon our farm for any reason since I was the only hope to accomplish the mission and responsibility I had undertaken. Villagers praised me so much for doing such amazing work while going to school and I didn't want to fail them again praising me even more. I started all by myself in the farm, motivated me even more to work hard in the farm. I tried to study hard as much as I could and it made me happy that the farms last cultivation and preparation called *Ka'aba*[66] was coming to an end just when one week left for the beasty exam I was afraid of. I was very much shocked, for I couldn't get prepared as I wanted, but tried my best to touch base of all subjects I had to review for the exam.

Part 16
Dunked by Farmer Disease

When we were told the exams would be given tomorrow, my heart blasted with fear. The night before the exam, I decided to stay

---

[66] Softening and accumulating mud under plants as they reached waist height

all night long to review all the notes and books as much as I could, for I might not able to pass in case a question came from them, to do fast review, and I tried sleeping really late, just before cocks called. In the morning, when I woke up, I found that my friends had already left without waking me up. I was late for the exam day it looked. I stood up fast and ran to school without any breakfast, fearing I wouldn't be accepted to exam. I regretted studying all night long when I supposed to be in the school by 7:00 AM, for the exams started at 8:00 AM. I ran and ran, none stop for ten minutes from my house to school compound to find no single student in the school yard. The empty yard of students shocked me, for they might be writing exam, I feared. I knew I wouldn't be accepted at all, and lost my chance to write it.

When I entered the class, I learned that the students had already completed one exam and they were writing the second one which was about to end soon. I pleaded to an examiner that I was fallen asleep by lamp, studying hard all night, and no one had waken me up. I asked to excuse me and displayed my being so sorry for it. The examiner was also sad about my luck, but said, "The exam wouldn't be given to you at all, just go home, it was unfortunate you lost this time your chance and no exception if you are not on time." I was freaked by examiners' order, and dashed shouting, "I had lost my entire life's learning" and hit something so hard with my forehead. I was so dizzy to find blood and blacked out to darkness like I was in a graveyard.

When blackout was better, I was still in the darkness trying to understand what hit me, where I was, and searched for blood over my face. My eyes wouldn't see anything at all found it very strange why dark and I didn't see any teacher or student. I found I was still in the dark. What was going on? Why was I in the dark even though my head was not in pain? Then it looked as if I was still in the studying hut of my friend's house by the lantern. I tried to walk to the door to see if indeed I was still in our studying hut and opened door to check it. There I found that I was in a dream to hit the pillar of the hut. I couldn't believe myself the whole thing was a dream my heart still rocking, but hitting a pillar was because of a dream, lucky

I ended up with swollen forehead. There was still a chance to write my exam. It was still early dawn, and I slept only couple of hours, and a rooster didn't shout to wake us up. Nay! My heart still in turmoil like I lost the exam, and I was mad and woked up my friend Muste to ask him why he didn't bother to wake me up for the exam, to complain their actions. They told me that I was crazy, suggested me to go back to sleep. For I had already tasted and seen the loss of my exam, I couldn't risk to sleep any longer and trust my friends to wake me up; and I decided to continued my studying till 6 am. Then I got ready my pencils and erasers for the exam and washed my face and headed to school without having breakfast. I didn't think I could swallow anything at all even if I tried for fear air already filled me up. On the way to school, I was focussing more on the exams, thinking and trying to rewind, and reviewing things I thought I needed to know in my mind.

School and the exam had never been so intense in my life and my thought of not passing it would be disaster in my future. My body was trembling like in cold winter. My teeth were colliding like loose pipes in a truck. Then we arrived in school yard and the bell rang and my heart chirped faster and faster. As I entered the class, my hands were frozen and there the examiners entered in the class holding that scary bundles of exam sheets and my heart cracked like shell exploded on it. I said, "This is it!" when they opened those packages. They told us about the exams rules, and what we had to follow, and then they began putting them in front of us. We were ordered to start after examples were done first. As soon as I read two questions, my fear left my heart and I began to worry about time if I could finish on time or not. I found it little harder, but somehow, I had completed on time.

After we finished all of them, we discussed about some questions if they were hard or not, on our way home. I was glad it was over, but worried about the result if I passed, or not. I told myself that now the worst was over, all that left for me was to struggle with my spade to dig that farm like *Kunbursi*[67] for about two months and wait for the results to arrive. In the mean time we formed team farm work like our villagers with my friends, I was happy and excited that the ground was crying to leave it alone when I sank and sank my V-shaped spade and thrown the mud under tall stems of sorghum and corns roots. The more and more I bent my back, in the end, I was unable to stand straight being so tired and seemed to me that my waist was crooked and cut in half. My hands were so sore and bruised, and my palms even became an island of little water balls. Some exploded and my fleshes under skin were smiling at me. No way to stop now, the more I dug the sorer and fleshy they became. My hard skin earned before as a farmer began to disappear after a while. I was astonished for the farmers who did this for living and their hands bled and wounded and finally gave up to the pressures and no more became like me. Their palms were as hard as a sole of the boots and I wished and desired their hands to dig our farm now. I brooded that I might be like them one day if I kept digging for long time who knew I might not pass the exams.

I was afraid my father's dream of getting me married at seven years old and becoming farmer might have come true since I was having such strong palms for our farm similar to many peasants of my village. After long period of severe digging in the farm, my belly button area developed severe *Hida Handura*.[68] I had difficulty breathing, it bent my back as if I was old man walking up hill. I couldn't wash a mud that smeared up to my knees being so sick and tired.

I was very moody because of my sickness and hard work. I liked my sisters to respect me like King of Jordan to give me water and food. I was proud of myself being the only head of the house. When my dad came home and saw the work I had done and he hailed me. He was surprised that I was able to keep our farm flawless like my uncles. I was excited to see my dad was happy and proud of me seeing our farms full of green vegetation as tall as me forming green dense

---

[67]   A fat, white worm as big as a shrimp found in pile of decomposed dungs of animals

[68]   Most common abdominal pain farmers cry of

cloud. When he said that son you have made a great job I could not have done myself, his comment made me felt I was the super child in the entire Village if not the entire district of Haramaya.[69] I was even began to be scared to walk in it, for hyena, fox, and rabbit could be hiding in it. When I was seriously ill with this Hida Handura, everyone around the villager heard about it. They believed that digging farm had to do with it and my dad was concerned and rushed me to a doctor in our town, but my situation was not improved even I was given treatment. Then I was afraid, it was going to be the end of my life. I began to accuse our farm for trying to send my soul to deep space with *Israfil*. I had prayed to God to spare my life this time until I saw my grade eight marks so that at least I knew the truth to the grave. This pain that twisted my stomach beyond recognition and wrecking it made me sworn, not to touch the spade again if I only recovered this time. I learned that this farmer disease was indeed the most terrible thing to face in my life and I regretted to dip myself in it. I got a little better after a month, but I was as heavy as a piece of paper. My legs became skinny like mosquito that a wind blew around in a lake. I was scared to leave my house. My skeletons were laughing like white donkey's teeth that lips were mauled off by hyena.

My ribs giggled at my family and they were already mourning as if I was ready to enter grave. I was afraid I had tuberculosis, not farmer's sickness. I was shocked; it was the sign of good night to my beautiful farm and people. For two weeks, I was saying goodbye to the trees, farms, families, and birds singing and calling my mother's name. I was listening to the hyenas if they cried like humans to confirm my death from night to night, for they were one of best creatures to give me sign of death like they usually did for everyone dying in the villages. I had also listened for howling of dogs since they were smelling and forecasting the coming of dead body in our village because I heard my parent and villagers were cursing these animals and yelled at them to stop crying as humans. Still worrying of my death, I got a little better than before and tried to visit our farm, for I missed it so much during my ailment. I was afraid to go alone and

---

[69] Lake view

called my seven years old brother whom I loved more than any person in my family to go with me so that I relied on him as a protector from dangerous wild animals hiding in the farm. When he agreed, we then slowly entered the farm in the morning while my heart was beating hard as if a hyena was about to jump on us. The sorghums in our farm were bearing fruit and some of them became like barren, very good to eat like sugar cane. Then I sank my teeth at elbow of each plant to see if they became juicy enough to chew. Upon finding the best one, I asked my little brother to uproot for us since I became like an infant with my strength, and he did help.

While we were sitting and chewing this cane, I heard a voice, like someone calling me from afar saying Abas, Abas…and I couldn't reply to it, for I was not sure what it was and I kept listening. I was afraid, it might be jinn who were calling my name, and I didn't want to reply to it. Since I was hearing a story from people about sometimes a jinn might call your name, and if you replied to it, you would die instantly, or they would abduct you right away and took you for good to their underground world. For these reason, you should never reply to it at all and I kept listening without replying while fearing that it was after me. Once it also looked like a voice of my class mate, Muste whom I doubted it could be, and I tried hard to recognize it. He might be calling like he saw something new, or exciting it seemed at one point as a voice was getting near and very urgent. Indeed at last I confirmed it was Muste who very excited to find me in the farm, but I didn't know the reason at all. He ran and ran like hyena splitting corn and Sorghum plants toward us, and I finally replied, "Yes, Yes, Muste, I am here! I am here!" I was mad at him for not paying attention to my reply and calling me hundred times.

"Why you call me like crazy guy hundred times today?" and I tried to calm him down many times with my sickly and skinny rat voice, and he didn't hear me well. It was my nature if someone called me twice and I said yes twice, and on the third time I would get mad, and never replied again. Because of this rule, I became silent and ignored him. I sat quietly and was listening his calling from the shade of sorghums. When I knew he was going further away from where we were, I told my brother to shout to him, to let him know where we were. And then he ran and ran toward us and I saw him covered with heavy sweat running down his face. "Why was he running like mad person?" I murmured.

As he saw us, he looked excited to tell something and shocked by it. I wondered what kind of rumor he was going to dump on me in the farm running and sweating like he came from far away. Then he said, "Abas, the final exam result had come. Some students had already got their exam card."

Then my stomach cracked open and I asked, "Did you see our marks, if we pass, or not?"

"Go and get your result this evening from director house," he added.

Again I was terrified, "I must have failed it. There was no reason I passed it, for I didn't study very well at all. If I went there and found that I had failed, I wouldn't be able to return alive. So why don't you go there and bring our marks?" I suggested.

"They wouldn't give it to me, only owner can take it," he explained. He pushed me to go for myself to get it as if he didn't get his, or he wanted me to find my result first.

I said, "Let us talk a little about it at home and go together." He agreed and we went home discussing about it while my worrying got very serious that I had gotten bad headache thinking all scenarios what if...how much I had gotten...all the way home. I suggested to him we go after sunset, in the dark, so no one would see and laugh to us at all if we had to cry of failing results and not to come home with shame in the broad day light.

We agreed and marched in the dark toward town with my mosquito legs. The more we got closer we got to the director's house, my heart began beating and beating hard. We entered the director's house fence with my heart suddenly dropped to my *Hida Handura* to worsen my pain as if it was touching my belly button. I knocked his door lightly with fear, and his wife came to open it. We asked if the director was home. She said, "Yes, he was home." She informed him about us and he allowed us to enter a door. We entered greeting him and he welcomed us inside, then he grabbed bunch of cards that sit by his side started looking my name in it saying, "You failed the exam. You were lazy!" My heart was ready to explode in my belly, and I was ready to run as fast as I could after I confirmed and knew my failing from his words. He then found and looked at it and repeated again, "You failed, take it!" and handed to me. I snatched it from his hand quickly, and I looked at it being curious by how much I failed and started reading to find fail word on it. Then I saw *passed* word on the card that my heart exploded with happiness, shooting electricity through my veins from toes to the hair standing like Porcupine, I didn't know where my shock and fear gone. I couldn't believe what I saw because of what he said. I feared I might be reading the word passed in dream it looked. The director said, "I was excellent student" and praised me for being top student in the class. I couldn't believe my marks were the highest in the school and the word I passed was not a dream any more. The shock of my happiness kicked the shock of sadness like soccer ball out of my anus and saw it bouncing out his door, never to see it again.

I was suddenly cured of my farmer's illness. He recommended me not to waste my good points by going to the night high school taught in the university of our town. He advised me to go afar to regular high school during the day at our capital city of Harrar, or another high school of Dire Dawa about sixty kilometers from my home town to finish secondary school. I learned that Muste had seen his marks before me, and he didn't tell me his secret passing to grade nine. Thanking the director, we were both excited and we went out with our skinny legs and I couldn't believe that we reached our village in five minutes, or so rather than it usually took us about fifteen minutes walk. I couldn't wait until I could break good news to my dad. When I showed it to my dad, he was so happy that he almost jumped like grass hopper, and became so proud of me to achieve such high marks in the class even though I was working in the farm to help them. I told him the advice my director gave me to go far away and I worried we didn't have any relatives to help me in both town as moving there was required. We were not rich either to rent a place, etc and couldn't afford four years of learning expenses.

Then my dad said, "Son, do not worry! We have your grandpa's sister, in Harrar. I am going to ask her to let you stay with her for four years." I was excited to hear this news of my relative I had never heard before in my entire life that she could help at all. This news was another source of happiness that moved my eyebrows up and down. I was breathless of things happening for me. This seemed too good to be true, dreaming of going far away like my director advised me to study in regular high school then after go to university from there. The excitement of the whole night made me feel as if I had never seen sickness before. My mosquito legs and body gained several pounds of fresh muscle, looking like a normal kid. I couldn't sleep at all the whole night imagining moving to town I had never seen before.

Next day, I woke up healthy and told my dad if she didn't agree to take me, I wouldn't mind to go to night school in the university with my best school friend who had no relative in town at all. My dad was mad to hear me saying this and advised me to go to one of the two cities like the director said rather than dying here on the farm. As he said, one day he left for Harrar to ask my aunt, and he learned that she had no kids of her own at all, and her husband was too old to work. She became dealer of Kat in the town to make money for their living. She warned him that I might die of hunger, for no one would take care of me. He came home angry with bad news; after all, I wouldn't be able to go to Harrar, city of my dream. He was mad at my mom, for her aunt refused to accept and help me finish school there. They had an argument and fought over my school. I was so disappointed that my regular studying and dreaming shattered in a few days. My mother was happy that I was not going away to useless school, for she felt that no one would work on the farm, and they might starve to death if I left them since my dad was useless on the farm. It looked her prayer was answered for me to stay with her, but my dad never gave up and he said he would try a relative in Dire Dawa where his sister used to work as a maid for fifteen years after someone had voodooed her marriage. I remembered she used to bring her master and family to our house once in a while to visit, and my dad used to make big splash party for them. After Somali's war came, she left them and became Kat trader between our towns to Dire Dawa to make her money to survive, and she had never married again. He advised her to go with him so that I went to school there.

My hope of going to regular school dream became alive again, but it seemed too good to be true, for they were not related to us by blood and also her master was fled to Saudi Arabia, leaving his wife and eight kids. Hearing they were not rich like before losing their business to workers who took over after war of Somalia with Ethiopia. I thought my chance of them accepted me there was shabby. Then again I heard there was another aunty of my mother in Dire Dawa, she married to an East Indian for many years, and there was some reason I didn't understand why my dad didn't like me going there. I didn't know the true story why they didn't bother to ask him for my stay there, but they preferred my aunt master's home like relative, and my aunt decided to ask them since she had been going to that town for her business. She told my dad, she would request first and get back to him. Hearing my aunt and dad worrying about me, I was afraid they wouldn't be successful, and I suggested them to abandon their worrying because they again would be rejected. I advised them to stop, and my dad told me not to interfere in their actions, for they knew better than me. Once Faddum gave the green light to my aunt to come with my dad, he planned to help her with grain from our farm to cover food expenses if she agreed for me to stay at her house since she had tough times to help her eight kids.

Then my dad and aunt went together and came back with good news that she had agreed to help me stay there with her kids. I was exhilarated knowing that I was going to big town, but leaving my best friend Muste and farm behind saddened me a little. I asked my dad what Dire town looked like, and how big it was, and he explained that it was the biggest of all around our province and more beautiful than Harrar, where I was initially suppose to go if my aunt didn't refuse me. I was super happy to hear that I was going to the best city of our province at last. I was excited more to learn that there was a train, something connected together like long anaconda which ran between cities. Now I would have a chance to see it, for the first time in my life. I saw my high school in my dreams that night: many students were riding bikes to school; it had many trees and gardens in it like paradise as I was sitting in it to study, take a break, and relax. I also saw myself ride a bike to school, and when I woke up in the morning I couldn't believe I was still at my house with my mother in the countryside. I was shocked and laughed to myself like crazy. Before I left our farm, I tried breathing more fresh countryside air, and looking around to make my provisions. I was sad, for I might not get a chance to eat the fresh corn from our land anymore. My heart was gone to Dire Dawa to study, but my body still in the farm. While I was trapped in these thoughts, leaving behind my family, farm, and friends, school doors were opened, and it was time to leave with a new shoes and dress.

CHAPTER 2

Journey to be a Real Cat Boy

My dad and I began our journey, taking *Nama-Nyaata*[70] bus toward Haramaya town on a long trip to Dire Dawa. I was excited, but worried, for this was my first time ever to go far from home into the unknown town, leaving my family and friends behind. We first reached Haramaya, a close town to us, and my dad decided to put us on a fast taxi, I had never taken before. I was amazed to sit in it, for it was my first time in such a small car. It was running faster than a bus, and it scared me with its speed that I felt I was going to die in a car crash. All the bushes and trees were also scared of it like me as they were zooming behind us faster and faster, with the land and mountains. Watching everything running weird in the window made me feel sick and wanted to throw up. Then, I read a sign by the window written in red that said, "Spitting will make you nauseated." I was hardly holding down my food and worried when it would end so that I would get out and empty my stomach content that scrambled like an egg for breakfast. We came to a place called *Jello*,[71] and there were many winding roads around the mountains like very big snake for miles and miles. Every twisted corner made me sick, going around these high mountains, with their deep valleys

---

70   Man eater
71   Twisted

which also scared me that we might fall off their cliffs anytime adding to my anxiety of death. I tried to control my urge to vomit as these conditions got worse and worse. I told my dad I couldn't hold any longer and he opened the window for me to toss out my snacks from my belly sack. Outside heat and smelly trucks exhaust made me even sicker. Breathing of this unpleasant air added to the misery of throwing up. I blamed my dad to bring me on this deadly road that made me unable to sit and enjoy the little car ride. I didn't know why my dad not let us walk on foot rather than die like this. I wondered when this bad road and feeling going to end, but my dad said that we were approaching our destination, just I needed to hold little longer.

I wondered and asked, "How did people able to travel such crazy road with very dangerous drivers every day to this town?"

My dad replied, "This is your first long trip made you sick because you lack experience of travelling by car."

As we finished the twisted mountain and came to a little flat land like desert and straight road, I felt little better and safe except black smoke ejected on our car as we passed them. I had to cover and hold my mouth and nose with my shirt to avoid breathing this bad smoke, but my shirt and hand couldn't stop all of it. This made me as if I was drunk and dizzy. I was tired and sick, but as soon as I saw first Dire buildings, I began to scan them left to right. I was surprised to see many houses made of stones I had never seen before. The town was very beautiful and I was happy to lay my eyes on many of its breathtaking buildings. I had never seen such a big town before. Then my dad showed me three big buildings at entrance of town surrounded by stone fences and a lot of trees to be my high school. My eyes were stuck on them, but fast-moving car robbed my eyes away from it. I saw many hundreds of cars running about and thousands of people walking on foot like ants in our farm. Seeing its beauty, my heart was jumping up and down with happiness to see something new and exciting, for the first time ever. I liked its houses and trees designs that swallowed all the troubles of this trip. My dad suddenly said to the driver, "Stop this taxi!" Then my heart popped and fell down my legs, to get off soon and reach my destination. My dad instructed me to follow him and I started watching everything around on foot. He frightened me to watch out for many cars on the road, not to eat me. I was scared and ran to hold his hand. He dragged me like a cow after him, and we reached Fadduma's house at last. He knocked on a door of a big gate and we were welcomed with happiness. Fadduma spread a nice colourful carpet to sit on which I had never seen in our village. I was glad to sit on such beautiful carpet like King of Jordan for not being rough on the bottom like our cow skin. She was a nice lady pushed us to chat and asked my dad, "Was he a little boy running and hiding from us when we came to visit you with Momo last time?"

My dad confirmed, "Yes! Indeed, it was him who run and hid like mouse behind a large gourd of water." I was embarrassed by this news while all of her eight children were listening and watching me. They gave us a town food which was different than our country side how it was made and I ate a lot of it liking its' flavor. I had to sleep the night on a very nice soft bed different than our umbrella bed and cow skin, in the nice mansion made of stones and cement bricks, saying goodbye to our tin roof which had many holes in it, letting rain and sun shine through its' walls made of mud and trees. I used to sit on a cow skin to eat my meals, but now I sat on a nice gold plated chairs and tables. I was amazed by many things changed for me and all I had to do was to just learn and eat good food. I said to myself, "What a life they live here in town! Maybe this is paradise."

In the morning, we went to school to register with my dad, and I was excited to see thousands of students in its yard. I also learned that there were many students came from other places to complete their high school just like me. We had to go to separate window to register. The line up was too long for us to register quickly, and I was sorry for my dad to stuck with me, and then told him to leave and wait at Fadduma's house. He agreed and left me there to register and I had to wait in line the whole day for it. I went home happy after registering and my dad was glad I knew the way back home, too. At last, he departed from Dire leaving me behind, and I was sad to see him gone. Fadduma and her kids saw my sadness about my dad leaving, and they tried to solace me by saying, "Please do not worry, you are at home, we are here to help you, you can go to visit your family once a while on the weekend." They made me feel better. Next day Abukadir, one of Fadduma's son asked me to go with him since he was going to grade ten of same school. I was glad to go with him suspecting that he might be friendly with me. I felt I had to glue myself to him like my own brother and dear friend more than anyone in the family. I saw his face smiled at me more than anyone in the family for me to accept him as true brother as Oromo say, "*Biddeena namma quubsu qibbaabaa irra beekannii*[72]." He was the third born child, the oldest to be a girl that was going to grade eleven of the same school, not interested in me and the second oldest boy, to be Ilyasu who was going to grade eight, not to the same school of us. Even though I liked and cared for him, he didn't seem to be interest in me like Abukadir probably for not going to the same school with us. I was astonished why older brother going one grade lower than younger brother when he was as old as me and should go to same school and grade as me to be my potential friend. The fourth to be Naju, a beautiful sister, going to grade seven, and the rest four kids were young kids attending elementary. With Abukadir, we went to school several days without starting class, and I learned that I had to take seventeen subjects which was a new rule of the government for grade nine students which Abukadir didn't face in previous years. It was the most shocking news to me studying these many subjects in grade nine. I was scared if I could pass this grade at all. We had been told to come, two weeks in the morning and two weeks in the afternoon.

It was truly a strange moment of my life, many subjects to study, only half day to attend school for all these subjects. Abukadir had his own unit, beautifully decorated with pictures of Rambo and Indian films super stars, in the compound where he studied that took my breath away. I found it being a very special study place to him that detached from main house. It attached to two other units one being a wash room and other kitchen where no one would bother him while he studied there. He invited me to join and study with him and his special friends. His brother Ilyasu was also welcome to sit and study

---

[72] When you see Injera on a pan, you would know whether it will satisfy you, or not.

whenever he felt like it. This little house became our main studying and sleeping place without need of bed. Only Ilyasu was the one who went to main house to sleep after study. Sometimes Abukadir liked to sleep in the main house where he had special comfy bed. I would be the only creature left to study and sleep in his tiny unit, for I liked it. As those seventeen subjects became tougher and tougher to study, we needed to chew Kat to keep us awake and strong all night long. Abukadir was the best candidate and associate in chewing this leaf and studied with me. We became in separable at all times. After we were tired of studying, we would go out to watch American, Indian or China's karate movies. Then we would come home to eat food from the same plate like twin boys and went back to study in our room. Now I could study very hard having electric light which was better than our gas lamp that darkened my nose and eyes with black smoke and no farm to work on. I had no worries at all besides studying hard and relaxed in this room. Sometimes I would study until dawn, for I did not go to school in the morning. Sometimes I studied all night and got to school straight. I had no problem at all, and it was my happiest time ever, being a true dedicated student. On the weekend, I would go out to visit different part of Dire to learn its beauty which I liked very much.

After two months, I missed my family and village so informed Fadduma that I wanted to go home to visit my family. I told Abukadir if he wanted to go with me and he said, "Yes." We then board a huge bus from town center to Haramaya and my friend was so happy to see a big lake of our town, which he had never seen before full of boats and birds like swan in it. After we took that bus we called "man eater" to Bate town where I walked him inside our towns' agricultural university for him to see. And then we walked to my village on foot where we were welcomed after long time. He was so happy to visit everything and breathed fresh air of the countryside that they didn't have in Dire Town especially walking in farms of ours where all vegetables grew. I was glad he founded out where vegetables and grains they bought in town coming from. I was very excited to bring my best friend and brother to Haro to visit my family and enjoyed himself. At night, I was sad to see him sleep on our cow skin which made him uneasy while those fleas bounced like basketballs on his belly and hit his skin like popcorn in the microwave and bitten him all night long. For they knew I was living there, they treated me like I was their old friend and they didn't eat me as much of him. I heard them said that we loved Abukadirs' virgin skin, fresh town guest meat with fatty and juicy flesh than me. He was rarely bitten by bedbugs of Dire as he told me, but these two legged night beasts didn't care if he was my best friend. They actually thanked me for bringing him. He was unable to sleep the night scratching all his body with those long nails that he had grown like girls that surprised me. In the morning, he showed me all his body that was stained with blood and many dark spots where they had bitten him. He joked, "You know! tiger was created in your village and now I resembled this animal just in one night." I was shocked and embarrassed about it, and sorry for him, but nothing I could do. I wished I didn't bring him with me, for his body was darkened and totally different than I saw before. I was afraid his mom wouldn't be happy with me, for turning him into tiger. I was afraid every one of his family and friends might blame and laugh at me when we returned, or at least I would be tortured by their criticism.

After we ate lunch, I took him to the blue lake, full of birds to swim with, and gave him sorghum cane which was special in our area. He was very happy, enjoyed everything besides tiger body that made him little uncomfortable. I was so happy to see my family and friends, and for my best friend to visit my birth place, and finally we returned back to school with less stress. Like I was afraid, he announced to all his friends and family where all the tigers of the world were coming from, and recommended them to go to my village to see them. We continued our study and the year finished with strong relationship between us, and I passed to grade ten. Then my friend decided to go back with me to my village for the second time to spend the rest of two month break time to become the mother of all tigers. We were inseparable for anything and everything in our life as one soul. He was part of my life: he ate, I ate; I ate, he ate; he farted, I farted; I farted, he farted; I laughed, he laughed; and he laughed, I laughed. We were meant to be together forever, stick together like crazy glue. The only things differentiated us were I was little taller than him and having cobra head and he was little shorter and having a warthog head. We spent two months, helping my dad in the farm, digging potatoes and playing with Muste.

When break was over, we went back to Dire having relaxed for two months. This time, with fresh mind and getting used to seventeen subjects, I was not afraid to learn and study more than ever, for I had already one year experience. My objective was to get good marks so that I could pass to grade eleven where I could choose electricity as my first career subject that I felt in love about learning current flow in wires. I decided to go all the way to university to become electrical engineer. If this was not possible, my second choice was to be mechanical engineer. As I heard and confirmed it, I had to be top dog in grade ten to choose one of these subjects in grade eleven or deal with the cows and pigs careers which might disgust me. Also another benefit of being top student in grade ten would offer me the opportunity to take only eight subjects in grade eleven. These chances motivated me to study very hard to reach my dream subjects and I had to compete with so many tough students came from out of town like me rather than town students. The competition was escalated to beat each other and I focussed more on electricity to be my major field, and tried to beat all students. I got excellent marks the first half of the semester. When I started the second semester, I arrested all my desires and extra fun to be the best student of all grade ten classes.

One day, as usual Abukadir started his fight with his family. He was especially very aggressive toward his elder brother, Iliyasu whom he chased with knife and Ilyasu locked himself in the bedroom for hours and hours if they had a small disagreement. It was not possible to cool him down once he started the fight as if there was category fifteen earthquake in the grand villa. I was observing all his fights over a year with most of his family and he had never taken on Naju before today. She looked very scared and desperate to save her life as I read in her beautiful eyes. I couldn't believe she deserved to be beaten like that. She needed me to help her. I asked my best friend to stop beating her expecting he would care and listen to me like his dear friend and true soul brother. Then he suddenly used bad articulations on me given to females in town, *Err! Anchi galla zim bey*[73] and came toward me to punch me, showing his kung fu muscles. My heart ringed with fear and surprised if he really meant and came to hit me just for saying to stop hurting his own sister. I couldn't swallow the word *galla* he had thrown on my face that ripped my heart out and cut my head off like rooster running around with blood gushing out of its neck. I couldn't believe he had taken steps toward me to rattle my face after he ripped off my head like that with bad insult. I waited to see if this was really happening. My heart whispered to me, he wouldn't hit me. I was his life and he was my life. If he was hungry and got bread as small as my finger nail, he brought to me and broke in half for me to eat with him. I doubted he wouldn't punch me today. So I waited until he reached me from twenty-five meters away where I shouted to him to leave her alone. He then ran toward me to teach me a lesson for opening my mouth and bent me like those logs he practiced on in the compound. He seemed so confident he dashed toward me without taking a knife like he did for his brother. I respected him as if I was his guest at his home, it wouldn't be appropriate for me to hit him back, or defend myself. Moreover, he was my hero and life as I saw it to wait for him patiently. Yes, there was no doubt; he landed one fist on my eyes. He was ruthless; he was acting like Bruce Lee in his fenced yard, smashing woods with his palms edge and forehead. Bruce Lee was his hero, he got some muscles and his forehead was black like charcoal of hitting woods. Now since he rammed me with his fist, millions of little lights sparkled and spread in front of my face like galaxies. My heart knew one eye had gone and I must defend and protect the other before he took it out. "I had no hearts, but at least a hollow lungs," and I challenged myself.

At last I threw a few fists toward him in self defence. Iilyasu jumped in the middle of us to stop the fighting, and his mother ran out of house madly uttering some words, "How dare you hit a kid that stay in our house, shame on you!" When Ilyasu got mad at him, he ran to beat him, they threw many punches at each other,

---

[73] Oh! Sissy *galla* (derogatory); shut up

and he couldn't defeat Ilyasu as he wanted, for he was stronger and bigger than him. I felt sorry for him that his brother attacked him for me, and I jumped in the middle to stop the fight. Then he ran and grabbed his knife from his drawer as usual to cut Ilyasu, and Ilyasu ran from his knife to a bed room as usual and locked himself up. He was banging on the door for Iliyasu to open and threatening by the door for him to get out. I was lucky he didn't come for me with knife. I went back to his study room with sore eye while his mother tried to cool me down. From here on ward, he had never stopped insulting and disturbing me while I studied, and never bothered to talk to me like his brother. He gave up going to school with me and abandoned his little room altogether. Any time I arrived from school, he would say a bad word so that I got annoyed. His older sister, mother, and Iliyasu tried to stop him from giving me hard time, and he gave them insult from time to time. He labelled them as supporters of *galla*. He couldn't pass by my door without saying something like I was a lady, or part of a woman just to upset me. I was unable to focus and study seventeen subjects like before and my goal to get outstanding marks from grade ten became unrealistic. I tried to befriend and talk to him, and he ignored and kept on harassing me. Any time he saw me helping Naju with her school work which his mother requested me to assist all the kids, he added more insult for us as if she became *galla's* wife. She was very beautiful girl and friendly toward me, and directing his big gun toward her because of me so many times made me very sorry for her. He instigated my intentions to marry her some day to make his insult reality. She was becoming the only person I assumed in my heart and soul to become my wife as he continued this assault on us day after day. He seemed he was on a mission to kick me out of their house, and threatened me to discontinue my high school there. I began blaming my dad who brought me to this inferno; I didn't expect to happen at all. Now that my best friend Abukadir was on the rampage, Ilyasu became a little more friendly who ate and drank with me. He stayed in the little house to study with me for a bit then left as usual. I was left alone in Abukadir's room and mostly I was lonely by myself. I could only paid attention to study about 25 percent and my body was there rather than brain, but from time to time my heart and brain was mostly occupied by his images running inside me saying bad things.

One night after Ilyasu left me to sleep about mid night; Fadduma went to the kitchen for something I didn't know about. She found out that all the raw meats to be cooked next day were suddenly disappeared from the kitchen. She shouted, "Oh! God! Oh God! Where are the meats? They were all gone, meat! Meat! What finished it! What happened to it? Cat!" she shouted. She wanted to verify what happened and there was only a tiny bit left on the counter. Hearing his mother shouting about meat and saying, "Cat" at last, Abukadir ran out of his bed and said, "Meat! Meat! Cat had eaten it! This is not a normal cat Mom, it is a big human Cat in the compound." Blaming a human black cat in his room so that I would be in trouble for eating raw meat from her kitchen. I was shocked by his comment becoming a big black cat that stole meat from them. He was relentless when attacking me with anything. I thought I should be better off stay back home going to night school so that I wouldn't be called cat man that stole meat from someone else's house. I cried like never before in my life as tears shot down my face like golf balls and wetted my note books. I thought of all the things we had shared together in the past, the friendship, the food, the laughter, the study and above all the promise that we would be friends for life. He was my soul and I was his soul. How come he was able and dared to give me these kinds of insults. It made me cry for a long time like river and I thought I would run out of water in my body fearing I would be a dry patch of grass. What should I do now? These insult of stealing meat as a cat from their kitchen with name calling of galla became intolerable.

I thought of quitting high school in Dire and going back to village and finishing my secondary at night school. I informed his mom about my intention to go back to my village. She tried to advice me to stay and finish school with them. Despite my friends' assault, I gave a chance to her saying at least to finish the rest of grade ten with patience, but he continued to harass me any time we encountered in the house. I prayed to God day and night to end my suffering and to separate us sooner than later, for it seemed impossible to face him for two more years in this condition. I wanted him to be friends again, and he looked not interested at all, for he had not stopped his slaughter toward me. He was shrinking his face anytime he saw me in their compound. While I was in this face, the second semester exam showed up for grade ten. I didn't get excellent marks as desired because anytime I opened my books to study, there Abukadir showed up like Satan even he was not there before. This nightmare of him and lack of any focus, I only managed to be one of the top ten students in the school rather than first over all. Then I heard a rumor from classmates that there was a notice on the school board about opportunity for top ten students in the entire school of grade ten, to be able to register for technical college of Addis Ababa, in the capital city of my country which was about five hundred kilometers away from Dire town. Those chosen must only pay forty birr for apron cost. This news made me happy and I dreamt to go to capital city, leaving Dire for Abukadir, but this news became too good to be true if I had family there to help, or the government gave me lodging for it. I went to check the notice board and I found it to be true, but it looked unlikely that I would register there anyway, for it was impossible to have a relative that lived there, or government to give me help in such far place. I was lucky even to come to Dire Dawa for my aunt used to work for Fadduma as a maid and I wished I had another aunt worked in Addis Ababa as a maid so that I took my chances to escape my friend's insult and study the subjects of my dreams. The notice had stirred the desire and opportunity for me to go. It was only a dream which I wished to tell my dad. Could my dad afford to pay for rental place? With this thought standing in my brain and desire to go to Addis, I completed grade ten and went back home for a break with intention not to return to Dire school at all. I told my dad what Abukadir had done to me and just continue night school with my friend Muste at my town's university. Hearing this conflict of my friend and comment of not returning to Dire, my dad got very mad at me. Anyway I told my dad the news about the opportunity to go to capital city if I had any relative there while expecting he would say sorry you did not have a chance to go there. Then my dad again shocked me, "There is another relative of your mom that lives in

Addis Ababa and I will go and ask for you." I was surprised to hear this news which was the most amazing thing I ever heard. I tried to confirm, "I have another relative lived that far which I didn't hear about it all my life!"

My dad replied, "Yes." This news flashed in my brain like lightning, but I recalled that my mom's relative had already slammed door to my face first time my dad asked her in Harar. I said, "There is no way this time this relative could say all right to me."

Then I was curious to know, "Who is the relative of my mom who lives that far?"

Dad replied, "My mother's another aunt had a child to East Indian marriage." I loved so many Indian movies and stars, I was able to sing just like them and I was glad to have this uncle who was half East Indian and half of my mother's African blood. Then I asked my dad to hurry up with the request before the registration was over and to bring my dream come true so that I even sang for him a few Indian songs and probably learnt the meanings of my songs. Then my dad planned to take my grandpa as a helper. I recalled that another Indian brother of him in Dire, which my dad refused to ask for help in the first place and I wondered why this time he wanted to ask the one in Addis. Everything about this request became unreality for me. I prayed to God to make him say all right and help me to finish my school there.

The next day, I went with my dad to grandpapa's house to listen what he would say and a chance to enjoy that white injera and drink smoked milk that I was dreaming about for a long time. Then he agreed with my dad to go to Addis and my hope of going was alive once more as they took on the journey far away hoping they would come with green light for me. After I filled my sacks, I left back home alone to tell my mom about it, but she was scared I might never come back to visit her again, for visiting wouldn't be easy any more. I was afraid I might come once a year to visit her, and I saw she was already sad if my uncle said all right. Then my dad and grandpapa returned back with good news that I could go ahead to tell Dire high school. It was one of my happiest days of my life being able to show my behind to Abukadir rather than my cat face he hated so much. I could breathe from his insult now, and I was excited to go to capital city so sooner rather than later. I did not know how I would live there with my Indian uncle and what subjects or field I might take. Everything became like a dream.

Next morning, I ran to Dire to register and paid that forty birr, and out of many students registered, I was accepted with other four students to go to capital city. I kicked my behind like rabbit with happiness, and I bragged that the cat that finished meat from Abukadir's kitchen would be going soon and went home with excitement. I thanked my lord who answered my prayers with this happiness and I believed. "There is always a light at the end of tunnel," as people said. Abukadir threw a stone at me, but it became a cake after it hit me. Besides, I was going to capital city to learn ahead of what I was planned already. I broke the news to Fadduma and her kids, and they were sad for my leaving, and I thanked them to help me all this time, but Abukadir was happy to hear that the cat ate all his meat had gone, and his dream to kick me out came true for him. I said goodbye to all of them and went back to my village. I spent two months of break time with my family, trying to get fresh air and enjoy them until I left them. I was very excited and couldn't wait until I sat on the train for the first time, or take bus for the whole day ride as I heard it. I had a small doubt my uncle becoming a beast toward me like Abukadir or his children to give me hard time; and there was no choice than to leave Dire behind. When three days left for school to open, I rushed and washed myself with bucket water my mom got from river and combed my catty hair for the trip. My heart drummed for this long trip I had never had before to the unknown part of my country. My mom face darkened like charcoal with sadness as if she would never see me again to a trip she opposed from the beginning.

CHAPTER 3

Cat's Trip to the Capital City

While being shocked, I started packing; my mom cried holding her mouth with a rug spread over her head. It moved me to cry with her seeing how much she loved me and it shackled my feet. While we both sobbed, my little siblings also began to cry. My dad's crocodile eyes never let out any tears and he urged me to go on. Now that I had some experience of going to Dire by bus even though I felt little sick with gas fumes and heat, I began worrying for this long trip to Addis which I heard might take the whole day by bus or train.

We went and said our goodbyes to Fadduma and her children, then headed to a train station. I was shocked to see the chaos of at least eight hundred people trying to buy ticket to ward Addis. We had to stand end of the line and I feared we might not get a chance to get on a train at all. Many soldiers were beating these crowds behaving like animals just to control them in lines and keep peace as some of them were trying to push, shove, and cheat each other. After my leg was frozen standing for a long time, we finally reached the window and got tickets in our hand. I was really excited, but we had to go to another tiring long line to get in train. As we approached the gate of entrance, we saw security police searching the bags of everyone for contraband items and let them go one by one. Some were protesting when items were taken, but these police relentlessly beat and shoved them to the carts like bees. My heart beat since they were taking new items and I was worried my new pants for school were going to be taken away. As soon as I arrived to them, they checked my ticket, and then told me to put down my bag and taken out my new clothing with books. I told them I was student and not to take my clothing's and they did not take any of them. I was relieved from anxiety of getting robbed there and we happily jumped on long anaconda train waiting on the railway. I was tired standing all day and there again I sat in train cart till the sun said, "goodbye" and my bottom strained with blood. I was almost shit on myself as train horn went off, having not heard such loud sound before and to make matter worse, it moved back ward first and dropped my gut behind me. Then I felt better and sounded good as it moved forward the way I expected it. There I felt leaving Dire and my province, for a long journey in the night as train began drumming its legs in the dark, moving faster and faster, making *choo, choo, chugga, chugga*[74] sound which I liked it and made my head swung and danced like lizard.

The train didn't care of my feelings of losing Dire from my view and the town began to disappear from my site in the darkness. I began to watch the mountains and trees run behind me so fast, but not easy to watch everything. I wished the trip was in the day light to see everything in detail. I tried to move in the train to watch the scene in the pitch darkness as much as I could, the faster the train ran, the faster Dire disappeared from my site like a devil had taken it away becoming things of the past, let alone see my village which became like a dream to see it again. Again not giving up, I tried to move in the train to watch in the pitch dark night as much as I could, but my dad urged me to sit and chew Kat[75] to watch it later. He feared that I would be getting tired doing this all night. It was true as my dad warned, my eyes dried and filled with tears, watching over and over again in fast moving train. I didn't know how many to see and leave for everything being the same and it made me very dizzy.

---

[74] Sound of train
[75] Green chewable leaf discovered by goat that makes people high and strong, sleep depriving leaf.

After I got tired of watching no man's land and many vacant mountains, at last I sat down to chew Kat with my dad who joked with me about wasting my time watching everything. After I swallowed bitter juice of Kat, I got energy to stare through the window of a train to see more of the country. Then the train slowed down coming to a small town where electricity was absent and only a few houses were made of stone while the rest were mostly made of mud. I asked my dad, "What is its name?"

He replied, "Its name is *Hurso*."[76] It made me smile and he added "everyone must be permanently snoring in it." A few people got off, and some got on. We stayed very little time as if the train was scared to stay longer and moved again. We passed countless little towns and suddenly at one of it many police began running in the train checking something in every opening and corners of all carts which was different than before. Whoever had worn two shirts must take off one for check up and all females were crying in such an anxiety especially getting naked in front of many. They checked my bag and I showed my student letter from my school immediately. Again they didn't take my clothing and I was relieved, but found that trip on the train was torturous and scary.

After cops were gone, I began watching more of the areas as some travellers were tired and slept on hall ways of it while some others were slumbering where they sat. I wanted to slumber and sleep myself, but I wanted to see more and more of the country and I didn't want to miss anything. My dad was not tired he kept chewing his Kat and I asked him if we were closer to capital city and he replied that we were not even close. "To reach the city, we must travel the whole night and whole day again," he appalled me. I didn't believe my dad at all. I decided to sit down and take a rest for a while and watch from the window as much as I could, but my eyes, hands, and legs were swollen and my shoes were tighter than before. I wondered why I was changed from lean to corpulent kid just in one night of travel. Socks teeth were sinking in my skin being very tight and lines formed on it becoming socks itself. I got up to walk around to stretch my body

---

[76] Snoring people or land and mountain.

and making it better, and it seemed unlikely. My back began to hurt badly, but I managed to insist on watching and walking around once a while and then we reached a very deep valley with bridge which was very scary to pass on it by train. Those who knew its danger started to pray to God to pass them safely to the other side of it. I was petrified by them and bridge, and went to window to see for myself as the train was not slowing down. When we reached on it, I looked down and I felt I was flying in air. There was nothing on both sides of us. I was troubled by not making to other side, but I was relieved when the train quickly ran over it to other side. Everyone exhaled, so I did same. I was curious to know its name and my dad said, "Awash valley bridge" one of the biggest valleys of Africa. I hailed those who dared to make such a bridge, risking their lives and able to connect the two mountains. I totally lost my breathe seeing such a miraculous thing for the first time in my life. Then about morning we entered Awash town and a train stopped at edge of it. There an order came, "None of you should get off from it. There would be another checking here." Again military invaded all the train bellies like monkeys entering a farm, and taken many items from people who might be smuggling things to another city. Again I showed my letter of school, they didn't take any thing from my bag, but they made me to watch items they collected as their keeper, and later let us get off the train. I wanted to get off to see around town for a few minutes, but my dad ordered me to stay on it, for there were hundreds of thieves that jumped on the train to rob everything that we had on board. Then I looked around the train and I saw many of them hanging on it.

Some people were afraid to get off, and they bought their snacks and drinks through its window. We did also buy same way. I was very sad not be able to get off a train, and visit the town because of many thieves surrounded the train. Then I saw one big thief was looking at my watch to cut it off, and I was prepared to hit his hand with water jug if he had attempted, and we gazed each other eye to eye as if he wanted to be a tiger creeping after a rabbit. I kept my eye on him, seeing his eye stuck on my hand. Then he decided to look at another window, seeing my eyes on the guard of him. On other side, I heard ladies shouting loudly at thief who snatched head scarf from them by window. I was amazed how tough they were to make many passengers cry like that face to face making me laugh in the action. Knowing that these were their professions, and how many of them roaming around a train surprised me. I was scared of a whole town youth, some like me, and some older than me being pick pockets, and I gazed each of them one by one running around. There were also many little kids shouting trying to sell injera, oranges, mangos, guavas, nuts, and alike to make money. This town seemed over heated with volcano and all of their activities including police and residents. I was curious to know if we reached Addis Ababa yet, but my dad said that we just completed our province; and now entering Shewa province which we had to travel the rest of the day to reach Addis Ababa, our destination capital city. I was already exhausted with lack of sleep, I felt travelling anymore would be fatal. I was worried I might not be alive to reach Addis.

I realized that our country was bigger than I thought; wanting the trip to end soon. I was happy to see many towns, but train stopping and sitting at each one of them for a while disgusted me, and more tiring. As the dawn approaching and morning air began rushing by my face, there a train sounded its horn to leave and everyone ran to the train and those standing and walking inside of it started to sit down. I was happy to see that we were moving, but three thieves hanging on the car by my side were watching my left hand like cat looking at mouse. I held my water container on the guard to smash their hands in case they attempted to cut my watch from my hand. I was wondering if they were going to go with us hanging by train, or just hanging temporarily until they got chance to cut my watch. Then before train sped up, one stretched his hand toward my watch, and I was scared and hit his hand, and he let the train go.

My dad said, "Didn't I tell you to sit so that this wouldn't happen?"

I replied, "Yes! You told me, I wouldn't put my hand on the window anymore." I asked, "Is there anymore military search to come?"

He assured, "No, no more search left until we reach Addis."

I was happy, at least to hear this news. The sun was to appear and the birds were dancing as they sang. I began watching those unique animals of Shewa park that only found in our country. There were thousands of them doing their chores in the vast field, and I was extra delighted to lay my eyes on them for the first time ever. I felt, I just began a new trip, for seeing some small mountains in the open space with animals in broad day light as if I was not tired at all. I saw we were running in parallel to many huge trucks and buses on the open straight road. I tried to compare trains' speed with them which one ran faster. While I was occupied with this comparison, a train went off sight of the trucks. I was amazed to see all wild animals like zebra and antelope which I had never seen before in my life. They were running away from the train as if they were scared of it.

While enjoying all these new towns and animals, at last I saw the tip of Addis city at far land which my dad confirmed for me, but I wondered of the villages and farms closer to Addis to be its suburbs. My dad added, "This is the entrance of the city. We will soon reach Addis tall buildings and many traffic lights that you had never seen before." I was happy to see big buildings, its flower, many amazing gardens, and statues in it. They took my breath away as if I arrived in center of the universe. We headed to taxi, to take us to my uncle's place. When we reached that part of my uncle's wooden houses, it was not as beautiful as other areas of the city I travelled in. The roads were paved with muddy stones and houses had old tin roofs which I thought we were in the country side of it, not realizing that we were almost in the center of the city's famous market area. Then we stopped by tall and faded wood fenced compound and got off taxi. As we entered its gate, I found the wall of two houses made of wood and mud mixed with dry grasses smiling at me. I was surprised to see this kind of house in the capital city and not sure why they had done it. My dad then greeted my uncles' wife Faddum, and she welcomed us. Then she asked her maid to give us some water to wash our feet, and I went outside in the compound. Then kids from two houses adjacent to my uncles' house began to watch me like gorilla just arrived from the bush. I questioned myself why they looked at me as my legs were swollen like pigs' thigh, and washing them I thought I was washing some one's else's feet. I finished the water given to me, but was not sure if I washed them at all, but went in the house with

141

my legs drumming in my ears. I had difficulty climbing up a stage about one-meter high sitting area of the house where we supposed to rest and chew Kat. I wondered and asked, "Why did you on earth make a tower look like to scare the crow in a farm, in the middle of small house?" And they laughed at me with no answer.

To the point it was going to make me fart like donkey, I managed to climb up and sat down letting heavy breath out of relief. I thanked God for arriving safely to my nest and decided not to travel by train any more. They gave us nice injera with a finger licking sauce I had never seen before. I was not able to indulge myself, for my appetite was shut down by train travelling as if air on a train had inflated my stomach. My uncles' wife suspected that I did not eat it, for their injera was ugly. I denied this was not a case, and I explained that simply my desire to eat was shut down. And somehow they pressured me to try it, and I managed to taste it twice. The house was very small, only with one bed room, and our sitting hill had small bed next to us. I didn't see my uncle and his kids yet, but I was afraid they didn't have any kids at all since they were not at home this late evening. I asked where about of my uncle, and his wife told me that he would be with his friend to chew Kat, and he would be home about eight in the evening. We began to chew Kat we brought with us with my uncle's wife, and she was very glad to get a Kat from her birth province of Harrar. She cried, "I missed this Kat very long time." And she seemed excited and thanking us for this. Then she gave us Kat from Addis and I was surprised that it looked very different than ours having broad leaves like spinach. She warned us that this was not tasty, but it might keep us up all night depriving our sleep time. If this was true, I liked its news, for my interest was to study all night long. Then I was shocked to hear that I was not permitted to sit past ten pm for any reason because it was rule of the house. It was not good news, for I could not take advantage of this Kat to help me study all night long as I was going to need it.

When I began chewing this Kat with disappointment, it was really very strange bitterness to it, but not as bad as I thought it was going to kill me. There I saw an older man coming in the compound, walking with cane in his hand, moving side to side like a tree swinging by hurricane and grinding the rocky floor while breathing like snake. Then Faddum broke his news to us that Zaku, my uncle was coming like that. I could not wait until I saw him closer to my face for the first time ever. "Good evening," he greeted us reaching the door. I saw his light skinned, rounded tiger face of India. We greeted him back, "Good evening." My dad got up and shook his hand, but I had to kiss his hairy right hand as respected elder relative. He did the same special hand kiss to me which he supposed not to do. He was surprised, "He had grown up so much from last time I saw him." I was flattered about it because I had no idea he knew me at all. He verified with my dad if I was indeed the one he saw before, and my dad agreed with him. All his hair was totally white as if milk was lightly spread over his body. He was old and really handsome for his skin and face had East Indian flavor which I liked it. I could see his scalp through very soft thin white hair trying to say goodbye to him. He seemed to me very kind old man, but his left leg was shorter than a right leg like hyena. This might be the reason he was swinging left to right breathing like killer whale in pain.

I wondered how on earth the East Indian descent, came from another planet so far away and married my mothers' aunt in the country side of Ethiopia where almost no cars and plane were visited before and none of this race existed. I loved Indian movies and its actors when Muste and I went five kilometers away to watch cinema at Haro movie theatre from time to time. I believed they were special beautiful people from far away land and my mom even used to say my son would marry Hindi girl any time my dad bothered me to get married at age seven to beautiful girls he might have seen in our area. Anyway I did not know where my mom saw Hindi girl as she had never seen any Hindi movies or girls at all as far as I knew. I wondered how Zaku became my uncle, and he did not look like African black Cat like me, or my mom, but I was proud of myself having him to be my uncle and loved him so much like my dad. I extremely glad that he allowed me to come to his house, in the capital city escaping the trouble of my friend Abukadir in Dire Town. I was shy to say to him thank you so many times, but thanked him enough in my heart. I dreamed to help him financially after I graduated from school and repaid to his kindness like my father. After his warm greeting to us, he went in a little room breathing hard and came back breathing hard, fully changed his dress without his walking cane to sit with us. We tried to make space for him to sit in a tiny space which was not enough for four of us. He apologized for living in such a small house, and climbed on the small bed next to us, with his Kat. I painted his worry about little house by saying this would be enough for the time being until something happened for you. I made him comfortable as much as I could about the little house.

He was glad I comforted him and told us a story of his ex-wife which had kicked him out of a big house without his dresses and kids when they had a fight and then divorced. Now he married to Faddum in this little house, and I was sorry for him to hear this troubling news. While chatting and chewing Kat, he began lecturing me about the rule of the house. I must sleep at ten pm because their maid slept in the same living room with me so that I did not disturb her. He made it clear just like Fadduma and dad laid on me earlier and this to be very critical issue. I was sad again unable to study the way I wanted which was now confirmed from man of the house and I had no choice, but agreed to it. Over all, they seemed to be happy with my arrival, and I was glad to see them they were happy to have me despite the rule which I had to abide to it. Then we stayed chewing Kat until 11:00 PM, and my dad and I slept same place we chewed Kat. Their maid also slept on a small bed next to us while Zaku and Faddum headed to small bed room. I found the city colder than our area and I had to put a few blankets together to be able to sleep. I was so tired and did not know where I was in split seconds, only to be awakened by my dad in the morning. It seemed I was clumsy to get up, for my body was very tired to move and somehow got up very hardly, being very shy, not to refuse my dad because I was new guest. I found myself to be in that mud house of Addis for the first morning. I realised I had to go to school, and I asked my uncle who would take me to school to register. He said, "I would find someone to take you to register." He found and introduced me to the neighbor kid, Gallatu Abduro who was as tall as me to show me the way to school. I saw Gallatu to be an excellent character, and he seemed to be very happy to see and take me to school with his big smile. I found him learning at other school, and I asked him to be my friend from now on and he agreed with me. After we had our breakfast, Faddum with Gallatu decided to take me to school and we took a bus there. When we arrived, I saw so many students that came from different provinces standing in line, waiting for school to be opened. The school looked very big and beautiful, and I could not wait until I registered. When opened, I went to register and they wanted to know which Kebelle[77] I stayed in, and someone to be responsible for me in case something went wrong in school. Then, Faddum signed and became my legal guardian. They warned her that she would pay for anything I broke or lost in school.

I found these warning to Faddum to be strange in the capital city. I was able to register at last, and we went home so happy even though I was scared of the dire warning to Faddum. The city was covered with low heavy clouds at all times, and it rained very much day and night. The sun rarely said hello through the cloud for a short period of time. I was little astonished by this weather and clouds that I did not know when sun rose and set at all, but over all I was one excited cat to go to school in the capital city far from my birth place and Dire Dawa's trouble. They told me there was a short cut to school if I wanted to walk about twenty minutes. Knowing I had to spend all day in school, we discussed what I should do about my lunch time. They suggested I took my lunch to school, or I could come home to eat it and go back to class, and we agreed on the later. My uncle again said, "You are required to register in a Kebelle of us as a new resident." He took me to the Zone's office. I didn't completely comprehend the reason, but little scared of this registration like animal in the zoo, in my own country as if I was not allowed to walk, in the zone, or sleep at my uncles' place.

After we went home, we chewed Kat all day, and about the evening I wanted to go out to visit the city, and my uncle's relative who came to visit wanted to show me around. We walked as much as we could, and when tired, we went back home. As we reached

---

[77] Zone

home, my dad broke the bad news; he wanted to take the evening train to leave me behind in Addis. I was shocked, "Are you really going to leave me here, and going back home?" I asked to confirm. He replied, "Do not be a fool! Without worrying, follow and focus on your school." I began deep thinking about back home, missing my family. When I lowered my head in sadness, my dad got worried about me. Again he said, "Do not upset me. You are not a kid anymore." He tried to make me patient about his leave. He got up to leave; Gallatu and I decided to accompany him to a train station to say goodbye. When we arrived, there was heavy line up in the train station, and we waited until he got his ticket, and made difficult goodbyes to each other and he went away. I discussed with Gallatu how we went home by bus, or on foot. He said, "Your choice," and I replied, "On foot," to see the city. We walked on foot in the beautiful part of the city which had tall buildings and nice streets for hours. I found the area we stayed to be worse than country side, and Gallatu confirmed that we lived in the worst part of the city where there were muddy streets, and the house looked like rotten tin roof and fences were made of old woods. I was so happy to see the beautiful part of the city. We went to restaurants to have a tea and drinks, and after we got tired we went home about nine in the evening. I was worried how to go to school in the morning, and I mentioned to Gallatu, and he was willing to go to school with me and I was relieved from tensions.

When morning came I washed in very cold water while I was scared, and I ate breakfast and Gallatu and I walked on broken streets to school straight from uncles' house. I found it easy to go to school, and when we reached it, there were a lot of students in the compound. As my friend said the school was not started yet, but the students were talking about which subjects they wanted to take, and some said there were nine subjects to choose from in this school. We stood there and listened all their discussions, and I had a deep thought which subjects I wanted to take, for still no one had told me which subject I was about to take, or they might force me to go to any field which they thought all right for me. I did not understand how the school operated, and all I knew was to be registered at this school. Hearing the students talked about subjects like: auto technician, electricity, welding, drafting, television and radio, wood work, general mechanic, building surveying, and machinist had got me interested. I wondered my imagination which one to take. When I was a child I wondered how buses and turtle cars able to move, and I had a desire to learn about them: how they made, how they move, what were inside of them. Auto mechanics might be interesting if I got it, or choose it myself. Electricity was my second choice now which I desired all my life. "I must get one of these two fields," I murmured. Then I realised that there might be a reason why I was kicked out of Dire Dawa for the opportunity to come to capital city to study my favourite subjects. I said that even if I was given any subjects by school officials, I didn't care as long as I completed in peace.

I prayed to God for everything to be perfect, and we went back home hearing the school would start in two days time. Still I didn't believe that I held books in my left hand and went to school in Addis. "Yes, still possible," I feared. "From now on, I must stay strong and study hard," I encouraged myself. Couple of days later, there I was excited holding my books in the left hand and walked straight to school on the same street Gallatu showed me. Sometimes being happy and sometimes being shocked about what to happen in school, I was somehow able to reach the school, and waited at its gate until its door opened. When gate opened, there were only a few students who headed to notice board and I followed them. I found out that they were looking at their names and which classes they had to go. I was also curious and checked my name if it was there. Then I saw my name and next to it written auto mechanic class, being given by school for top students from each province. I couldn't believe my eyes what I was seeing to be auto technicians, one of my dream came true subject since child hood. After we sang national anthem where they showed us, we headed to that vacant and ghostly class that abandoned for two months for the first time. We kicked out all ghosts and Satans attending our class, and sat down eagerly waiting for the teacher to arrive. Then a teacher came and told us very strict rules of school and learning procedures of our field. He said, "Before noon you must attend academic classes for regular high school, and in the afternoon participate only in automotive field." I found taking these two classes in one day to be very hard things to face. When half day was done, I was able to go home for lunch, and Faddum welcomed me with big arms, and she gave me nice lunch. It was my happiest day ever, and I went back to school for the afternoon class feeling much better than before, being able to come home and going back to class safely without losing the way. I was less strange, in the afternoon to be in the auto class. When our teacher welcomed us to the class and taught us many amazing things about automotive I had never knew before, it made me lose my breath. I was more amazed even to be here that first day was gone in a flash of lightning and I went back home like king of the street. I realised that I needed to study hard in two areas, first for the morning academic subjects, and second for my main field of auto technicians. As I feared, the rule of my uncle house to sleep at ten pm stroked my brain. I was little unhappy, for I wouldn't be able study and finish everything by ten O'clock. I planned to study hard on the weekend, but my weekend was also going to taken by compulsory Kebelle's youth participation which they were forcing me to participate in it, or risk being arrested as I heard about it. I found most studies time was taken by their rules, and I tried my best to study hard. I wished there was no curfew on me from my uncle and Kebelle sides, but found myself lucky at least able to go to school.

CHAPTER 4

Cat Trouble in Addis

While I was doing my best following house rules and studying hard, one evening, my uncle came home very shocked with frowned face, breathing like rhinoceros. He broke the news to us that his million-dollar friends were in trouble with the government. One of them, the most dearly friend to him whom he chewed Kat all day long was already arrested. He feared his well of money to dry up soon like stalk. He commented, "I might be unable to support you from now on, I need your dad to help you. Please write an urgent letter to him." I was shocked by this development, and wrote urgent letter to my dad. I gave it to a broker lady that came very often to my uncle house from Dire Dawa so that she passed it to someone in Dire who would then pass it to anyone going to my village, or Bate town. I was afraid this might take several months until she got a chance to see someone, for she was a busy business lady. Every night, he came home; he was grumbling how other families supported their kids to study at private school spending a lot of money for them. They bought them all that were needed like shoes and clothing etc., but my dad was not doing these things so far. He kept blaming my dad every evening as he came home, and he was verbally torturing me, "You didn't look like student in the capital city at all." He repeated many times, "Why didn't you bother and inform him about the cost of living here."

Then I tried to explain to him that my dad was a poor farmer, and not rich like others to send money every month. He, then said, "You would be in trouble to complete your school." I was surprised why he was saying these things to me while he was the one promised my dad to assist me until I finished my two years course since he had no kids to worry about anymore; and now accusing my dad he abandoned me in the capital city.

One day, I came home from school for lunch, and I saw Faddum was crying and very distracted by some thing. I asked, "What went wrong?"

She replied, "Zaku, this morning, after you left, he threw your bag of clothing outside in muddy compound while raining by saying who would this garbage bag belong to...? While pretending he did not know it, and I got mad at him for doing this on purpose. I asked him to stop throwing your bag outside and he insulted me as *Kotu*.[78] He then began beating me, for saying do not throw his bag and our fight escalated to the point Gallatu's mother showed up to stop our fight. I was stricken on my ankle with a coffee cup, too." I saw her limping. I was astounded they had a fight because of me. I was sad and blamed my dad who had brought me to this trouble far away from my home. I thought this to be worse than my friend in Dire Dawa, for I had no place to escape from him. The lunch she gave me was hardly passed down my throat, and I went back to school feeling morally and physically down. I asked myself, "Why did he do this before my father replied to my letter?" I had many questions, but I had no answers for them just puzzled by them. I began to masticate the story Faddum told me about her son whom she brought from another marriage. She said, "I married your uncle with my son, and he used to live with us. Then the *Derg*[79] government suspected him to be participated in opposing students' parties, and they kept coming to our house to look for him, and Zaku feared that he would be arrested and killed because of him. We had many serious fights when he threw his food in the toilet rather than he ate it. At last, he chased

---

[78] Farmer (derogative to Oromo)
[79] Military of Ethiopia

him out of house." She was crying about so many things my uncle did to them. I realized she was again burning because of me, for it seemed that I was on his menu.

First time, she chatted with me about her son's story being no longer in the country because of him and government, I did not think I would be affected at all. I wondered why my dad did not reply to my letter, and prayed to God that he said something soon. All day, I was taken by many thoughts in the school, and I came home worrying to what would happen when we faced each other. Lucky, he was not home as he spent the day at his arrested best friends' place. He came home swinging in the evening about eight pm, I was worried what he would say as he entered the door. Anxiety fell over my head as he entered door with tiger face, without saying, "*Asala mu aleykum*"[80] that he usually threw at us. He went straight to his bed room, very quietly to change his cloth, and I kept quiet expecting some commotions to happen. He came out and asked the maid for his dinner, and he went straight to bed. Thank God, I was safe for the night.

When morning arrived, I tried to talk with him to make matters easier, and made him feel all right. Our conversation was normal, and I couldn't tell how much his anger sack was filled and what he planned for me. After we had our breakfast, I headed to school. I suspected that he wanted my dad to give him some money perhaps some grains to support me at his house. He didn't stop me from eating and staying with him, but from time to time, I saw him rattling his lips in his desire to get help from my dad impatiently. I was asking why he did not show up quickly. I suspected that he was trying to send an urgent message to my dad. While I kept going to my school, I felt more anxiety, day and night about my uncles' actions. One evening, I came from school and sat on a chair facing outside door, thinking about my dad, and I saw someone strange walking to our door as if I saw a person just came out of a grave yard. He had a long dirty coverall like greasy monkey, and his face was badly burnt, his eyes were as red as a flame. His face skin was flattened to the bones like pistol's handle, and his hair seemed unwashed and uncombed for twenty

---

[80] Peace of God with you

years. He had a walking cane on his shoulder carrying something, and I thought what kind of beggar born from earth trying to enter uncle's house. I was somewhat scared and watched him curiously. I wondered how come this beggar knew, directed his head toward our door. When he approached more to our door, he had a feel of being my dad's feature on his face. I doubted if this person was my real dad I had known before. Then he greeted us, "Good evening!" sounding similar to my dad's voice I heard all my life. Now I thought he came to me as a ghost. I stood up to hug him while shocked to his appalling situation. I asked him, "Are you my dad?"

He said, "Yes, I am your dad!" Immediately I felt dizzy seeing him like dark ragdoll. I lost a word to say and tears filled my eyes; seeing his cheek bones were laughing at me. With that horrible face, he himself began to cry for seeing me alive and I also cried to see him come back from his grave just awoken by someone, or something. He asked, "Are you all right, son?"

As if someone filled him I was already dead in Addis after he had gone, bombarding him with urgent calls that he should respond to my call. He flew and came like battered eagle from the way he breathed. For almost two hours, I was deeply and sadly screened his body to figure out what happened to him to look like worn out rug. I could see Faddum was also swallowed by his condition to come like that and she lost words to say by our situation.

We were all in the state of sorrow as if we lost a loved one and wondering what went wrong trying to find what to say. Before we say anything to each other, Zaku arrived and greeted my dad, "Hello" and then he changed his dress, and jumped on the bed next to us. First he welcomed him, then he said, "I request you, to support your son financially. You never returned to see him again. I warn you, from now on to aid him, or take your hand off him, and never return to see him like your son." I felt that he was to force my dad to give up on me so that he would adopt me like his son. My dad was shocked by his demands, and he replied, "I was sick for three months, and never left my bed to do any work, and you can see how I look. I got your message and ran here. Otherwise, I am not a type of person to give up on my son, or to just ignore you." Then Zaku did not seem to worry about my dad's situation and he pleaded, "I am not the same person you knew before. My friends were arrested, and I no longer have the ability to support your son and myself. I am old man now, and I want you to give me one hundred Ethiopian birr every month." I was listening to all this and wondered that my school completion might be hampered by my uncle's demand. My dad lost words about funds demanded, and then, Zaku went outside and grabbed the neighbor as a witness and said, "Please be my witness that I am passing his son to him at your presence if he does not give me a hundred birr every month, and my demand is final! I will not take any more responsibility for him." He gave another option to my dad, "If you are unable to send the money, I can let him sleep in the house, but you must provide food part, or he must find it somewhere else with school supplies." The neighbor was shocked by my uncle's speech and asked my dad to do something. Then my dad thanked him to help me so far, and told him that he might give me ten or twenty birr whatever he could even if I had to eat a dry slice of bread. Then my uncle again repeated he was willing to let me sleep in his house, and he had no problem about it, and he gave us a chance to talk about it so that we made our decision. He should let him know about it as neighbor left us. I was very sad to see my dad in this situation, and lost a word to say, for what to do next. Now, I realised that my school was about to end. We went to sleep with so many headaches to discuss in the morning. I was unable to nap whole night thinking what to happen and what we should do.

In the morning, my dad walked with me to school without breakfast. I was curious to know, "How did you hear my news and come?" He replied, "I heard you phoned Dire Dawa and left a message with someone to tell me that I abandoned you in Addis and how you were dying of hunger and sleeping on the street because your uncle kicked you out of the house. You were also on the verge of death and urged me to come in a hurry!" I was shocked to hear him say things I didn't say and no doubt uncle was already at work while he was bothering me. I confirmed to him, "I didn't call and left you any messages, but I sent a letter to send a sack of grains and vegetables for support. Did you get it?" He replied, "I didn't get it." In the mean while, we reached school ground, and I could not be absent even for one day from school which might result in heavy penalty for me so I told my dad to go back to uncle's place for us to discuss this matter later on. He agreed and stayed back and I went in class planning to get permission from teacher to leave early. Students left class early for break saw my dad and told me he was indeed outside school gate.

I was shocked and asked a teacher permission to leave because of my dad was still standing by fence all this time. I was upset to see that he did not go home. Some friends asked, "Is he your dad?" I was very embarrassed the way he looked, but no chance to lie about it and said, "Yes! He was sick for a long time and came for emergency reasons." I was embarrassed and said to him, "Why did you stay here? Because these students were staring at us. They could laugh at me, for the way you looked." I urged him to leave the compound area fast before more students see us together. Then he replied, "You under-estimated me. Next time I would show up with worn out sacks of grain!" I was mad at him trying to embarrass me in the capital city. I saw his focus was only the problem of my uncle, and we walked together out of compound, discussing about it.

Then he told me, "I borrowed five hundred birr from your aunt, Momo, what should we do?" I was more upset hearing he took this money from his poor merchant sister of his, without a husband with two twin kids, and she had no farm like us to depend on.

"Gracious! God," I was baffled.

He asked, "You tell me where we go from here? I must go back to take care of matters."

Then I urged him, "Please return three hundred birr to my poor aunt, and just give me two hundred, I will try to stretch it until end of the term by buying only a cup of tea and slice of bread since we can't afford my uncles' demand of hundred every month. I will be fine as long as Zaku did not kick me out of the house. Even if he kicked me out of his house, I would not mind to sleep on the street to finish my school by eating Amhara's *kollo*."[81] I encouraged him

---

[81]   Food like popcorn

to take it easy and go home. He was very worried; I could read on his face how much this was hurting him. I tried my best to ease his worry, and after a deep silence he agreed to leave. He then gave me that two hundred birr I demanded and sadly headed to the train to go back home. I did not go to uncles' place for lunch, for the first time, and stayed the whole day at school deciding not to eat at my uncle's anymore. At end of the day, I went home knowing things had changed for good. Faddum got mad, "Why didn't you come home for lunch as usual? We were waiting for you!" I replied, "My dad would not afford the funds my uncle requested. This was why I did not come." I tried to make her understand my decisions, and my dad had also left city. She felt sorry said, "Sometimes I have a few birr I get from broker's ladies, I will help you, just ask me when you need it and hungry." She reminded me, the story of her son happening to me.

I said, "Yes, you are right, it looks like my turn now!"

In the evening, my uncle came and asked, "Where is your dad?" I replied, "He had taken a train this morning." "What were your decisions?" I had detailed my dad's condition to him first, and sadly explained, "I will eat from my pocket if as you said allow me to sleep in the house." He was amazed by our action and said, "Ok! It is good if you can do that, you can only sleep here." I thanked him for this; at least I had a place to sleep. He seemed he was happy; I would no longer eat at his place. I doubted that he was not really poor person, hoarding thousands and thousands of birr for retirement: to munch on it little by little until he died. He gave his wife two birr for daily food expenses which was barely enough in the capital city. This was also one of their reasons why they argued like hyena and lion almost every day. She was chipping in, with some funds of her own, while he was being like mad cow disease, picking on her for every little thing he saw of her, just to make her mad. I began taking tea and consti-pating bread for my daily rations that was very low on nutrition, but glad to make a trip to school every day without to deal with my uncle's nagging for eating at his house. Every day, I worried about my dad's deteriorating health if he would make it alive, and saw him again. I advised myself to be strong and patient with everything, and tried my best in school despite these new challenges I was facing. I became friends with some of the poor students going to strange place in town where there were shaggy little houses that sold strange and cheap *Atmit*[82] drink which disgusted me the first time I saw it, and then went back to class burping its gas. I thought this drink was exactly what the doctor ordered every day, for my small pocket funds so that I did not run out of it. I tried to study hard very quietly, but there was no privacy, or quietness in the house, for they did not know how hard I had to study with a malnutrition brain. They pressured me to talk and laugh with them, but I tried going along and focusing, for I could not tell them to keep quiet at all.

While I put up with this, my first year was done and I was able to dash to a train station to go to my family to spend two months of break time. When I reached our village, I found that farm lands were over taken by a small pest socialist peasant association that was formed in our area before I left for Addis. Everyone was in serious trouble of living to survive day by day. Some were forced to join the party when land was taken. Some refused to join, and they had to go far towns every day to their *Kuli* job where the wage was not enough even for one daily meal for their family. Some of them also arrested for refusing to join while others were arrested for coming close to the association farms. After they were released, they were given a very small portion of land that not producing enough grain needed for their family. The lands taken by the association were hardly culti-vated and mostly became barren with those little farms abandoned by refused villagers. They had also taken our irrigated land, and I spent two months of break times with sadness for our land and the villag-ers who lost them while worrying what to happen when I returned to school. My dad was able to get some funds for me to go back to school. This time I was comfortably returned to it knowing that *Atmit* and dry bread were waiting for me with tea. While worrying of my family surrounded by socialist party, I arrived for school's second year finding Faddum and uncle fighting seriously over a cloth dealer that went bad. They were not talking and not treating each other

---

82   Fermented dough drink

like husband and wife at all. He was insulting and disrespecting her more than ever. She had stopped sleeping in the same bed with him being so disgusted to be next to him. He began to insult her as *kotu's* wife and even sometimes called her *galla's* wife to stab me alive. He heard me calling her mom all the time, and I loved her just like my own mother and she was almost four times my age. I was disgusted by the way he acted toward us, but still tried to mediate and bring peace between them. Again, he didn't count me like a fly landed on his stool. I tried to be friendly and treated him like my blood relative, but he kept insulting me indirectly with Hindi bad words, *mannel panchur sallam karnarre.*[83] Throwing these bad words from his mouth like a missile, I suspected that very soon he would kick me out of his house like a soccer ball. I kept wondering, and scared of what to happen next. His insult to me and his wife as *galla* and *kotu* became heavier and heavier like a million Mt. Everests. I respected him being my relative and senior person. I became patient like Canadian people and ignored him as much as I could, but I started to drag myself not to come home early evening so that I could minimize his insult and sleep quickly. His wife had lost words about what to say and she had never said anything to me.

One day, on top of his ugly insult, he began cursing someone, "Let God kicks this guy out of my house!" I feared he was talking about me since I was the only guy in the house with him. His desire to kick me out of his place was hitting my brain day by day as he intensified his watching me from his wife. I was worried where to sleep in case he decided to kick me out. Suddenly another problem was cooking in the horizon when the Ethiopian Derg government declared that all youth to be registered for war to save the country from the so many rebel groups that getting stronger day by day to overthrow it. One day as we were lining up to sing national anthem to enter our classes, the school administration informed us to go and register our names with the government offices and get identity card. They warned us if we did not get this ID card, we could be arrested walking to school. All students were gone to register after break time

---

[83] Who penetrated mother and gives salutation to his dad.

and I went to my Kebelle office to do it. There I saw females and males of all kinds in line up. After long wait, I got my small paper ID card for registering and went back to school fearing that they might call and stop me from my course I was about to finish. I thought I was immune from it because I was attending special college course that ended soon. Then we took mid semester exam, and the school was closed for two weeks' break. At least, I wanted to visit my family for two weeks, but I was afraid this might deplete the little money I had for my atmit and I would also stress my dad more than I already did. After I bent my mind so hard whether to go, or not, I decided to go and visit my family, but I needed another ID card from the Kebelle as rules of travel got very strict from government. I headed to the Kebelle to get it, but the officials thought I was to disappear from the city and hesitated to give it to me. After I explained my desperate financial needs to continue my school, they were unable to trust me, but at last gave it to me. I headed to train station showing the new ID, and embarked on the train. I reached Dire Dawa about evening, but scared to move on fearing my friend the hyena to jump on me. I didn't know where to go, besides Abukadir's house which was the only options I had, or I had to go and face my darling hyena from my town fifteen minutes' walk toward our house in the country side where hyenas were running around to eat something. Then I remembered my voice had been changing to an adult and could scare hyena. I felt it was wrong for hyena to dare me anymore.

I encouraged myself to go after so many contemplations to go, or not to go. I made myself strong while my stomach was shaking, and took a bus toward my town from Dire. I hoped to see someone who might walk toward my village and defend me from hyena in case my voice was not sufficient, but I looked around and found no luck at all. I hopped on the bus to my district of Haramaya while my heart was full of doubts on the way to facing hyenas. Once I took another bus to Bate, which was five kilometers away from Haro, my heart beat doubled as if I faced several hyenas who seemed not to be afraid of me. I got off at Bate bus terminal and now there was no return, my heart went wild; I wished I had *sabata*[84] to tie my stomach and chest together to help me walk from there. I was not lucky to find someone going north with me. I started praying to God to keep hyenas away from me. Once I looked behind, once to the right and once to the left, and my heart was pounding as if I saw it every step I had taken toward my house. I had aborted so many babies on the way and reached my home without seeing any of them. My prayer was answered and I entered my house safe only to find my mother with kids. I learnt that my dad was in Harrar town working as carpenter building tall towers after he felt better from his sickness. Then couple of days later, my dad came home to visit and he was surprised to see me. I was glad that he came because I was planning to visit him in Harrar in a few days. We discussed about several changes that was happening in the country, how government was registering and taking youth to army by force to fight those rebels. He was concerned that they might take me in the army and I would be killed as some others who lost at war from our area. He felt that I would be next when I returned there. I had no choice than to go back since I was close to graduate from my school. I made my mind not to stay at all. He asked me about my uncle's situation, and I told him that he was stretching my catty skin more than ever and he pointed all his heavy guns to my head and his wife. Then my dad was concerned and advised me not to return there and stay home with my mother as if I would be safer in the village. He was afraid of Zaku would hurt me by planning very bad things. My mom also agreed with him, I should stay with them. I refused to stay since I became so skinny trying to finish my school I had started and I insisted to return and finish it. My dad went back to his carpentry work while he was disagreeing on my return.

When my two weeks about to finish, I decided to visit him first, to say my goodbyes to him. My mom asked, "Where are you going?" I answered, "First, I visit my dad and then I go to Addis from there."

---

[84] Long and fat fabric belt of woman used to tie belly after childbirth, or just hold dress on the waist

She was then concerned and said "I will go with you to Harrar." I encouraged her to stay with the kids. She insisted, "No, no, I will go." We took a bus from Bate to Haramaya where we needed to catch another automobile to Harrar. When we were about to take a taxi to Harrar, she saw an old lady walking with cane.

She asked me, "Is that my mom?" and I looked at the old lady, "No, she wouldn't be your mom as far as I see her."

She insisted, "She is similar to my mom."

I suggested, "You must be crazy if you think all old ladies with cane are your mother."

"You must know, she is like caucasian, beautiful, and never walk with cane, and this one looked like her face was covered with gore!" I tried to discouraged her, not to go to the old lady she was thinking her mother. She had refused to enter taxi when I tugged her hand very quickly to get in and sit. I jumped in taxi, and pressured her, "Come in."

She went straight to the old lady; they began to hug each other.

I felt she might be right and got out of the taxi to see them. Indeed my mom was right, it was grandma. They were crying and hugging each other. "My son was taken by soldiers this morning, he might be somewhere close by in the compound," she moaned. I was shocked to hear that my brother was taken and we went to find him. We learned that all youth were taken to a compound near the bus station herded like goats inside a huge wall. Soldiers were only allowing families to see their kids one by one through the hole and no one was allowed to get in to see their boys. When we got our chance, we asked, "Where is Gemal?" They brought him to us through that small opening and hugging was not possible. Mom and grandma were weeping like dying wild boars knowing that he was already dead. I cried with them being very shocked and saw him gone forever. I felt that this might be the last time I would lay my eyes on him until doomsday when God would reunite us. I gave him some money to help him, and said, "Goodbye, brother, I am going to Addis from Harrar, hope we will see each other someday, *Insha Allah*[85]!" It was a bad day, but

---

[85] God will

160

I had to move on since door was jammed between us sooner than we wanted. I advised my mom, "Please stay with grandmom, and take her to her village," because I was afraid that she might not make to her village alive and safe with her gory appearance. Then grandma worried for me, and said to my mom, "Take him to Harrar! I will go with my villagers who also came for their kids."

Mom agreed, "All right!" Then we made hard goodbyes to grandma and my mom came to Harrar with me while crying in the bus for my brother as he was going to die in a war.

When we reached Harrar, residents were also crying in the same way, and the situation was appalling that many youths were rounded up in the whole town. We walked through this chaos and reached my dad's work place. He asked, "Why did you come?"

"I came to visit you, on the way to Addis." Mom began crying heavily. My dad asked, "What was the matter?" She told him, "Gemal was forced and taken by soldiers for war from Gode village!"

There, my dad also cracked, "My son, my son…if you go, I will lose you, too. You will be next in Addis." They became a brick wall, refusing me to go to capital city. He threatened, "Do not go, stop your school," as if they could hide me in their den. The whole situation was bad, and I was confused, but there was nothing I could do. I decided to go to my school, I thought no matter what, and besides, I gave a reason. "I am a college student, almost finished my course, and they have no right to take me away from it; and a law would not allow them to take me!" I spoke like someone who knew the country's law about students in school so that they would let me go even they caught me. About evening, we heard that all youth taken from all districts were brought to Harrar.

My dad and mother went to see Gemal and I stayed in the construction compound. They were unable to see him, for there were thousands of families came to disturb the compound, and soldiers were refused to let them visit at all. I was unable to sleep the night thinking of my sad parents and school. When morning showed up, I made up my mind to go, and I headed to the bus stop. Both of them came along crying until I got a ticket. I said, "Goodbye, Dad! Goodbye, Mom!"

They were crying blood for me not to go and made their appeal to listen to them. It was hard for me to leave them in the same condition, but I had to take my chances. I looked at the ticket number to find where to sit on the bus, and pushed my heavy heart like elephant and found it to be by a window of *bal-anbesa*.[86] I gazed them from there, carrying sense of guilt to leave them while they were crying; and they approached me by window. They began begging me to get down, and cried some more, and more. Tears run down my cheeks like balls and I was choked not being able to say anything at all. I wished the bus driver drove me away fast from their sight and grief. This made me mad at him, for he was not around, or in his sit at all.

At last, I turned my face away because I could not bear their crying. I pretended to read information notes on the bus card until driver came in. Some passengers informed me that my family were calling me from outside, and I ignored them pretending I did not hear them, or know them. Then, the driver hopped in and he started to move as my nerves were frozen by shock to leaving them. I showed them my palms, and they raised their heads not feeling to say goodbye. I was not feeling all right rejecting my family, but I was excited to be on *bal-anbesa* for my first time to take such a huge bus with the big pictures of leaping lions on both sides of it. The bus was extremely fast as its name implied and took me away from their sight. I was excited to see many mountains that I had never seen before by train. I was glad to take it, moving very fast toward Addis while I was tickled by many thoughts and problems of my uncle and what awaited me when I arrived there. Then a lady began to labor on the bus and everyone was disturbed with concerns and this was strange enough to keep me forgetting my worrying until I reached Addis. After I got off this bus, my feet tackled for no reason, and my eye brows and lips were ringing and shaking like old moon shaped phone. I feared strange things to fall on me very soon. I had no good answers, but what it would be. I could not guess besides blaming devil's handy work. I tried to make myself calmer and stronger as much as I could

---

[86] Head of a lion

on the way to Uncle's home. The closer I got to my uncle's house, the more my stomach twisted.

When I reached my uncle's house, only Faddum sat on the hill, gurgling and puffing her *gayya*,[87] with her maid sitting like rabbit by her side down the hill. I said, "Hello! How were you doing?" Faddum replied, "We were all right except troubles of Zaku." I had nothing to say, but whispered, "He still not got better, and changed his behaviour after I left for two weeks." I sat down on the stool next to the hill without taking off my shoes, engulfed with many thoughts. After twenty minutes, a revolutionary guard appeared with a letter on his hand to our door. "Where is that kid leaving with you? Did he not come yet?" asked Faddum.

I was shocked by his questions as he might be inquiring about me, and I looked at him. Faddum replied, "He is the one," pointing to my head. He was happy, at last, to see me like cheetah saw an antelope, and he asked me to sign a paper for him. "What paper to sign?" I was shocked to verify. He replied, "I do not know it was an order from the government, just sign it for me." Then I came to suspect what he was saying was not true, and I did not feel right to sign it since they supposed to force me like my brother I thought. The letter seemed fake to me, but I was still scared and got mad, "I do not sign, I am college student. I came to learn here, but not real resident of this zone, you can't force me to go!" I tried to stop him. Then he said, "I was ordered to make you sign, you can talk to officials in the morning if you wish," he urged me to sign for him. Faddum encouraged, "Please sign it otherwise you will be facing troubles if you don't do it." After I signed it, the officer added, "You must come to the Kebelle office in the morning!" I was astonished.

Now I realized why my lips and eye brows were shaking and I stumbled on the door. Faddum said, "The whole week they were looking for you." I was very sad for my school knowing that it was going to be interrupted before I finished it. I might have no chance to be back here as I would be a dinner for a vulture in the west and north of Ethiopia, same as I heard many people were already eaten by them.

---

[87] Hookah

I heard that school did not care anymore once a student had gone, or come back alive. This made sure that my education had gone dust to dust and ash to ash forever. Thus an unimaginable sadness invaded my body from toe to my hair. I had seen no more city lights like I was in a black man's graveyard, talking to angels, and getting punished for all the sins I had committed so far. The cries of my parents by side of *bal-anbesa* now became true sin I was facing. I regretted my stubborn head, what if I had listened to them, this would not have had happened to me. I was fallen in deep thought that it looked my neck was hanging by thread. I recalled many youths were chased and grabbed from the street and houses by guns in my Harrar province, but here only letter was given to chase and grab someone like me. The thought of whether going to school in the morning first, or go to the Kebelle became hard on me until my uncle arrived from his friends' house. As he entered the door, he smiled without greeting, "Were you contacted by an officer yet?"

I replied, "Yes!" but he didn't seem to be surprised at all, never displaying any remorse about it. He added, "How come they call you! You are a student…" I informed him my brother was also taken in Harar. I was wondering why he talked like this while his face was relaxed and seemed to enjoy the moment than ever. Then after we chewed Kat, he suggested, "We will go together to my friend, a revolutionary guard called Adam to help you free from this." I agreed and astonished that he was going to be my hero after all and true uncle who cared for me at bad time. After he satisfied with Kat, he asked me to go with him in the dark, knocking a ground with his walking cane as usual and we reached his friend's house. Lucky he was home and said, "Welcome, Zaku, come in, sit down."

Then my uncle explained, "He is the kid that stay in my house, relative of my mother, and his brother was also taken from Harrar in the army. He was going to technical school; please try your best to free him." He seemed to beg him for me, and his speech really impressed me that after all I was his true relative.

I began to thank him in my heart as I was listening. Then Adam said, "I was the one put his name down to be selected, and I didn't know that he was your relative. Now it is too late to remove his name from the list, for his name had already been transferred to a district office. The only way he will be free is if and only his medical test failed him to be accepted."

"My being free is not going to happen," hearing all these explanations from Adam. He warned me, "Don't try to escape, for the army is very strong these days, and they can snatch you out of any hole, or bush you might try to hide." He discouraged me as much as he could. "I can't do anything to help you, except God!" he stressed on me. From his words, I suspected that he was the one to recruit me on purpose. When we were about to leave, my uncle quickly reached by door and turned around, and stressed to Adam, "Take care of my business, be strong about it, do not drop on the ground!" And I heard Adam agreed, "All right." I wondered about what Zaku meant, and little felt it if they were talking about me and planned by him to take me away. He breathed heavy sign of relieve, and we went home.

I could not sleep the whole night thinking about it, and I had a serious headache. When morning came, my heart was divided into two: whether I went to school, or headed to Kebelle. My friend came to accompany me to school as usual, and I told him the bad news. He was shocked about it, and encouraged me to go to the Kebelle to verify things first. I had agreed and gone madly to a Kebelle, holding my school books. At the Kebelle, I asked a president of youth there, "Who is looking for me?" and the president instructed me to go to the district office for I was selected to be in the army. I asked them why they put me in the army knowing that I was going to school, and he said, "We can't do anything for your selection." Then I got upset and asked them for address of district office to complain about being drafted and everyone in the office got mad at me. Understanding that I was very serious going to district office, they suggested I should follow kids at their office who were going there. I decided to run home, to put the books back and returned to Kebelle, to go with them. We went to the district office, and we saw hundreds of youth, some standing in line, some sitting down and being sorted by district, they came from. I heard from someone, mentioning that one important district leader was sitting afar by a building. I wanted to talk to him if I could leave the line up which was not possible at the time. Suddenly he got up and decided to walk by sides of our lines to check us out like oxen for sale.

When he was a few feet away from me, I quickly left line and ran to him and I said, *dallalagh*[88] before I finished my statement, he right away countered it, "*nigigrih cheeka naw,*[89] go back to the line," he then dashed to hit me. I was scared and run back to my spot very fast. He continued his cat walk, without saying anything to me, and I brooded what went wrong, or I said to offend him. I was also afraid that I might pronounced his name wrong. While I was thinking many things might be gone wrong, they called my name, and I was given medical exam form to be checked with different departments.

First, I went to their eye specialist, and he showed me many writings I had to read, and I read everything correctly. When he got to small ones, I could not see them, and he told me, "I was a liar and thief." He hit me on the head several times with his pointing stick, and forced me to say right thing. Then he said, "I passed the eye test." Next, I went to line up for body exam, and I saw *dallalagh* coming. While being scared of him, I said, "My Lord, *dallalagh*!" I hoped to get his attention. Then he replied, "Yes! What do you want?" I began, "I am technical college student came from other province…" He did not accept this as a reason to let me go. I continued, "My brother was also taken away, and how come the government takes two people from the same family?" He shouted, "We take even ten people from the same family!" He added, "We can make your mom and dad a soldier, too." I wanted to explain to him about my problems of school, and I wanted to know what a law said about taking all family members especially two brothers at the same time. Because of his replies, I ran out of what to say, and I kept silent for a few seconds. He commented, "Your teeth were crooked, you don't pass the military exam anyway! Why do you afraid of military training."

Then he headed to where people names were being called, ignoring me. While I was shocked by his comments and actions, I finished all medical tests, and returned the examination cards to

---

[88] Sad face
[89] Your words are like mud

their appropriate place. They instructed me to return next morning, to get all exam results whether to ship me to war, or not. I was so sad and jealous missing my classes for the day and chances to learn new things which made me very sick to my stomach. It forced me to check out what the students had done all day even I got one word of it. All students were surprised to hear me saying that I was being forced in the army while none of them had experienced what happened to me. They were in grief and shock for me and commented, "You were about to graduated with us and this was not fair at all." After I learned that I was the only student in my school to be taken, I decided to argue and fight for myself so that I finished school like them. I sat in the class like a doll while everyone was paying attention to the teacher, sipping and eating his new teachings, I only saw his moving lips. Half day was done while I was looking at my smouldering corpse in the war zone. I went home, not feeling very well about what to happen in the morning, and it was difficult to sleep the night turning the pages of my problems. Morning came; I went to find out my fate, knowing that I was fit to go like horse, when they gave me the letter of appearance on the a specific date. My heart dropped down to belly, filming that rebel soldiers were about to kick and stab my pumpkin dead ass. My dreams to graduate, get a job and support my dad and aunt were going down the drain. I had no chance to study and prepare myself for exam anymore like my class mates. Knowing that I had to appear at the meeting hall on the date specified in the letter to be taken away. I was shocked and unable to go home like mad cow, got in and got out of many restaurants and parks for six hours, and then went home very disappointed to sleep the night.

Next morning, I decided to go to school, unable to give up being student and learning new lessons. I only held a few note books until a day of departure while feeling like drunk person going to school. The students were taking notes feeling very happy in the class, but the teacher saw me sitting like dull cat, doing nothing. Then he asked, "Don't you take notes like other students?" I had no answer, I pretended to take notes to show him I was on it, but I was like writing my notes on an ocean surface. I didn't see the benefit of taking notes since shortly I thought my brain would be gored out with bullet, or shell and ended up in a mud. I was unable to stay away from school while knowing it was not good for me anymore, but I dreamt of completing all courses in a few days if possible. When I tried to write, I could not finish one line as another teacher popped up in the class, then same thing happened over and over. I went to school being jealous of all students who were learning happily.

One afternoon, I decided not to give up on my school and went to argue with the commissariat at the medical exam building trying to free myself. With fear, I approached one person looked like a king cobra I had never seen before. I said, *endaminachew?*[90] He was not as furious as *dallalagh*. He replied, *endaminachew?*

He gave me a friendly face. I sighed! I started, "I have a little problem to tell you." He said, "Go ahead" I showered, "I was chosen to come to Addis technical school from Harrar province, and I am about to graduate in six months time. If you force me to go now, I had no chance of coming back to this course again. I want you to help me so that I finish this course." He seemed sad for my situation, "Please return in a couple of days." I felt better getting this response from him, but I did not know his rank and power in the army if he could truly help me, or not.

For two days, I went to school with tiny light in my heart, but I sat like a statue doing nothing. I was only copying some home works from my friends to show the teacher that I was still a student. After two days was gone, I went back to look for that king…and I could not find him at all. I realized he played me and I sadly went back home. I heard there would be a test for a very complicated math chapter which concerned me about it. I decided to go to my friend's place on Saturday the whole day to learn from him whatever he could teach me, but I found that he was not allowed to sit in a room of where he stayed so he decided to come and study at the park very close to me and I just sat with him to watch and listen what he was saying. He was solving tough questions using difficult formulas

---

[90] How are you doing?

they learned, and I did not have anything to say, but only watched him in vain.

He encouraged me to pay attention to him, for he thought I might get a chance to be free, but my mind was seeing my body jumping on a bus, or military truck taking me to unknown land. I said to him, "There would be no chance to stay and I do not seem to grasp such calculations even I try." He pushed me to write a letter to a chair person of our Kebelle, and I thought it was a good idea and I tried. After a few attempts, once I got hold of him, he said, "He could not help me at all." I told my friend it didn't work and he said, "You lack someone who knows the chairman" and I informed him that I tried my uncle's friend, but my effort failed, for my uncle already begged him not to let his matter down. He had never said anything since the day we went to his friend's place, knowing that I would be gone sooner than later which was clear for me by now because of the way he ignored me. He did not even bother to ask me what was happening to me. We only saw each other during bed time, and he had never said anything at all. I gave up on writing a letter when only four days left for the day we had to congregate to leave from town hall. My departure to the army was clear to me by now, but I didn't give up on where about of a cobra guy who gave me some hope coming back. I skewered my eyes over hundreds of people in the hall to get glimpse of him, in case I saw him, for he might be working there. I did not know his name to search him by name, and I regretted not knowing his name, but I might only remember his face. When I didn't see him, I was disappointed and went back to school without any focus at all.

In the afternoon, I searched for him from Kebelle to district, digging all the holes possible, for the day of departure approaching faster than I wanted it. At this point, it felt so serious that I entered Kebelle youth office with force finding its door was slightly opened. I found some workers who knew my story and problem and they also encouraged me to write a letter to the chairman of Kebelle so that they would give to him to help me. Then I ran home and brought the same letter which the chairman refused to see if they could put their magic hands on it, but I informed them about his refusal to me. They read it and said, "This letter is useless! Go to commissariat office and complain and tell them your story." I asked, "Where is the commissariat office." Once they gave me direction, I got mad at myself one more time and ran there in a hurry like an ostrich by dumping past fear behind me. As soon as I approached their office, I found two police guards in front of the door stopping and kicking back two other youths trying to enter there. This made my heart shrank as a pop corn and feared that there would be no chance to pass these two huge bulldogs as if they were tied there by chain. Knowing that I had no other options left, I was furious like a cat to the dogs and kept going at them to see commissariat while my heart was drumming hard they might hurt me. Then they ordered me, "Stop!" I didn't feel stop was the word I wanted to hear at this moment and something made me mad and I shouted at them loudly, "I do not stop." I saw my skin hardened like wild cat and pushed myself with force. As they ran to push me back and hit me, I suddenly saw the face of that guy who told me to come back in two days. Seeing his face gave me a boost and resisted the dogs and forced myself to the door and the guy suddenly told them to let me go in.

As I entered, I was shocked to see so many commissariats, but my eyes were stuck on the same person who insulted me my talk was like mud. He asked, "What do you want?" I started, "I have left about five months to finish my course and I am going to technical college…" before I finished my statement he quickly jumped in, "Even if you are in university!" made me lost my words to say that I was important student. I continued, "I have left only five months to graduate."

He replied, "Why not you left one day!"

And I continued, "How come I leave my school…. Again" before I finished the sentence he said, "Is the school better than your country?" He always interrupted me with something, and not allowed to tell my problems and story. I cleared, "I know school is not better than my country, but the slogan says, "Military service is obligatory and you have also a right and you are forbidding my right." I shouted to him with anger so he understood. He shouted,

"No, you are going! Are you *galla*?"[91] He wanted to know my race. I was shocked he said this to me being a colonel. He ordered me, "Leave the building right away." I said, "I am not *galla*" and he said, "Harrar *kotu*!"[92] This was another mind blower for me. As I was mad and reached the door to get out, that guy who said come back followed me to outside and offered to help if I could assist him with some money. He encouraged me to write a letter right away so that he gave it to *dallalagh*, the insulting colonel. I was excited and ran to the Kebelle to get the letter I gave them and passed to the guy. Then he passed to *dallalagh* and he said, "This letter was not written to us, but for the Kebelle. You must be present at the hall for departure!" I was shocked and disappointed that there was no chance to be free and went home very sad.

Next day, I spent all day in school, and about evening I went home to learn that my uncle's friend was released from prison and they had gone to another city for vacation. I doubted this to be his plan so that by the time he came back I was long gone and he would have clean home. The night before appearing to a hall of army, I could not sleep the whole night worrying about losing my school just like that and being dead soon. I couldn't even said my goodbyes to my family. In the morning, the time had arrived to push myself to the hall and found thousands of youths herded like cow. Then the officers came and started calling names one by one, and they gave each person a red card and told them to come next day with their family to the goodbye location. They must show soldiers at the gate their red card to leave a hall compound. With my heart drumming so hard, I was listening for my name to be called next, and then next. It was my worst day ever. I wished the earth swallowed me right there. More than two hours past, my name was not yelled, and officials went for a break. They continued after break for a long time, and still I didn't hear it. I was afraid they put my name at the end. At last they were done calling names, and tired officers left except a few of them.

---

[91]   Derogatory insult to Oromo
[92]   Farmer of Harrar another derogatory instead of Oromo, treating farmer as ethnic group.

Those officers left wondered how some of us left there without red card and they began checking our names with Kebelle's house numbers. It was shocking to find their names were yelled, but they didn't hear them. They slapped them one by one on the cheek as thieves and cheaters and given those red cards and kicked them out of the compound. I was afraid I would be next to be beaten like them. I was surprised I didn't hear my name. Then the guy who wanted to help saw my face and came toward me grabbed my hand, took me out of the hall. He said, "I let you go today, but we will get you second round, now run and finish your school quickly." I couldn't believe what just happened. I felt billion kilograms of burden were lifted of my neck and thanked him very much. I ran home like horse and told my uncle's wife first so that she would be happy.

Next day, I didn't know how I reached school and told my friend who was so excited for me. He was willing to help me to catch up giving me his note books to copy for missed classes. I tried my best to study hard and catch up. My uncle returned from his trip and shocked to see that I was still in his house. He breathed hard, "Didn't you go to the army? You are still here!" "No, I did not!" I replied. I was afraid he would have heart attack from his actions, seeing me as huge gorilla still sitting in his house. I reminded myself what he said to Adam, to keep an eye on his matter and the curse he uttered indirectly for me has faded away. Shortly after, he jumped again on the wagon of nagging and insulting me. I was seriously concerned of what next on his menu for me, but I stayed mostly in the park to study for big exam, for I would not be at peace and trying to minimize contact with him as much as possible, and only showed up during sleep time. Again coming late, he didn't let me sleep well. Understanding these problems, Gallatu,[93] my neighbor's friend came up with an idea for me to stay and study behind his house wall and fence. It was very narrow and hard space to fit the body where many rats and lizards ran by wall. If I could get peace from my uncle and able to study quietly, these creatures seemed friendlier and I would survive them. I didn't mind even they laughed or mocked me there.

---

[93] Thankful

We put old cartons on the ground like carpet and covered fence with it. It looked like we made a little room of boxes. He then got me a small gas lamp for the lights. I was able to study as much as I could, sometimes all nights, besides rats and lizards that distracted me a little bit by making noises around me. I was little scared of my health when a black smoke from the lamp darken my nostrils like chimney and dark fluid began dripping on my notes and pages of books I was reading. Also rainwater from the roof hit the ground next to me and splashed on my face, and ran down my cheeks as tears. I tried to keep myself as close as possible to the wall of house so that I did not get too wet. Even though I was little beaten by cold and rain and creatures ran over me, I was happy to escape my uncle's insults and stayed there free from him.

Now we only saw each other at Gallatu's house when I got in to chat with them after getting tired of studying. He was not concerned for my stay outside. His wife was so sad to see me living like wild cat unable to do very much. I made her understand I was only feeling little weird about rats and crawlers becoming my roommates and now I could study harder by getting away from my uncle. I continued my study, but the Kebelle's officials again forced me to perform a peace keeping duty at night which became more obstacles for my studies. I struggled with Kebelle's rules and tried to study for final exam as much as I could in my carton's unit. When I was tired, I laid in it looking at its design and roof with my condition and amazed by it, even some times it made me laugh like dear friend. After a while, we got to be very close to each other, leaving it for school in the morning made me think about it. My dad had no idea I was staying outside in the rain and became friends with creatures. In my letter, I had never mentioned to him about my new place, but to send me some money if he could. While I was in this struggle, the final exam approached and I tried to study hard, but the rain got very heavy and made me soggy than before. Most of my blanket and note books were wet making it harder to see and read. I tucked them under my body as much as I could from heavy rain and warned a small stream ran by me, not to come closer than it was. When I was tired, I slept by it and woke up to greet it. When hungry and tired, I went to my tea and bread house and came back quickly to open its plastic door where I had no guests, and continued my study as much as I could.

After academic exam was done, I was much relived from studying hard, but auto training sessions continued from my watery unit being little relaxed than before. This gave me a chance to cruise the city on foot. When this training was done, we heard a rumor that some of us had to work for ministry of defence. I did not want to stay in the city until all results came, but I decided to visit my family, this time jumping on the bus. They were happy to see me graduated, and I told them what happened, and they were astonished and shocked by it. I also gave them hope that I would be working soon to help them, and they did not need to worry about me after all. I assured them that I was no longer obliged to participate in a military, for I would be working in the ministry of defence. They seemed to be convinced and excited about it with little doubt. It was the happiest time of our lives. The worst and bad times were over besides my brother was sent to *garamulatta*.[94]

After a few weeks of relaxation and break, I began my journey back to Addis with that long anaconda train. I embarked on it, this time with little happiness that things looked more clear and hoping that I would be working and free myself from rats and rain, renting my own place with my school friends. I arrived to my uncle's compound and I greeted Faddum first, and went to Gallatu's house to greet them as well. They were happy to see me, and then I wondered if my shaggy unit was still intact behind their house while I chatted with them and I went to greet it pretending I went out to toilet. I found it as I left it and I was very excited it was still there. I was amazed, "My room was still there!" They laughed, "Yea! It was still there. Gallatu was using it like you!" We spent chatting until midnight and I went to sleep in it.

When morning came, I decided to visit my dear classmate Charnet, but as I left my compound, he also showed up to see me. We were excited to see each other. He joked, "You now became fat

---

[94] Mountain seen from many places

by eating vegetables back home." I asked him, "What did you do all these times?"

"I also went to my home town for a while, and I got bored and came back," he said. We went together to school to find results, and we both happy to pass, but did not know yet where we were going to work. We went home after we spent all day looking for place to rent and unable to find it, but we asked some people to help us. We spent several days and heard from school that we were given a place to work. Out of thirty students, we heard that ten of us with my friend given ministry of defence as rumored, rest twenty with ministry of transportation. We were so happy and left school with excitement, not knowing when we were going to start it. We then cruised in the city with happiness for our celebration. In the evening, we went back to my compound to learn that the Kebelle's officials were looking for me, hearing that I stayed behind Gallatu's house to force me in the army. All night, I could not sleep; they were after me again to force me in the army. I wanted to fight for my right again as I would be very soon working for the ministry of defence.

CHAPTER 5

The Cat Was Scared to Die
(Claw Cutting)

I went to a Kebelle and they gave me a letter right away to report to exams and tests like before. This time, I tried to tell them I would be working for the ministry of defence and I was exempt from military. Again they had nothing to do with my talk and I must explain to higher district officials. While my stomach was rattling and drumming, I decided to go and argue with fierce eye commissariat for my right the second round. Fearing the worst from them, I reached their office door, but lucky there were no army guards to stop me. I was relieved a bit; at least I got the chance to face them. I hesitated to enter without their permission and I stood by door for a few seconds. Then suddenly my human right gland exploded and forced me to enter as my legs were shaking with heartbeat. As I dared and scanned their faces from one end to the other, my eyes ended up on the same bad commissariat whom I had trouble with. "Why did you come?" he asked in a harsh fierce voice and frown face while others were focussed on the paper in front of them rather than my talk. My mind was ready to argue for my right and I began with, "Like you recall me before I am technical college student just graduated and got a job," and he did not let me finish what I was saying and he stressed, "What work? Work is not better than your county!" He planted boulder word in front of me so I did not talk.

Then my mind whispered, "I cannot argue with this person what I should do?" I halted to talk then I felt I should argue. As soon as I started, "My right has to be respected."

He quickly uttered, "What right? You are obliged to protect your country from enemy."

"Yes, I know there is obligation on me, but can I also ask for my right?" I tattered. He then said, "Yes, you can't ask for your right." My word was lost by his comment and I stood there thinking what to say and do next. He said, "Are you Harar *kotu*?" Right away *kotu* word sliced my heart like Italian pizza. I was mad and answered, "I am not!"

"Are you *galla*?" He again crushed my heart like elephant stood on it. Even my brain melted like mozzarella cheese. My lips and body shook, "How come you said these words? You are government official! You have said these to me last time I came here too."

Seeing my anger and buffing saliva like camel from my mouth, he then asked, "What are you then?" While fearing I could be in trouble, I threw these words, "I am pure Oromo! I do not know the *kotu*, or *galla* you talking about, you poked my heart saying these words." I feared I might be in trouble with my word Oromo. He said, "There are east groups that call themselves Oromo, collaborating with Somalis to fight us." I explained, "I told you only my ethnic group," while my intestines were twisted in fear. They gazed me with fierce eyes as if they wanted to chop my body. I was afraid I might be in trouble just like others who disappeared from the planet because of Oromo name. I doubted if I went out of there in one piece. I found myself drowning in the Atlantic Ocean saying my ethnic in their faces. While my stomach was grumbling in fear, they looked at me for a while and one said, "Go home now, and we will discuss about you." I went to my shaggy house in panicking state they might come after me as supporter of the rebels they were fighting in the country side. My brain was about to explode with many thoughts and bad things to come as the lizard on my wall shaking its head and weeping at the same time.

I deeply thought the purpose of forcing youths in the country to war just to kill their own people who might have been oppressed and I was not happy to fight them. I had seen before useless war of Somalia brought devastation to innocent people, not a single benefit of liberation, or freedom came out of it. This time, there were only our own people the government had to kill, and burnt our own forest which I would not support. Beside my life would be in danger of being Oromo, which was going to send me to prison for torture, or being killed like others. I couldn't nap all night long while weighing the benefit of hanging around in Addis any longer. At last, in the morning it forced me to run away to the train station while looking behind me as if security officials were following to catch me. I was sad on the way to a train to leave my capital city, the job about to start, and all the future opportunity to come for me in Addis. This fear tickled and pushed me to go on if I just made it alive to my family. I stood in a line for ticket, looking back if soldiers were coming to get, or stopping me from going and its anxiety twisted my kidney. It didn't seem real, leaving the city I loved so much and going to spend the rest of my life: working and raising my own family. I was engulfed in many thought, what if this didn't happen and why it happened. I was not sure if I was standing in the train station at all. There evening arrived while I was waiting for ticket; I could not wait until I got it and embarked on a train. I prayed to God to take me safely to my family. As ticket selling began, several hundreds of people started to scramble for it forming a long line up. I observed yelling and shovelling of each other, far ahead of me as some people started to cheat. I pushed and pushed people ahead of me as if I could shovel them in train to get my ticket faster, feeling pushing them was not fair. At the same time, I was scared I might not embark on the train which made me uncomfortable standing there. I told a person behind me to hold my spot in case I returned and my heart started to drum for going to the front area if I could be able to sneak in the middle like others. I stood beside the front line for this opportunity, observed what was happening, but afraid to jump in front of them they might yell at me and I could be beaten by soldiers. I begged a few to let me in and they refused me.

Soldiers began to beat those causing havoc with stick in the front to bring order and calm them down. I was slashed a few times along them and found that cheating was not possible at all. I ran back to my spot to save my skin and then some began screaming not to let me back to my original spot. I argued, "This was my place."

They said, "It was not yours; you should go and find your place." I tried to argue, but I doubted I might be wrong for I did not mark a person's face that I told to hold my spot. I was extra confused making a simple mistake not remembering where exactly I left from. I said to a person, "Didn't I tell you to come back to my spot when I left?" He replied, "No, no, go find your place!" I felt I was ripped off by these people, denying my original spot and they really made me mad. Then again I felt I was completely messed up and I did not come out of alleged space. I began searching my spot very seriously strangling my neck why I left my place and I approached a few of them carefully to see if I remembered them. Some even mocked and laughed at me as pick pocket. I wanted to insult them back, but I cared not to have more trouble there. I was not happy at all, for them to think I was thief, and I began looking again with little patience. I guessed a guy to be the one and I pretended I knew him 100 percent and made my move to enter in front of him by giving him my warmest greeting, "Hi, I am back!"

"Get out," he shouted with harsh voice.

"What happened? I was here earlier!" I tried to convince him. Other's yelled and yelled at me to leave. Then he informed me I was there and pointing to my spot. Then I apologized to him about my mistake and thanked him. I was afraid they might not let me in and dared to enter it quickly by telling myself there would be no other choice. This time, I was ready to fight and argue if necessary since last guy confirmed it for me. I faced some resistance, but at last able to stay in my right place.

I was relieved to return to my position, but I was afraid I might not get to the ticket booth, for there were many people ahead of me. I learnt my lesson not to leave again no matter what. I had minor urge to push them like boneless worm, but I had gone nowhere. After a while as I got closer, one soldier said the train was full and my stomach cracked like water melon that smashed on the ground. I said, "There! I can't make it to the train." I lost hope, but prayed for God to help me. "There were only a few people left ahead of me. What a bad luck, for them to stop now," my heart bled. Suddenly a soldier said, "We only need ten more!" I counted heads before me and I was the tenth person. A little relief, there might be a chance for me after all. I said to them, "Come on, come on," and several times in my heart started to count one, two, and three…as they began moving people ahead of me. I could not wait until I was touched on shoulder to enter. I pretended to push them by slightly opening my leg and a soldier hand stopped on my shoulder to halt me moving because all seats were full. I bubbled I was the tenth person, I should go in, but unfortunately they ordered the rest of us to leave.

I was devastated a hand to stop on me and I did not believe this had just happened. My heart shattered, suddenly they declared one more while I was in a shock of my life. My heart kicked with a little joy, but still I did not feel it to be true that I would be on the train until I got ticket and enter it. Then I paid for the ticket and boarded it, the miracle I had never expected I was leaving Addis. Now sadness of leaving the city I loved kicked in. The feeling of those looking for me and my safety forced me to say goodbye to Addis and sat down on the train.

There a train began moving while I was drowned in many thoughts and I saw soldiers with gun coming toward me from other cell checking every one for something. I cried, they were coming to get me and I had an urge to run from them, but there were no place to run and hide, besides sitting as a cold stone in my spot. I got socked by sweat all over my body. My heart beat was added to the train noise, only to learn that the soldiers were following a ticket checker. I doubted and looked in their face and how they were reacting with one person who was talking to them. They seemed friendly and I watched their conversation. He had very wrinkled and scorpion skin and his face was like crocodile with red eye and I was astonished by it as they seemed to know him. I stared and watched them. Then one lady shouted, "Father of Derje! What do you think of these soldiers? Talk about them." He replied, "We call these cold shivers!" He took one hand out of his pocket. It was round like a small children's basket ball which scared me. I was curious to know what happened to his hand and began staring at it while listening to their conversations. Some people started to laugh to his talk as if they knew him before being funny. I was contemplating why he said to the soldiers "cold shivers." Then I learnt that he was a smuggler to Addis Ababa and soldiers knew him very well. He raised his hand to leave him alone and began swinging his hand at ladies next to him as if he wanted to distract soldiers from taking his items. They began crying and running away from him as they urged him to stop. Many others were laughing by the action and I was concerned he might touch me with that hand. I asked one lady why they ran away from his hand and she informed me that he was a leper.

Now I was very scared to be infected by him. A lady shouted, "Who would provide you a shelter once you go to Dire Dawa?" He then passed his bald hand on his nose and eyes, and began talking, "I do not know anybody in Dire Dawa! But first time I arrived, I was stranded looking for a place to stay. After I was tired, I asked some one where to find a brothel. Once I got lead and entered one, a lady asked me, 'What do you want?' I replied, 'I want to spend a night!' She agreed and went to make a coffee. I was afraid she would see my hand when I drink so I cancelled my hand under bed sheet. When she brought and poured it for us and invited me to drink, I was unable to take out my hand. Then I asked her if she has some water to drink. When she went to get water, I quickly gulped down a hot coffee which cooked my throat and put back my hand in a bed sheet with tears filled my eyes. When she brought water, I asked for beer and she requested ten birr for everything and went away to get it. Again I quickly put ten birr and drank some water and hide my hand. After she brought a beer I pretended to be a gentle guy and sat by beer. Then she asked if I want to eat food and I urged her to cook for us. She grabbed the money and went to buy meat. I began struggling to finish the beer and water. After she cooked, she spread nicely cooked meat on injera and put on the table brought water to wash my hand. I was afraid she might see my hand, and encouraged her to enjoy pretending that I had already had a dinner even though

I could eat a whole cow. She appreciated my kindness, and began to eat all while I watched her with my evil hungry eyes. I was so hungry and afraid that I might not be alive and see next day light. At last she wanted to put food in my mouth with her hand and I said to her that if you do this for me, it shows your kindness. She then wrapped meat in injera as big as golf ball and stuffed in my mouth and I swallowed it. Again she asked me to repeat it and I said, 'All right, I do not mind,' and she did. My starvation cooled down, and she wanted to do a third time and I said, 'No, I am done, you go ahead,' she insisted to give me two more time and I was very satisfied. When she took plates in a kitchen, I quickly removed my clothing and jumped on her soft bed and waited for her. She took her shower and came dancing and I was so excited." Then almost every guy laughed on my car and the ladies began to disgust about his talk, "Who would sleep with this creepy leper!" Some I saw covered their mouth with rug and giggling like small hyena.

My mind was drowned in laughter and commotion with Dereje's funny story. It made me forget my fears and why I was on a train. He added, "When she came close to my bed, my heart began to dribble and she asked, "Are you already in bed, and did you asleep?"

And I said, "Yes, I am in bed, but still awake, and tired from a train trip."

She acknowledged my point and turned off a light and jumped next to me. Right away I dropped my round feet on her leg and loaded my circle hand on her back and squeezed her to my chest very tight. She wanted to know my name, for my hand and leg was heavy on her, and I told her my name, they call me father of Dereje. Then she said, "Father of Dereje, your hand is very heavy on my back, and she tried to remove it by grabbing my bally hand off her. Then she freaked and screamed, what happen to your hand, it is cut and round?"

Then I explained, "Please do not be afraid, I was a soldier during Somalian invasion, fighting in Ogden and as soon as I saw a few Somalian soldiers, I took my hand grenade and threw at them and it took all my limbs with it."

She was sorry for me and quietly listened. Then a soldier commented, "Dereje father, what if she suspected that you have a disease and run from you?" Then he said, "No problem, I was already prepared and planted my heavy trunk legs on her body and my steel iron hand grabbed tight and she isn't go anywhere from me. She bragged and excited that no one had amused her like me and she even invited me to come back any time I was in town without paying her. There is my home where I go to..." He made us entertained and I saw myself reaching Awash town far away from Addis listening to his story. I was surprised that at least I was closer to home forgetting my worrying for long time.

We took a break in Awash and returned back to my car feeling much better as if I was already back home to my family. I went all the way to Dire town listening to never ending Dereje's fathers' story. I was very much relived reaching Dire Dawa and heading to that bus stop which would take me to fresh air of my town that I could smell from here. After going through that dangerous terrain, I was glad knowing I would arrive soon to my village, but I began to worry what the villagers and our enemy were going to mock us with, just for returning home in vain. Besides, I was afraid of shocking my mom and dad who were not aware why I was coming back, might be for good. I expected them to be disappointed after they spent so much energy and money specially my dad who had been swinging from building to building like Tarzan while being pierced by nail with ugly and worn out socks and his skin was faded out like rag becoming skeleton just trying to help me finish my school. I was ashamed thinking what to say to him when I saw him. All these thoughts almost exploded my brain. I was back empty handed without work unable to repay them what they did for me. I advised myself at least becoming farmer and being safe was better than getting tortured, and killed. My family was indeed shocked with my fear of the government and being back in village. Then this worried them that they might come after me and it was a dangerous season in the village, too. I was in a dark state, day and night with my family, but at least I was lucky to eat fresh corn and millet canes with them again and perhaps they would see and say goodbye to my cadaver.

While we were in such bad time, the local association committee told my dad that it was time to demolish our house to relocate it to different place with many others because of socialism idea roaming our area. They wanted to unite everyone in socialism to work together and share everything except their spouses. It was widely talked idea and plan to stop and distract rebels groups not to come to villages. Things were getting worse and worse for people to enjoy their freedom and everyone losing belongings to the association. I was brooding all day long as if dark clouds with tornado were moving in. About 5:00 pm in the afternoon, there the association chairman and companion leaders with many soldiers came to our village, looking for place to settle for the evening. I heard they chose my uncle's house about sixty meters from ours down the hill which its door faced west. This news from my family scared me why they came to us! I was curious and came out of our house, and looked toward my uncle's house to make it sure it was really true. His house was at the edge of his farm and there was a huge peculiar tree behind its back. I heard they were demanding poor people of our village to bring Kat, milk, cigarette, and food for their party and meeting there.

At the time, drought was creeping on residents and they were in hardships barely making day by day what to eat. Some of them who had been little lucky with cow's milk, they must sell this milk in the town to get their flour to eat. I was very mad when I heard that they were ordered to give up this milk and little food they had for their families. A villager's committee aware that some of the residents had to beg from better residents for their meals and still forcing them to bring what they did not have made me even more upset, besides forcing them work in their farms turn by turn. On top of all these demands, they were asking $50 Birr to be given to them by each resident so that they support the soldiers forced from villages to fight the rebels who might be at *mulatta* mountain. I was devastated hearing this order and I could not imagine where these poor people who had nothing to eat could come up with this amount, on top of losing their food and milk, etc. Then residents were running around in fear that if they did not come up with this money, they had to be arrested and facing serious consequence. Mohammed, one of the poorest people in our village, lost his little land to the socialist association and his kids were walking bare naked bottom. His wife had to sell some disgusting weeds no one dare to deal with by walking twenty kilometers to far town so that they got something to eat. They mostly lived by begging for food and they had to come up with $50, extremely boiled my brain seeing him running around in fear of them. I felt to run to my uncles' house to tell and stop them from this poor man how they troubled him, but afraid they might back fire on me. I lost my mind in anger and thought about the idea to throw stone at my uncle's house, but I could not find any at all scanning the ground in a darkness around our house while I was scared if I was caught they were going to hurt me, and hesitated for a while to do it. Mohammed's suffering did overwhelm my fear of them and I felt like drunken person and must do something. I could hear some heavy chat came from my uncle's house about 8:00 pm. I ran my hand on the ground in the dark, not finding anything to throw and suddenly I thought breaking dry mud from our house wall which might reach them. I dared to go at the back of house while scared of scavenger hyena being there. I found large pieces of cracked wall and grabbed two in my hand and returned to my point of gazing my uncle's house.

My heart began beating more than hundred fifty times per minute to throw it on my uncle's house and scared what to happen to me if I was caught. My hand was shaking vigorously in fear, I was almost unable to hold mud and put it down by my foot. I tucked my hands in my pocket to minimize its shivering like a person who killed cat. I stood there contemplating to throw, or not. If I threw, I imagined soldiers rushing out to get me. Being so overwhelmed by Mohammed's suffering and their ruthless orders, I picked a mud and swung over my head a few times with severe heart beat. When suddenly I saw Mohammed crying, I didn't know how I let the dry mud fly hard toward my uncle's house. They exploded on my uncle's house tin roof one after the other just like asteroid bombarded the moon. Its noises was so loud that I thought I had thrown a grenade to it. I heard a big commotion inside uncle's house and soldiers were pouring out of the house with flash lights in all directions. Some dropped themselves on a ground like making fortification, charging their guns to fire anytime they saw someone by there, or whatever thing they saw did this noise. I stood there watching activity around my uncle's house and unable to move in a shock. Once their flashlight was toward me, I thought they saw me and I wanted to move back home. Unable to stand outside any longer, with fears, I slowly shuffled back home expecting they were after me. I tied my exploding brain with rugs, and covered my body with bed sheet; I had lain down on a bed, groaned like ailing old man. I breathed so hard expecting they were coming in my house at any time since they were doing heavy searching in all directions. Suddenly I heard someone crying by my uncle's house as they might be kicking and beating with their guns. I was sad for him and tears ran down my face when he screamed like mouse caught in a trap and dragged all the way to association prison. I was afraid he might be at wrong place at a wrong time. I got up and sat on my bed in great sadness for him to face this trouble.

While my tears flooded my mattress running down my cheeks, suddenly our door banged open so hard by someone, and I said to myself there, they came for me, too. It was my father who dashed from my uncle's house breathing hard to see if I was the one who was screaming. He asked, "Were you all right, son? Did you scream? Were you the one beaten?"

I said, "No, not me."

"Do not go outside! Today someone hit your uncle's house with something loud and bad, and they got one guy, looked like Yuyye son. They beat him all the way to prison and they were looking for more running around." I could see big fear on his face. He asked, "Did you do this?" I said that I was sick and in bed, nothing to do with this trying to calm him down. If I told him the truth he might go through serious heart attack. He ordered me just to stay in bed until things calmed down. "We faced something dangerous today," he seemed scared and almost farted on himself with everyone as I read on his face.

I asked him how much damage caused by this thing! "This thing did not look like stone. At first we thought it was a bomb thrown at us, and then stone enter the house, hit a lantern and some people. We were running in the dark for cover and searching for a place to hide and we were very shocked," he was speechless, unable to describe it well. Then he went back quickly to my uncle's house and I laid in bed. My mother doubted and scared for me to be arrested since she knew that I came from outside. My siblings were feeling very unrested and I ordered them to shut up and sit where they were. I gave them fierce eyes like tiger that arrested them where they sat.

Our village looked like war zone, no one moved, and no words were spoken, besides my uncle's house which was in commotion with loud voices. I got up and stood in the middle of our door and tried to understand what was happening and I could hardly see in dark, but found that soldiers were still in their fortification guarding my uncle's house from more attacks. As some people began to leave, I went back to my bed knowing that I was still not safe. Shortly after I was in bed, my dad had returned home feeling shaken and scared and sat by lamp. I got out of bed with fear and sat with him. I asked him the condition of my uncle's house and he said, "The leaders were very scared that the suspected rebels had come to rob them the money they have collected and they were escorted out of my uncle's house without collecting all of it." I was surprised that they decided to leave at last, and I asked my dad, "How about Mohammed a poor guy? How much he paid?"

My dad said, "Mohammed complained that he did not have anything, but at least they were sorry for him, but asked him to get only $5 to borrow as soon as possible which would be hard for him even to repay it." I was livid hearing this and they were collecting money without receipts. If people didn't pay as asked, they would be jailed for a while and then taken to socialist association barren farms to work for two weeks without pay as a punishment, and after that they must pay added penalty on top of requested money. If still not paid at all, they would be sent to district office to be jailed as anti revolutionary for a long time, facing all torture.

My fear they would come after me from Addis as Oromo supporter and being caught by association took toll on me night and day. I had seen myself in prison, or getting killed which filled me with the decision to leave my country as the only option. Leaving the country was like day dream because I was going to lose my mom, dad, sisters, brothers, beautiful country, relatives, and friends. I kept this option to myself and I didn't try to burden my family as I was not sure where to ran and what would happen even if I ran somewhere. I was drowned in the ocean of thinking for a while without sharing with anyone. Two countries to run to pop up in my mind: Somalia and Djibouti, which I thought neighbors to us that I could walk on foot if I made to it alive. Running to save my life was easier than said and done as my parents never allowed me under any condition even if it was a good idea to save my life. I thought about telling my dad in secret without upsetting my mother, believing he would agree if I convinced him enough first by taking him outside. Then I moved him out of house and told him all the troubles I faced in Addis which I did not tell him yet. I explained to him my best solution of survival was only to flee to another country. He was shocked, "This is not all right, son, and your mother would be shocked and not agree with it. I did not like your schooling in the first place, your safe arrival here is the most important thing. Don't worry, I will protect you. I know so many people and I have my own tricks just stay with us." He tried to convince me to be with them. "What you said were excellent and I like it, but surely very soon they will come for me, and my life is in danger. You just bless me to go without hesitating and we will not tell my mom. Do not worry about me if God says, we will see each other again. If not, like our religion says, we will meet after judgement day if we have a chance to enter paradise together. I will then have a chance to explain what happened to me while running for my life. Running is the only option for me right now for me to survive." We argued for a long time and finally I convinced him to flee. I begged him to be strong even though it was the most difficult thing to do for him and my mom. I suggested to him, I might go to either Djibouti or Somalia. I could see his face was darkening like bruised liver when this bad news sank deep in his body. I wanted him to inform my mom so gently so that she would be not shaken hard. I preferred to escape without telling her, but thought she might even have heart attack and the consequence of not saying goodbye at all. I was afraid she might be devastated as I looked from many angles. I did not find any other solution and what to do. My stomach was shaking and trembling as we returned in the house and what to happen to my mom, seeing my dad face already flipped outward like fried gore. He did not seem same person I had known and he worried me. "Once you live happy and once you being sad, and what a crazy life. What was the reason of life if you never seen your family again?" I murmured to myself. My mom wondered why we stayed out so long, and I was shocked to tell her the truth. I said to her, "We were talking about something not important." She doubted us, we were up to something and she wanted to know. We denied her, nothing was going on and my dad asked her, "Where is dinner?" She went on to get it while I kept my eyes on her sadly.

While we were eating; I scanned every one's face one by one like my last dinner and provision, holding food on my palm as I might never see them again. They pressured me to eat while I was swallowed by many thoughts and unable to put food in my mouth like ill person. A curtain of sadness blocked my appetite. After dinner, I went to my bed thinking about what I told my dad. I could see my father breathing hard as he was walking in the darkness toward his bed. I thought it was better if my dad would tell her about it tonight, for I might be leaving in the morning. I began brooding in about my journey and for things to happen and would be facing as if swimming in the ocean of thought all night long without any nap. The chickens and birds announced that the mourning had come. I opened door to verify that birds were right, and my dad cried, "Who is that…?" I claimed, "It was me." And my stomach cracked, to scare him like that. He asked, "Where are you going?" I replied, "I am going to farm for wash room action." He did not seem to trust me and got up, keeping his eyes on me. I swore to him that I was not running, for him to go back to his bed, but he kept watching me in distrust. He warned, "Do not run."

"No, I will not run," I assured him.

It was still dark and scary for me. My friend hyena might be still around farm and I scanned it from side to side before I entered it. Then I saw one small bird, on a leaf of corn, crying in distress like

ABAS HASANTU

it saw something horrifying. My heart wobbled not to go forward remembering the story of Muste how birds accumulated around animals and cried in distress which we proved together and I tried to find out what it saw this time. I said this bird not crying in vain unless it saw a beast, or animal under vegetation. This bird's cry must be for a danger I thought, it had seen my hyena. I stood and stewed in the darken farm and suddenly more birds appeared one by one, making that distressed calls. It looked as if they wanted it to go away, or warning me not to go closer. I was badly needed to pee, but afraid it would be the hyena. I wished my dad came to help, but I was shy being about 19 years old. I felt I should be using my adult voice if it was enough to warn it now that I became like man, it should respect and fear me. My instinct urged me to go forward to it, and again I doubted my voice was like a girl for the reason I did not know, but trying to push my throat to make my dad's voice might not convince Mr. Hyena I was grown up. I was still vulnerable boy that baffled by fear to go forward. I heard that hyena was very clever animal; it could read ones' heart as well when someone approached it.

As I kept wondering what to do, birds increased more than before. I guessed this must be extremely huge male hyena that could sink his long sharp teeth in my body and would run with it very fast. "My dad and villagers would have no chance to rescue me," I murmured. Being so frightened, first I wanted to throw a solid mud in case it ran away, or to find what it was, but then recalled a story that someone died in our village after hyena had bitten a rock a villager had thrown to it when it had snatched and ran with a goat from his house in the evening. I urged myself to throw a fine sand so it would not able to bite it, but I still feared it might not be good idea in case it might be able to gather it and bite it. I tried to get little closer to see what it was, and I was unable to see because of dense bean plants. I dared to throw a fine earth and jumped back wards as my heart ordered it expecting hyena running toward me with fear, or anger. The birds flew away when I showered the area with dust and my heart dropped down to my crouch. Then I saw a beast running from there to be my sister, the pussycat. I was surprised all the noises and gathering of birds were for this small harmless family member.

I was sad to chase it and I could not believe I was almost pooped on myself. While I was shaking, I sat down with sadness and deposited my feces as a fertilizer gift to the plants in our farm for the last time as a farewell gesture.

After I finished my business and still shaking, I wanted to indulge myself with sorghum cane and fresh corns which I would never be able to see and taste again. I wanted to say my hard good-byes to them as a provision. Calming down my fear, I collected them as much as I could while watching for hyena and returned home looking behind me in case hyena was following me. Reaching home safely, I saw my mom's face was upside down and her tears were running down her cheeks like water from a gutter. I was shocked by her condition and feared that my dad might have bombarded her with my news. I asked what went wrong and she kept weeping bending neck down. My father was wiping tears from his face while begging her to stop it. Seeing my mom's situation, tears began running down my cheeks like balls and I grabbed my mom's hand from her face to verify why she was crying. She was unable to talk to me and pushed my hand aside as I gesture to say leave me alone. I could not say, or describe what she was feeling. I did not know what to do, but just cry along her standing by her. My dad was begging her to calm down crying, being the better one. "Mother, mother…I did not die, I am still alive, please stop crying!" I begged her as much as I could. I wished to take her with me, just a vain dream.

My dad encouraged my mom to get up and cook something for provision and she got up and limped to the kitchen wiping her tears. My sisters and brother were sitting like monkey in sadness for the situation in the house was not amusing to them and the reason they did not understand. I stood and gazed them like my mirrors and scanned them while saying goodbye to each of their body for the last time. I asked my sister to peel the corns and toast them on fire while I began chewing sorghum canes. My father sadness was gotten worse and worse, and he laid down on his bed appeared having hiccup from crying. I distended myself with corn and cane as if I would never see them again. When my mom brought the food, I told myself this was the last meal with my family. As the sun came up with a few little red legs, I went to farm again to collect Kat to make me strong for my journey. I stuffed some in the mouth, began chewing it like my grandfathers' gorilla style and brought home a big bundle of it. I worried what to wear for my trip and thought of a trouser might cause me to be killed as Amhara's dress and insisted to go with peasant skirt and ugly shirt to look like country side people with a matching shoes while concealing Michael Jackson's green pants that I liked under it.

CHAPTER 6

Cat's Flee Journey

I dressed up so ugly to such extent no one would think I was student, or someone who had seen town at all. My heart began drumming with legs trembling leaving our door. I doubted if this was veracity I was facing, running from my family and fatherland. How could I say goodbyes to them? My heart would not allow my mouth to say these words! As if Mt. Everest was grown in my throat, unable to say goodbye to them. I stood and looked at my mother's face. She said, "Are you leaving us?" I said y…e…s like sick old man. She was rattled, and I could see her heart shrunk like chicken in dejection. I was powerless to talk to her and leave the house as a chained *Masujedal*[95] in the seven oceans. I was dizzy and confused what to say and do. I threw Kat on my shoulder to help for a trip and began staring at each of them. Two sisters knew what was going on, but others had no idea, just looking at me. I scanned every one's faces for the last time and I could not see my dad's face covered by blanket who was groaning like pale aged lion. I was freaked out by his noise and went to check and said, "Dad, Dad," but he replied with oxy cry. I repeated, "Dad, Dad, are you all right?" He replied with tiny mousy voice. "Goodbye son, goodbye," I was unable to hear him very well. I didn't know what to say and how I could fix him. After watching him

---

[95]   King Devil waiting to be released from deep ocean on Jesus's return.

for a while in his blanket weeping, I went to my mom to say goodbye and tears were running down her cheeks. She began crying, "Are you just leaving us?" She was unable to grasp it like I was already dead. I was unable to bear their grief and crying anymore and without my desire something pushed my legs toward the door. I was unable to turn around and kept going even though my heart was glued to their body and swallowed by depression and hating myself. Fear of death kept me going toward east of *Eggu* mountain, a familiar war time hills. I must go on if I wanted to live. I nodded hard goodbye to my family and villages knowing never to see them again as my legs were unhappy to take steps forward like a cow to slaughter house and my skin became heavy like an elephant. I could see my mom crying and my father's face faded, then I began blaming myself as these must be a curse of some kind befallen me. I recalled all his suffering, beating his fingers with hammer and all that happened to him to take care of me, and now losing me forever dropped me in the ocean of darkness.

When I looked back my mom and kids were following me, I waved them to go back while my brain was exploding with sadness. The more I went, the further I was from them, my heart wondered to go back and see them for the last time. I felt that it was bad idea and kept going far away from them. As I turned on the main street, I saw my aunt, which was equal to my dad began to make things even worse. She was shocked the way I dressed and she said, "Why did you dress like this?" I did not want her to know the truth. I took another beating, adding insult to injuries. I felt electric shock from my toes to my hair, and I was unable to say any word to her, besides I preferred to lie a bit so that she did not suspect by saying, "I dressed to remind myself of farmers' life." She applauded, applauded, "Good boy!" She wondered, "Are you going to town, or near village?" I managed to tell her, "I am heading to *Eggu* village, and if I didn't return, please do not worry and someday I would be back to visit you!" I tried to make indirect goodbye to her. She read me well that I didn't say the truth, and pressured me to know more. I was unable to lie and I admitted to her that I might go to Djibouti or Somalia. Encouraged her not to worry at all, for I would be back someday. As I uttered these words, it looked as if her waist was chopped in half like an onion. She lost her conscious and dropped the bag of Kat on the ground and she was about to hit the ground blind folded. Then I threw my load and ran to catch her from crashing to the ground crying, "Aunt, what happened? Are you all right?"

I grabbed and hugged her from falling, begging her to awake and to talk to me. I began cursing myself why I did tell her that now she might die with my news. I begged her as much as I could and cried to Almighty God to save her for me and the sake of her children who had no father to support them which I was preparing to help after I got a job for all her good deeds. I would never be able to forget as long as I was alive.

As I held and begged her to come back to life again, people passing by were sorry and asked me if I needed help for they thought she was very sick, and advised me to drag her in a shade from scorching sun. Then we pulled her under a shade of tree continued to turn her here and there, and begged her to come back to life while blaming myself for what happened. She had begun to move her head and opened her eyes, and I was excited that she was going to make it today. I tried to solace her even more by assuring that I was not going too far from here, I would be closer to you guessing the country I might go was not too far. I lent her my sincere advice to take care of her kids. I wanted to convince her that our separation was meant to be by this unpredictable life which we could not change somehow, and I assured her she was my second dad, who had been there for me. I asked her to bless me and my journey with open heart. I begged her not to worry and think too much about me not to affect her health.

Then she got better and better as I explained I needed to run to save my life. She finally blessed my trip hugged, and kissed our goodbye for about five minutes. Her prayer and goodbye made me feel better and I was somewhat excited to have her blessings to the unknown land. I had no regret that I did not see her and said goodbye which meant a lot to me. I began marching forward as she let me go and every ten to fifteen meters I turned around to see her tall body for the last time while stumbling. I went further and further waving my hand and we began to disappear from each others' sight. My eyes were full of tears unable to see what left of her body in the distance as if a fog blanked my sight and my stomach were filled with some stomping things I did not know. While brooding about her past memory, I made my goodbye with her several times in my heart. I opened my brain to scan the landscales, new villages, and roads that were built after the war of Somalia. I also made my hard goodbye like I would never see them again, hoping to see them some day.

After about two hours, I reached the mountain of *Eggu* asking strangers new roads while being scared of getting caught by soldiers and area Farmers' association dogs. They became armed during war times and now the government urged them to keep peace in the area without taking their guns away. They could arrest or question anyone for ID cards and why someone travelled in their land. I was surprised seeing how they were empowered and had the will to do whatever they wanted to do. Seeing them ahead, sitting under tree, on the road with gun frightened me. Then as I feared, they stopped and asked where I was going. I was appalled and told them name of *Eggu's* village. They then checked my ID card and asked me who I knew there and I told them my relative's name. They then allowed me to walk saying they knew that name. I walked and walked doubting the way to my relative's village going up and down the mountains range and finding them difficult to reach there. My nightmare from war time had returned and I realised it might be not easy for me to reach Somalia or Djibouti. I kept on the roads I thought I could remember while shaking and doubting if I was on the right track. I was also afraid being stomped on military camp and prayed not to face it as they might suspect that I was with the rebels and they might send me to prison as wanted fugitive cat.

While all these conquering my head, finally it seemed to me that I reached the bottom of the right mountain and village. My heart smiled a little bit, feeling I might have arrived and seen it. I remembered the big trees next to village that I used to sit under to watch the war and happiness knocked in my brain. I climbed it up while doubting a little, and there I saw down the newly constructed town of *Kombolcha* which impressed me how it looked after eight years. I was sure reaching the village; I started to call children's names. They were surprised how I was able to know them, being stranger with tattered cloth. I asked, "Is it Bakr's house?"

They said, "Yes!" I was super excited to be there, at last. I stood on the door only to see a small kid that I had never seen before whom I did not know his name. I asked, "Where is your mom?"

He replied, "She went to get cattle from a farm…" I sat thinking, "Shall I move on, or wait for the family to come home?" While my gut urging me to move on toward *Fellana* to spend the night there, my doubt to reach there, forced me to ask for direction first. I was restless to wait until his mother came, so I went to neighbor's house to call her for me if she was nearby. Then in the mean while her older daughter came home from fetching water. A neighbor then informed me that she was indeed her daughter if I knew her, and I told them that I came here when I was young at war time and I did not remember her face and name very well. They giggled at me for my talk, and encouraged me to talk to her. When I went to greet her, she freaked out with my greeting. She asked, "How do you know me?" When I mentioned my place of birth and name being her relative of war times who came here, she recalled and saddened to talk to me little harsh and apologized to me. She then invited me to come in house and sit. I asked where about of her mom and dad. She broke in tears her dad had passed away, but mom was still alive. I was sad for the moment and I cried with her not believing the news which my family did not tell me about it. After a while I inquired who would help them in a farm and she explained how they begged villagers to help them with their land.

After sitting a while with sadness, I begged her to call me her mom because I was in a hurry to go to *Fellana*. She said no to my trip there and begged me to stay the night with them. I worded the importance of reaching to *Fellana* before the sun went down, and I stressed and begged I needed their help to get there fast. She insisted I stayed with them and to stop saying I was in a hurry. I was unable to explain the urgent reason to go, but she insisted about my not walking alone. She then went to call her mom and they came together. We greeted and we were excited to see each other and she was surprised how I grew more after the war. I was shy for she said that, and

I gave my condolence about Bakr, and the trouble they were in. I encouraged them to be strong with their life and blessed them to live in peace. After I stressed my desire to go to *Fellana* before sun set, she had also wanted me to stay just like her daughter. After back and forth argument between us, she agreed for me to go on a condition that I ate and drank first, and I had a chance to tremble my body with Kat and tea just like my home. I was ready to fly to *Fellana* like small plane. She regretted not able to accompany me to *Fellana* for her children would be alone, but gave me excellent directions that I needed. I said a sad farewell to them, and began my trip hesitating and sweating if I could reach *Fellana*. I began galloping like horse, feeling sadness after sadness of losing my country, stride by stride.

I went up and down mountains as I was told and once shocked by a few donkeys and group of men on a road. I held myself together not to panic, and headed to a few shepherd kids to confirm my way. Then I saw a beautiful big river and nice breathtaking trees and vegetation along the way. I stood and enjoyed it for a while, and then headed to kids. As I tried to talk to them, they were startled, and began running and screaming like they saw a mad person. They made me giggled and I looked at myself if I looked anything like Jinn. Villager's ladies ran out of houses to see what was happening to their kids, and I was afraid they might beat me thinking I was hurting their children. I could not help my laughter while fearing consequences and parents tried to calm down their children after seeing that I was a poor dressed and harmless boy. I stood and watched their actions for minutes while laughing to the whole situation for being some kind of terrorizing animal that arrived about their village.

When they walked toward me in a peculiar way, I searched for a stone on the ground for self-defense in case I was attacked by them. They then screamed and dashed to their houses like I was going to hit them. Their actions giggled me again as some of them peeping from the windows while others stood by their doors, warning their children to stay inside. I was afraid that the situation might get worse and fathers of the kids in the farms might hear and attack me with sickles and swords, I decided to go on without asking any information. I prayed for someone nice to come on my way to ask direction. When the villagers saw that I was going away, one said, "There crazy boy had gone!" I turned around to check and one shouted, "He might be back." I replied. "I am not crazy as you thought. I am sorry for my action."

One of them said, "Where were you come from?"

"I am from Haramaya. I am going to Heyban village to visit my relatives." I asked, "Which is Heyban Village?" They pointed it to me. I was glad to see it, at least a thirty-minute walk from there. I was excited and thanked them to continue my walk. I went in the direction of that village and reached there, but confused about which house was my relative's since there were many changes made after the war of Somalia. A small kid walked toward me while I was wondering and I asked him, "Hey, kid, where is Ibrahim place? Can you show me please?" I felt better as he led me there. My heart cracked as I entered, "Good evening!" Greeted Ibrahim and his wife. They both jumped from the floor, and excited to see me especially Ibrahim whom I loved very much used to come my house once in a while when I was small kid. He was astonished to see me grown up so much. He wanted to know if I was married, yet. I smiled, "I am still young to get married!" Then he asked his wife to give me something to eat, thinking I was starving from a journey. Then Ibrahim left and came back with full load of Kat on his shoulder and piled it up in front of me like an ox eating grass. I had never seen such a beautiful leaves of Kat before and began masticating it like monkey eating banana, thinking never to see it again.

It looked as if I was chewing them for doomsday. I was so full with Kat and tea that I was unable to eat my dinner which they tried to force me to it. Then they forced me to drink milk so that Kat did not affect my system. It looked as if I was killing myself that evening. I was scared to go out to relief myself, for I heard that hyenas were infected the area. I did not want to go out and repeat the hyena incident of *Godde* that made me cry like baby. This time at Ibrahim village, I didn't want to cry and ashamed the family, so I asked him to accompany me while feeling shy. We indeed saw many of them hanging around house and I was little scared, but managed to throw my babies out and felt better.

In the morning after we had our lunch, he took me to his farm where he got those nice Kat and his farm's Kat trees were breathtaking I had never seen before. It looked like tall paradise trees, not easy to climb to collect its branches. He climbed like a monkey and began cutting their branches and I had a chance to eat them for the second day while I was worry if he could help me to leave the country. While hesitating and fearing, I dared to ask him, "Ibro! Can you please help me to get to Somalia or Djibouti, for I have to escape to save my life?" He was dumbfound to this news and asked me why I wanted to run away. I explained all that happened and he felt so sorry for me to run like this leaving my family behind.

After his deep thought, I was shocked to hear him said that he did not pass Jijigga if I wanted to head to Somalia. He guessed it might take about two days walk from Jijigga.

I asked, "How far Jijigga from your village!"

He guessed, "About three days."

Then I said, "I could go to Somalia in five days?"

He exclaimed, "If you walked very fast!"

"How many days will it take me to go to Djibouti?" I asked him just to know.

"I had no idea at all."

Then I was confused, "What should I do?" As he was thinking, my brain had rotten like inside of a pumpkin with headaches that I had never seen before. Then he breathed like a cobra, "I am afraid if I can take you anywhere soon because of something happening."

I asked, "What is it?"

He mumbled, "An order to relocate us to barren land near big mountain just announced, and there would be severe punishment for those who did not comply soon, and I am scared to go with you at this moment." His words cut off my neck as if I was bleeding like cow. My brain revolved three thousand times per minute feeling no chance to get away soon.

I brooded and brooded to go by myself if he would at least tell me the way and direction to run, I tried to encourage myself. I was curious, "How about if I go by myself?"

He feared, "It is very bad terrain and many mountains to cross, you could be lost easily and end up in a wrong place and fell in danger." I was even more appalled and no option left as if I would be dying there. I saw in his eyes, he was deeply troubled by my problems and order to move his house. I continued with fear, "Could you at least take me a little bit down toward Somalia?"

"If we climbed that big mountain with flat top, I could see down to direction to Somalia," he refreshed me. Then I began shovelling Kat in my mouth like hungry cow eating grass, and contemplated about going to Djibouti might be easier by recalling a monkey valley that I heard leading straight to it when I was travelling with my dad during war time. I kept hallucinating a chance that it might be closer country and better place for living.

I felt Somalia to be my best choice even though it seemed very far, but I worried about what the country might look like: if they had farming lands like us, what did they eat and how they might make their living, what would be my life look like, what would be cooking for me! "If I go there safe, the rest, do not matter. Definitely I would die here anyway, why not run and try my chance of survival," I solaced with any advice I could lend myself. After a few hours, Ibro made me speechless saying, "All right! I would show you a way to Somalia if you like!" I could not believe what he said. I agreed since Somalia was easy for him, and I felt it. He encouraged me to get ready. I began chewing and swallowing Kat as if a Jinn forcing me to it, faster than I could, knowing I would not see such Kat again. He wanted to show me the way and direction we would take, and we started to climb that long mountain next to us. When we reached flat part, we looked down at shining and breathtaking range of mountains in the horizon. I inferred I saw Somalian mountain. I asked, "Which one is Somalian mountain?"

He pointed that way, "None of them you see is Somalian mountain."

My heart had beaten like horses' shoes galloping on cement being disappointed. The sun was saying hello just behind our mountain every morning. Now seeing the blue sky looked attached to another mountain, jumping behind many others backward terrified me. He pointed to a tall mountain far away, "If we reached it, we could walk from there at least a half day to be among some speakers of Somali and Oromo languages. After you reach there, no one would bother you, where you come from or going to, they do not mind helping strangers." I was excited hearing this news and some motivations started to hunt me, a desire to kiss those little hills around it.

Then we returned home knowing the direction, but many questions were bothering me: How I could go there? What if country side police arrested me? What if I stepped in the military camp? Having no relatives in Somalia or not knowing anyone, how would I be able to survive? Where should I stay? All these questions strangled and chocked my soul! I became a blind bat flying in the darkness. While I was thinking about these things, it became 5:00 PM. I had no idea when I should leave. Then for my curiosity, I went outside to say goodbye to my friend hyena, looked around if I saw it. I stood on small high ground, in front of Ibro's house, and stared at side of the mountain where there were big rocks; locals called it "hyena's home." I also pierced other side down the hill where there were many animals grazing by beautiful grassy land surrounded by trees and green vegetation farms. I wondered how they would come home if these beasts had already began running around. Being so worried for their safety, again I checked rocks for any signs of hyena rushing down. Suddenly as I looked the other side, there I saw one lamely baby hyena staring at me, which I had never seen in my life. My intestines dropped to my bottom while I was excited to see such little one, but quickly grabbed a small rock to scare it. It backed off to the direction it came from carelessly of my action. I was afraid to throw the stone at it in case this little one might also bite it, and put my life in danger since no one had told me about it. Then it turned around walking slowly toward me, and I began trembling in fear that this one might hurt me. I quickly grabbed a maize stem and threw toward it, shouting with scared voice, "You coward!" It dashed in a corn field and some what I was little relieved. I felt I was strong and chased it.

As I kept looking, there one big one jumped up hill and stood by my side. My heart cracked and water filled my bladder. This one might be mad and wanted to revenge the little one, and it was going to chop me in pieces since it looked at me face-to-face. As I quickly grabbed a huge stone from the ground, it had freaked out, thinking I was about to hit it, and then it ran away. I pretended to chase it about ten meters and it went down in the farm. I stopped not to dare to enter farm because this could be a booby trap for me. Then I was very afraid when they were coming in numbers, and returned home very fast and told Ibro that I was scared. He encouraged me they were cowards, and not to worry about them. I did not trust him to tell me the truth at all. While we were talking about these hyenas, soldiers of their area entered his house, and I knew they were here to arrest him, for he did not show up to their order to build a relocation camp. They asked, "Why did you not appear as we told you?" I sweated; they were going to harm him because of me. He tried, "This boy was my guest, related to me, came from very far to visit, and I had forgotten about it." They did not care at all, and taken him away to prison. My dress became as wet as a rat jumped in a water, sweating and sweating as if small river flowing out of it through the door. I wished it washed away those soldiers. I regretted coming to him with these troubles. His wife shocked, the house became as dark as someone's grave. The beasts running around made a matter worse for me as I was the only man left in the house to defend it. I was afraid they would come to knock a door and say hello to us. My heart almost stuck in my throat. When one big hyena stood by kitchen where Ibro's wife was cooking, she asked me to chase it, for a hyena being so smart and did not naturally afraid of women and kids. She had no idea my heart was so light like ladies and children, when it came to this creature. She did not hear my heart was beating two hundred times faster than normal person.

I found myself in deep hole, and refusing was not an option. "I must dare to stand to its face no matter what happens," I encouraged myself. I recalled some of my friends were already married and fathered children, and they were not as pigeon hearted like me. "Shame on me," I insulted myself. I shied away and grabbed Ibro's sickle, and went toward beast while my leg was shaking badly, to proof to her that I was indeed like a man. Hitting the ground so hard with the sickle, I shouted with strong voice, "You donkey! Go away!"

It seemed to back off a little. I said, "I could not give a chance now that it moved."

While the sweat was pouring of my face, I moved forward carefully, and found a root of a dry maize, left over from cows' mouth. I threw toward it like bazooka, and it ran away in the dense farm. I thanked God, for saving, and giving me a small victory. "I had to be a man from now on," I encouraged myself. It kept coming back again and again, and I had to keep it away until she completed her cooking. It was my first time we faced each other like this. Ibro's arrest with Mr. Hyena's restless around house gave me so much headache. I thought about heading to Somalia by myself if Ibro was not released because I was afraid my safety was in danger from two sides: The government and a master hyena that did not badge to anyone. When dinner was ready, she asked me to go with her to deliver it to Ibro and I was worried what to do if Mr. Hyena decided to attack us. It was another nightmare I had faced, but I must go with her, for there was no way I should say no to her. As my legs were shaking, I held Ibro's *Mencha* that I found might hurt, or scare hyena and we went to prison to see him while my body was shaking vigorously. Lucky I did not face any of them in a short trip that we were walking. Ibro was happy to see us and he said he might be released with a condition very soon. There was hope he might take me quickly to a person he knew for some time who could help me toward Somalia. I was excited to hear this news and next morning he came home. After we relaxed and chewed Kat, he decided we should march toward that big mountain. I was excited and my heart began to tremble, for fear that I might be caught and the reality of losing my country and family even if I made it to Somalia.

While being scared and melancholic, our steps went into full gear. My skirt became a little obstacle as I walked faster and faster than before making me mad. I wrapped my pants up under it like pita bread, fearing I might be caught by soldiers if they saw it. I tried to tie my pants with long grasses on my thigh, but my muscle movement cut it loose, and the pants kept running down my leg. We went down a little mountain and lost sight of the big one. We went up another and saw that big one again and my heart was beating hard any time I lost it. I was so tired and thirsty to go anymore. I pushed and dragged myself as much as possible after Ibro. Then we saw a small road lead to a house. We went to beg for water, walking like tortoise. My mouth was hard as dry wall paper; I was unable to say a word to a lady. I pointed my finger to my mouth for water, and she ran and gave it to me. As I sipped cold water, full mouth, it began burning it and I quickly gulped down to get rid of it. It stuck in my throat like gulf ball, when I tried to force down hard, it made my throat and esophagus wounded. I drank about half litre that caused me serious stomach pain.

She asked, "Were where you coming from?"

I replied, "I came from *Fellana*." Then she looked very sad for us.

"Were where you going?"

Ibro said, "We are going to visit our relative in *Dida Walled*." Then he asked, "Could we stay the night with you?"

She then advised us, "Wait until my husband comes home to get his permission." As we rested, her husband came home and surprised that two strangers were sitting outside his yard. She told him about us and he allowed us to stay a night. We thanked them for their kindness and giving us some Kat to chew and dinner.

In the morning, they also gave us lunch and Kat before we left and I was extra happy that I would have energy for the trip I did not know. We thanked them again, and began our trip mouth full of Kat and my legs began to shake like earth quake. I was worried to be caught, but became so happy for the journey. We walked so hard and fast we were able to reach that huge mountain and so scared of it, for there were no houses. It was covered by small trees and strange to look down from it. I was so scared if we made it alive from there down. Now the trees were different, being small sizes and I realised to be similar to desert mountain. No one lived here except big birds that were flying about bushy hill. We sat to take a rest for a while, being alert in case any dangerous animals ran toward us. After we finished this mountain, we came to a very dense scary place, and I was seriously on the lookout for dangerous beasts. After we completed this area, we saw at far some villages, and I was very excited. I was very tired and wanted to rest, but determined to reach those villages and kept going at it. I saw a lot of camels for the first time in this area. I thought I had reached Somalia. I was excited a bit, but Ibro said we must pass this village for some reason.

We pushed and pushed until we reached the second one. The sun was setting down as we reached it. When we got closer to it, I heard some Somali language was being spoken and some of them were whistling as others shouting. I did not understand, I thought their yelling to be fighting. Then I was scared to go closer to them, and Ibro dared to take us in the village. when he greeted a house, they allowed us in. I saw a guy and an old lady. Ibro said, "Yasin!" and introduced us as his dear friend. I was excited he might be the one to take me to Somalia. Their house was made like ours with mud and grass, but they did not have a skin of cow as carpet. Instead he spread empty sacks of grain as a mat, and we sat together chewing Kat from his farm. The way he talked Oromo language, his kindness, and actions made me so happy and breathless. I was able to understand him. He wanted to know why we came to their area and Ibro told him the truth. He was sad to hear my story, and I asked him if he could help me go to Somalia. He was willing to help me if I waited for two days. I was concerned, "Does the Ethiopian soldier, or army come here?"

He laughed. "There were no soldiers or army here and you are very much safe."

"How about association guards, they might arrest me!"

He said, "No one would bother you here even you stayed fifty days. If someone asked me, I would say you are my relative." I felt so good that my worries and tiredness were crushed on the ground like pumpkin, and my body became lighter than cans of tuna. I was excited like resident of a village being somewhat free with only little worries. His mom made a desert porridge I had never seen before. When I wondered and looked at it in a very strange way, before I put it in my mouth, they clarified it to me it was the grain given to them by United Nations aid in their area when hit by draught. Still I was hesitated to eat it with a wooden spoon they gave me and I held it in my hand and began shaking about it. "Eat men!" Yasin pressured me.

I replied, "I have never eaten with such big wooden spoon before." Feeling shy that the spoon itself was disgusting, for everyone must use it by taking turns. He had no idea that I had never taken any body's saliva which made me threw up when I saw them doing it. He laughed, "Okay! Eat with your bare hand." I felt shy and began putting wooden spoon in my mouth, the wrong way while gagging. They laughed and showed me the right way to put in the mouth and how to eat it. I liked its' crunchiness and tastiness of porridge and filled my sack until swollen like turtle shell. I tried to keep it down not to lose it.

After dinner, he asked us to go to the farm to sleep in the open as if it was a windy hotel. I was astonished why we had to nap in the open sky, but recalled that during Somalian war time I was also kicked out, so I didn't ask the reason today. While I feared this outside sleeping order, Yasin explained, "Wart hogs and monkeys were ruining the farm eating sweet potatoes and corns so we have to chase them." This shocked my cradle they might hurt me as I slept. While my heart was weeping of these two beasts, he added, "We have lions come from time to time." I was appalled than ever since lion had no mercy even for their mother. I feared my body being torn apart right in their presence. "I do not want to be eaten alive while I sleep!" I raised my concern. He said. "Lion would not come closer fearing the fire we mostly burn in the farms and we make a lot of noises which they do not like." He tried to cool me down, but fears fire was burning inside me. Somewhat I regretted being there, for it was possible to be pricked by wart hogs, punched by monkeys, or cut into pieces by lion's teeth.

When he got up and went outside, I had no choice than to follow Yasin and Ibro. Like he said, I saw many fires in the farms and I was happy to hear people shouting in their farms as if they were going to protect me, but their skinny loud voices irritated my laughter inside. "What were they saying in Somali?" I needed to know. "They were scaring beasts not to show up, and to let them know they are here." Then he lighted fire like them and got some corns from neighbor's farm, we toasted to eat them. I was glad to eat by fire, but unable to sleep the whole night in the farms surrounded by thorny fences looking through its openings for beasts to bite my head off.

I was tired to get up in the morning, but happy to be alive once again. I promised to help him dig in the farms quickly so that we finished things in couple of days for our journey. After chewing Kat, I was excited and worked in the farm like never before, and he was excited to seeing me work like horse with different style and speed that surprised him. "You are very strong and dangerous farmers," he commented. "You are right," I flattered myself. He seemed interested in me to stay forever by saying, "I want you to be like my son, get married, and I will give you lands." "Thank you for the chances you would like to give me, but I am afraid for my life, no guarantee from anyone that I would be safe around here, besides I would not be able to handle your tough women! I would fall in serious trouble!" They cracked in laughter. He said, "If you insist to go, the way we were working, we might be able to finish tomorrow a second farm, and then we would have a chance to leave after tomorrow, *Inshallah*!"[96]

Next morning, I got up with eager to finish that small farm, and we finished it in about six hours. It made me walk like ninety years old hunch back man that farted every five minutes. He never thought this was possible, under mining my desire to get away from the country, taking on a trip. He was so happy that he asked, "Would you like to go on a trip in the afternoon?" I was so excited, and I did not care how tired I was and said, "Yes, sir!" I had to say my final hard goodbye to Ibro who was my last relative I saw. We marched in the afternoon toward mountains in the east. He made me walk up and down many strange terrains and mountains while I was already tired of farms' work. We reached very dangerous bushes, full of beasts as he warned me to stay closer to him. He cut a tall base ball bat like tree for self defence, and I put it like him on my shoulder, ready to hit any beasts that might charge toward me. I followed him with fear, but happy walking and acting like Somalis. We passed many mountains, then the biggest one I was aiming to reach fainted from my sight. I felt I was far from my place of birth, disappearing from my country.

---

[96]   God will.

Sadness began to sink in my soul if I ever came back again to it. Then we saw many Somalis on the way, going with sacks of aid grains and I asked where they got it. He said, "They got it from Ethiopian aid in *Chinakson.*" I was curious, "Where is *Chinakson*?" I never heard this place before, but scared that there might be Ethiopian Army.

I begged him not to take me closer to it. He assured, "We will not go there." I felt much better hearing this news. "Do you know how many more towns left ahead of us?" I asked. "There is only one more to pass, and there are so many soldiers in it, but after that we are free all the way to the border," he mumbled. This began to rock me as if I was going to swim in the army. "I will show you this town from afar," he seemed hesitated. This answer made me feel better. About evening, when we climbed a big mountain, he pointed at it a town that was surrounded by the scary mountains. As we walked a little bit, it was getting dark. I worried, "Where would we spend the night?"

"We are closer to my Fiancé's village; there will be no worries at all." I was relieved. When we arrived, there were many people in the house, and they welcomed us to sit. They began talking and I did not understand what they were saying. I kept wondering if they were talking about me as they were glancing me from time to time. I waved my hand to say, I do not understand. Yasin's fiancé spoke with me in my language, and at least I was glad to understand her. I wanted to know, "Are we in Somali speaking area from now on?"

He assured, "Yes! It is rare for some to understand you!"

"Does this mean I am in Somalia from now on?" I wanted to verify it. He replied, "No, not close at all." I was startled. "How many days you think left for us to go?" He guessed, "We might have to walk another two more days from this village." I was amazed the lands I left behind were not still enough to reach Somalia as if it slapped my face. Yasin shocked me, "My fiancé's father is Oromo, and mother is Somali, but she was orphaned at young age. I will marry her very soon." While this news saddened me, she gave us dinner, and we chewed Kat all night long. I asked, "What time we have to leave in the morning?" He said, "I want to see what my fiancé says first! I think we might stay one more day." In the morning, we had our lunch and he took me to visit his fiancé's farm. It was bigger than his, but it was not properly taken care of, since she had no help from villagers to take care of it. Weeds and grasses made our walk a night mare. Yasin promised to trim them after he took me to Somalia. Then we got some dry Kat from her farm to chew all day and she wanted us to leave in the first light.

About 8:00 AM in the morning, we marched on the road with her, the action that I did not expect from her. We, then came across many young men with guns working on the road that scared me, I felt we were doomed, but they spoke with Yasin as if they knew each other. Then he said, "You need not worry about them at all, for you are safe from here onward, and this is normal from now on." It was little shady for me why his fiancé came with us, but I wondered if he knew where we were going since she was leading us. I feared we might be in trouble if she was confused where we were going. We walked all day long, and I was so tired when we reached top of very difficult mountain. When we saw a very flat land as far as eyes could see, my heart suddenly wowed and I lost breathe, for I had never seen such flat land before. There were no trees, but a kind of village, made of rugs like igloos stood little far away. Seeing hundreds of whirling tornados with its children running around also surprised me. I asked Yasin, "What is the name of this flat land?" He answered, *didawalled!*[97] We then sat down to take a break on this big mountain and chew Kat we brought under shade of a tree for energy while looking down to Dida. I enjoyed its view like I saw a Mecca of flat land. As we were taking rest, a stranger walking on the road, seemed to greet us, and said something to Yasin and his fiancé. After he left Yasin told me that the stranger warned us that there were Ethiopian and SNM[98] Soldiers' check points ahead of us in a flat land. We might be getting robbed and many other forms of troubles. He advised us not to go by day light. We should stay until evening, by first village that we came, and only passed them in the pitch darkness.

---

[97]   Wide, flat ground
[98]   Somalian National Movement

Hearing this news began to shake me, and we got up and walked down the mountain with fear. When we reached further down, we saw many gun men that freaked me, but they were from the same area we had come from. We then reached the first village of clustered grass igloo huts that Yasin said, "They are area residents." We then stopped there. I was surprised to see such a strange form of houses which we were invited to enter. I wondered how they slept and cooked in them, and Yasin told me that these would be their mobile house that they took along on back of camel from place to place. I had seen my first nomadic people of our country to the east that I learnt in school. My eyes wept of the smoke inside while we chewed Kat and taking rest. I was surprised to learn that we were sitting at Yasin fiancé's aunt's unit. He then slapped my face with the news that these villagers very often going to Somalia for business of smuggling items across the border. I was afraid this might be the plan for me why his fiancé had in mind when she came along with us that I could go with these people across the border. I kept imagining this place to be a camel ships that I might embark on to Somalia. Yes! Indeed, I later verified from Yasin that I had to go with the clans if I wanted to make it across the border. In addition, the *gadbursi*[99] Clan settled around border were worse than SNM, Ethiopian soldiers as they would kill, or rob people of all of their belongings, they would even take shoes. If they felt it, sometimes they might take you to the Ethiopian army on the pretext that you were running from the country so that they got grain rewards from the authority in the border.

All these findings made me scared and I came to learn that Yasin and I alone, or a few people would not be able to cross the border from these areas. They wanted us to wait for another larger group coming from Somalia and then waited for them to go back so that I hid myself among them. Hearing this news, the Kat I was chewing became bitter in my mouth. My hope to cross the border dimmed like light, coming all this way. My mouth dried like stalk of a corn and I was so thirsty. I begged for a cup of water to relax my mouth, and then I found a cup was very heavy in my hand. I was curious to

---

[99] Somalian tribe around border

know why it was heavy in my palm, but I had no time to question it because of my mouth and thirst had grabbed me by neck. I sipped a mouth full so quickly, and it was as heavy as a yogurt, and then felt muddy taste. I felt not normal at all, since I sipped in the dark hut with not enough light. I feared to swallow and dashed out, and spat it on the ground. They questioned why I ran out. I replied, "You gave me muddy water that kids put in a cup to play all day, and I spat it out!"

Then Yasin explained to me, "This is their normal tasty water they use and drink every day. It is rain water that collected in holes of *dida-walled*. Even camels and animals drink from same place for there were not any sources of water in the land." I was shocked; no wonder I tasted cattle urine and droppings, mixed with mud. "They had to travel very far even to get this," he added. I was sad to hear that there was water shortage, and this was what they survived on. I had no choice; I sipped twice, to force it down my pharynx just to make it alive. I recalled my village water to be from paradise and it would no longer come back to me. For tea, I mixed it with sugar as if I was gulping sweet potato soup. They brought head biting porridge that was made with same water that I had no choice, but to eat it. After we ate, Yasin wanted us to go to his uncle's village who might help us even more. He then requested for someone to show us the way there at night despite their initial warning of danger and advice to wait for the caravan group to come from Somalia. He insisted they called a boy about twenty years old to go with us. His fiancé stayed and did not want to come with us. Then three of us marched in the dark. He encouraged me not to fear at night, for the soldiers would go to town at night and back in the morning to the check point as if he heard this from locals. He felt confident that it might be the safest time to march to his uncle's village. Seeing his minor confidence, I felt little better and began praying for safety.

As the boy walked ahead of us, we followed him in the flat cold land while tornado sung to us. There was no obstacle at all, besides little bushes of grasses like soccer ball kicking my legs from time to time. I was happy and stepped up my strides with them. We walked about six hours in the dark plain field to reach that village at last.

Everyone had slept, besides camels that burble in the dark. Then Yasin woke up his uncle, and he took us to a nice house to sleep in. The house was made of tin roof and looked nice, very unusual for the area. I was a bit glad at least this house was better than what I saw so far. Yasin told him the reason we came for, and he uttered the same thing. We needed caravan to go with to pass those beasty border clans. I was terrified that this was not going to be good. He informed us that there would be a caravan group to leave in three days; we should have to wait for them. I was little relieved that at least now there would be hope to pass the border as planned before. I wanted to learn more of this tough *gadbursi* clan's story from Yasin's uncle. He explained, "These tribes were not governed by Ethiopian and Somalian law. They are free to do whatever they want at both sides of the country. They rob you of your belongings either by setting a post in the middle of road, or they hide along the roads here and there and hard to know where they would be. They even take your shoes so that you walk bare foot on rocks to Somalia. If you dispute, or resist what they say, they will shoot you." I had about four hundred Ethiopian Birr that they asked me to convert to Somalian shillings for the journey since this Birr was not good in Somalia. They informed me that it would be more than ten thousands shillings which should be cancelled on the back of camel from these looters. Yasin's uncle gave us an option to stay with him for three days, or go back to Yasin's fiancé's village and then come back in three days. Yasin then stimulated my decision on this idea and I was concerned about waiting too long since Ethiopian army and towns were closer than comfort going backward. I tried to see if there was another way out. After vigorous discussion with Yasin, he let me sleep to discuss it in the morning.

All night, I brooded from every angle about escaping these robbers and army, and the sun smiled at me. I was so disappointed, unable to keep going as I hoped before. I washed my face with cold, yogurt water, and then ate that heavy porridge. I asked if there was Kat and cigarette in the area to relax my body. Yasin begged his uncle to check and we got very skinny leaves of dry Kat for two hundred *shillings*[100] taken from my well. I was also shocked that a pack of cigarette would cost the same. As we were chewing Kat and chatting, I wanted to know if we had any other way of going to Somalia as soon as possible. Then Yasin's uncle went to check nearby village for another caravan that might be going to Somalia, but he came back empty handed. He again suggested if we found someone related to *bursi* clan, he could easily sneak me to promise land. After we agreed with him, he went and found someone who demanded more than one thousand shillings he offered him. When this idea didn't work, they came up with bewildering plan for us to go to the border by leaving all the money and expensive beautiful watch I loved more than my life. They planned to bring them after I crossed the border with that caravan we were waiting. I didn't understand where Yasin's courage came from to take me to Somalia by himself, but I couldn't resist his action having no other choice. I doubted if I made it alive to Somalia and ever saw the face of my watch and shillings again.

Next dawn, we decided and marched in the open field where the chilly wind and bad feeling were beating my body. We walked and walked in that wide flat earth with many doubt that Yasin might be on the wrong way since he came a long, long time ago as he enlightened me. Then we saw a lady on the way whom I thought he asked for direction as I read from her gesture as she was pointing to the west side of us. It looked we missed the direction we supposed to go by a great deal. When we faced to that direction, it made me little happy, for we at least headed to the right road. Now he recalled going the other way about nine years ago that took him about a town which we were trying to avoid with any cost. He said, "This town is closer to Borana, a Somalian border town where residents were using both countries' currency." Hearing him commenting this, I felt I was already arriving in Somalia. I began staring in the direction we were going and asked Yasin, "Are we closer to *gadbursi* tribe yet?" He feared, "We might be in their area by night!" When Yasin put stick on his shoulder like them, I also did the same to pretend I was

---

[100] Somalian shillings

one of them while whispering to myself, "I wish I have spoken their language."

The field was getting longer and longer than I expected. I thought I was walking backward, or standing at one point all day long. While I was dragging my legs like old turtle, we came to a pool of blue water about three in the afternoon and able to see a small mountain at the horizon of the field surrounded by a huge ocean. I asked Yasin, "What is the name of that ocean by the horizon?"

He smiled. "It is just dry air and sun ray that fooled you." Then, as I was thirsty, we came across a well. Yasin said, "You have to drink it since this is all we got here." I was not expecting muddy water, but it was just full of green algae.

When I looked deep inside, I found many frogs and tadpoles with variety of worms. I asked, "Are you really going to drink seeing all these creatures in it?" He said, "Yes, no other choice. Go ahead and drink it. This is all you get from now on. If you don't, you might die of thirst." When I saw him drinking, I was freaked out even animals in our area would throw up seeing this water. After hesitating for a bit, I scooped it like Yasin with an ugly, old can laid by it. Then I covered a cup with my shirt, trying to avoid swallowing those toad poles, worms, and junks. I filled my tank as much as I could. I advised myself no time to be sad and throw up this water feeling I must bring myself to safety first. Holding myself together, we headed toward those little mountains. Yasin feared we might see *gadbursi* about those mountains. Hearing this, my heart began beating hard and my wounded legs were shaking.

At last, we reached that first mountain and my eyes caught a person who cracked my heart and made blue water sweat run down my legs. I felt we were doomed right there. Yasin greeted when we approached him and I scanned him for *gadbursi* texture and a gun he might conceal under his sheet. Then he asked him for direction and he told him the way to the mountain. I was relieved, he was not a dangerous man, but I prayed not to see others. Yasin increased his steps even more than before and I must keep up with him having no other choice. After a while, I begged him to slow down a little bit, but he was afraid it was going to be dark soon so we did not want to face those lions that might be in the area. "We must reach a place called *bakke* where we can find tea and rest," he urged me. Fear of lion also boosted my energy and I began leaping harder and harder after him to be safe from a beast that I didn't want to meet face-to-face. I continued running after him like old fox. We climbed the mountain on top, limping very hard. Then there I saw chains of mountains in front of us, and my brain almost blown out of my head. "Are we going to go up and down all these hills and mountains?" I wanted to know. He then guessed and pointed to one at far to be a Somali border. I could not believe all these with little delight seeing a Somalian mountain, which I tried to confirm several times. He also repeated the one covered with a cloud to be its Alpestrine. I dreaded to reach there in one piece. "I would better see border and pass it," I said to myself. Then I saw pictures of fierce soldiers with cannon pointing at me from both sides of the country and first to face *gadbursi* muggers.

Yasin then dropped bomb on my head, "We have now reached *gadbursi's* zone!" I repeated what he said with panic, "What? You said *gadbursi's* zone!"

He confirmed, "Yes! Sure!" I began squirting thousands of eggs and children from my belly like horse fish while staring and scanning bushes and roads for them. I wished I flew over the mountains like crow to pass them across the feared border. After we passed about five mountains, we saw an old man sitting under a tree near a house. Yasin talked to him to confirm the way if we were on track. I thought it was bad idea to talk to him, for he could be dangerous, too. He said, "He is an old man, we can handle him." He made me laugh a little bit. I hesitated to stay back a little bit expecting we would be under fire from the villagers rushing with guns toward us. Yassu greeted him, and he got good direction from him. I was happy that we were safe from old man and village being on the right way. He increased his strides once more, walking very hard. My feet were so sore and its pop corn suppurations made it worse to go forth and began limping very hard. We went very far, not seeing any danger, then came to a small village where we got water from kind *gadbursi* ladies. They encouraged us, we were closer to *bakke*. I was delighted to hear this news that became my Vitamin supplement. Then after a few leaping strides, we saw a strange wooden houses built with mud to be *bakke* town.

I was so happy to hear there was no Ethiopian army closer to this town even if it looked very spooky to be in it. I asked Yassu "Is this *gadbursi* town?"

He feared, "Yes!" I was then worried, "We are in danger Yasin!" I freaked, "We are going to be safe for the business caravan and some other groups come here for rest and a danger would be minimum." I felt better hearing that the gun men might hesitate to enter at night fearing so many people around here. This news gave me some hope of survival as we sat in wooden tea house where there was only one scary young boy running the place.

Watching his shark teeth, strange hair, and a face of *gadbursi* started to worry me when Yasin was talking to him. He gave us tea and rice that Yassu ordered. I felt we were his customers and hoped that he would not attack us, or call his friends to rob and slaughter us. After we ate, Yassu bought nice Kat I did not expected to be there, and we began chewing by fire side warming ourselves till night. I was little happy, we were still safe and alive. Then a noisy caravan arrived in town, to make my night better as Yassu informed me. I felt that they were what doctors ordered for me. I hoped they would go to Somalia so that I hid in the middle of them. About early morning, we were tired and snoozed a bit where we sat. Then we woke up at sunrise, and Yasin met a guy who was heading to Somalia. I felt they knew each other from somewhere in the past. We began marching in a very nice sandy valley that seemed to drag my legs backward. Seeing I was dragging behind, they encouraged me that there was one tea place two hours walking distance ahead of us to rest if I kept up with them and it was bigger than last one. As I was trying my best with happiness, a guy who was passing informed us there were many *gadbursi* thugs before towns' entrance. Suddenly my face turned to kidney size, pouring urine to bladder. I was concerned and asked, "Could we avoid these brigands if we go another way to escape them?" He confirmed, "There is no other way to go! This is the only way to Somalia in and out." He asked, "Do you guys carry a lot of money?"

Yasin replied, "We have about five hundred shillings."

He said, "Not bad at all!" I kept worrying on the way until it was about two in the afternoon, then we came to very bushy camp area surrounded by thorny fence which seemed gang hiding places. They confirmed, "We are here!" My gut was right. Then my heart raddled and stuck in my nose. I was about to shoot my soul to the heavens. I saw many of them carrying machine guns, my body rammed like watermelon, my shoes repleted with sweat, making farting noises. We headed to a tea house as they cast their eyes on us while my heart was swinging, feeling they would come to drag me away. I quickly pretended like Somali not to stare at them so much while I almost rinsed myself with piddle. I was expecting something to happen while we were drinking tea, and once my eyes were locked at them. I quickly turned away as if I didn't mean to see them. My heart beating was quadrupled. Yasin and the guy kept talking with others in their language; I had no idea what they were saying. I was expecting to be grabbed, robbed, and mugged at any time while I was praying to God to keep them away from me. After we were done with tea and got some break, we went outside to buy Kat.

We saw many people came from Somalia town buying Kat and some sipping tea while sitting under a tree taking rest. Yasin got us two bundles of Kat, and the robbers were watching us. When we started walking out of town, two of them came toward us questioned Yasin, "Where are you going?" Yasin said, "We are going to near Borane town to visit family." They miraculously let us go without harming us. I was relieved God might have sealed their beasty hearts. I was more worried and asked, "How far we have to go to this town of Borane?"

They said, "There is a chance we could enter it soon." I was happy, but curious, "Are there any more of these robbers in it?"

"There might be area youth! Otherwise we are safe from now on," they made me feel better. As we increased our speed, we managed to reach a group of people with donkeys and we mixed with them like sugar in a tea.

I was surprised how far I had gone to leave my country. I came to realise that our province was bigger than I had imagined and returning back home would be inconceivable. I asked, "Are there any towns of Ethiopia and army close by here?"

They assured again, "There will be no more of them and town close by, but they come here from very far town to check the borders' safety from time to time." I prayed and hoped they would not come today until I passed the area. After we walked very hard a couple of hours while massaging my heart, they broke a news to me, we passed a check point of Ethiopian army and we had arrived at grounds that not controlled by two countries. I was astonished hearing such land had ever existed between two countries, which I didn't know before. As I was getting hammered with this new learning of border situation, they pointed to a mountain who said, "I am Somalian land." I was so happy to see Somali's mountains, but I was worried for their check point if they allowed me to pass them at all. I feared, "What would they say when they saw me? What would their town look like? What kind of life I will be facing once I arrived there?" While I was trying to find answers to these questions, I said farewell to my country filled with sadness if I ever saw it again. Tears of another loss washed my face looking back wards at far mountains for the last time. After a while, there we were climbing a Somalian mountain that I saw from afar. We went down its hill and passed two more small mountains to face Somalian check point. I was scared seeing huge guns on top of these mountains pointed to the heavens. I pointed and asked, "What are those guns?"

They said, "These are guns for Ethiopian aircraft in case they attack." They warned, "Do not point any finger at it, they might take you as spy for Ethiopians and kill you. Just go quickly without staring at it." My heart almost banged my ribs in shock; I hoped they didn't see me and I prayed to God once more to seal their eyes. I asked, "Are they going to stop and question us?" They assured, "They do not bother us, and care about these people going in and out." I was excited and amazed by it if they told me the truth. As they said, there we passed them like wind inside a tree.

At last, I was in Somalia leaving my country like snake came out of its shell and at least felt free from being arrested and get killed by soldiers. Then I was shocked to see extremely short corn and sorghum trees that were unable to hide even my knees. While I was wondering about these things, we came to about six houses made of mud with a few Somalian automobiles in it. From here when they pointed at Borane town, I saw it to be very big and beautiful to my sight. They polished my heart, "These cars arrived from there!" I was so excited and being in Somalia, just sank deep in my heart over writing my fatigue with joy. I couldn't believe I was in Somalia. We decided to take a break at mud tea house and chew our Kat feeling much better. The owner of tea house warned us, "Kat is illegal around here and you must hide it. I would be killed with you if soldiers saw us." I was scared hearing this news. He added, "No one chews Kat around here and it is controlled substance."

We quickly chewed and washed it down with a few glasses of tea as if we had never chewed Kat and got enough energy for the rest of the trip. We marched about half an hour staring at Borane and there the first cargo truck full of people caught us. Yasin waved and begged it to pick us up and we jumped on it. We were hardly fit on it with full of men and women. I was happy to get ride beside crazy driver who never slowed down in the bush where there was no road at all. People were screaming being afraid of to be thrown out of truck like bread dough on the spatula. Some hurt banging heads with each other and began cursing a driver with bad words I had known from back home. I held on for my dear life hoping not to be killed this way while some people actions also made me smile and giggle a little bit.

CHAPTER 7

To Die in Borane

I was excited to arrive in Borane, first town of Somalia. It has beautiful modern building designs and many garden trees. Surprisingly, not too big of a town, but I was amazed seeing such town close to border being very sophisticated, not being made of only mud houses. Stone and brick houses blew away my beliefs that Somalia cities were not as beautiful as my country's towns. "Judging by Borane, others big towns and cities must be better," I guessed.

We got off the truck and Yasin said, "We must go and register our arrival at city security office and if not we can't stay here, we might be arrested, or killed as spy from Ethiopia." I was shocked to hear this. He steered me to that way and I began watching everything, starting with many Somalia soldiers just like war times. Many memories of 1977 war time invaded my brain. Then, we came to a compound with armed guards that tickled my heart. Yasin said some words to them and they let us sit and wait under a tree on a stone chair. Two guys approached Yasin and questioned him about us. He seemed to inform them about our arrival, and we needed to register with them. When they said something to me, I did not understand. Yasin came to my rescue that I didn't speak Somali. He became my interpreter, but I felt he couldn't be the best one. One of them babbled to me in Amharic, and I was shocked how he knew it assuming that Amharic was their enemy language as I guessed. I tried my best to talk with him even though I was not perfect myself. I was little happy at least we could exchange some words like monkeys. He questioned, "Why did you come to Somalia?" I explained, "I came to save my life!" He seemed to tell others what I said, and then one of them tried to talk to me in funny English accent thinking I might understand it. I exchanged some words with him; we seemed to understand each other. I was proud to go to school, for at least I could speak some words of English too. They informed me, "Security officers not working on Wednesday, you should be back tomorrow to report yourselves!" Another one added, "We should stay overnight in security compound, for there was some problem going on in the city. If you have any money, you must go to restaurant to eat and come back." We agreed to return and headed to Restaurant. Then two of them decided to accompany us.

Every thing became strange; I was overwhelmed being in new country, eating their food. After we ate, we went back to compound as they told us. One, who spoke with me in Amharic, warned me that in the morning those security officers would yell and pressure you to return to your country. They would also give you a hard time. So he wanted me to be strong and not to fear so much. I was scared to hear this bad news. I was afraid that after all, I might be kicked out of Somalia. I was also worried, "How am I going to survive if the security allowed me to stay? I do not know anybody, have any father and mother to assist me. I have no enough money to make me survive longer." Yasin said, "There were some Oromos who live in this town that came during war times, and they might help you. I will try to take you there. If they refuse you, you might then have to work as a watch man for rich people." I expected challenging things that blew my brain off. While I was beating myself with these worrying problems, one said, "There is no bed for two of you to sleep here tonight; you should go to a motel to sleep for the night." Yasin told him, "We do not have enough money for hotel bed."

He informed, "No worries the government will take care for it, just follow me." We followed him to a place and they requested our identity card which we didn't have. Yasin told them we had nothing with us and we just wanted to stay for one night.

Then a guy told them, "They are refugees and we would be responsible for them." Once they knew he was with security department, they led us to a room with two beds in it.

In the morning as we woke up, I found myself in Somalia, not my country, and my legs were seemed severed to walk again. Yasin's pain was the same and it made us laugh and we mocked each other. He wanted us to go for a tea and bread for breakfast, but I wanted him to save the last two hundred shillings that left in his pocket for his provision to return home. After he had taken me to the security, he planned to take off right away to Ethiopia. I was burdened with additional worry to be on my own and he had to go back by himself all the way we came. I was afraid something might happen to him which would kill me. I had no penny to help him as an appreciation for his tiredness and suffering to bring me to safety. These sacrifices he made for me torn my pouches of tears. As tears kept dripping from my chin to my shirt, we walked to security office. They told us to wait until big guys arrived to the office. When they came, one of them spoke Amharic and asked me, "Where were you born?"

"I had born in Bate, Haramaya!" I replied.

He questioned, "Why did you come to Somalia?"

I replied, "To save my life!"

"What's your ethnicity?" I was chocked to say Oromo in case he did freak out hearing this name, and I might not be allowed to say it in Somalia, for they used to call us Somali aboy! During war time to annex Ethiopian country to Somalia the ethnic name they gave us. While I was brooding what to say, and pretend to babble something in fear, he uttered "Oromo!" and I was relieved that he knew me. I was still feared he might hurt me, but said, "Yes" amazing how he had known it. Then he asked, "What clan are you in Oromo?" I replied, "*Nolle!*" I wondered why he wanted to know me, deep inside my blood content. While I was banging my brain with all these questions and fear, I was surprised he didn't know this clan. "Were you student?" he asked. "Yes," I replied. "Can I see your School records if you have them?" When I showed two of them, he looked at them and gave them back to me. Then he left quickly without saying anything as if these records contaminated his hands and chased him away.

We sat eagerly and waited for his return. I was curious and asked Yasin, "Why did a general officer run like that after he saw those documents?" He replied, "I have no idea, we have to wait for him until he comes back." After a while, a guy who was standing on a door gave as the answer, "The general refused to accept you as refugee, so both of you must return back to Ethiopia right now." I was blasted out of a hole like squirrel by cannon. We sat perplexed as if I didn't hear what he said. He repeated, "Go…" bombarded me several times in a fierce manner. I lost word for it and began crying while saying, "I am in danger if I go back to my country, kill me right here if you like, going back will be death, and I might as well die here." I was stuck there like dry wood, finding no other solution. "They might have to drag me to the border." I whispered. This fierce order of a guy at the door for me to go back looked different than the advice I got previous day to be strong. Shaking my kidneys, rattling my heart, I was troubled very badly and needed to develop barrier, or armadillo skin from this guy's order to leave. Yasin had also lost words what to say bringing me all the way here. When the guy at door saw my tears ran down my cheeks like Nile River and we were not leaving; he suggested we might want to talk with two other people sitting outside the compound, under a tree of the street. We went out; indeed saw them across the office, sitting approximately thirty meters away from us. Abusalam who might have seen my documents, run out of office and said, "Do not move, stand there!" He ordered us not to approach the officers, but asked me to give him my school documents. I gave him while being scared of what he was going to do with them. He said, "Sit and wait under a tree."

Yasin seemed he had enough of waiting and he wanted to go. He asked Abusalam, "Can I go if he has a chance to be accepted by you?" Abusalam nodded his head to him. I was little better feeling that they might let me stay after all. Yasin said, "Good luck! Farewell." I thanked him for his help and begged him in tears, "Please try to bring my watch and shillings when you get a chance from your uncle." He agreed, "All right." He showed me his back, and hoofed facing west. There I was by myself, a cloud of fear covered my body and the sun was kicked out of my face.

Yasin vanished from my sight and I wondered what they were going to do, or say now. They might arrest, or kill me after all; no one would ever see my dead body, or trace of blood. I expected many dangers coming my way, or they might take me to that motel again. I thought of everything. I waited under a tree for a long time, staring at the security office, and my bottom swollen like pumpkin. While I was wondering what was going on, I saw an old man, with cloudy hair and beard, very paunchy walking on the street swirling his cane. He said, *Wariyya! Afka Somaalii, magaraneeysa?*[101] I knew what he said; my aunt taught me before. I replied, *Affmagareeney!*[102] While twisting my palms like scissors, *Hagge ku dhashee!*[103] I thought he was asking me where I was born. I could not say more, but I wondered why he was bothering me. I suspected he might be another security official, or he might be stranger wanted to help a homeless and hungry person. When he waved his hand to follow him, I was scared to move, not to violate Abusalam's order to wait. When he insisted that I should go with him, I decided to follow him fearing that he might have had an order to move me from security compound.

I kept walking and walking while suspecting something bad to happen, or he might take me his home to give me something to eat. Then he led me to a suspicious area, looked very weird to me. I was scared and wanted to run away from him. When he faced a kind of store, I thought he was going to buy me a candy or something for himself. I waited by door feeling little better, he might be a kind man after all. He again waved his hand to come in a store. I entered doubting many things, but a young man working in there looked like he was from Ethiopia, having their features. I felt that an old man brought me here for interpreter reason, or to help the young man in a store. He spoke my language; I was excited to see him and hearing the words I born with. I answered all his questions for him to know me, and informed him that I did not know anybody here to help me and I came to save my life.

---

[101] Do you know Somali Language?
[102] I do not know.
[103] Where were you born?

Then he took me to a kind of busy vegetable market where many ladies were doing business. He asked one of them, "Please take this boy to Sheik Mohammed Kalifs' *Hadra*."[104] She inquired me, "What's your language?" I speak, "Oromo." She freaked out hearing this word and her face changed colour like chameleon, then she jumped up like tiger pocked in the stub. She cried in Amharic, *Ere inne yisheh al-heedim!*[105] I feared she was not Oromo, or she might not like this word "Oromo" being said there as if it could put her in danger. She was really mad at a young man's order. He seemed to stress to her the importance of taking me there. News of taking me to Hadra had shrank my face like a raisin and the way lady acted broke my collar bones. Hadra's life style was not the one I wished for anyone unless one chose to live by it, but it might be better than dying in vain as a last option. She nagged, *Min-chenekeny*.[106] She repeated, "If you like, you stand there like tree!" My eyes were full of tears to burst at any time. My throat had risen like small tomato threatening to choke me. Then my tears were flown like lava down my neck. I could not resist crying, for all things that were happening. I realised that the old man to be working with security officers from the way they tried to put me in Hadra for the place to stay, but the reason they chose for me a place like Hadra amazed me. I felt their actions of singing and crazy dancing which led them to pass away for some time until a specialist came to the rescue with weird possessing power. I also imagined eating camel hump looked like brain of human which I disgusted even looking at it.

All these invaded my mind on the way there, with crying lady. We walked very far to the edge of town and I saw those huts made of grass like *dida-walled*. I wondered where she was dragging my head while she was questioning about my clan and place of birth. She feared I might not be accepted in the Hadra and she cleared herself not being member of them in case they refused to let me in, or be in trouble. Then I saw a big white mosque as if it made of yogurt

---

[104] Compound (especially of a sheik)
[105] Oh! No I will not take you with me.
[106] I do not care.

wreathed by many houses of different sizes and colours. There was a big bus in compound. I stood outside of fence while the lady had gone in to discuss about me. Wondering what I was facing, tears began washing my face. Then a few women flooded toward me as if the lady gave them my news. One of them being sheiks' second wife. I was scared and wanted to run for my life seeing many of them, but nowhere to dash away. I stood my ground to see what would happen. They began to interview my tribe and where I was born, and how I came, all that they wanted to know. Miraculously they took me to Sheik's second wife house and gave me tiny injera which I had never seen before. I feared ant people should consume this, not hungry men like me. They then clarified that the compound to be Sheik's Hadra who came from *Fellana* village during war of 1977 with Somalian army. This news brought my old wounds of the area I was running around to save my life during war. I was surprised they were still here, but they told me the sheik was passed away three years ago and buried in this compound.

They informed me that his three wives, children, and many followers lived here and all these houses belong to them. They also told me that many Oromo people came here to rest either from Hargeisa or from Ethiopia when they travelled in the area. One day, two people came here to stay, and they went to the shop in the market and an owner of store saw the Ethiopian currency in their pocket. He then informed security officials and they came to Hadra at night and arrested them. These people also found with many identifications and passports to be Oromo Liberation front members. After this incident, they did not trust anyone came here, but they would let me stay since I was brought on the order of security officials themselves. After I ate and finished a tea they gave me, the second wife told a guy to take me to *ustad's*[107] house. I didn't know why he would take me to his house and what this meant, or going to happen. When he took me there, he said, "Ustad is not here, he went to *dida-walled* to buy cattle, and everyone who comes here must stay in his unit if accepted by a compound." Then I joined a few strangers like me

---

[107] Teacher

227

sitting on plastic carpet. He added, "When Ustad comes back, you will be staying with him as long as you are here." I began screening everyone's face if they were like me while pondering about my situation. After a while, a man introduced himself to me as Abdullah brought food and said, "All three sheik's wives ordered me to pick up food for you by turns. This one is from the first one!" I was happy to hear their generosity and thanked them for caring for me. About sunset, I met a boy named Jamal who had a Range Rover arrived at the compound. I discovered him to be the brother of sheik older son's wife. He was very sad learning that security officials dumped me at their compound and seemed to care and like me. He enlightened me, "Abusalam is very bad and dangerous security official in town, but you might be all right since he was aware that you are here. It is important you should go to his office for help from time to time." I agreed and could not wait until the sun rose.

Next day, after I ate my breakfast from second wife, I headed to Abusalam's office. As soon as I arrived; a bomb from Abusalam mouth hit me. "Don't come again until I call you!" he shouted. I was shocked and said to him, "All right sir!" I hoped he would not harm me for coming, but I wondered what he meant by until I called you and how long he was going take for this. I went back to compound shaking and pondering if he really meant to call me and time came at all. Then a lady I had never seen before introduced herself to me, "I am Sheik Hindiya." She asked, "Did you already see Abusalam?"

I said, "Yes I saw him this morning." She cried, "You should not go there to bother him. He is very tough and bad guy. He might arrest you and no one will be able to release you from jail, or he might give an order to kill you as spy from Ethiopia if he wants and your life would be wasted." She seemed to know him more than anyone and I had almost peed on myself. She added, "I would beg him to release your school documents if he listens to me. In the mean time, you go to river with kids and wash your stinky clothes, start on the prayer, and never leave the compound." Now I had no choice than to follow her advice, removed stains from my wings like bird as much as I could at the tiny river down from the compound and started my prayer since prayer was one qualification I needed to keep me with them. At least the Hadra was not as dangerous and crazy like the one next to my elementary school.

After two days, while I was walking outside a compound, a lady seemed to be from the compound asked, "Where are you from?" I replied, "I am from Haromaya!" Then she said, "I would give you your daily munching from now on if you fetch and bring me firewood." I thought this to be a good idea so that I didn't worry sheik's wives. I was not sure where I went to get firewood, but I agreed if she was serious about this. She went away, "I will show you my house later." Abdullah brought my lunch as usual about mid day and I pondered and pounded by Lady's idea all day long. In the evening, Abdullah came without dinner in his hand. I was surprised to see his bare hand. He then said, "Why didn't you go for dinner?" I was strangled by his question and asked, "Which dinner you talking about?" He reminded," Do you remember, you were talking to a lady in the morning about giving you banana every day."

"Yes! A lady said something like this, but she didn't show me her house. I thought she was kidding me." He was breathless and stroked my head, "A lady was sheikh's third wife, Hajji[108] Kamaro!" I was embarrassed for not knowing such a respected lady in the compound and she was already sending me food with him from time to time. She now interested in me to work for her. "Do you know her house?" I replied, "No I do not." He dragged me, "Come, I will show you." He took me to her door. I realized this was going to be serious business. I knocked her door and entered while feeling very shy. She stressed, "I was waiting for you!" I was embarrassed, "I didn't know your house; Abdullah just showed me your house." After she gave me a dinner, she reminded me about bringing firewood in the morning. I agreed and returned to Ustad's house. I worried all night long where to get firewood because no one told me and I was shy to ask its place. I had no idea what I was facing and what would happen to this thing. Morning came, I was eating breakfast at her house and she said, "I will introduce you to group of ladies that you go with for firewood." I was happy to hear at least I had a group to go with, but my becoming

---

[108] Someone who made pilgrimage to Mecca

one of the mom hovered over my head because a man fetching firewood with female was very unusual in our culture, or tribe. She gave me a long rope to load firewood on my back like donkey and I rolled up the wrinkled shirt and *marto*[109] to begin the job. She then led me to group of ladies ready to go. They ordered me to follow them as the rope was hanging in my hand.

We began our journey and went very far from town. When I looked back, Borana disappeared from my sight, and I was not sure how far we had to go, but I was already very tired walking with them. My brain and legs were started to crack fearing if I even made to where firewood would be found. While I was weeping and groaning from inside, we started to climb a very dense, big rocky mountain for about three hours before we sat for rest. Then they got up and began collecting dry branches fallen from trees and they showed me how to do it. I made a huge bundle, tied it together like them. When they put on their back like Mule, I put mine on my head thinking I was a man and it would be easier. We began returning home with our loads. It was so heavy that my head almost bent forty-five degrees with wind twisting my body to the other side. I wanted to take off some weight, but felt shy of them and kept my dignity as man. I sweated and sweated, and very tired while I was holding myself straight, not to fall down. It was the worst day of my life to earn my bread for living like this. I also wondered what men would say seeing me carrying firewood with ladies on the way to compound. I encouraged myself as part of earning wage to survive. We travelled almost all day to arrive at the compound, and I was so hungry and tired for the first day.

Next day, I had to go again and I faced the same situation. This became my routine work every day, and I became friends with ladies, established my spot as a woman without breast and long hair. My head was swollen like hump of a camel and my shoulder was torn with shirt. Then I decided to carry like them, on my back since there was no difference between our genders anymore. I could not sleep every night, for my shoulder pain was excruciating sleeping on any

---

[109] Skirt

side. I had no way out of this trouble, just felt nightmare after nightmare while skinny plastic carpet hurt me even more than a firewood. To make things worse, a few people were asking me if I contacted security officials yet…They added fuel to fire already burning my brain. Once Abdullah saw my wounds, he became very sad for me. He advised, "You should bring a lot of firewoods one day so that you go every three days with them."

I replied, "Good idea, but I have already exceeded my limit and more would be deadly to me." He then commented, "Nothing can be done. You must continue your duty. Why security officials didn't say anything at all, holding your documents." I became little restless hearing this as if he was indicating that my only way out of this firewood lady to be in the hands of those officials. I felt like running to them right away, to complain to them, but I recalled sheik Hindiya's advice not to endanger myself by going there, hesitated to face that Abusalam since she said that she would get my documents from him. When I heard rumor that this official had sold documents of some people for cash, and there were some students and people who had never seen their documents again, I freaked out. In some cases if he wished, he needed bribe to release documents.

Fearing I would never see my papers again like others, gave me a little fuel to go and face him. I felt I was lied to for him saying, "I will call you." But before I ran like mad dog to him, I tried to discuss with Hindiya to respect her words. She encouraged me to look for work in the city like watch man, or gardener as some did it before. She suggested that if I was lucky, I might go to Hargeisa when some people arrived from there to compound, or going there for celebration. I liked her idea, but I questioned why officials delayed the release of my documents and never did anything all these times I was suffering. Then she guessed he might want me to pay him for my documents first, the same story I had already heard. Since she knew that I did not have any money, she would beg him for me as a poor boy as he might be sorry for me. I better wait for her to do the job to avoid some troubles. I felt she might be wrong about getting my documents and I did not feel she might go to him anytime soon. I feared I would be rotten in this compound and I felt to go and try my chance next day. When the sun woke me up, I decided not to go with ladies assuming previous firewood would be ample for two days and discussed my problems with a guy in the compound from a refugee camp that arrived day before. He was sorry hearing my story and decided to go with me in case I was arrested by security official so that he would bring news back to the compound. We then headed to the security office as my stomach was shaking and as soon as we entered a compound, we saw Abusalam. He right away said to my companion, "Where did you come from? Where did I see you before?"

The guy replied, "I do not know where you saw me!"

Abusalam, with fierce voice said, "Yes! I know you! Do you think I do not know what you do?"

Then a guy added, "Did you see me doing something wrong?"

Abusalam added, "Did you just come from compound?"

The guy said, "Yes, I did!"

Then Abusalam bombarded him, "You sometimes go to Djibouti, sometimes come here, so come inside" arrested him right on the spot. He forbade me not to follow them. I was shocked and asked him, "What did the guy do?"

Then he said to me, "I know what he did, and none of your business, you go back to Hadra right now!" He chased me out of office to the street like rhino chasing a lion. He made me shit on myself and I was sad to bring a guy to this trouble. I quickly ran to the compound for help while my heart was beating like Hadra's drum. I felt very nervous to tell sheik Hindiya now that, what she told me came true, I put a guy in danger. I had no choice, but quickly told sheik's second wife. She then had run to sheik Hindiya with the news since she was the only authority in the compound to handle matter like this for Hadra. As I feared, Hindiya ran to shoot me with her bullet words from hell. She came with sharpened tiger claws and magma face and started, "You! You! Did I not tell you not to go there? Look what you have done now! You made a guy arrested!" She looked as if to swallow me alive. I had no place to hide from her, and tears filled my eyes because he might be murdered and I disappointed her. I prayed and prayed for him to be released safely even though she was skinning my body for what I did. She then dragged me to go with her to the officials. On the way, she started torturing me with words and while she was insulting Abusalam himself and it looked as if she wanted to get her teeth on his ass and fingers.

When we reached his office, she stuck her face to him, and began screaming, "You arrested one of our compounds' members. You are a bad dog! How come you are after us every time? Last time you found those bad people in our compound. Since then you expect all our members to be bad. How dare you arrest innocent guy? You are a loose rubber body!" I was amazed she insulted him from his head to his feet; including his body wings and ugly disfigured hair. She warned him, "Leave us alone, or else I would show you the heavens!" She threatened and gave him hell like he had never seen before. I was surprised he was scared and apologised to her and he had no idea a guy to be their member. He begged her to forgive him, and opened the door right away for the guy to come with her. I admired her power over security and thanked her in my heart to save this guy's life. On the way to compound, she marinated my body in a bag and fried it in her mouth so that I would never do such things again. Now knowing that she was one tough cookie, I was little happy and hoped she might get my documents from him some day if she opened her door on my case. Realizing how dangerous the security and Sheik Hindiya were, I continued pulling firewoods and never to go back there to mess up things. Everyone heard this incident and some gave me two thumps up to keep pressure on Abusalam until he gave up my documents and probably help me like some refugees while some others warned me to stay away from him. They drove me so crazy from all sides and I did not know what to do. Hearing there was a refugee camp, I wanted to go there hoping I would have better life than carrying firewood for my bread, but I did not know how or when this would happen for me since I was hearing the security no longer send anyone to refugee camps. This also seemed a farfetched place to go. While I was dreaming of this refugee camp and struggling with firewood, a new guy arrived and stood outside compound's fence. He looked like beggar, but someone saw and let him in. As I chatted with him, he informed me that he came from Ethiopia and settled in refugee camp where he was arrested and beaten for some reason he didn't tell me, but somehow escaped and came here. I was sad and shared my story with him and we became like friends. I explained how I got my food, and willing to share with him so that he did not have to worry for what to eat.

Next morning, I left him for wood collection. When I came back; he was sitting with a lot of Somalian injera in a bag like lion sitting by his kill. I was amazed he even got some clothes while begging for food. He invited me to eat with him. I appreciated his kindness, but I had never eaten begged food in my life. When he insisted I should try it, I shied and tasted it. I would never dare to put begged food in my mouth if I was in my country, besides I did not want to demoralize him eating begged food. We discussed about going to Hargeisa one day, but we had no money for transportation and the arresting of my documents became another obstacle. Then I suggested to him that we go to officials to help us go to Hargeisa or Tug Wachalle refugee camp and also release my papers.

In the morning, we dared and went to security and saw Abusalam. This time he didn't try to rip me apart with my friend. I complained and showed him my wounded shoulder that caused by firewood gathering and the pain I was going through. I begged him to send me to a safe place to live and sleep, but he said, "I don't mind you doing firewood collection. Please continue to be a good boy and live with it." I pointed to my friend's filthy appearance and skeleton body that we were both living like African wild dogs and please have a mercy on us. I tried to convince him as much as I could to help us. He then said, "Return tomorrow morning at 8:00 AM." The words I did not expect him to say to us. We returned to compound contemplating what he was going to do, or say, but little excited that after all he might help us with something. We doubted he might send us to refugee camp which we said it was fine if true at all. Now that he was little softer than before, I hoped he would give my documents very easily.

About midday, another new guy arrived at compound, He was darker than me as if I was a white man compared to him, his face was covered with ugly pimples, having many holes like the surface of the moon. I was scared to look at him and all his clothes were smeared by heavy grease as if his body was a dump ground. He carried very ugly torn blanket on his shoulder. His hair was short and strong like porcupine; I feared he might threw them at me. I was surprised to see him sitting by Ustad's house lowering his head like bird hit by stone while worrying of his troubles. I asked, "Where did you come from?" He replied, "Dire Dawa!" I was shocked he was from there, for I did not see anyone like him there. I was afraid he might be those who lived under bridges of Dire Dawa that were robbing residents. He said, "I was working Dire Dawa's gas station, washing cars and repairing them." He explained why he looked dirty.

I understood why he looked like this, but I was breathless he brought all this mess to Somalia. It was hard to swallow what he said to be true. I was worried to make him my friend. I asked, "When did you arrive here?" He replied, "I stumbled in Somalian military border camp to sleep and they caught, tied my eyes, and put me in the hole underground for nine days thinking I was a spy. They then took my watch and all the money I had, and threw me in prison for almost a month. The security just released me to come to this compound." He displayed wounded legs and hands where rope cut him. He was poorly ill and disabled. I was sorry for him and shared my lunch with him, enduring his greasy gorilla fingers which another monkey might not allow it in its dish. In the evening when I invited him for dinner, he informed me that he had already been eaten begged food.

In the morning, we asked him to go with us to security official and he refused, for he had enough of them. As we were told, two of us went and sat under a tree and waited for Abusalam to show up. As he entered a yard, we saw eye to eye. We got up went to him. I began greeting, "Abusalam" He screamed, "Why did you come so early, I did not make appointment with you, just leave!" I was shocked and went to him. He pushed my chest away and tried to hit me. I wanted to get my paper from him and I did not want to leave without it. Seeing I was ready to stand to him, a soldier jumped between us, to stop the fighting. Abusalam then ordered a soldier to make us leave and we were ordered to go.

My friend scared and I waited near a tree trying to get my papers from him and bother him as much as I could. Then a guy, who had taken Yasin and I to motel first day I arrived, saw me crying under a tree. He was sad and said, "You are the most mistreated refugee I ever seen." Then two others came and talked to me in Somali and I had no idea what they said, but they seemed sad for me. I indicated with my finger that I didn't understanding what they said. "Do you speak Amharic?" one asked. I replied, "Yes!" I was happy to talk to them. They asked my situation, I told them how I was suffering and what Abusalam was doing to me. "We will get your documents from him and send you to Hargeisa," they splashed me with good news and took me to nearby restaurant. They asked, "Do you smoke?" I lied, "No I do not smoke." I wanted not to be a burden on their pocket so much. They assured me not to be distressed, for they would be around to assist me. Then they let me return to my compound with happy feeling.

When I reached village of sheik in the afternoon, I saw all members and children in the farm, harvesting very weird skinny sorghum and I went to help them. It was very tiring job and while I was wobbling around, there I heard some noise in the sky. They were terrified, "We are doomed today! Where are the Somali soldiers to defend us?" I wondered and feared they might say we were going to be killed by this plane in the sky. I looked up to verify that if indeed this was a plane came to attack us and it was a fighter jet that I had seen in my country during war times. I could not see its shape for it was flying so high and I saw a trail of white smoke coming from behind it. I laughed at them to fear an ordinary commercial plane that usually went so high in heaven leaving a white fog behind it. As I was enjoying its milky trail behind it, suddenly a loud boom to the skirt of town made my ears erected like rabbit. My heart ordered me to run. They shouted, "Come back! Do not run! If you run, they will see you and bomb all of us!" They wanted to kill me for running. When I came back, they ordered me to put my head down like them. I was as if my baby was pushing out every time loud boom shook my body and still alive. For fifteen minutes, this had continued from all directions of town. I swam on the ground like cat fish while ears were deafened by explosions, discharging watery things on my part. The blue sky and town were covered with white foggy smoke. Farms' air smelled like gun powder. I was still in one piece and heart was beating faster. No bleeding, arms, legs and head in place, my intestine and stomach not found on the floor as I tried to verify them. When explosions were stopped, no one was hurt in the farm, and they informed me that Ethiopian planes sometimes enjoyed coming here to destroy this border town. I was traumatized by this news.

After all, it looked to me that I arrived in war zone, not a place of peace. I suspected that my grave would be in this Borana Town. "After all these explosions, how many people did suffer from fatality in the whole town?" I asked to understand the incident of today. They replied, "No one died, there were no bombs fell from Ethiopian planes!"

"Then where did all these explosions come from?" I was surprised. They pointed to the many mountains' anti aircraft guns that surrounded the town, which I had never seen before, pointed to the heavens, their mouths wide opened. I could not believe these things made such crazy noises which terrified me to the point of death. They informed me that in the past a plane had killed several children in elementary school and some town residents. Knowing danger of Ethiopian plane coming to fart bombs once in a while and this miserable life, I wanted to get away from this town more than ever. While my intestines were sweating of these explosions, we finished harvesting and I went home very scared and tired. My friends were terrified as well.

In the morning, I went to my duty of collecting firewood as usual and came back in the evening to find out news from Yusuf that the other friend had gone to Hargeisa after he got enough fare begging all day long. We realized that he escaped from the explosions. I said to Yusuf, "You are going to do same to me if you get fare money!" He promised, "I will never do this to you, I had regularly disclosed to you what I get and I will never leave you, you do not know me well." He tried to make me understand his loyalty to me. I had also promised him not to betray him at all. He clarified, "Our Lord will help us! We will be all right and go one day!" I agreed with him, "Yes, once we have the money, and my documents, we will try to go to Hargeisa!" Next day, when I was back in the afternoon with firewood, I learned that Ustad returned from his trip with cattle. He seemed to like me hearing I was a firewood worker for sheiks' wife. He had no problem for me to sleep in his unit.

When the evening arrived, Yusuf came to sleep with us and Ustad did not like him as I expected and he was told not to sleep with us. Ustad might have been filled by rumors of compound people that he had leper disease which was serious business and they were warning me not to go and eat with him. They were saying he was limping from leprosy, his left hand middle finger so dark and its nails long like lion, his face dark like pot with many holes, he carries many contagious disease and his ears full of dark beetles why he adds oil from time to time to calm them down. He informed me before adding oil to his ears for the dark creatures roaming his brain. I doubted they were right and he even scared me from time to time, but I did not want to discard him for any reason. I believed this was why he was kicked out by Ustad to the street. I was very sad and went outside compound laughing with him for how he was treated for his looks. I encouraged him not to be despaired sitting and sleeping outside until something happened for him and we would be joining again. I went back to house to sleep worrying for my friend being outside.

In the morning, I decided to get my documents in case I had to go with my friend who might be going soon since he had no place to stay. When I reached security office, I did not see those people who wanted to help me. I pierced office door eighty miles an hour like typhoon as if I had no option left to get my documents. My catty moustache rose above my eyebrows to appall Abusalam and one huge general with stars on his shoulder whom I had never seen before was there. I was little scared of his stars, but it was a time I should be very bold to get my documents. I didn't want to be discarded by my friend's legs which I felt were ready to walk out of town. These fear cancelled my patience of waiting any longer. After I greeted him, Abusalam asked, "Why did you come?" I replied, "I am in trouble, give me my documents and help me please." He seemed had enough of me and gave me one of the documents. I said, "Where is the second one?" He replied, "The other one is not here and I will give you another day." He seemed to give me crooked answer, I was afraid he might have sold it. I questioned, "How come you say not here?" He replied, "I looked around and I could not find it, maybe it was lost." I was mad, "How come you say to me it is lost in the government office? It is impossible!" He replied, "There are thousands of papers come in and go out every day to the garbage, may be lost in this process!" He tried to convince me. I strongly objected, "I do not believe you say this." "Please give my document right now!" I urged him. He again replied, "Come back after tomorrow. If your document was written by typing, I will surely find it, but if it has been written by hand, I will not find it!" He tried to make me go away. I agreed to come back and I was happy at least I got one from him. I kicked my ass like donkey to the compound. I did not want to inform Sheik Hindiya about it, not to put myself in hell knowing that I could do it by myself from now on.

In the afternoon, I prayed in the mosque and stood on its door area and watched two students reading Quran[110] with a compound member standing there. The two kids asked me, "Can you read Quran?" I replied, "Yes! A little." Then they criticized me, "The way you sat in prayer was wrong. You didn't look like learnt at all." Then they challenged me, "Read opening chapter of the Quran." I replied with pride, "I could even read the last two chapters of the Quran for you." Since it was the part of Quran I mastered the most after war of Somalia, which I liked how it read. They were surprised I said this, but criticized me again, "You don't read Quran from last pages." They tried to shame me and then our arguments escalated. We agreed to ask the teacher to settle the differences. Any way they wanted to see if I could even read those areas at all. I began, *Bismillah rahmani rahim*,[111] *alif lam mim*.[112] They cried, "You read wrong."

"I am right," I shouted. Our argument jumped over the cloud. We decided to go to their teacher to find who was at fault. He said,

---

[110] Holy Book
[111] In the Name of Allah, the most gracious and most merciful
[112] Opening letters (for some chapters)

"It is all right to read from last pages." At least he confirmed my point. He did not criticize the way I read. After we argued more and more, but their teacher advised us not to fight about it. Then I went to Jamal and saw a few compound members with some Somali friends. They sat to chew this ugly Kat probably Sheik Hindiya got them left over from some Somalis, which surprised me. It looked they were getting high to fix Jamal's Range Rover later on. I was happy they invited me to chew with them like goat, and it made me laugh and we had a good time. Then the two argumentative kids came and sat by door. They saw a poster of motorcycle on the wall written in Arabic and English. They challenged me if I could read the Arabic part since I learnt Quran. I said, "This is Arabic language, and it is not Quran."

They argued, "Its Quran writing." Once again we started the fire. I told them, "You are crazy, and want to argue for everything." The radio in the middle of us was speaking in Arabic and they told us to shut up and listen to *hadith*.[113] They asked me, "Do you know what the radio saying?" I questioned, "Are you saying this radio is talking about religion? Where did you come from? You were talking trash."

Then Jamal advised me, "Do not argue with them, everything they hear and see in Arabic seemed Quran to them."

Then he was mad at them, "Shut up!" Then a guy who did not understand what we argued about was curious to know from Jamal why he was angry toward them. He explained to him what they were saying and their being students at the compound. Then a guy started, "Long ago, I was student came here with sheik of the compound, I wanted to be a super sheik, studying day and night, but living is so hard, and I had to work to make my living. It is not easy to be a master sheik because you need to be dressed, eat, and get married. There are many obstacles on the way to stop you and you will not be able to achieve your goals. These things stopped me from being sheik since I came here. I see you are new here! I do not think you will be sheik in this country by begging for food. Do not drink too much

---

[113] Explanation of Quran, or prophet

water here! If you want to learn Quran very well and you are serious, you better go somewhere else. Now you better stop this nonsense, go search for work before it is too late for you." I seconded, "This guy told you the truth, you better do as he said." Then they attacked me, "You do not know Quran, you were praying in vain! All you know is some science which is very bad thing." I was mad at them to make my school useless. I tried to show them science is good thing, "Do you know our world is rotating? Tell me how day and night is created if you know." They replied, "No one knows if the Earth is rotating. Day and night was God's creation. People that believed our earth is rotating are scientists who are unbelievers. You are one of them!" We argued and argued that vulgar words were thrown at each other like rockets.

At last, I released the words like a bomb, which I was regretting "God does not exist at all, the universe just created out of the blue, or nothing." I assumed what some scientists say which I couldn't prove even if they asked me to explain it. My comment "No God," which I didn't mean from my heart added gas to the fire. I was saying, *Istafurulah!*[114] in my heart which they didn't hear it, but I gave it to them being upset with them and to fend them off. Once they heard that I was denying the existence of God, they slammed the Quran on the ground and got really mad. If they had known Arabic Quran they were reading and its meaning, they could simply mention chapter 21:30 to defeat me which says, "Do not the unbelievers see that the heavens and the Earth were joined together (as one unit of creation), before we clove them asunder. We made from water every living thing. Will they not then believe?" Also Q21:33 says, "It is he (God) who created the night and the day, and the sun and the moon; All (the celestial bodies) swim along, each in its rounded (Orbit) course." Since this verse was thousand years older than my recent knowledge of rotation of earth around the sun, which I came to know that made me comment there is no God and I am better than you. They could have argued I was wrong and God had given this knowledge of night and day creation that happened by explosion of matters from one

---

[114] God forgive me.

place as above verses. I recalled my dad said, "We, especially non Arabs who read Quran, not knowing its meaning and what it says are like donkey who carries a honey to town." There was no doubt I was a donkey and they were a mule that were kicking each other on the things we didn't understand and had no knowledge of. Anyway, despite our ignorance and arrogance, we both had about God and school we went, they asked me to say *Istafurulah*, which I had already said in my heart which God already knew, but I refused to obey what they wanted me to say. They began crying non stop for some time. At last we reconciled of this argument, and I explained to them that I was not serious about denying God existence. Then they asked me to read *Sura*[115] *Ikhlas*[116] chapter 112 three times from the Quran, which proved that there is only one God to be worshipped same as the first commandment of moses in the bible, or torah so that God will forgive me for this sin. After discussing that Satan had caused all these arguments between us, we blamed him for it and we all separated with happy face.

About evening, after we were high on Kat, Jamal went to fix his Range Rover with Somali friends and I went with them to the yard. When they couldn't fix it, I found that its carburettor needed some adjustment which I was glad to help him without any charge. I realized that Jamal was very happy with me. Lucky me, I learnt how to fix when engine got hiccup, or some pain. After that as usual, I went to Ustad's house to sleep, but I found that compound members were going to celebrate religious things in his house and I could not sleep there. I discussed this problem with Abdullah, where to sleep for the night and he asked permission from Sheik's older son for me to sleep in his Range Rover's back seat. This seemed strange, but I had no choice and laid at the back seat of it. I was not comfortable to nap all night long even for five minutes, turning here and there especially with the noise coming from Ustad's house. After Compound members performed early morning prayers as usual, the sheik whom at first the kids took me to verify if I could read Quran had passed

---

[115] Chapter
[116] Purity of God

by Range Rover. I heard him calling Mohammed Nur so loud that it lifted my head up from a seat of car. I looked through window of the driver to find out what had happened to him. Mohammed Nur was shocked by his name called so loud that he cried back, "Yes!" He continued shooting his name like machine gun million times per second, "Mohammed Nur! Mohammed Nur!" Mohammed Nur also replied with "yes" million times per minute.

Then the guy added, "It is urgent! I have to tell you something. This boy bringing firewood to Haji Kamaro said, 'There is no God' to the kids and insulted them too yesterday. God will, in the morning if this is true story, and kids tell you as a witness, please send him to the government. Let them kill him." He then threatened Nur, "If you do not get rid of this boy, leaders of your compound had warned me to leave for good." To my surprise, Mohammed Nur seemed to agree with him, "If it is true, I shall do as you said." Hearing this, my heart fell under the seat of his car; I would be killed in the morning. I could not believe that the matter we had settled with "*Istafurullah*" now coming up and I would be killed for it. I was very mad at him being very ruthless and wanting me to be dead. I got up and sat in the car knowing that my end was in the sun rise. I screamed from back seat so loud, "How dare you say this? You are so cruel; I did not expect this from you!" He did not know I was in the car and heard him all that he uttered. He then heard a little shouting coming to him from the Rover in the dark in a fierce way. Right on the spot, I wanted to come out and swallow him fresh like Eunectes murinus. Once he saw me in the car swimming with anger toward him, he threatened, "If this is really true, you will see what is going to happen to you!" I countered by screaming, "You are not a lawyer for God. He didn't say kill anyone who spoke like me, we will see!" I tried to defend myself even though I was terrified to perish at sunrise. I thought about running to save my life fearing the government would not spare my soul once they laid their hands on me, but I was confused where to run.

Returning to Ethiopia was jumping in alligator's mouth I ran from and now Somalia was becoming my grave yard very fast. No matter what I decide to do, death opened its mouth from both sides. Djibouti crossed my mind, but I did not know how to go there and

I had no transportation funds. I murmured, "I saved my life to come to Somalia, now I die here!" I did not expect my mouth talking about science could end my life. I envisioned vultures pulling my eyes out and ripping my skin. I brought my soul to Somalia to live a long time and die in peace, but now was going to have those sons of guns dance on my body and send me to grave. Death was becoming a reality, it came faster than expected before I could marry a Somalian girl and see what this life would be like in Somalia. I gave up, no place to run. I was shocked more than ever and I needed a miracle to save my life. It was a chilly morning, I wrapped myself with blanket in the seat and sweat dribbled my belly as morning got closer and closer. My body was shuddering; my brain was bustling about death. I brooded, "Mohammed Nur is going to take me to the Somalis, no, no! He will not do that! Yes! He will do that because they gave him an order. He agreed in fear that his father's compound will fall apart if he did not do what they said." So I had no chance of being spared and there would be no miracle. I just waited for my death.

At day break, I got out and sat by Rover. Not all members heard what happened and what was going to happen. When I saw Jamal was going to start his Range Rover to go to work, I went to him to check the carburettor if it was still going to be all right. As he opened car hood, Mohammed Nur also came toward us. The guy who wanted me to die showed up with the bigger sheik to ask me if I really said those words. I did not deny what came out of my mouth, but I tried to explain how I said it and again repented to God for my mistake. Hearing these, Jamal got mad at the kids and explained all that he heard. I saw bigger sheik unhappiness on his face and they returned to mosque. Mohammed Nur said, "They wanted me to take you to Somali, but if you go away, I will not pass you to them." I thanked his desire to save my life, but I told him my document was in the hand of security, and I had no money for transportation. I begged him, "I appreciate if you can ask them for me to stay until I get my document." He was concerned, "They were very upset and difficult for me to let you stay any much longer." Regardless I was very mad and decided to get my document in a hurry. I went to Abusalam said to him desperately, "I have serious problem and must get my last document right now." I begged him more kindly. He seemed little kinder than ever and began searching in the pile of papers. "Is it written by hand, or typing?" He wanted to confirm again. I said, "By typing, but it was a copy document with my picture." He showed me one, I said, "No." He showed me another one. I said, "No." Then he said, "I do not see another one!" I was shocked to hear him say this. It looked like there was no hope to get it since he searched sincerely for it unless he was lying to me. While I stared at him, he again tried to show me many more and I said negative to him. Seeing I was not budging, at last, he showed me one, no doubt it was happened to be mine and it tickled my heart. I shouted with a big, "yes" to it. My heart lubricated with joy when he handed to me. I thanked him very much and told him that I am being kicked out of the compound and asked him to help me. Then he said, "You have your paper now, just go wherever you like! I cannot help you." I left kicking the globe with my heel.

I went back to compound, and informed those who did not hear the news that I was being kicked out of compound. They seemed little venomous toward me, but they understood that I was sorry. I was shocked to hear from my employer, Hajji Kamaro that sheik had told her what happened. She gave me some food to eat anyway and ordered me to feed her donkey with sorghum trunks from the farm. When I was going to a farm, I saw a Somali sheik that I told the information using an interpreter, I should not be killed for what I said especially after I apologized. Then the guy who wanted me to be sent to Somali to get killed showed up. We had a chance to discuss the matter and he seemed to cool down little bit from his anger and for me not be kicked out fast. He softened Mohammed Nur to let me stay until I got ready to go away. Yusuf was happy to hear this news and suggested for us to go to Hargeisa as soon as possible. I asked, "How are we going without transport money?"

He suggested, "Tomorrow is Friday, we go for Fridays' prayer at a big Mosque and beg for money since there are many people come there for prayer." I agreed with him if this helped us leave town. When Sheik Hindiya saw me, she also gave me hell for what I said. She advised me fasting for forty days to wash away my sins. "I couldn't fast forty days being homeless and I have already asked my God's forgiveness, he can see my heart," I said to myself.

When the sun red feet touched the mountain to west, I hesitated to go to Hajji Kamaro's house for dinner since I thought she was in trouble feeding the sinner like me even though I worked for her. Yusuf and I ate the injera he begged for dinner. Then as usual, I went to sleep at Ustad house and they informed me that another compound celebration was to be held. I was again sent to sleep in the Range Rover. In the morning, Yusuf woke me to our plan to go to Friday's prayer and beg for transportation funds, but I was afraid that he specially shouldn't go to pray in the mosque with dirty clothe and stinky body I had ever seen on this planet that he had never touched with water for long time since he arrived to the compound. So we decided to clean up ourselves for the historic first time prayer at very unpleasant slimy green algae pond, full of tadpoles as soap. We then headed to find mosque while green algae swung from our hair. Then we saw a mosque filled with people and hundreds more covered its' yard and streets like bee on its beehive. I spread my wrinkled bed sheet on the dusty and rough ground. Yusuf did the same with his ugly jacket while town people had soft and silky Arabian prayer mats. "There is no time to wish for this kind of mats and be jealous," I whispered. As we began to pray with them, there we found some tadpoles swam in our cloth and dropping out like lice in front of us as we bend down and then prostrated on the ground.

As prayer ended, Yusuf began shouting, *Liban,*[117] *Liban, Lillahi warasul.*[118] The words I did not understand, but I was impressed by his nice voice and how he sang it. He might be saying very compelling and heart softening words to the worshippers. I lost my words how he begged in Somali like professional beggar who had seventy years experience. Then Somali shillings began falling on his jacket and I believed we might have a chance to get fare money we needed badly. I had never begged in my life and I was ashamed to shout like him. I had also hesitated that no one will drop money on my rag

[117] Alms begging sign
[118] In respect of God and his messenger

like him. He urged me to say like him and I had no chance to sit back and watch him like I wanted. At last with a tiny kitten voice I meowed, *Liban, Liban, Lillahi warasul.* Someone dropped a coin on my sheet. It made my heart smiled and moved my ear lobes a bit at least getting something. When some of them just looked and passed me, I was demoralized for I might not looked a good beggar, or had poor people's face like Yusuf, or I didn't shout enough at them. I tried to shout more and more, and then a few shilling bills began to fall on my sheet. I murmured, "I am not a professional beggar like my friend." As we were sitting and begging, Yusuf got up and held his jacket like big satellite dish to the heavens and began shouting and running around until everyone cleared from prayer area. His sophisticated begging and running around action made me laugh at him.

When begging was over, I counted forty shillings and reported to him. I asked, "How much did you get?" He replied, "I only got sixty shillings."

"After all that crying and running around, you were only twenty shillings richer than me," I taunted him. We earned total of hundred shillings which did not make us happy since we heard that we each needed two hundred shillings for fare to Hargeisa just to take a cargo truck. We agreed to beg more until we had enough money and he continued his Liban on our way from mosque about town. I was and kept my mouth shut while going back to compound. Everyone lent him, *Allah kusiyyo!*[119] and he didn't get any Penny. His actions, again made me laugh even more. "Stop laughing and beg like me, you have no mother and father to help you here," he tried to push me. When we came to a house, I said, "Liban!" to make him happy. Then a girl popped out to verify who said Liban. Then she got a big spoon of rice in her hand. I stretched my palms together as a plate and I was shy and hesitate going to burn me. She then went back home and put it in a grocery bag for me. I was happy at least I got a rice to eat. It encouraged me that begging may be easy after all, I might get something if I begged. I kept begging and begging, got nothing, but lost Yusuf in the process. He suddenly disappeared from my sight.

---

[119] Allah grant you (somewhere else)

While I was looking for him, I begged more and more, but nothing hit my hand. I found myself in town where I had never been before. I heard a lady was calling me. I thought she was going to give me some money and I was little delighted. As I went to her, there I saw Yusuf calling me, and eating spaghetti in the hut. "Is that you, Yusuf?" He said, "Yes?"

"What on earth are you doing?" I asked. "I was hungry and bought pasta." "What extra things did you get?" He asked me. I showed him, "I only got a cup of rice in my bag; I hope you were not spending the shillings you begged for our transportation!"

He said, "Yes! God will give us later on!" He invited me to his $20 Shillings that left in his pocket. I asked a lady, "How much for a plate of pasta?"

"Full plate is $40 shillings, half is $20," she replied. I ordered half plate, to add to my cup of rice while regretting the loss of our transportation funds. We went to compound with the feeling that I became a beggar person. I could not believe being beggar for the first time in my life and experiencing what those beggars felt in my country: their tiring, battering, suffering, and rejecting that created severe migraines. I was lucky my Uncle Zaku who kicked me out of his house didn't see me because he could have shouted at me like those beggars: look at this boy, his muscles and physique, you come to rip me off an old and lame man like me, and he could have hissed at me like snake to make my life gloomy. From time to time, I was filled with coyness and laughter from the first time how we begged and all actions that happened while we sat under gutter of Ustad's house. Hajji Kamro's children came to chat with us and we asked them a favour, "Could you please get us left over Kat?" They then ran and brought us tiny bit left from people. We chewed it to relax ourselves. Yusuf had already spent forty shillings on pasta, fifteen on smoke. I also spent five shillings on a single smoke. It looked we were having bonanza with the money that could help us to leave Borana. After a while, we saw Jamal leaving his room that facing toward the mosque. He picked a kind of stone from a ground and threw at something which we could not see from our angle. I heard him say that *Inatachuhun biddu, hiddu,*[120] *Indih aynet negar atadirgu!*[121] He seemed to be upset at some people whom we had no clue about. I could guess bad people since we were sitting at angle of the wall. It also seemed to me that he wanted to kick some kids off his property that were doing something wrong. We continued chewing Kat until the sun said goodbye to us.

At sunset, I asked Yusuf, "What are we going to eat for dinner?" Since I felt that I had no place to eat for the first time. "Let's enter town to beg," he advised. I suggested, "You go because you were not afraid like me; I stay here and wait for you. You go and try your best!" He then advised, "Why don't you try your best, I don't think I will find food that enough for both of us since it is dark. You must help me." He tried to convince me to go out. I agreed with him and we both decided to go different route. I was shy to go for begging and waited until he was gone. Then I got up pretending to go to washroom out of the compound. After I cleared the compound, I covered all my body with sheet like mummy except little opening for my eyes so that no one will recognize me at all. I hoped it would help me act like a good poor beggar and headed to the area of town where there was no much electricity, and huts were fenced by thorns. It was nerves wrecking to stand by huts fenced by thorns and had small lanterns and candles light in them. Then I saw one huts' gate of thorn was already opened. I entered with caution and said that Liban, Liban again with tiny voice like kitten so that I do not disturb, or scare residents. I was astonished only a kid came out, hearing these tiny noises. I seemed to freak him out a little how I was covered and he looked at me like dead body wrapped in white sheets just came out of grave. While I feared his dad to rush out with sword, or gun to attack me if a boy cried thief, or danger, he went inside and came out with a small plate as if he was carrying a larger hockey puck on it. My heart giggled as he walked toward me with it feeling that he brought some thing for me. He said, *farisoo, uun!*[122] showing with

---

[120] Mother whooper, get lost.
[121] Never do such thing again
[122] Sit down and eat

hand gesture. I figured out he wanted me to sit and eat it when he put it down on the ground. I couldn't believe that this black thing on a plate was food to eat. I feared that this kid was giving me a black stone to eat and he was playing a game with me. After he went in the hut, I bent down my head and first smelled it to see if indeed he gave me food. Then it smelt like some kind of boiled dark meat. When I caressed it, I found it to be my favourite juicy oxen tripe cut floating on a watery soup. I regretted I was not able to take this wet meat to Yusuf since I was ordered to sit down and eat it. I drank soup under it first, and began chewing little by little in a hurry, for I had to go fast out of yard. Before I finished it, a kid came back for a plate and I grabbed it on my hand and gave him his plate while saying, *galattomi*[123] in my language hoping he would understand. I tried to chew even faster and faster to leave the yard quickly.

As I found it hard to finish quickly, I decided to put the rest in my mouth so that I softened it faster. Once I believed that it was masticated enough, I decided to swallow all and it did not go down my throat as I dreamed of it. I pressured little harder and still there. I pushed very hard and still swallowing was not possible. After a few tries, still it was there around my throat. Now breathing became harder and harder and I was concerned that I was in danger. I tried a few more times, but it looked I was running out of time. I was about to die and could not move to house for help being scared and not knowing the language what to say. I ran and ran around fence, my eyes were like gulf ball to come out with pressure from pushing down. At death point, I put my finger in my mouth to find that some of my molars were holding fibers of chewed gut. I tried to reach with my finger to free it, but unable to reach those fibers hanged around my teeth. I realized that I was running out of time as I was barely able to breathe. I saw angel Israfil flying down through the clouds toward me with his shinning fingers to pull my soul out. At this point of my soul coming out, I jumped two meters in the air like Michael Jordan dunking a basket ball and pushed down so hard rather than dying there. It opened my throat and esophagus like baby Godzilla being

---

[123] Thanks

250

born toward my stomach. I was able to breathe again, but I suffered severe pain all the way down. I was ashamed and scared, for almost lost my soul in vain which I brought all the way to Somalia by ox's gut. Realizing that I could die as beggar, I sweated and sweated and returned to compound to tell Yusuf about it. He was sad for what happened and shared his tiny begs. We heard Hadra's party would continue for the night and I decided to sleep outside close to mosque where Yusuf was sleeping to taste a cold night with him. While shivering in the cold and talking, grinding teeth with cold, we arrived at the dawn.

After the prayer caller ended his call, he saw us lying by mosque. He told us to leave the area right away like kicking out Satan. Sheik Hindiya saw me and asked, "Why did you sleep outside?" Before I answer her, the prayer caller waved his hand vigorously to take here attention away saying to her, "Come! Come!" As if he did not want us to hear him, by whispering to Sheik Hindiya, "Jamal had stoned the kids yesterday because of this boy who brought firewood for Hajji Kamaro. The head sheik and children were upset and going to leave the compound unless Yusuf and this boy are gone." She advised us to leave rather than talk to Jamal which I understood very powerful and feared because he was brother in law of compounds' owner. She realized that the compound would be ruined because of us. She ordered us to go away in the morning. She only worried, "You did not get your documents yet!" I sadly told her, "I have already got my documents."

She did not give me hell for going to Abusalam this time since she wanted me out of Hadra rather than it ruined by us. She was happy I got them and suggested we go to Hargeisa and stay in a mosque. She advised us never to stay outside, for many people were killed there and it was a dangerous city to stay outside. She added that we kept our mouth shut if we wanted to be safe. With her comments, I was very shocked; we were going to die with no place at all.

I was little happy that she kicked us out of compound by herself, but we had no money for transportation to go. It was as if she was pushing my body through a needle eye toward Hargeisa. My cerebrum collided with my skull like moon with earth. No place to stay, no food, the sky and earth darkened as never before. We stood behind Ustad's house, wondering where to go, but Yusuf began aping how prayer caller told sheik Hindiya about kids. He cracked a loud laughter like I had never heard before. Even the neighbors came out to see what was happening. He made me exploded with him that I had forgotten the trouble we faced losing another Mother India. I said fare well to some people who cared for me. I headed toward the unknown with Yusuf. We found ourselves in a city center to beg truck drivers to give us a lift, having no money and no language. If they refused, we decided we had to go on foot to Hargeisa. "It was too early to beg truckers, in the meantime lets beg for breakfast," Yusuf said. "You remember I was chocked and almost died. It is up to you to make us alive," I polished him. "Sorry, I will not feed you," he reacted in funny way. Then he took me to the nearest tea house and spent the last shillings he had on small bread and tea. Not satisfied at all, we headed to three empty trucks waiting for people to embark on. There was no one there including drivers. Little later on, we saw fare collectors arrived and they asked us, "Are you going to Hargeisa?" "Yes," Yusuf replied. "Two hundred shillings," one proclaimed. Yusuf declared, "We do not have money! Can you take us please?" Then they madly said, "If no money, go away, nothing is for free." I predicted there would be no luck at all. I whispered, "In my country no one will take you even you are short five cents, begging these truckers to take us for free in Somalia did not seem reality." I found this hope to be crazy. Yusuf moved from truck to truck like a mad dog while I watched him rejected again and again. I felt his pain of being kicked in the groin several times and advised him, "Please wait until drivers, or owners arrive."

As I stood there in despair, I recalled those people at the security who said they would help me. I told Yusuf about it and went away to return quickly. I ran around in the market, entering several tea shops, but I heard some people calling me *wa wallan*[124] while fearing Yusuf might have gotten a truck and left me. The vision of being left alone in Borana urged me to stop looking for those guys and ran

---

[124] lunatic

back to Yusuf very quickly like hyena while my gut was saying that he might have left me. I felt better seeing him still standing by truck and begging a driver. As I got a few steps from him, he began climbing on a truck. My stomach dropped on the ground like pumpkin, not believing what I saw. He then urged me to beg a driver from the top of truck which engine was running as if it wanted to go. I didn't know how to ask and what to say, but I ran to him and said the only word I heard and knew, *wallaloo*[125] raising my hand with very sad face. Having a cat face and mouth, he knew I did not speak Somali language, and stretched his hands to give him fare. I pulled out my last five shillings left in my pocket to say this was all I have. He then disgusted and rejected showing anger toward me. The day became night, looking up my friend on a truck I was unable to see him clearly, knowing that I was left behind and regretting why I left him. I had no choice, but to keep up *wallaloo* in a crying state. My eyes were full of tears, for I saw losing my friend. A driver repeated, *la-akta*[126], *la'akta*, again and again as I pulled the five shilling to him, for I could not explain and made him understand my problem. He ordered me to go away displaying very fierce face that I had never experienced so far I was begging him. I had no choice than to with stand his scaring face and commands, but I increased saying *wallaloo* hundred times per seconds very desperately while thinking that I was about to be eaten alive, or die in Borana if I lost Yusuf. Then a driver was pushing me away while I looked at Yusuf and threatened him, "You are going to leave me just like this." Yusuf pushed me to beg him and I kept begging fearing the worst to happen under the tree and get murdered by dangerous people.

When a driver began to roll his truck, I increased *wallaloo* a million times per second while displaying to him the same five shilling, trying to soften him up and have mercy for me as a poor beggar. I spoke my language in a crazy manner, "The guy you picked up is my friend and I will die if you leave me here." My tears ran down my face as he increased speed of truck tires and I increased speed of my

---

[125] Brother
[126] Money

legs to keep up with him. Now my mouth ran faster than ever saying *wallaloo* a billion times per second, my heart falling down on the ground. All organs one by one left my body while running by side of truck. At last, he threw a word like a bomb, *wariyya fuul.*[127] It was one of my dearest moment. I dared to climb fenced side of the truck like a Monkey, the talent I had never knew I had in my life. I thanked God and a driver in my heart, but I did not thank Yusuf considering he betrayed me just like that. I questioned him, "If this driver did not pick me up, you could have left me, eh?"

"God did not separate us!" He tried to calm me down. "I saw what friendship promise meant to you anyway!" I tried to make him feel it. I realized the kindness of a Somali driver who just picked two of us for free of charge which I thought impossible before.

We were lucky once again to be together, but now a city we were going to worried me more: what would happen? How we were going to live? We might be staying in a mosque as they told us in Borana. Yusuf said, "I heard my best friend is in Hargeisa. Do not worry! As we go there, no more problems." I asked, "Who is your friend?"

I did not believe him saying these words he never said before. He replied, "His name is sheik Billisa!"[128]

"What! Sheik Billisa?" I tried to verify being shocked about it if he was the same Billisa that I knew who had a compound near my elementary school. He added, "I used to buy Kat in Dire Dawa and go to his compound." I was even more stunned, his compound was just three hundred meters from my elementary school's fence. My class door faced north to his compound which I gazed every single day. Everyone scared of him in my town being such a powerful figure there. You could not refuse him whatever he wanted to take of your house, or business store. I guessed this was how he made his living with his members stayed with him. I heard if you refused him to take whatever he wanted; you would risk losing a lot in life and your business by his curse. If he took it, your business would increase in profit many times. He also beat anyone he liked and no one dared

---

[127] You, get on
[128] Sheik flash walker

to raise hand to him. His members were possessed by some kind of Jinn anytime they danced at the compound and passed out with drums while praising his name. As a child I used to scare of him with everyone in town. He was not God and not a true religious person as far as I knew. Once you enter his compound, you would become his property. He could do whatever he liked with you: beat, kill, force you to eat, get married to compound members, stop you from eating, or make you finishing a meal. If Yusuf was right, Billisa was really in Hargeisa and we had to go to him, it started to bug me. While we were hiding in the mountains and running around during war of Somalia and Ethiopia, I was not sure where Billisa had gone. I doubted my friend might be right. At least I was little happy because we might not starve to death if Billisa forced us to eat like I heard. If you declined to eat, he would hand a stack of food while slashing you with cow skin. However, if you were not satisfied with what he gave you, he would also slash you in anger while wailing that he could not fill your elephant belly.

While we discussed about him, laughing at how we were kicked out of Borana, the bumping and shaking of truck on a dusty road, I heard that we came close to Ethiopian border. I was scared we entered war zone since Hargeisan freedom fighters were close by with Ethiopian forces. There we faced tight checking of Somalian army from station to station. I was relieved after hearing that we some- what headed toward center of the country from border area. Then from gravel and rocky roads, we entered a nicely paved, smooth tar road which felt very good on my behind to ride on truck. We went little deep in Somalia while watching its' country side and farmers all being different than my country. We travelled all day long, at last we came to a big city of Hargeisa that pleased my eyes. Beautiful stone high rise buildings and houses sandwiched between two moun- tains were taking my breath away. I began to smell fresh city air that excited my feeling not knowing what was sizzling on a grill for us. We got off the truck not knowing where we would go. I challenged Yusuf if he could take us to his friend Billisa using his chicken head size Somali language he could say. All I could do was just to follow him with my ugly dresses. I was very shy about how I looked for a big city, but I whispered no one knew who I was. We were very tired, thirsty, hungry, and ran out of gas. I wished to get something to eat even not to backing down from Billisa's torturing style of feeding me. We just kept walking blind in a city. After a while Yusuf asked some people where about of Billisa and they didn't know. I endured many evil looks on us. We cut many street corners and houses and kept walking and walking searching for compound of Billisa. Then suddenly a young man Yusuf asked said just go straight and turn right, then we would come close to Billisa's yard. We were excited to see Billisa's compound, but worrying began to settle in my soul for the reality of facing dangerous character in the universe.

We increased our steps feeling we were getting closer. As we turned another corner, we heard our language being spoken and extra delighted feeling we hit a gold mine. First guy we came to informed us that Billisa's compound area was where people gathered and pointed to a tree for us. I was happy that Yusuf was right about Billisa and he was indeed in Hargeisa and we found his friend as he said. We felt happy that we were going to eat soon, but I warned Yusuf of Billisa's life style. I knew we might be better begging rather than stuck inside his compound for good. He laughed at me for saying this. I suggested Yusuf to go ahead and find out while I waited across the street of the compound by people sitting under a tree. I saw gun men popped out of corner like wart hog and stopped Yusuf at gate. I was shocked that Billisa's compound was well guarded here by heavy armed men. I felt his power in town and Yusuf came back as if he was rejected to gain access. He said, "The guards asked me where I was going and I told them Billisa was my sheik in Dire Dawa and I am going to see him. They informed me that he is not here at the moment, but to wait under the tree to come back when he arrived." We found that the tree across his compound was a big apartment building for those people not allowed to enter his compound. We mixed with them like sugar in coffee and sat there. There were no children and women living there, besides at least thirty people of all sizes and shapes, some sleeping and some were sitting. Everyone had a dusty flat box that wrinkled like old lady's forehead and dug spot in the ground as a hog. There were many tin cans and garbage littered around these apartments. I was surprised how so many people ended up here and besieged the ground. I wondered if they just arrived, or people that came here long ago, or people who might be kicked out of the compound. I also assumed they must be waiting for a turn to be admitted to his yard just like us. Their conditions were very appalling.

While we were wondering when his friend would come, there about sun set he was getting off his car with heavily armed men. There were very scary creatures surrounded him like China's wall with heavy guns. I was afraid Yusuf might not able to penetrate them to talk to Billisa. Yusuf, raising his long donkey ears like never before, got up and ran as rhinoceros toward this wall declaring, my Billisa, my Billisa…. Seeing this filthy dark guy, Billisa's guards were ready to shoot him down from getting to close to Billisa. "Where did you come from?" Billisa inquired. Yusuf replied, "I came from Ethiopia to see you my Billisa." Then Billisa asked, "What is your tribe?"

"I am Jarso!" Yusuf uttered. Billisa replied, "Jarrsos are garbage! What do you want?" Yusuf explained, "I used to visit you every day when you were in Dire Dawa, delivering Kat to you. You are my sheik. I am very hungry and desperate of shelter. I want to get in your compound." Billisa shrieked, "I do not know you, you are crooked! Go away and sit under the tree with those people!" Yusuf enticed him, "I can wash and take care of your cars! My sheik! Let me in please!" Billisa was really mad, "Get lost, boy! Guards keep this man away! Do not let him approach my gate." Yusuf walked toward me broken hearted where I stood and listened to all that said. I cracked with laughter seeing he was kicked out badly. I felt I was glad not to talk to him, for he could have insulted me like him, for my tribe *nolle* meant to him that we were spies of Amhara, which he did not want to hear. My mother's tribe *alla* meant "filthy," which my friend did not hear of before. Yusuf was sad and said, "Too bad! Let's go to the tree!" I said, "You were saying Billisa, Billisa, and praised him so much. I didn't feel this to be good from the beginning anyway. At least, now we don't have to suffer in his hand." We faced the reality to help ourselves as Yusuf's dream was shattered right there. There would be no more snugly compound he dreamed for us. We had no choice, but to settle among tree people.

CHAPTER 8

Cat Becoming Tree Hog

We sadly walked to those wild hogs dug under huge tree and they wanted to know if Billisa agreed to admit us to his complex. We said, "He chased Yusuf away." They explained, "He refused to let us in and we have no place to go and made this tree our lodging. He will admit you if you are his clan, or you should know someone in there who will come to get you. Otherwise you have no chance to go in." We then had to settle under the tree like them finding unoccupied space like room. They added, "Sometimes he brings us food that rotten for five days on purpose to feed us and if we refused he would beat us until we finished it. Once in a while he brings leftover food sitting for days from his members which they eat with bare hands while licking them and it tastes the grittiest food ever seen. Besides bad food, if he feels, he will put you in the hands of Somali officials as spy of Ethiopia. There were many jailed and perished this way." Hearing all these, I got scared and little mad at him that we might be soon facing these songs. We asked, "Why were you here and how long did you live here?" They replied, "It is very deadly to sleep outside house in Hargeisa for security reason and there are many muggers. This tree is the safest place to stay in town. Thanks for Billisa's compound and his power in town, beside guards were watching this area twenty-four hours a day. Few of us came from refugee camps nearby to work in town to earn some money for clothing and other needs. When we didn't get a job, we became members here. There are some new comers like you." They gave us old and dusty flat boxes with torn news papers and we dug hole in the dust like them. They encouraged, "You must beg for food if you want to be alive here." Again I had no choice than to ask Yusuf to beg for us, for I had already tasted death in Borana being not a good beggar who lacked knowledge of little Somali language. He agreed and made my life easy for me.

After sunset, there we were hungry and tired. Yusuf was scared to go alone for we were new in town. He suggested, "Can you at least go with me for the first night in case I get lost? You might recall the way to get back. You don't say anything just follow me." I agreed, "You are right, two heads are better than one." We blindly walked in one direction and saw that most houses had high brick or stone fences with iron gate that confused us how to get in and beg. We walked and walked there were no people in the yard beside those walking on the street. After we were very tired, we decided to return, but on the way we came to a big house very deep inside the fence from us. We hesitated to say anything for the house was too deep inside the fence and no one would hear us saying anything. Because of our hunger, I knocked its gate in case they saw us and came so that my friend would alms them. I knocked and we waited for response and no one heard us. No one seemed to hear it for a while. I did knock again and suddenly a guy came out, but not paying attention to me as if he did not hear my knocking. I knocked again to let him know we were there. He was freaked to see us standing by their door and dashed toward us, calling us burglars and thieves from what I read on his face. He was as angry as a lion and going to call soldiers to arrest us as thieves. We quickly dashed back to our tree and told other hogs how we came close to being arrested. They laughed and warned us never to go at night to milk this town except mid day. We regretted why we did not verify with them before we had gone. We wrapped our tails around thighs like hog and laid down with hunger under tree while hoping for left over to come from Billisa's compound since we heard that sometimes at night the guards generously bring, porridge, or boiled grains in water if the hogs begged them. I was so tired and hungry I hardly slept with cold.

About midnight, they woke us up for Billisa's porridge like I dreamed. My hands were very dirty, but there was no choice than to get up and eat like a pig to stop the hunger. Later I saw my hand was so shiny like moon and slippery to touch. I asked what it was. They said that Billisa added a lot of oil on purpose. He used to force you to drink one to three litres to oil you up and satisfy your body. They made me laugh I got my first lube like gear box of a car. I appreciated soothing of hunger and lubrication that I might be needed soon or later. It made for me easy to roll back in the dust to sleep. It was the first night to be on the street of Hargeisa. Being among so many hogs made me comfortable knowing that I was safe from much harm and able to eat begged food. I was happier than living in Borana to roll in a dust like a donkey believing no one will kick us out, and no trouble of carrying firewood as if I was excited to be free under this tree. Just close to dawn, there was commotion around tree by the hogs which woke me up and I wondered what was happening. They calmed down my fear by saying not to worry this was happening every day to get ready to start begging. They encouraged Yusuf and me to get up and keep going for the duty, but as usual I asked Yusuf to go for us. Some of them who did not know about my story asked me to follow Yusuf. After I told them my problem, they let me be a watch man of their holes and card boxes. I agreed they might pay me with some begged bone with meat on it.

After they left, the wind began to blow around their boxes and I tried to keep them together from dispersing while counting cars with people running by me. Then Yusuf appeared with a lot of injera in his dirty clothe. We ate injera without any sauce. I asked him, "How begging went for you?" He said, "It was very easy to beg here than Borana. I found most people were nicer. Only a very few people insulted and said rude things to me." After we ate, we craved for smokes. The hogs advised us to wrap a tobacco with a dusty news paper, or cut a piece from wrinkled boxes that we sat on the floor. Entire area filled with stinky smokes that made every hog cough like dinosaurs. I blamed this cough on hogs' tobacco factory.

When lunch time arrived, they gave Yusuf an empty dirty milk powder can to bring food in it. I was little afraid if I was going to eat out of this thing at all. He put it under his armpit like them to fill it with food for us. I watched them dispersing in different directions like wolf hunting for food with cans under their arm pits in a professional hasty manner. That made me laugh a little, but also sad for this kind of life befallen us. Then I was amazed to see that they brought rice, injera mixed with spaghetti and meat sauce. Varieties of breads were also present as if they brought so many provinces together. I realized that the container to be a federal government needed for all types of food to join their arms together to please us. I could not refuse to join them even though the container disgusted me in the first place. I had never tasted a bread and meat in a long time which I missed so much. I kissed and ate until I bulge my ball with them. We hid the rest for dinner in the thorny fence next to us like fridge and protection from danger since we can't beg for dinner. Some hang them on the tree like stars in heaven to shine down on us. It was amazing to see cans were everywhere swinging on top of our heads.

About evening some strangers talking our language came to visit us as if we arrived from another planet. They claimed that they work as security guards and gardeners for some rich people who never lived in them because of many reasons. They also informed me that there were many students from Ethiopia live in Hargeisa, but they did not know where they were at all. I thought I was the only student who came from Ethiopia. If they truly existed in town, I wished some of them came to visit me so that I got information from them. A guy told me to go and verify from others who might know more than him, but he suggested I should first go to Hargeisa's security office for registration as student. It was mandatory for me to go there and avoid many troubles that might arise if I was caught as a student living under the tree. I was scared and decided to go there the next morning, but Yusuf refused to go with me and headed to begging duty for us. I begged a hog to show me the security place and he agreed to wait outside for fearing the place until I was done. When we reached compound's gate, it was closed and I was confused how to enter. Then I saw a Somali guy who was talking through the hole in the gate and then got in. I realised I had to do the same and saw a guard through a hole. I said to him "Hello" in English and he asked, "What do you want?" I told him, "I am refuge." He then opened the gate for me to sit on the chair and wait for security to show up. I was scared what they were going to say until they came. When I was tired of waiting, I had an urge to go and talk to someone, but I did not know which office to go, for there were many offices in the compound. Suddenly a guy came from outside heading to office talked to me in Somali and I indicated to him that I did not speak. He then spoke Amharic to see if I could understand it. I was glad and said, "Yes, I can!" He then said, "Why are you here?" I said, "I am refugee from Ethiopia." He ordered, "Follow me to my office!" My heart shrank a bit to what he was going to do to me since now I doubted that he was probably an officer I came to see. He questioned, "Where did you enter Somalia?"

"Borana," I replied. He asked, "Where is a letter they gave you?" I replied, "They gave me nothing." He asked, "Where are you staying now?" I said, "I live under a tree by Billisa." He said, "I will send you to Mogadishu soon, for now just go back and hug your tree and come back tomorrow morning." I was happy he gave me this news and this security office was nicer than Borana, but I stressed, "You know I was suffering under the tree of hogs and eating begged food." I said it in case it helped me to soften him up some more. He advised, "Be patient, do what you need to do and come back as I said." I was happy with the news and went back to a tree, feeling excited to go to capital city where I might be sleeping like King of Jordan eating cake for breakfast. I trusted him from the way he spoke to me to be very serious. I told Yusuf they might send me away and he was happy for me to go, but he made clear to me he wanted to stay in Hargeisa rather than go to capital city. While I was sad to leave him soon, we ate what he got as if it was our last meal together. I wished he was student like me and now we were going to lose each other.

Next day, after we ate what he brought, I went back and saw many armed officials and colonels, sitting outside office like Ducks surrounded by AK47. My heart wiggled they might do something bad to me. When I was about twenty meters from them, the officer let me in said, "I sent a telegram to Mogadishu for you to go and they refused to accept you. Instead I suggest you go to Wachalle Refugee Camp." I was shocked and disappointed about not going to capital city where I had an opportunity to find a nice bed and food. I didn't know what Wachalle meant and how I would get there, but when I inquired, he said, "Go away, It is NCR's job to take you there, it's somewhere North." He didn't care at all, by not saying very much. I never heard this name NCR before, where it was and what they did. I went back to tree saying NCR, NCR…on the way so that I did not forget it. When I arrived, I did not see any one beside an orphaned kid. I asked him, "Where is NCR?" He said, "I didn't hear it before and where it is located." Since he spoke good Somali, I asked him to go with me to north direction if I could somehow stomp on it. As we were going north, several locals wouldn't know, or heard this name.

After we were exhausted, at last we found someone who knew it and sent us to that building. During my interview, they asked me for letter from the security, but I wondered why the security officials did not give me a letter required by NCR. When I returned to security, they told me to be back in one week to pick up a letter. I returned to my tree getting another hope. By now my hair was very dusty and badly messed up. My clothes were filthy becoming cannibal junkie. A boy from my home town saw me there, but he didn't bother to help me at all. Every time he just passed me by tree as if he did not care at all. After one week I went back and did not find the guy who promised me a letter. I asked office personnel who said they had no idea where about of him. I checked the next day; he did not get a chance to make it ready, for he had gone somewhere urgent. He seemed sorry and asked me to come back in another week. With my brain hanging by thread, I trusted him and went back to my beloved tree.

By now Yusuf became professional beggar. He began begging for money to buy his cigarette. Some time he went half naked above waist and earned a name crazy beggar. One day he was bored and bugged me to follow him. I shouted very fast with him in our language *sadaqa nu kanna*[129] for fun and they seemed to be confused to what we uttered. Then we added our favourite signature sentences which we had no idea what it meant, but seemed amazing *Tigrigna*[130] *Chihin karre kai, Ney mistir lakkum, Uwwe.*[131] Then we cracked in laughter as if we were doing our own comedy talk to them talking Tigrigna language. As these words flew and hit their houses, mostly ladies reply, *Yaa maha tree*[132] and then Yusuf repeats, *Chihin karre kai, Ney mistir lakkum, uwwe.* They kept, "Yaa…" again. They didn't get what he meant. We smiled seeing they were tired of these strange words they didn't seem to understand it. At last, they threw their answers, *Allah Kusiyyo, Wa-hassan.*[133] I again laughed and replied, "Yes! My name is Hassan." It sounded like my last name Hassan, I thought they figured out my last name, but we were two different tribes, one from Jupiter and the other from Pluto. Then we went back empty handed to our tree with only laughter and headache.

Next day, Yusuf went alone and got a whole sheep head with its tongue intact, cooked in rice that I had never seen before. Yusuf didn't feel like eating it. I was scared to touch it for a while, but then hunger and desire to eat meat won me over to pick it up in a strange way and held it in my hand. I found it a little heavy and I began to remove tiny red muscles from its top area with my fingers. I was laughing to myself eating such a weird meat from sheep's head that I had never tasted before in my life, holding it in front of me. Two Somali girls were passing by and saw me eating from this skull and said, *Yaa allah! rer galbet mehay unneyyan!*[134] They laughed hard and looked down on me like some kind of two legged scavenger ransacking a sheep's head under the tree. Once hogs told me what they were saying, their actions twisted my brain and I had forgotten being in

---

[129] Please donate alms.
[130] Tigray ethnic language found in west province of Ethiopia.
[131] Meanings of words we do not know, but it sounded like Tigrigna (one of Ethiopian ethnic languages). For me I was saying we are poor beggars to let you know our secrets, yes indeed.
[132] Yes! What did you say?
[133] God will provide you, or bless you
[134] Oh, God! People of the West, what do they eat?

someone's country and said, *kan anna kariyye?* [135] *Issini bilcheyse ruza wajjin nu kanne!*[136] I stood up fast and felt to throw it after them by swinging over my shoulder. They dashed like frightened chicken saying, *Allah hoggey, wa uwallen.*[137] I was surprised by their reactions and many hogs were spouted with laughter around the tree. Even my action made me my bottom wiggled with a smile. I managed to hang on my meat after they were gone and continued snacking on it. After I ate this scary meat, I went to NCR again and they told me to return in a week time. My shirt and sheet were torn out badly. My face became so dirty and disgusting. The smell of my body disgusted ants and insects passing by me holding their noses. We hardly got begged enough water to drink once a week, let alone to wash hands and bathe with. Hamid, one of our members, sometimes bought charcoal from Somalian camels passing by and selling to some residents. As if he set up his hog business under the tree, he also went to neighboring houses to mop floor for money. He was funny and very pudding headed person. He told Yusuf that craziness will be cured and turned off if he had removed his front two teeth which looked like a mouse. I would be cured if I got some cash. Some hog would be fine if they got a lot of begged food while some needed to get married to resolve their madness. Everyone loved his show like opera to kill the time. We had a good time even if we looked very disgusting and messed up animals. I went back to NCR after five days as I was told, but I was unable to find a person I was looking for. I kept going there almost every day hoping to see him.

One morning as we woke up, Hamid could not find his pant to put on. He cried very loudly, "There was nine hundred shillings in it. Now it's gone. My money...." Every one stunned to hear this and became very sad for his loss. It looked as if the king of the wild hog passed away right there. Our jaws wide opened this could not be true. Some feared that a new guy I was not aware of slept with us the night. He might have taken off with it early morning before we

---

[135] Did I cook this?
[136] You cooked and gave us with rice (my language).
[137] Oh my God, this guy is crazy.

were awoke since he was not there in the morning. Some hogs ran in all directions to find this suspected guy being too sad for Hamid. His craziness doubled this time more than before. He ran with no pant on, in search of a thief to catch him in case he found him at the bus stop. Hog's tree foundation had been shaken with category ten earthquake for his loss. No one had a feeling to beg, or eat this morning. Doubt fog covered the tree and everyone became smog. Being confused with many things, I went to chase my letter and I found no luck.

When I returned back to our sad house, still there was no sight of Hamid's money and pant. Hamid told his loss to people he knew in the area. They doubted Yusuf to be the culprit. They promised Hamid to help him continue his business. Hamid didn't calm down and kept telling everyone about the story including Somali residents he worked for. They went and told Sheik Billisa since their relation were strong with him. At midnight, Billisa ordered his guards to kick us out from the tree for good early morning except Hamid. We were in disbelief this happened to us. Early morning as Billisa was passing by tree, he saw we were still there. He didn't seem to forget what he said at night and shouted toward us, "Despite my order you still here!" He yelled at guards, "Why are these people still here?"

"Leave immediately!"

They shouted and ran toward us with gun in a threatening manner. Now everyone knew this was very serious business and quickly grabbed their torn flat boxes and news papers and began running fearing that we might be arrested or beaten by guards. Yusuf and I also ran for our lives. It was the darkest day for me in Hargeisa, for there was no safe place to sleep and stay as we were told before. My vein with the tree was severed. I was sad and mad to see many young kids and seniors to be dismantled from their units. Billisa didn't care if we all suffered and died.

Having no choice where to go, Yusuf and I with three other people agreed to go to NCR to force them to take us to Wachalle refugee camp as soon as possible hearing to be a safer place for new arrivals. If they did not send us there, we decided to stay in their compound fearing our death to be imminent. As we waved our torn shirts and clothes all the way to NCR, a soldier tried to stop us from getting in the compound. We told him that we were in serious danger and he let us wait for an officer to arrive. When officer arrived, we told him we needed to go to Wachalle to be safe, for we were kicked out by Billisa. He told us to come next day to do something, but we told him we had no place to sleep. We could be in danger, and we must sleep in this compound to be safe until tomorrow. Then he decided to take us to a place he thought safe to sleep until next day with one person who was a speaker of our language. Then the speaker welcomed us for the night in the compound he monitored, but advised us to leave early morning before the owner of the compound found us there. We agreed, at least we were safe until morning. Yusuf and others went to beg early morning for breakfast and I waited outside that compound until they returned.

When I was tired of waiting for a long time outside watchman's compound, I decided to enter close by teahouse seemed owned by a soldier. An owner felt that I was kind of beggar and ordered an employee to give me pasta. When I finished it in a very greedy way, he ordered more to be added to my plate. When I said enough with my hand, he insulted, *un abba hawas*[138] I knew this insult and offended by it just for food. When he ordered tea, I raised my hand to say enough feeling shy and robbed his Café, but he bombarded and blessed me the same way. I filled my tummy with his kindness and insult and at last gave up being mad at him. When I told someone what happened, he detailed for me that this was how a Somali guy would treat you whether he liked you, or not. They themselves blessed each other this way and once you understood their language you would understand that it meant nothing at all. They would also call you and each other the way you and they appeared rather than names: *Sanka yare, Afaka balladdan, Ga'amow, Indolle,*[139] etc., and no one got mad at all. Thinking about all these names, how the insult was accepted and they said Yes to it, cracked me with laughter even though I was suffering with problems. Then Yusuf came with oth-

---

[138] Eat! Father F…
[139] Small nose, bigger mouth, arm less, blind.

ers empty handed and starving, but I was lucky for being insulted and eaten very well. Then those guys came with Yusuf took us to a hut made of sacks, torn rugs, and canvas to sleep the night that was owned by someone from our country. We spread on ground the news paper and boxes we brought from hog tree. I slept very well until morning since I arrived in Hargeisa because there was no cold wind to beat me like it did at hogs' tree.

Before dawn, we had to wake up and go outside the hut so that the owner could have his privacy making his tea and breakfast before he went to his work. It was so cold at this part of town being on the hill, we had to wrap and smoke old card board to warm up our lungs until morning came. Then Yusuf asked me to go with him to find breakfast. I again begged him to get me as usual because I didn't feel to go with him. He said, "I can't bring to you here, at least you have to go to Billisa area to get it." I said, "This is a bad idea for Billisa was already mad at us."

"That place is very lucky for me and we might see new comers, too." He tried to convince me, for he wanted to hang around there and he felt it to be the best place for him. He added, "If you remember last time, I made fifty shillings around Billisa's compound which I bought cigarette for us by fixing a car for someone." He tried to lure me in, to hang around there until we left Hargeisa. He seemed not to waste his time coming too far away to bring me food. To ease my hunger and let him win, I agreed to hang around there and go back to a hut afterward. When I arrived at Billisa's about 8am, I didn't see Yusuf, but there was only Hamid sitting under the tree, but a clothe hanging on the side of the tree looked like Yusuf to me. As I approached it, I found it to be Yusuf's sheet. I wondered where he had gone by hanging his dress there, but I found food in it which I ate for breakfast. I went to search for him fearing Billisa might have arrested him. After I searched for him for a while, I saw him to be safe. He told me to get the food he hanged on a tree with his clothes. I told him, "I saw it and already swallowed it, thank you!" He was happy I ate it. Then I decided to hang around him until lunch time. When he left to beg for lunch, I waited there for him. After we ate lunch, he didn't want to go with me to that hut. In the evening, Yusuf arrived with only one guy while others didn't show up.

When midnight approached, we still didn't see others and we were worried about them. I decided to go to NCR in the morning, but first I wanted to try security personnel why I didn't get a letter to NCR from them. When I arrived, I saw other person like me with a security guy who was rejected by Mogadishu. My dirty appearance and worn out clothe didn't make me like normal human being which seemed to filled him with sadness that I read on his face. I begged him to help me for I was in a dangerous state. He right away grabbed a form, told me to fill it, and bring to him in seven days. I broke the news to Yusuf when I met him to eat breakfast. He said, "Initially I want to leave Hargeisa because we didn't have place to sleep, but finding that hut where I can nap, I will never leave Hargeisa. While begging for food, I might find a watch man's job to set my life here." This was a clear cut for me that he wanted to stay in town. If I stayed with him, he would never get tired to feed me with alms as usual, or he was willing to let me go to Wachalle if I wanted.

In the evening, one of the lost guys came, and I asked, "What happened to you?" He replied, "I found a nice place to stay with a few who left hog's tree and I stayed with them, but when I inform the guy that there was also one educated boy kicked out with us, he asked your name and I was unable to tell him even where you were born. Then he felt that you might be related to him and I came to get you." I wondered who could be saying this thing since I had no any relative in Somalia as far as I knew unless he might be from *Fellana,* Grandmother's birthplace where we ran with my family during war times. When we went there, we did not see him, but someone called him from a place he went and he just said my name as he approached me. He seemed to recognize me even though I had no idea who he was. He, at last confirmed to me that he was related to me by grandma of *Fellana* and I was happy he said this. He could not help me very much, but he took me to a place he knew I could at least take a shower. It was luxurious marble house of rich Somali that took my breath away, but its owner might have not lived in town, or country. I was glad to take a shower in a long time and able to put down dirt as thick as hippo skin that moved on the ground like snake. I released some dust off my torn clothe with water only. He did not get his wage to help me with money and he had no food to give me either. I told him not to worry about food; for I had a friend who could beg for me. I found out that there were very dangerous gangsters who lived in this compound forcing people to bring them snatched tomato, potato, and onion from town for them to survive there. They were the most sophisticated thieves I had ever seen so far in my life. I didn't feel all right to stay there and I went back to that hut saying fare well to a relative person hoping to see him someday.

Next morning after breakfast and lunch ended, Yusuf and I were standing by small bridge next to Billisa's just relaxing. When five beautiful school girls were passing by us, Yusuf wanted me to pay attention to them. As I looked, he asked me to sing an English song probably wanting me to impress them the same way we used to do under the tree before we were kicked out by Billisa, for some men and women including school children were mocking and looking down on us. Sometimes they called us Abboy like we were lower quality people, speaking *budhu badha*[140] language under tree. *wariyya abboy! negedda*[141] *budhu badha* as if we were talking trash, meaningless language. Understanding this pain, I had to throw some words of English to stop them from saying bad things to us. Young and older passerby began to be impressed how this dirty abboy beggar from Ethiopia could speak English. Then they began to treat us like civilized black people from the west if not of Caucasian people of America, just little dark on the outside. Sometimes even young students stood there trying to talk with me in English and spend hours and hours smiling after school until a few bad ass and family come to kick them out, not to spend time around dirty beggars like us. Once a while I had also seen some students were dragging themselves hesitating to pass us to school being very late which I would blame myself for taking their time from school even though I became some kind of celebrity under the tree. Today, when Yusuf asked me to sing

---

[140] No meaning sound
[141] Stop

what I thought my favourite song of Diana Ross for these five girls passing by. I was motivated by their beauty and his encouragement. I started, "Someone talk me hide in the Night, jacha ra hibe,[142] I am just coast toast tin levy…babe, some more somewhere." I saw all five girls lost breathe right away. They were so happy even so I doubted I didn't get the song right. To all of us, I was sure it sounded great song that we enjoyed together. I repeated this song a few times and when I ran out of my songs, they headed their way north by taking a narrow bushy road. Yusuf and I spent some more time on the bridge. After feeling a little tired, I said, "Yusuf, let's go home!" He replied, "I want to hang around here until evening." Then I left him as usual going north toward the hut taking that narrow road and saw those five girls standing in the middle of this tight road I was going. They seemed swinging their tail side to side as if they were uncomfortable seeing me coming toward them. I hoped they had no issue with a boy just sung for them with his favourite Diana Ross song who looked very stinky.

As I came closer to pass them, my heart ringed how they were going to react, or say. When I reached in the middle, one smiled at me while some others moved to the side to let me pass, but one jumped like kangaroo to the side as if I was crazy anaconda going to swallow her. She cried, *wa huwallen*.[143] I stretched my hand pretending to grab her in a joking manner. Unfortunately, she stumbled and fell down on the side road, unable to control herself, for there was no enough room to jump from me. I was shocked and felt very sorry that this happened and tried to help her get off the ground. She screamed like fox as if I was going to suffocate her alive. Then I tried to calm her down from fear by putting my hand under her chin just like we do in our country and begged her in my language with respect being sorrow for her, *addee hin soddatin, anni humma sin goddu*.[144] She then grabbed a huge stone from side road very quickly and smashed on my leg below the knee. It shot me about a couple

---

[142] No idea what it means, maybe I screwed her song.
[143] He is crazy.
[144] Sister, don't be scared, I won't hurt you.

of meters away from her as her companions squeezed far toward a strange guy who was coming our way. He stood in front of them holding his waist with two hands. She seemed to enjoy and smile at how I held my leg and cried of pain while she got up and collecting her scattered books. Without threatening her, I swung my finger at her just like we did in our country indicating that she did bad thing to me while I tried to help her. Then I leapt away holding my leg and approached the guy who seemed from my country who told me they insulted him as *wariyya abboy* and they looked like disdaining him as they were trying to pass him. I saw him, he looked very angry at them. The girls stood there and watched us talking. Then a young Somali suddenly came from behind them and they filled him with gas and bullet pointing finger at us. He then dashed straight toward me ninety kilometers an hour with a tiger face. He seriously commanded me, *wariyya kaley*.[145] I said to him, *abbo dem- nurra*[146] in my language to show serious refusal. He didn't know what I said, but it was as if a zebra refusing instruction of a lion to come to it. I read his intention from his hand as a sign to say come with me I was taking you to prison, or beat me some where he liked. I was afraid he might take me where no one would see him killing me. I refused to obey him and ready to fight back in case he hit me because he was skinny mosquito like me, but little bigger than me.

Seeing my refusal and being very ready with dangerous fist, he put his hand in pocket as if to pull knife, or gun on me. Then his hand came with paper Id showing that he was a sergeant which I confirmed. My heart sweated and dripped tears in my belly. I knew I was doomed today. Then he repeated, *wariyya Kaley!* Showing me he had power to take me. I knew I was going to be arrested for sure and my heart pounded like dying pig. I decided not to go, but started arguing with my language which he could not understand that I was innocent and did not hurt these girls. I bubbled in many languages about what happened, to make him understand not my fault. I did not harm any of these girls. I showed him my bruise where she

[145] You come with me.
[146] Go away, leave me alone.

unfairly hit me. At last, he declared, *wariyya so'oo*[147] in a punching manner. I was relieved and jumped away from him hearing the word *so 'oo*. I said, "I came so close to danger just playing with girls and I never ever play with any of them again." When I was passing by their school, those girls saw me and ran away saying the crazy boy had come. Then all the kids on the street and in the school yard ran like lion entered some herds. I prayed to God not to bring another trouble to me. My heart drummed more and more. At last, I reached hut thanking my God I was safe.

On the fifth day, as usual I went to find Yusuf for my breakfast and I could not see him. While I was wondering around, I saw a car dashing toward me as if someone wanted to run over me. I ran as much as I could to escape from it to the nearest bush. It followed me as if it determined to kill me there. I made my Shehada[148] this was the end of my life and my heart cracked open like peanut. I knew that whoever doing this had serious intention to kill me. Then a car barely stopped by touching my knees. When I looked inside, I saw the security guy who interviewed me. He rolled down a window and gave me a form to fill, and bring it back to his office. I was so scared I was in trouble when he said, "*Fuul.*" I was uncomfortable to get on it, but no choice at all for this was an officer who had power over me. I jumped on loading part of a truck. Then he told me to get down and get in by opening next door to front raw cabin behind him. My stomach trembled about what to happen and where he was taking me. He asked, "Did you eat a breakfast?" I replied, "Not yet, I am just looking for my friend to bring me begged bread when you got me." He did not say anything. I was bothered when he took me far out of town to a remote building which had a flag on it. He talked to someone like authority there that he got me from living on the street the reason why I looked so filthy. I saw him to be very sad for me and he asked security to help me. A security then passed me to another person. This person took me to a place like office and interviewed me. He then passed me to a head commissioner who asked me to

---

[147] You! Go now.
[148] Confirmation of death by Muslims.

prove to him that I was student. When I gave him my documents, he could not believe that was me in the picture as if I had a face change, or stolen these documents from someone else. It took him a while to trust me and he was amazed by it. I tried to explain how I was suffering all this times in the town. My eyes were filled with tears hardly explained my suffering while choking on the truth. I sat quietly while tears were running down my cheeks. They told me to wait until mid day then the office was closed. They instructed me to return in two days to give me some help since office will be closed next day. I had no idea what this office standing for and what kind of help they would give me. I was happy that at least something was happening for me.

In two days, I had returned the form of security as I was told and headed to that help place and surprised to find so many students from my country as refugees. They gave me form to fill for the interview just like them why I came to Somalia. Then some officers came and asked, "Are you registered with us?" I said to them, "Yes." After interview, they told me to come back next day. When I went back, they gave me four hundred Somalian shillings and asked me to return next day to sign a document. I couldn't believe the money filled my pocket as if they had given me all shillings in the banks of Somalia. I had never had these much money before and it looked like I had kicked begging life out of Yusuf. I feared we did not need to beg again. I ran to find Yusuf to stop him from begging so that we went to our dream restaurant. Once I found him and showed all that money, he was excited and we entered a nice restaurant, but we didn't know how to say we wanted to eat an ox meat. I raised both hands over my head like horn of ox to order its meat. They didn't get it, but gave us very weird meat. I realized that we got a camel meat, which I did not like. When Yusuf dared and ate, I was surprised and shied to leave it, but tried a little while picturing and gagging the animal I was eating. It looked tasty, but I couldn't eat much with fear, it might hurt me, or turn me to a camel itself. I ate mostly the rice and they asked two hundred shillings for damages done by us. I was surprised that half of the shillings given to me were gone in one sitting. I realized the money was not enough to retire Yusuf from begging. I sadly

274

announced to him to continue his begging for us. Next day, I went to sign papers as they told me, hoping money kept flowing like Nile River to me onward from this building. When I came back next day, I only got one blanket not money and clothing I expected. After so many days and effort, at last I got the letter I was expecting to NCR. When I went NCR office with happiness to get a place to live and much more, they only dragged me here and there, from this leader to another. I complained that I badly needed to eat and a place to live. "Are you willing to go to Tug Wachalle?" They asked me. I replied to them, "Yes!" having no other choice and believing that it was better place where I could live peacefully and ate without begging at all. I left with happy face when they told me to come back next day. I decided to go, the only way to get out of these problems I had in Hargeisa.

Next morning, I went to NCR and they gave me two letters. One to take to Wachalle with me and other one to give to a place called Elu-Care before I went to Tug Wachalle which I had no idea where it was and the reason for it. When I asked someone, I was showed a big compound to be Elu-Care. When I got there, I saw the security head councillor at its' entrance. He saw my letter to Wachalle and shook his head as if the letter was invitation to the gate of hell, or wrongly given to me. I felt that they should treated me like student refugees. My gut was not happy, but I had no choice about my decision, seeking and dreaming place to rest and sleep even if for two days. I had goose bumps when he added a comment they should have sent me to sub office rather than Wachalle. He urged me to come back next day with my letter as if he was going to save me from shark tank. When I returned next day, I could not find him. After a few days searching for him, I went to his office, and guards let me in. Then I saw one white man I had never seen before. When I greeted him by shaking his hand, the councillor got mad, "Why did you come?" I did not know what to say as if he was against shaking and talking with a white man would bring something out of hiding, or disastrous things. Then he later said, "Go to Wachalle, I will give you cooking utensils." Since I heard a rumor that I would get them in wachalle, I told him not to give me here.

Next day, they took me to a refugee camp two kilometers from Hargeisa and gave me, one and half kilograms of rice, two hundred fifty millimeters of oil, and one palm dates for ten days until I went to Wachalle. I was confused what to do with it since I had no place and utensils to cook them. I ran to Yusuf with them so that he would not beg for food until we finished them. I asked a hut boy to cook for us. The next day, I had to go to Wachalle as they ordered me. I was unwillingly waved my hands to Yusuf and his begged little injeras with rice that I would no longer see. I could not hold my tears to lose them from my sight especially Yusuf who was like my mother. It was as if we were heading toward Ethiopia. My stomach began shaking for Wachalle to be at the border of Somalia and Ethiopia. I was afraid that Ethiopian army might run over us, or shell if war broke between them. When we reached Wachalle, I saw it to be little special and excited, but there was heavy dust war that wanted to crush my face. Tents were covered by dust and many new arrivals that smelt like fresh Ethiopians. I stood in long line to register, get tents and rations. I was surprised by fountain of families of refugees with sick kids crying as they covered with dust. A guy asked me if I was a student refugee and I proved to him with my documents. He informed me that there were two students in the camp which he introduced to me. Then those guys welcomed me with open arms that made me happy. They wanted me to stay with them until I got my own tent. They showed me the leader of the camp who would register and give me a ration. When I went to him; he asked me, "Where do you stay now?" I told him, "I am temporarily staying with students." He said, "All right, stay with them for the time being and later you will get a tent which you erect next to them if you want."

"Can I get utensils?" I inquired. He replied, "I do not have a key to the warehouse right now, just stay with those guys for now like others." I was somewhat excited to be with them having not to suffer like Hargeisa. They filled me in about many students that were not happy in this camp and left for Hargeisa, but some of them still coming back just to collect their rations and return back to Hargeisa. Some of them also left ration card so that those left in the camp would collect for them on their behalf to pick them later. They added that recently the authorities were on the lookout for those students leaving and coming back. Things were getting tougher and tougher especially leaving this camp. This news discouraged me from leaving the camp. I also heard that previously camp leaders were sending a lot of students to another camp since this place were not permanent one. The food given to them was not enough, but Abdu had three people rations while Yaku got twenty students rations that were left for him and became rice and oil rations billionaire at the border. When they cooked this food, I watched them and made porridge for myself. I was happy to prepare my food despite the ration was not enough for ten days. We had to fetch very scarce firewoods from far away, but water was brought to us to the camp by truck from the moon it looked. After we washed our clothes, we hang them between two tents to dry, and they quickly got very muddy when dusts of the border hit them right away.

When the numbers of refugees increased, they brought more tents and the camp became very big tent city. We went and visited many of them as they came and at last they began sending them to permanent place, for there was no enough water and firewood in the area. My new friends began to hate me because of these shortages. They sold their flours for cash and bought lantern. Abdu began nagging and started to cook and eat alone. He disagreed with yaqu almost on everything and at last moved by himself. He told me, "We cannot leave together at all." Yaqu also verified to me that Abdu didn't like me in the first place. They had several arguments with each other. When I asked for my utensil, a leader did not have anything to give me except a blanket. So I had to stay with Yaqu as camp leader told me and we used my tent for taking shower. I tried to cook in a can just like some people were doing. The food was burning and it smelt like rusted pan. I heard that utensils would be given at bigger camp so I begged a camp leader to move me to the bigger camp, or take me to Hargeisa to get them. I also requested to write me a letter to take to Hargeisa so I could show that I was refugee at Tug Wachalle and needed utensils. He then said, "I can't write a letter to anyone except NCR." Then Yaqu and I asked him to take us to Hargeisa. He did not say anything. After we bothered him to put us on a car to Hargeisa, he finally ordered us to jump on it. Then Yaqu and I were gladly jumped on it, but a Leader who might be from East Indian descent finished talking to someone and he saw us on a car and got very upset. He ran toward a car and ordered us to get off it right away. "We have utensils problem please let us go," we begged him. "It is getting darker now. The soldiers will stop me at check point and they will not let you go with me," he turned engine off and dashed toward us in an aggressive manner. As we tried to argue with him, he kicked us off. We then went to a camp leader and suggested, "We want to go to main refugee camp where we get items we need." He, at last said, "You can go wherever you want. It is up to you." I gave my suggestion to go to Agagub[149] Camp that I heard might be a good place to go where my friend agreed to go with me. I realized now why every student ran away from this miserable camp.

The next night, there nine trucks came to scoop refugees and we were happy to jump on it. The leader was surprised, "Do you really want to go with these people?" We afraid and hesitate, "Yes! There is no utensil here, better to go if we at least get cooking utensils." He said, "All right! Go ahead." seemed happy getting rid of us while knowing it might be a wrong decision on our side. They handed us a small roll of dates to eat for the long trip. We filled all nine trucks to Agagub. I did not know where we were going, but we passed many dusty, bumpy rocks, and mountains to the direction of Borana where I was choked by meat. This reminded me my nightmare at town of Borana and prayed not to settle anymore at border area. Many collided head to head, shoulder to shoulder, and children were weeping and whining as they suffered in the valley and hills by trucks hurting them. It was the most distasteful and bitter ride I had ever seen where dates shot out of our mouth like bullet toward each other as tires slammed with rocks and jumped in and out of holes. With this road condition, I doubted if we were ever reaching Agagub in one piece. We travelled whole day and night facing many scary checks points. We then reached a place called Darbahure a big flat town with many lanterns by side of a nice river. I hoped to be Agagub where I could dive like a duck to cool my burning stinky body. I was disappointed we passed Darbahure and went far to reach Agagub.

---

[149] Foot scorcher

CHAPTER 9

Flamed Claw in Agagub

Agagub was a valley with tiny bushes scattered everywhere like hair of bees, a place where ants cried my God! My God! What you forsaken me. White thorns exploded like popcorn and they began smiling at me from everywhere. The sun started frying my claws and testis, no wonder burning name was given to it. It had warm cooling river, surrounded by immensely huge bald mountains, grinner of my soul. I was dreaming all along to have a soap and utensil since I arrived in Somalia and I felt I would get them here for seeing this huge refugee camp as big as city. I could not have imagined seeing such place far away land of Somalia. Residents came out like ants to wave their hands as if we were kings of kings and queen of queens, but no energy left in me to swing my claws back to them. I was freaked out, when trucks passed this heavenly Jordan River I had feeling for which I thought they were going to stop by it. After all, I was sad that we might end up in a worst place. As we went little further, we saw other side of refugee camp where we stopped. I felt it, this is it. Now it looked real. I could still smell a river, which excited me believing that I was still around it. As we were trying to get off, they told us we had to go further more. I was shocked we were still not there and sat down thinking we might be going to a bad area. They told me we were going to real Agagub and this was not the one. I was also shocked knowing the area was dangerously scorching; the reason this name was given to it.

We finally arrived to our destination and it was not as beautiful as the area of Agagub I saw earlier. I was happy at least not very far from bigger village of Agagub and that river still ran closer to where they were dumping us. There were many new mud buildings and structures under construction with new tents being erected. Those came before us, still not settled completely, looking for places to be given. They moved us in a big compound surrounded by thorns and there we saw some Somali and Oromo speakers. The place looked different from what I had seen before. We bolted down and headed to prickly big compound gate so big it swallowed us. The soldiers put us like chicks under hen, not to mix with others so that they protected rations fraud from happening. We were unable to drink water, or beg for food from villagers. About midnight, leaders of the camp came to control our names so that it matched to the lists we came from Wachalle to give us rations. Some people were allowed to grab water over thorny fence. I was extremely tired and weakened with my friend. We slept like dead fish over stone and ground that were uncomfortable to the body and mind. I was hardly woken up in the early morning wind. They then showed us our new settlement area to make our nest. I started digging ground like armadillo and tossing rocks like chicken. I was surprised preparing my own spot and smearing my scent like hyena so far from Hargeisa to make my home. All I had and would have was only one ration, which would not be enough for one week which worried me more. My friends made spot little far from me closer to Somali speakers.

I wondered why I got spot little far from them making myself a lonely pussy. When I was thinking to get closer to them, I saw the little orphaned boy walking toward me who used to be the smallest hog member under the tree in Hargeisa who became my interpreter. I could not believe it was him, but he assured me it was him. He confirmed to me getting here via Wachalle when Billisa removed us from hog tree. Because he saw I was dying to eat, he ran and begged *borash*[150] and gave it to me as his hungry old friend. I was so happy to see him there and rescuing my life. After I swallowed those balls, we laughed and laughed as much as we could, saying *chihin karre kai ney mister lakkum uwwe* recalling about hog tree life that we had together in Hargeisa. While we were laughing, my friends showed up and invited us to stay together. We did not know where people got tree, but when we asked them, they said they got them from behind far mountain, which seemed had no tree on it. When they told us the distance and time it would take to bring one tree, it was like telling a camel to pass through an eye of a needle. My colleagues wanted to bring one bundle of trees each without bothering me which would be enough to build base for our place. I was relieved and happy they let me stayed behind. I questioned, "Is this really where I end the rest of my life?"

"No green tree! I was afraid my eyes will be pale dry, never to see green again!" Losing hope I would be the only person in my generation to live place like this. I recalled back home the gardens, the flowers, the vegetables, the big lakes, and the green grasses as tall as my height I could be hiding in it, variety of birds, the trees, and the animals. My eyes were like someone baked them in clay. I was afraid if they survived and lasted longer to see what they deserved to see like in my country.

My friends brought some woods in the after noon after travelling almost all day. Their faces dried like leaves and they were unable to talk like human. After they rested, we dug holes for posts and tried to build, but unable to do like Somalis. A Somali lady saw us and said, "You men of the west, you don't even know how to build a house!" She showed and helped us to build it. I was surprised how she helped us quickly with our place to sleep. I saw Somalian women being too strong, they built houses of all types and brought food to the table while their men, mostly just sat around with wooden toothbrush, or wooden toothpick in their mouth and played their games. Our suffering continued without utensil to cook and at night we stared to each other in the dark like owls. Suffering got worse

---

[150] Golf-sized flour balls, sometimes rounded as shape of an egg.

and continued even here where I thought it would be eliminated. I doubted I might die in Agagub.

My mind had almost blown worrying how to survive this miraculous new life. I compared the begging life of Hargeisa to this Agagub and hoped this might be better than begging. Despite little problems, I came to appreciate being saved under United Nations flag standing in the desert. I wondered how UN able to support these father and motherless refugees, young and old with no jobs at all. The amount of food that came every week by trucks was mind boggling. I didn't know which country, or countries called UN and give all these rations, but it amazed me while hoping they didn't starve their own people to save us all. I thanked those countries when I saw their names on the grains and supplies like Canada, USA, Australia, Britain, French, Russia, Germany, Italia, etc.

On the fourth day, at last, I got rations after they verified that I didn't get it second time. We made porridge without any dipping sauce for several days that kept being stuck in my throat like constipated rectum. We tried to make flat bread by cutting a can in half and burnt it. We had no tent, just slept on the open sky, counting droppings from the stars. When I begged a leader for shirt since mine was badly torn from front and back and looked like a rug of scarecrow. He said that all of us had the same problem and I must wait for it. He gave me three old grain sacks to cover one side of hut posts for the time being which was not enough to cover all. Winds were saying hello and kept slapping us from three sides. My toes were curling to the ground while my skirt shrank like elephant mouth.

Next day, I was awarded a pant that could swallow at least three huge men and a shirt that was made for sumo wrestlers of Japan which my body swam in it like mosquito. I thanked them at least I could say goodbye to my wrinkled and torn clothes. I was happy being able to take a bath at the river using sand as a soap to wash my new outfit and body. The sand scratched my skin and my dresses were faded, but using sand to wash my skin and clothes was the best discovery of my life in Somalia. I encouraged my friends to do same like me.

After two months' scorching heat and long wait, tents had finally arrived in the camp to be given, but they said only those families of three, or more could get it. I was disappointed that we were again given ten empty bags of flour to cover part of the hut, which made me sad because it would not stop the sun, the wind, and the dust completely. I had requested cooking pot, spoons, cups, and pail several times and the answer was the same, "I am not different than others." Luckily they afforded to give me a sweater and a sheet and they told me to move on. Our area looked like a new town as new tents erected by families and noises had risen like bees. I was happy with the changes and little progress of getting some items, but no cook ware. Again, I went to complain, but they told me to come back next day. When I returned, they gave me a big box to take home. I was happy feeling all utensils of my dream were in it, but there was only a pot. I felt I was given a wrong box and shocked that a big box had only one item in it. We enjoyed the cooking pot, besides our hut looked like chimney waving its wings on my head. When rain came, it whipped me up in the hut. I wanted to run away since I couldn't stand flashing of the lighting besides the fear of hyena, but I had nowhere to go. I thought about getting away looking for work as I heard that Zeyla was the only close town to Agagub where I might get a job. I heard some people went there to work, but it was very scary military town where soldiers could arrest me under suspicion to get away to neighboring Djibouti. They also checked everyone's movement in town and not knowing language, I could be arrested as spy from Ethiopia.

Hearing Zeyla being at edge of Indian Ocean, I was eager to see it since I learnt in geography, but too dangerous and risky business and I gave up the idea. I thought about going to Hargeisa if I got a chance to be a watch man, but it was only a daydream from there unless I begged trucks going there. I begged the camp leader to take me to Hargeisa. He wanted to know why I wanted to go there. I showed him my worn out clothes and wounded body. I tried to convince him that if I worked there and get some money, I might be able to buy these things and come back here. He gave me a reason, "I have only a private car, and it is not possible to take you there."

283

He suggested, "You might ask those trucks which bring ration from Hargeisa." The keeper gave me hope that the trucks came every ten days and I must try my chance. Then I asked for utensils and he said that it might come in a month, or so. I was happy with all these news and went back to my hut. When trucks came in ten days, I didn't like these ones and I tried another leader. He said, "I must wait for a person called Abdusalam." When he came and I asked him, he would take me in the morning. When I returned in the AM, his car was already full. He apologized to take me another day. When I saw him another day, he disappointed me again by saying, "I am going to Derbahare, I will come back to get you." I waited and waited and he never came back for a long time.

While I was waiting another ten days for a truck, there at last tent and utensils arrived and given to us. They were also blindly pitching something round that was tied together toward people which looked like clothes. I was glad catching one of it, believing it to be a nice dress for me. When I went home and opened it, I found them to be a lady items: socks, underwear, shirt, frock, and head scarf. I was so disappointed and wished I was a woman right away to indulge my body in them. I also found something similar to pants, which I didn't figure out if it was for woman or man. I suspected to be woman's trouser, but I put it on anyway since it seemed to me that it was not a traditional wear there. My mom's wish for me to be her beautiful girl in the past might have come true if she had seen me with this thing. The trouser I had before was full of lice. One day when I suspended on top of fire to kill these vampires; it was burnt halfway like meat. I kept my skin healthy with this new pants, and spread out the rest to ladies and kids in the area. We kept orphan boy's tent and mine, and put the others on the roof. I was happy to get all things, but my legs were shaking up with a desire to go.

When I went for washroom business very far to hide my testicles and whinnies the poo behind a small bush from view of the camp, my friends told me that a truck had already came and left. I was shocked by the bad news and regretted why I left and ran to find it just to make sure it had gone. When I saw it, it was ready to leave. I ran to camp office and asked them to help me. They slaughtered me,

"Where were you? You were too late!" I begged them very hard and he quickly wrote a letter and gave it to me. I ran none stop and gave to a driver. He scanned with his eyes quickly and gave it back to me and took off. I could not believe he ignored and didn't care what the letter had said to him. While I was watching its dust behind it, then it had stopped about five hundred meters by river. I ran like cheetah and saw him collecting fare from people. Again I gave him the letter and he threw at me asked for fare. I wondered what the letter was saying since it had been written in Somali language. I used an interpreter to explain about my problems, but he still needed me to pay him. My interpreter suggested I should sell my tent and make a fare money, which I didn't know if it was possible and enough money for the fare. I ran to one of my new friend to give me the money and kept my tent and utensils as bond until I repaid him later coming back from Hargeisa. If I did not come back, I allowed him to keep them. He refused my offer. Then I asked a neighbor to keep the tent and give me one thousand shillings for the trip and he agreed learning my problems. I ran back to the truck, but it had already left. I was disappointed and returned back to camp. I gave back the money to neighbor and able to sell my tent for one thousand and four hundred shillings. My cooking pot had also earthed four hundred shillings.

At last, I had enough shillings for the truckers that came from Djibouti, but due to heavy rain and flood I heard passing through the valley was not possible and why the truckers were unable to come. I had to stay three days more and saw couple of people wanted to go to Darbahare on foot. So I decided to go with them. When we reached Darbahare, we were exhausted, but could not find any truck. Again we decided to go on foot from there, but we heard that soldiers were restricting refugees going back to Wachalle to cheat on rations: some did it to get rich by selling rations as a new comer, or some didn't have enough ration so they registered under new name to get more food. I was surprised that there were some rich refuges in the desert enjoying and living comfortable life while others were trying to survive doing crazy things. Rumor of rebels in the countryside had also scared me because we might be taken and killed as rodents in their land they were trying to liberate. If not, military posts might shoot us assuming we were rebels.

While fearing these two groups, we decided to go on foot taking our chances. It was nerve wrecking to walk miles and miles where there were no trees and bushes that could hide us. My heart began to beat harder and harder heading out of camp, expecting to be caught at any time. We walked for four hours none stop and there at last soldiers drawn guns on us to stop moving forward. My heart popped, "Death came up on us." Then we were questioned, "Where do you come from?"

We replied, "Agagub refugee camp."

"Abboy?" one asked. We said, "Yes." Then a fire lit on his face. "You are going to Wachalle to cheat rations!"

"No! We are going to Hargeisa," we strongly answered. Miraculously he let us go without harm. We then begged army's truck that was already loaded with civilians to pick us from street. They refused and we continued to walk on foot being happy at least they let us go. It looked we had to walk on foot for whole day in a rugged mountains when rocks made me think this journey would be impossible. I learned that we had to be at Harirro before end of the day. If we failed to reach it, we could be a supper for rebels and Somalian army. Fear calibrated my muscles to go up and down the dangerous desert rocky mountains and terrains like I did during war time. I feared my family would never know where I was killed if something murdered me. After a hard journey, we saw long sand where we dug to get water to drink and met some people who told us that our grave would be here if we didn't make it to Harirro. They ignited more fear's fuel in my stomach like triple seven aeroplane and we began walking like ostrich as it was getting darker. We were at last happy to reach Harirro alive, but happiness had shrunken very fast seeing many RBG-7 with soldiers and trucks of machine guns running around as if they were ready to open fire. We had no idea where to stay the night, for we didn't know the town. Sleeping on the street didn't feel right how soldiers ran around and luckily they didn't say anything to us. When we found a teahouse to rest and ordered tea, soldier wanted to know who we were and we told them we were refugees going to Hargeisa. They told us to sleep where our country men were collected for the time being, or we faced danger at teahouse.

When we went where we were told, there were many people gathered like chicken as the town's guests whom army might had put them. It looked safe for us to sleep the night. I was sad to see people had nothing to eat and some of them were wondering around for months without help after they suffered all the way to come here with children. I heard the army might help them go to Wachale's refugee camp. Then I heard from these people that there was a clash between rebels and Somalian army the night before. "We were lucky to be alive from explosions," they said. I was now scared that we might die this night if they went at it again. I kept praying with shaking lips unable to sleep the whole night listening for gun sounds over my head and then the sun smiled at me. As morning sun shined, we saw a hundred-year-old military truck loading people to Wachalle. We begged them to give us a ride. They asked us to pay two hundred shillings. I was scared of this shaggy truck to end my life, but rather than suffering and getting killed by rebels, I decided to pay and go with them. I was not surprised that it began to move like turtle while making ailing sounds all over its body having very bad maintenance. It broke down many times on the road as I expected it. When it reached hills of a mountain, it had no energy to climb at all and we had been told to get off and walked along it on foot like turtle until we cleared a slope. After so many nerve wrecking moments and walking on foot, we managed to reach Borana where I was choked on meat and almost got killed. I was glad at least I reached Borana in one piece and we had been told to get off and stayed in town since it got dark and this vehicle might not make it alive. They then dumped us in one area while tired and got bitten by hunger through the night. I had no choice than to sleep while my intestines were twisted like tail of frozen fox with hunger for the night.

In the morning, being tired and flattened by hunger, I headed to that truck and we began another torturing journey to Hargeisa. After long day suffering, I reached Hargeisa to look for my friend and mother Yusuf, this time with little worrying since I knew the city. I hoped to find him where I left him if not having choice to go another place. As I guessed it, there I found him at same place. He was surprised to see me again and gave me one of his old sacks for carpet. Then he invited me to eat that begged food left over from him. Its smell punched my nose and I was afraid to indulge myself, but grabbed mouth full just to untangle my guts that stuck together. I was happy to find food. I again quickly snapped in my mouth from safe part and said enough to it. We had a chance to laugh again *chihinkare kai*...and reminded our self all that happened. He didn't try to find any work, but he said he acted like driver companion for one senior lady and earned a few shillings which didn't last for long. When he asked my story, I laid on him the stories from Wachalle to Agagub and now back here to find work. He criticized me for leaving in the first place and then hit me with bad news that exploded like grenade on my face, "All refugee students came from Ethiopia: Oromo, Tigre, and Amhara with some Somali were rounded up and sent to Arri-Addis, a desert camp toward Barbara. They are now under supervision of the military. If they had to get some water and collect firewood, they will be watched with eagle eyes, besides we heard the place was contaminated with poisonous snakes. The securities were threatening any student they find in city and if you don't go there, you will be in trouble. There was a notice posted on the security board about ten days ago for these students to leave the city immediately." I was shocked by this that my plan to find work and help myself was ruined. Since the securities were going door to door to hunt for students, there would be no place to hide. I was worried until next day to verify with security if this was indeed true story. Having no other choice, in the morning I went to security to meet my fate while my heart was drumming for what to happen. There I saw some more rounded up students were registering to be taken away. They asked me where I came from and I told them from Agagub camp to help myself. In this case they said that I had to go to social services since I was already registered there. When I went there, they ordered me to return back to it. I was disappointed and explained to them that there was nothing to go back to. "I need you to help me here!" I begged them. After I stayed there for a long time, at last they told me to go to a new camp of students. I insisted if they could help me in Hargeisa explaining the experience I had already at refugee camps, besides my concern to what I heard about poisonous snakes and suffering at this new camp, which could endanger my life. They then warned, "If something happens to you here in Hargeisa, we are not responsible at all because the rule for student to stay in town was restricted from now on." They even scared me more than I already terrified by news. Understanding the consequence of staying, I decided to go to a new camp as they said. I told Yusuf I had decided to go and he didn't mind at all. I begged him to come with me hoping it was better than begging here and we could be together again. He replied, "I would rather die here even if I do not find a job." He advised me to go for my safety hoping to see each other someday. I was sad again we were separating and I did not know what would happen, but to move on with my worn out nomadic sandals and a very cheap pant that even a goat would not wear.

Next day, about two in the afternoon, we jumped on a truck to new life of a desert. While we were waiting, heavy dark cloud greeted us from above as if breeding severe lighting which I did not like since I was young boy. My heart began singing sad songs to my grave expecting to be toasted on the top of open cargo truck. I doubted to make it alive to a new place. It reminded me when I was young, I was almost toasted twice, but here in Somalia where my parents would not find me made me worried more. I wanted to hide any time it flashed and my sight went blind, being another bomb that coming from heaven that threatened my life. I wished not to go today fearing to be fried alive as my teacher taught me that the lighting mostly hit moving object especially metal. I worried so much it looked like doomsday and the heavy rain began beating my head. My heart pumped harder looking at the sky like I could stop the lighting if it started and ready to jump from it when it flashed. Suddenly when they covered top of it with canvas, I felt little better, at least I did not face its flashes in my eyes and got soaked. We began moving and I had no idea where we were going and what kind of land we were passing through. I could only see heavy water that accumulated on top of canvas pushing me down as if a five-hundred-pound breast was dropped on my head. I tried to protect my head, but heavy to keep it away as if this huge hippo sized breast was in love with me while I was expecting to be hit by lighting anytime. The wind became another nightmare with its noise deafening my ears. Fear of crash and over turning tantalized my heart, too. After about forty minutes, the truck had stopped by checkpoint and the social workers got off to tell soldiers to let us go because we were refugees. After a while the rain had stopped and we got a chance to get off to look around when the truck was broken down. After it was fixed, I was able to gaze a direction we were going to be east where the sun came up in the morning. We travelled all day in a strange land, about evening we reached a beautiful town of Darbuluk where we were stopped for a break time. Then some people said we were going north of this town. I also came to learn that this town to be in the center of Hargeisa city and Barbara town. Then I heard town people calling us Habash, Habash which freaked me out like war time. Those who never saw Habash before began watching us like beast from the west coming to their land.

While they were astonished seeing Habasha, we left town alive and headed north on the unpaved road full of rocks and dust to the north. There were some small trees and bushes that could hide rabbits and turtles that I saw on the way with little hills, which made me feel better than Agagub. After about twelve minutes, we went down a hill and I saw very big refugee camp just like Agagub tent city. I said here we go again, but seeing a big high school in the entrance of it took my breath away and made me feel that this must be the most sophisticated refugee camp I had ever seen. As we entered, we saw a lot of people were welcoming us and we waved our hands for them. They then took us to a big compound looked like storage of things where I thought they were going to unload us for good. I was relieved that we only got off to get some supplies there. After we headed out of there to the remote area; I began to freak out that we were heading to be thrown in a bush after all. It looked as if we were going in the direction of Darbluk then headed east downhill. We saw more than hundred fifty erected tents other side of big refugee camp, where they told us to get off to be our destination. Seeing these entire students' tents made me happy that we were not alone in the desert and going to be in their community. It was getting dark. I was worried where to sleep for the night when the truck dumped us there. While I was worrying and looking around like monkey, there the truck came back with tents, which relieved me. They told us make a group of four for every tent and those who knew each other forged group of four very fast. I stood still for one to call me, and luckily three of them asked me if I would join in with them. I became exultant to confederate with them. We got some dates to eat for dinner and when we had some energy we looked for a place to erect our tent like others. When we had some confusion how to do it, those who had experiences saw us and came to rescue us.

Our tent was nicer than the one I saw before because it had beautiful furnishing. I was happy I didn't have to swim in a dust any more. We sat in the dark and ate dates again while fearing snakes to kiss us until midnight. At last, I fell asleep because I was tired and the sun woke me up alive in the morning without any snakes by my side like girlfriend. I went out to check where we were and the area. It was a kind of strange to be here, but happy as everyone. I saw huge rocks as big as a house around us. There was river flowing two hundred meters down from our tent. It made me felt exceptional and emotional as if we were brought on purpose to a little paradise: new tent, huge rocks and river. The rumors I heard in Hargeisa that soldiers guarding the camp and they followed you to a river were not true. I could see we could go to four to five kilometers on foot without any supervision at all. Understanding the area to be nice and safe, I returned to tent kicking my buttocks like donkey to masticate dates for breakfast. I heard that we were going to get ration before noon which also excited me, but we had no cooking pot yet. I advised my tent mates to use oil can as a cooking pot in the mean while which made them laugh at me. Previous students were very mad and disappointed not getting personal rations that they were promised which made them crazy besides cooking utensils. The leaders they elected from among themselves told them that we were not different than other refugees to get extra things and rations. They must take one ration as prescribed in the rule of refugees per person, which made them grumpy.

Next day, they gave us a blanket for each person, a single soap, two cooking pot, five spoons, two big plates, a lamp, one knife, five little plates, and cups for each tent. Generally, we were very happy for having these things we never had before. I was content to be with all these refugee students like me from different languages and ethnic backgrounds of my country. There were also some Somalis among us that I believed came from Ethiopia. The others from Somalia itself called us Abboy while they called Amharas and Tigrians Habash. Without any fight, we tried to teach them that we were Oromo not Abboy. We made them understand that we did not like this false name and they had at last stopped calling us Abboy.

After all, we all became one ecosystem of tigers, lions, zebras, hyena, and rhinos living in a tent city. There was still a little ethnic hatred that might have been dancing in the brain because of the past history. Understanding each others' language, we had agreed on common issues to solve our problems in the camp and elected a leader from each language. Being a neighbor to one of the biggest refugee camp of war times between Somalia and Ethiopia, we were known as Habasha that lived close by them. I learned that we could get firewood for cooking by walking thirty minutes from the camp around close by hills and area. Our job was to fetch firewood and cook boring flour porridge that had no honey, butter, or milk to eat with. When the flour that was given finished in seven, or eight days, we had to scratch our belly for two to three days with hunger. We had no lamp or light, just sit and eat in the dark like owl. When I learned that some who came before us were buying gas from neighbor camp to light their tent, I also used my money that left from my tent sale to light our tent for a month and then back to our darkness.

When we learned there were some Somali villagers in the area that came to our camp to buy things, my tent family agreed to sale one of our pot that we did not use for four hundred fifty shillings. Then we were able to buy a few things like milk powder and soya milk flour for our porridge which we tried to stretch it to last, but finished only in fifteen days. When a single soap given ran out, body stench came back, facing problems again. Some began selling their tent furnishings and tried to survive as much as they could. I learned that other groups like Amhara were able to get help from CRA to open some business in the big refugee camp tailoring and car repairing. Their money bought things we couldn't afford such as gas, charcoal, clothe, soup, and biscuits which we were jealous and drooling for. When they cooked, it was as if Hilton restaurants were established in the rock with us. I only licked the air passed by my nose and I wished to eat that kind of food at least one day in my life. I also realized that Somalis were able to buy things like onions, tomatoes, red peppers, etc. by using their tricks which made them better than my people. Those of us who had no support from any organization kept complaining to UNHCR officials who came regularly to check on us. They were recording everything we said and demanded as if we were going to get very soon, but they became like we were giving our message to the crow in the bottle. Hunger got worse when we started to sift worms and dirty particles that represent 50 percent from the flours given to us. We decided not to sift it anymore and declared, "Flours worms are flours, we can't lose its grams." We kept the integrity of one kilogram as usual. We baked, or boiled it with worms alive. I was hardly able to chew and swallow like my tent mates for the first few times. At last, I accepted as a reality and ate them while closing my eyes and gagging about it. After a while I became a member of worm eating machine like my roommates.

After a long time of eating worms and lack of necessary things, we wanted to go to town to work so that we got soap, shoes, gas, and clothing we lacked. We discussed and asked permission from our leader to let us go and he disagreed all of us could not go at once. He advised us to go one by one, or maximum of two at a time, for he would be in trouble to let everyone leave from the camp. I heard officials were saying the main reason they decided to dump us in the desert was because we student refugees were toxic to the land. This might have been the reason why we were not allowed out of camp for too long. There was a strict policy we must inform them when leaving and coming back to the camp. Not too long, one person left without advising leader, or anyone. Shortly after that the second one wanted to go, for the food was still not enough for us. We agreed with him to leave, but he had no transportation. Then we decided to sell the bag of our tent for two hundred shillings to help him. Then two of us left in a tent to deal with the worms and snakes. The one who decided to stick with me and worms said, "I pulled carts like horse and slept on street of Hargeisa and bored of that life." One of our neighbors had a flat pan to bake injera just like our country and we wanted to make like them. I started to beat the dough with worms like ladies in the camp which was a shame thing if it was in my country. I only felt that I was a woman with no husband in the desert and made a white mess on my face and clothing. We both tried to bake without any experience, a very strange looking injera with worms sticking its head and legs which said, "Hello, refugees don't be shy to eat me." We were able to eat a blind injera that had no eyes that I had never seen before after covering it with a little sauce we begged from the neighbor to help us swallow it. We bragged that we at least changed our usual porridge menu that bored us for a long time. After our friends left, we managed to use their rations and able to eat little better, but still was not enough to make through very well to the next pick up date. Sometimes we tried to sell a bit so that we get other things like powder milk, or sauce for our ugly injera we began to bake, since it was difficult to eat without sauce. My friend asked me to sell some utensils we had and I refused him, for we will be having problems like others who had almost sold contents of the tent and had nothing to cook with.

One by one, a lot of students left camp and the leaders were unable to stop them, but they tried to cut the part of rations for people who left. We were united and opposed this cut the day it was given to us. After two months, food trucks ceased to show up every ten days, but it came every fifteen and fourteen days. Sometimes it showed up after twelve days. They said, "There were shortages of trucks." We faced more hard conditions than before. We demonstrated, "Why not given to us every ten days?" They answered, "You could get rations every ten days if you go to bigger camp." They made it harder for us. One time, it did not come for seventeen days, which made us run out of patience. We all had a meeting to find camps' general manager by heading out of camp and luckily found him just close to our camp. We first demanded the ration to be given to us immediately, or we had to leave the camp for Hargeisa. He threatened, "We are not giving anything immediately and if you leave the camp, you will see what will happen to all of you." We scared; he was very serious to harm us. We went back quietly to our camp. Our leaders also advised us to stay put and not to jeopardize our safety by leaving the camp. Those who had extra ration left in their tent offered us to eat with them. We suspected that the reason the trucks stopped coming regularly was a kind of trick they were playing because of those who left camp.

When this continued, our leaders prepared to take some type of actions which they didn't tell us. We were then scared that a military might show up to deal with us. As we went to eat lunch at some ones' tent, two of our members disagreed on something little. One got angry and hit other one with stick on the hand. The attacked one went to treatment center to fix his hand, and complained to camp leader. He then brought forth a letter to the attacker to present himself for questioning by the camp's lieutenant who stayed at bigger camp. It was like bringing the attacker to the supreme court in the desert. As a family, we were scared for him and accompanied him to other camp to learn his fate, what the lieutenant would say. To mediate between them, we begged the lieutenant that the accused to return for questioning after lunch. The lieutenant agreed with us and we returned back to camp. Then we went to Jamal (accuser's tent) for talk and he assumed we were too late for it. Again argument escalated between those two, and they wanted to fight. We jumped between them and stopped the fight. Then it looked Jamal might have gone to accuse the attacker without our knowledge, for first letter. There three heavily armed soldiers came with the leader who threatened us about when we told him we were going to leave the camp if ration not given to us, right away. Jamal and his friend just pointed fingers toward two people sitting with us. Without any word, soldiers began hitting Kamal and Aliyi using both sides of their guns. Kamal laid flat and seemed dead from the hits which dropped our jaws and left our mouth dried and opened as big as rhino. They dragged him on the ground like corpse bleeding from his mouse and nose, then dropped him like sack of rice on the top of small truck. When my dear friend

Aliyi was hit a few times in the neck and stomach with a gun, he was angry and got up holding tip of the gun from attacking him. Then other soldier hit him on the stomach hard and he laid flat like lizard. Kamal being like dead on the truck, then three of them focused on Aliyi who seemed defiant and strong as turtle's shell. They kicked his stomach, head, nose, and back with heavy boots and guns so hard at the same time. He began to throwing up gore from his mouth and blood running from his nostrils.

When these made us kind of restless, fearing they were killing them in front of us, we made some resistance and they opened fire on us so that we did not try to help them. We were shocked and in disarray, we could not help our friends. We could not bear their pain; our peace was shattered in the camp. It was as if we were already in the grave. As gun fire escalated, I did run to save my life out of tent, while others already out of camp hiding in the bush. Some laid flat on the stomach to hide head from the bullets. They dragged Aliyi too, to the truck and threw him on top of Kamal who was almost laid dead there. They threatened rest of us to shut our mouth, or else. After they took them; they spread them like meat to dry on the ground in the sun at edge of the camp. They continued beating and kicking them there for more rounds. When they were tired, they threw them in jail as we looked on them. When things calmed down, we went there to check on them if they were alive, or dead, but we were again chased from the area.

After several days, our leaders managed to bring those beaten like hell to our tent, and luckily they were still breathing. They tried to calm down by mediation those angry parties so that this did not happen again. They also secretly went to Hargeisa to complain to the headquarters so that these soldiers' beatings would not happen again. We sold some of our flours and collected ten shillings from every one and able to buy them a meat for treatment, the only tablet we could purchase there. We requested UNHCR that the ration to be deposited and given to us from our camp. They were able to do this within a short period of time. Many of us realized that we might die in the hands of soldiers. Some had there already began getting away to near town and cities one by one. My friends and I had also discussed about going to find a job, to better our lives and get away to safety from camp soldiers. Then we heard someone saying, we could work on a ship, at port of Barbara. The wage was an earning of thirty shillings a day which was enough to buy six pieces of cigarette and sometimes free meal. We liked this news, but we had no transportation money to go there. I was dreaming to see Indian Ocean which I learned on geography even I did not get a job. Three more students, who had three hundred shillings, heard this news and they wanted to go with us. They suggested that we should go on foot to Darbuluk and beg truckers to Barbara with this three hundred shillings. Most truckers asked for two hundred shillings each and we were unable to get one until a big ration truck we begged wanted six hundred for all of us. After we had explained that we were refugees at Ari-Addis and we only had three hundred shillings, he felt sorry and told us to climb on it. We gave him, *Wat-mehasentahay*[151] and we headed east of our camp toward Barbara town.

The trip by ration truck was nice, but the draft of hot air began to burn my nose and face as we got closer to town. This was the worst heat I had ever experienced in my life as if the sun was pulled down on purpose to toast land and its occupant. Entering gate of Barbara town, we saw so many fierce soldiers with guns that stopped a driver and took money from him. When they stared to us, I was terrified that they were going to harm us. They verified with a driver that we were abboys on a truck and let us pass without heavy questioning. We were relieved to pass them, hearing that it was not easy to go into this town as it was surrounded by fence for a reason. We got off truck at town center and just headed toward ocean to take a look for the first time. I was amazed how the air and land were different from place to place in Somali land. I was excited to see Indian Ocean like I saw it on ball of global map of my school. I couldn't believe, what I learned came face-to-face with me after travelling so much distance from my country. There were so many huge ships as big as a mountain sitting in it while some appearing in the horizon far away just like I used to see in the movies. After satisfying with its view and fresh breathe, we

---

[151] A big thank you

returned to town and worried where to sleep the night. As we were wondering around, we heard rumors that there was a Somali *Abboy* camp in town where we could stay, a compound just intended only for foreign ship laborers. We were happy to hear this even though we didn't want to be called *abboys*. Then we saw an Ethiopian person and asked him, "Where is Oromo camp?"

He seemed confused, "I had never heard Oromo camp." Realizing that we made a mistake, one of us said, "Where is *Abboy* camp?" which he might know. He was happy to give us direction and we split in group of two pretending we knew the town very well so that we were not questioned and headed toward its direction. As we got closer to it, we then saw an *Abboy* who was willing to take us there. A compound walls were badly eroded and faded, encircling adjacent many little mud rooms. Most people furnished flat boxes under tree and on the ground, making their spot similar to that residence of hog tree in Hargeisa. I was surprised seeing hundreds of people in the compound mostly speaking our language, half naked body marinated with sweat and salt like black chicken cooking in the heat of the sun. Whistles were hanging on their neck like coaches of ships ready to do soccer match on the ocean.

Some of them were already heading out to ships as we arrived. We tried to verify if we were allowed to work and they shocked us, "If you don't work on the ship, you aren't allowed to stay in this yard. Compound leaders only consider hard working people to work and stay here." We were happy to hear this believing that we were strong enough for this job. Once some learned that I could write and speak English, they suggested that I could get a clerical job on the ship, but first I had to discuss this opportunity with Kadir, worker's supervisor. At the same time, only a few of them were concerned I might be arrested as spy of Ethiopian since they had never seen any student like me among them. On one hand, I was excited to be learned and got clerk job, but on the other hand, I was terrified being arrested as spy. Anyway I tried to convince them that the government already recognized me as a student, or political refugee so they didn't bother me about it. Two of them who returned from ship gave us flat boxes seeing that we were new and poor for the compound and other one gave us a fat cement bag allowing us to sit in the yard. The heat melted my body and sweat ran like river. I was very thirsty and begged for water, but they sent me to water pipe in the yard. As I ran it on my palm, it burned my hand like volcano. I jumped back word ten meters crying loudly hot, trying to cool down my hand while blowing with air from my mouth. I told them I needed cold water, not this hot water. They laughed at me by saying this was our cold water. I couldn't believe it. Again I tested on my feet and the result was the same, it scorched my feet. So surprised and disappointed, I went back to my sleep, unable to drink it. Seeing my suffering, someone gave me fifteen shillings and I bought a bottle of cold water from *Abboy's* teahouse. I felt little better, but in few minutes my stomach began to burn as the bottle I just drank squirted out of my skin and formed a very white powder like salt on my body. I doubted to be salt and tasted. It was indeed a real salt I was producing from my skin. I thought about collecting and bagging them at compound and then going down to marketplace to sell it for cash if I continued to produce like this. Then I realized every man was going bare naked upper body and looked a gray donkey covered with salt and no one would be interested in mine. I was afraid if I survived in this town at all in this condition. At night, the flatten box under my skin got very wet with sweat. I kept turning around, feeling not comfortable with heat and sweet, but it meshed up like sweet potato and stuck on my skin. I began to peel them off like hippo skin. When all this boxes gone in a few hours, a person next to me gave me a plastic bag, which again got very hot with sweat burned my skin with forming hot ocean. I was unable to get a good sleep the whole night, the same as my friends. I wondered how these people were able to survive all this time.

As the night was over, we wanted to go with workers going for morning shift and they told us they only work in group of ten and they could not take us with them. Since we were only six new comers, we need four more people to join us. They advised us we must wait until more new people arrive to form our group and inform Kadir about it so that he would authorize us to work. While we were waiting, I saw groups that returned covered with grey dust from head to feet looking like donkey that swam in volcanic ashes. They told me that they worked on cement ship. I wondered how they survived this mess and still walking about while their lungs and belly were clogged with this powder. Their eyes were also red like tomato while eyelashes were like white brush. I was really scared this was going to happen to me. We waited until midday for Kadir. When he didn't show up, we decided to visit the ocean again. As we reached there, I ran and threw myself in it with clothes on. Just to cool myself down, I dipped my head in it first; my eyes and nose were burnt like someone peppered it. I informed my friends about being razed and tasting the worst salty water I had ever seen in my life. I felt that residents might have purposely or mistakenly dumped thousand kilograms of salt in it. I begged them to taste it and said, "We didn't learn in school the ocean to be very salty like this." It became a miracle to me why the whole ocean became briny liquid. Then someone suggested, "If you drink a palm full of this water, it will be beneficial to your health." Having no doctor and medicine for almost a year as a refugee, I felt he might be right and scooped and gulped it down. It rocked my mouth and stomach so bad that I almost fainted and fell down in it. This made me to think that it was poisonous water to swim in it. I got out quickly so that I did not ruin my skin. When we returned at the camp wondering about the ocean, my body became so white and powdery than before. There was no doubt I turned white donkey from now on since my skin changed from black to white ash.

While I was looking at my body, about in the afternoon, Kadir showed up. We raised to him our interest to go to ship. "Where did you come from?" he asked. "Arri-Addis camp," we replied. He stressed, "This job is not easy and you have to work hard. Once you start, you are not allowed to run away." We bragged, "We came to work hard, not to play around. We had nothing to eat right now and not eaten since yesterday. We need to work." We begged him to put us to work right away. He lamented, "When you are new, you suppose to do the worst and low paying ship work for the first year before you go to good paying one, I let you go to good one to start today." We were so happy and thanked him, but the group he told us to go with got mad knowing that we were given nice one too fast before suffering on the ugly ship and its work. On the way to ship, some of them kept throwing bad comments and crying. They complained while we went with them and we even did not possess previous experience for this exotic boat as if they were upper class ship workers and we were lower caste. We were surprised that there were such things exist here as good and bad work and higher caste and lower caste. We walked on foot from camp to the harbor where soldiers stopped us by gate entrance. Then Kadir freed us saying we were new workers and he was taking us there.

When we reached at ship dock, those who knew ran and climbed one and we did the same. We went through many doors like Super Mario, hallway to hallway, one door to the other, too many strange doors and things I had never seen before. It was surprising and confusing to walk in it as if there was something made me lose control of my body. At last, we reached a hole to enter work area. I was shocked to see that the ship working area to be a very deep big hall I couldn't imagine that existed anywhere. Every one turned around their face and climbed down the long skinny ladder very fast like monkey going down long scrawny tree. Seeing it very deep, I was so scared to go down. Those behind me lost patience and yelled, "Go down!" Because of their pressure, I tried to go down a few step, but my gut appalled and urged me to back up, for I believed I could not make it all the way down. When I looked down where they were, I could only see their dark circle hairs as a full stop at the end of a sentence among many hundreds of sacks. I was afraid, I would crash like an egg if I slipped going down. I had never, ever had seen such scary deep place in my life with very long skinny ladder that seemed to go down forever and ever. I contemplated to go back out of ship and cancelled my work there, but was scared how I was going to survive at all, seeing my friends went down. After so many pushes from my friends and encouragement from people, I tried to go down a little, but my stomach kept shaking with my legs. I was stuck somewhere in the middle, unable to go further, and then there my worn out slipper flew way down off my feet. While I was thinking, I was going to fall like my slipper; there some came down rushing the ladder giving me a nightmare to push me down. Without any due care for frightened cat like me, they pushed me aside and I almost fell off and hanged on the ladder for my dear life. I was shocked to fall off if this continued. At last went down while my heart was drumming and sweating like never before. I realized this was dangerous job with height and not worth to lose my life. Then I watched how they put rope on the ship floor and they arranged about twenty sacks on it. Then from high above a crane operator sent down long line with hook and picked the sacks. They then told me to run for my life to the corner to save my soul because the sacks might return down. I felt another dangerous way to die there. They also warned me to be aware of avalanches of sacks would kill me there which I must watch out for while working. My fears were increased by one thousand times. I realized I was there to die than making shillings. I exclaimed, "This job is very dangerous one!" They informed, "Many workers' souls were already flown to deep space as objects going up wacked their head." The sacks kept falling off as ropes not strong enough for the weight it seemed. I kept running to the corners. I was so tired before we took out thirty ropes while those who had experiences taken out about eighty. My fingers were so wimpy that it hated even to touch the bags and my back also hurt as if someone stabbed me. I was so tired running to corners of a ship to save my life while coming back to make stacks of heavy sacks again and again which almost made me fell on my face.

Seeing we were so weak and tired, those jealous eyes about us getting the job had begun yelling to us to work faster and harder. We learned that their leader could kick us out of this ship if he wanted too, since this ship was a special paying load per sack. We were not going to be paid if not worked hard at the same pace with them. We made one huge stack to please them and it came crashing down on the floor. A crane driver shouting from high down and we were frustrated and began working hard to make it right. We tried for a while and after a few arguments about our experience, we tried to work by grouping with them. Then we were able to learn tricks from them how to tie sacks and finally became happy moiling on the ship. When they saw a wooden pallet, they scrambled to get it as if they tried to make extra cash by selling it. We could not compete with them, but at least our first day, we were able to survive it. I worried how to get out now that shift ended. They started climbing out like ant while I stood there watching being jealous with anxiety. I wished they carried me on their back like baby. I slowly went up after everyone cleared to test myself while my legs were shackled in fear. As I went little up, I looked down and trembled more. Having no other choice, I went up to the middle and felt dizzy looking down. I held hard on ladder and kept going. At last, I made it to the top at the point I dropped my baby. I wondered if this thing really made by human creature, thinking they could have made it easily accessible, or have some type of elevator to go down with it if really they had a good brain at all. "How did they put this thing in water in the first place? How could it carry all these weight without sinking?" I murmured. I understood that getting in and out was not easy, lucky and happy to get out alive. There was no easy money. We ate corn powder that we begged neighbors by rolling like gulf ball as they did. Then, we took showers with that hot water and laid down on my shirt as carpet, for there were no boxes. I was so tired and slept like dead snake in the heat. When I woke up in the morning, my body was dusty with my hair and I looked like a crazy person.

CHAPTER 10

Death in Barbara

The next day in the morning, we went back to a ship and they told us to work on a cement one. They informed us for every sack, we got twenty-five cents. I was afraid I was going to be a cement head like those I saw. I must pull at least twenty bags of dusty cement just to buy a piece of cigarette. Realizing that we were just working for nothing and unable to buy anything, my friends encouraged me to take wood pallets like others so that we sold them in town to make money for a meal. After getting tired at end of the shift, we ran and got wood pallets and put them on a crane with some bags. When we took it to the yard, no one bought it from us. I was happy to have all these logs, but no luck to convert it to cash, and we were hungry to go back to work. We told Kadir we were very hungry and no energy to work and he lent us three hundred shillings for food. We were then able to eat a little bit and went to cement ship. This time, we were happy to work by ourselves with four new arrivals. We rarely made a mistake, but overall very happy with our work. I looked like a mouse fell in a bag of cement. When I drank water it dropped on my skin and my body became a cement mud. I was afraid the dusts inhaled would mix with water and stuck in my intestine and would become cement belly. I was afraid I might die very soon. I realized that there were many dangerous things to kill me more than ever. Once I brooded, it might be better to stay in the camp and eat my porridge and wormy ugly injera in the place where no one would tell me where to go and what to do at all rather than endangering my life. When we got paid minus our loan, we got only two hundred shillings for all of us which was not enough for lunch. Those who had experience got about five thousand shillings each and they were complaining about it. When we sold our wood, we made thousand shillings, which made us little happy. We ran to eat lunch at restaurant and able to buy cold water with it to cool ourselves.

When the mother of all ships came as people verified it, we heard it was carrying refugees rations. The pay was only ten shillings, or enough to buy only two pieces of cigarettes for working the entire night removing thousands of heavy sacks. Everyone hated to work on this ship, for pay was almost as if putting air in the pocket and its work very difficult and tiring one. Shortly we heard that there were some more ships docked from Saudi Arabia, which had housewares and a variety of clothing as if these items would be treasures they were going to pocket them. They were extremely excited if they got a chance to work on it, they might fatten their pockets with more shillings just like selling those woods. They also said that refugee ships provide good opportunity to steal things like rice, flour, and dates, etc., to keep them alive. Moreover, if they ate as much as their belly could hold while working in there, no one would complain, or say anything. "These were why we were able to work and survive here," they excited. I wondered if I could do like them as if I was climbing Kilimanjaro mountain. As people say, "If you are in rome, do what the romans do."

When we went to work on those ships, we were luckily sent to that Saudi one called *yarew*.[152] It looked much different than others. No ladders to climb down and easy to get in the loading area. Goods were arranged in an easy way to pick and put on the fish net for crane to pick them up. We were excited that this had to be the easiest work so far. A group began chanting, *gel gel fulle*[153] then others replied, *gadi*

---

[152] Little
[153] Camel climbed camel

mayee.[154] I liked this song and its melody. I was interested to know what they were saying and asked those who knew. They interpreted the first one saying, "A camel climbed on a camel" and other replied, "I can't reach them." It made me laugh so hard that my anus bulged like golf ball. I was unable to grab items as if I had lost my muscles for several minutes while laughing and thinking of very tall poor creatures on top of each other. I was happy to sing with them even though I didn't want to mock these rounded belly animals.

Everyone seemed to be in an excellent mood especially those who had amazing experience of concealing things in their body while it made them sing like crazy. I heard them saying sometimes they got away with what they had stolen and sometimes they were caught by guards at yard's exit. Items stolen were taken away from them without being arrested. When the load fell down at the seventh shift from the crane, some juice boxes were exploded at crash site and they ran and started refreshing their belly. I dared not to do like them fearing it belong to some ones' else and I would be in trouble. Then order came from supervisors; we must finish the remaining loads in six hours, for the ship would be going to leave soon. I learned that they were going to pay us only ten shillings for every shift. They encouraged paying us extra shillings as an incentive if we started working so fast to finished it. A big boss also began yelling at us to hurry up. We rushed and rushed to finish it. I couldn't believe the way we finished the whole ship very fast. It made me so exhausted more than ever before. We managed to finish it and again they moved us to the refugees' ship without a break and energy to suffer me the most. When they paid for seven shifts of yare, we got seventy shillings each not enough to buy anything at all. We asked where about of that extra payment promised to us, but they denied it to be only ten shilling per shift for this type of ship. Their lies made me very angry. I felt someone was taking advantage and not being honest with us. I sang anger song in my heart, "Oh! Yare! Oh! Yare! What have you done to us?"

We continued Working on the refugee one with hunger hammering my stomach like ocean's fifteen-feet tides. I was tired and

---

[154] I can't reach them

exhausted, so hungry to the point unable to move at all. This desperately forced me to scoop spilled raw grain of rice from the floor of ship to my mouth and began grinding it raw. I tried to grind it as much as I could and it sounded as if a dog was crunching a bone two yards away. I had never chewed such strong grain before and I wished I had hot water to help me with it as the grains refused to obey my teeth. I couldn't believe I dared grinding raw grain with my teeth just enough to stop myself from dying there. I got to drink some water after a while and able to wash it down which made me little uncomfortable, but better than before. I hoped it would break down with stomach heat and acid, and not to damage my organs.

Our cement ship wage was not paid because some suggested that the leaders feared that a few workers might run away from town after getting paid. We again borrowed two hundred shillings each to drink tea and bought dry bread and continued on the ration ship. We heard rumor that good ship would come in about three months, or so to make a little more shillings. In the mean while we thought these ten shillings to be harsh. We thought about returning to our camp as soon as possible. One of our members, Abdulle had lost his patience and left us by saying "This is slavery work." Once he looked like skunk swam in the ashes and his eyes were as red as a red pepper which made him unable to see any of us. I was almost similar to him and wanted to leave, too, but I had no money for transportation. We returned to rations ship having no other luck. When we finished our shift; I saw almost every one taking about two kilograms of rice to cook in the yard. My friends encouraged me to take at least one kilogram and they tempted me while I was feeling ashamed to do it. I had never taken some thing not belong to me before. I then wrapped a kilogram of rice in a flat box to conceal it from guards hoping no one would see it. My heart was drumming all the way as if I was going to the gate of hell and prayed guard's eyes sealed by God. When I reached to the guards, they didn't ask me to open my carton, and I felt free to go with it. I thought I got away and ready to cook it, but when we reached biggest exit gate, a soldier asked, "What do you have in the box?" I said nothing being hard for me to explain in their language. Then he said, "Tell the truth!" I tried to explain my way, but they ordered me to open my treasured rice. Seeing I concealed a kilo of rice, they ordered me to put it down by wall. I begged, *walla-loo!*[155] to let me take my rice by touching my stomach to show I was very hungry. Then I was hit by words as big as a bomb, *wariyya tug, dhik, so'oo!*[156] My body was more soaked with sweat and ashamed like never before for stealing rice and getting caught. I must put it by wall and go empty hand. Thank God my father didn't see me. At least, they didn't arrested, or beat me, for a kilo of rice. I was happy to go free, but I was deeply hurt and promised myself never to do such a thing again. I swore never to dare to take out even empty box from the ship as I headed to yard with shame. My friends and others were also caught; being told the same *tug* word and walked away empty hand. I continued crunching the same spilled raw rice once a while to cool down my hunger.

One afternoon, my friend went to beach of Barbara, and found nice pair of shoes. I was jealously asked, "Where is my share?" Mine was worn out and my heels were kissing the ground. He said, "Go and get yours; there are plenty at the beach." This encouraged me to run like ostrich to make my feet happy. I saw many shoes, but the one I liked very much was beautiful and smaller than my feet and it was only a single shoe lacking its sister. I was amazed that people here were richer than I thought throwing shoes at the beach just like that to find them easily. Rather than my heels kicking the ground, I decided to put on some not matching shoes that fit me, just to divorce the ground that was kissing me even though someone would laugh at me. It was my first day ever collected shoes thrown as garbage like those crazy people in my country. I labelled myself lunatic of Barbara and went back to camp with it.

When they paid me, I got only 425 shillings which defied my expectation of at least one to two thousand shillings. After I paid my debt, I had only left with 225 shillings. This made me very sad and I wanted to go back to my camp before I ran out of this fare money. I didn't want to wait until I collect 170 shillings left, wanting my

---

[155] Brother
[156] You, thief, put down and go.

friends to bring to me. I felt ashamed going back to the refugee camp with shoes that I got on the beach rather than thousands of shillings. I was not able to replace even my torn out shirt which was messed up worse than before with cement and dusts of Barbara. A few of us returned to camp empty handed, looking so bad physically and mentally. Camp residents laughed at our conditions: toasted by heat, fingers and waist wounded, clothes stained by cement, back bent like old man. We defended ourselves, "We at least saw big ships and Indian Ocean, while you sat here doing nothing. I also got shoes on the beach for free looking like a cat that slept in ashes and brought five shillings." Hearing beautiful beaches and tall ships enticed others to go to Barbara to see them and they left after one week. My shirt was so badly torn that I didn't have even a needle and thread to fix it, but my friend Abdulla asked me to bring a long thorn of a tree as a needle and made hole at the end and we pulled thread from canvas. He managed to put back its flesh together as much as he could. I thanked him, for he made it little better. He was so disgusted by the situation in Barbara and sworn not to hear its name and ships again even one that came with full of gold and he would not return there. I felt the same showing him the cement that became part of my toes with my clothes, which I was unable to remove at all. I even rubbed it with sand as soap at the river and it refused to let my skin go. My hair became cement dreads and combing was not possible. While I was dealing with this pain of Barbara, my other two friends came back from the port, specially the one who couldn't bear being called Abboy and he fought with Somalis each time they yelled to him. Our friends and some others helped him with fare and he returned with them. We agreed to stay in our camp rather than being called Abboy, having enough of it. Compared to Barbara, our camp was like heaven where we could take baths in the river and bake our wormy flour for survival.

After a while, we got four blankets and six soaps, which made us happy. We were able to sell a blanket for 150 shillings to people who came from another refugee camp. This gave us a chance to buy a couple of sandals and some sauce for our ugly injera that we baked. We were excited about eating injera with a sauce, but the sauce that was smeared the worms didn't last a week. We returned to boiling corn that had no salt. Once we were tired of boiled corn flour, we made its injera, but its sauce was also the same flour mixed in water, they became twin sisters. Then we heard that there were disagreements between Ogden, an Ethiopian Somali and Isa Musse, the Somalian refugees who lived in the big camp. We heard that Ise Musse was preparing to attack Ogden especially when fetching fire log out of the camp. We scared to go out of our tent to collect firewood. Once they began slaying each other in the refugee camp and bushes, the military arrived to keep peace. They began arresting some of them, and we were very scared and frustrated to live in the area. Learning the story of their tribal feud and fierce hatred for each other surprised me while being the same ethnic group. I heard they knew each other just by some word in their language: when Isa says, *noow*,[157] Ogden would say *agga*.[158] I was prepared to throw away *noow* from my mouth if I saw Ogden and *agga* if I saw Isa's tribe to spare my life even though I spoke very little Somali. Their roots were the same; I did not know why they treated each other like wasps and bees. My heart began hammering anytime I saw any Somali person since I couldn't identify who was who that I was facing.

While I was worrying about all these things and possibility of dying, there came heavy rain and wind blew off our tents. I only saw we sat in the open field getting stabbed by thorns and blood poured from my lips. My eyebrows were also caught by hooking thorns as if rain was fishing on them. I made loud cry when pricks piled on my body. My blanket was also full of thorns when I found it far away. I became a porcupined cat when thorns pricked my entire body. Golf-sized hell also hammered my body as I bled in the rain. The lightening I hated to see didn't feel shy to say hello in the desert adding an insult to injury. It was one of the worst times in the camp so far. I then discovered that our area was mostly covered by Isa tribe who didn't like refugees very much. They were causing shortages to their supplies of logs they needed to build houses and those dried fallen

---

[157] What!
[158] What!

branches they used for fire woods and their live stocks were depending on trees, too. I was sad hearing their concern as I went to a house with one of my friends who claimed to be of Isa tribe. I saw how they lived and how trees were important for their survival. I felt they were right to stop us from damaging their environment. I felt not good to collect wood from them unless it was fallen dry branches which was not needed at all. I was confused with all these problems. I didn't know what to do and how to live in this camp that got sour day by day. I wanted to run somewhere, but Barbara was the only choice that came in mind. On top of these, Ramadan was getting closer and we didn't want to sit in the dark, having no shillings to welcome it. When I heard from my friend that Abboy camp in Barbara was getting much better than before as they got a small Abboy room of their own, he pushed me to go back with him. I agreed and Abdulle gave us one pot, cup, and plates with some rations so that we had utensil to cook there. Ibro promised me that we were going to come back to our camp for Ramadan. All these enticed me to return back to Barbara for the second time feeling it was getting better and different than before which surprised me even to think going back to it. We did finish three ships in short time and I was very excited being very fast, but so tired working harder than before.

Many ships arrived and there was quarrel among groups who would take the coming ships. We somehow got the one with a lot of sacks in it. I had to work with a very lazy skinny boy who was very hungry, grumpy, and tired all the time. He dragged me behind saying, "I don't want to die for ten shillings and I must work slowly." I was afraid a crane guy would yell at us soon and tried hard to make a pile on the rope. We managed to pile a load and the crane lifted up. I was so tired standing as usual and I decided to sit down for a minute on a sack. As I was sitting, I watched other crew across me being so sluggish like me that they were barley standing. Suddenly I felt like I was in a dreaming state, seeing that their lips were moving at about three thousand rpm looking at me. They probably saying something to me which I didn't hear a word of it. As if I was in a grave, I thought they were calling my name, Abas! Abas! Many million times per second. As I tried to say "yes" to them, suddenly I felt so much pressure on my head as if someone was drumming on it none stop having no idea what was doing this to me. I thought I was shouting hard resisting the things happening to my head and shocked about it. I then saw myself sprung up in the air like basket ball to be dunked and flying across the ship while shooting blood from my mouth like shell. My eyes were popped out like golf ball from its deep hole. I was unable to breathe as if turtle shell was stuck in my throat. I gasped for breathe while falling ten meters away. My brain and skull were flattened and my head sank down in my chest like tortoise. My ribs squeezed as shock absorber of a truck and pasted to my waist. I saw many people as ghosts circled around me saying something which quite I didn't understand, but seemed very concerned of my situation. I might go deaf forever, it looked. While I was gasping to breathe, I saw an angel flying with my soul to outer space in a cold cloud getting wet. I was trying to breathe hard to return my breathing to normal, but I found that I was indeed swimming in ocean of sacks like stingray.

I tried to stop my soul completely from leaving mother earth. Unable to swim in many stacks of sacks, I figured out that I was stuck in a ship. Many workers began showering me with water while making noise in a very distress way to revive my soul. I was in so much pain when they put my rounded body on a wooden pallet like grain bag. They were shouting, "Lift! Lift!…" to the crane guy as if I was a bag to be taken out with someone holding me from falling off like those sacks. I was scared to crash like egg as crane lifted and dangled me high bleeding from mouth and nose. Seeing all these made me say this was doomsday I was expecting. Lucky I was safe out on top of the ship and thanked God to make me out of that height, not falling down. They put me on top of SFD ship for a while and they then transferred me to a small bed of clinic in the ship that I had never ever expected to be there. They realized that they were unable to put me back together and urged them to take me to Barbara hospital. The spy of Kadir said, "I am going to bring a car, please take him out of ship." Then two people held my ruined body, in serious pain taking me through narrow hall and stairs of a ship, and laid me beside ship dock while crying like pig.

As a bee hive, more than hundred workers surrounded me by ship, making noises and yelling at each other to open air space so that I could breathe. Some showered me with water again to keep me alive. Then the supervisor brought taxi and they rolled me in like oat while I was crying of pain. When we arrived in hospital, they put me in a sick people room, on a bed until they got paper works, or permit from the port authority. I was groaning and crying from this bed until order letter came. The heat was scorching in a high ceiling hospital hall ways where only a couple of weak fans running there, unable to cool me down. After hours and hours passed, there a letter came to give me a treatment. A tall person, I did not know where he came from, arrived and informed me that Barbara insurance would come to treat me there. I was groaning from that bed for five hours without anyone showed up. My best friend then brought me spaghetti in a plastic bag, making it flat like an envelope. I wondered how he did that; he might have been graduated from high technology university restaurant, which I had never seen before. He tried to feed me like a new baby with soft spinal cord and neck. I was unable to chew and swallow with gored tongue and shifted jaws that seemed not part of my face. My leg swollen like an ox thigh, I could not move anywhere.

Several hours later, my best friends Ibru and Hassu came to visit me and learned that I didn't get any treatment. They got mad about no one bothered and cared to look at me. They went to talk and complain to Ilmmi, a person in charge of workers at the port why this happened to me. After sometime, a hospital general leader, quite very young man arrived, *Inanka aya kenne?*[159] as if I was kind of animal, or filthy rug that sat on the bed. He shouted, *wariyya abboy! ka'a!*[160] He pulled me down from bed like a pillow. I cried like wart hog bitten by lion with severe pains from my chest and neck. Knowing I was going to crash on my head, suddenly I tried to stand with my left leg and I was unable to stand on it. I switched to the right leg and I was a little better, but I was unable to stand at all. While I was crying and wanting to crash on the floor, he kept pushing me to the door with

---

[159] Who did bring this here?
[160] You Abboy get up.

fierce yelling. I hopped on one leg like kangaroo to survive while spitting blood. As I reached exit door, my friends came through gate of hospital and saw I was being pushed out. Seeing my desperate situation, they ran to punch the hospital guy. They shouted, "How dare you do this?" Then people jumped in middle to stop the fight. While they were in this commotion, dragging each other in side hospital, I fell down by the door area, unable to stand anymore. Falling and pushing doubled my pains and I was even dizzier that almost made me throw up in the yard. When they ended the argument, they put me back to that bed where I was kicked out.

Shortly the hospital guy didn't stop his fierceness toward me so my friends convinced that he wouldn't stop to harm me. So Ibro carried me on his back like my mother while I was crying of pain coming from my chest pushing on his back. We arrived at a place looked like a police station two hundred meters away from the hospital where soldiers pointed guns toward us and commanded, "Stop." Then questioned, "Where are you going?" Then Hassu spoke good Somali and explained to them how hospital leader kicked and threw me away without any treatment. We felt and believed that soldiers were going to summon the bad guy to the station so that he would give me treatment and leave me alone. Instead soldiers told my friends to lay me under the tree across the station street. It looked they didn't care very much. I had lain under that tree until it got dark. After a soldier advised my friends to take me to our camp. Ibru once again collected my body together like my mother and carried me all the way to the camp on foot as I was crying of pain and near my death. Hassu stayed back there to do something, but he didn't say what. I again sobbed so much for Ibru who had been carrying me so much around and becoming a burden on him. Any time I breathed in, it looked my crushed chest and ribs were expanding like mushroom coming out of a ground. I wished I did not have to breathe at all and cried in pain while I was suffocating to control my breathing.

Then Hassu came and told us that he stayed back to beat a hospital leader after his shift. He then said, "When I saw him in town, he apologized to me for his actions and bought me a pack of cigarettes and told me to bring you back to hospital." I thanked and appreciated Hassu for his daring actions and they carried me back to hospital in the dark. I was surprised when a leader came and said, *abboy, mahay uneysa? pasta, rooz?*[161] I was still mad for the pain he had caused me when he threw me off the bed as he was rushing me to the gate of hell. I felt like biting him to ease my anger, but I waved my finger as a sign to say I did not want anything to eat. To add insult to injury, he kept saying *abboy, mahadoneysa?*[162] He annoyed me even more. My friends, again came to my rescue, "Leave him alone, he doesn't need any food!" Only then, he moved away. After that they got me tea and bread for dinner. When they were worried about ship waiting with load and they might have to go, I encouraged them to go. I stayed by myself all night while groaning with pain without anyone cared to look at me except mosquito that came and taxed me for blood. In the morning, Ilmmi, the ship supervisor had gotten me medication needles to be administered from somewhere and no one came to inject me with it. They just simply slept next to me as if they were my girlfriends.

On the fifth day, my friends brought almost all compound ship workers to protest about my suffering and they filled inside hospital like bees on honeycombs. When they were about to take me away, a hospital worker scared and questioned "Why do you want to remove him?"

They replied, "He was in here without treatment for four days! Look! The needles were sleeping with him." Then he was scared, or felt sorry for me and pierced me with one of the shots right away. They were on fire for treatment I didn't get and carried me to the camp helping each other like beetle carrying rounded feces. The ship leader saw us on the way and they told him why they were taking me away. He then told them to take me to a clinic and they agreed. I became very big burden to my friend Ibro who had been carrying me to clinic every day while I was crying on his back with pain. I wished I was in my country for everything. Now my life was about to end in Barbara. I imagined my body laid in the grave by Indian Ocean of

---

[161] Abboy what do you like to eat, pasta, rice?
[162] Abboy what do you need?

Barbara. No wonder some workers were paralyzed and sitting in the camp while some others didn't make it at all. I was luckily crushed to small boy, but not lost my limbs. I encouraged myself, "I will recover from this and resume my *Kulli* again." No wonder people say, "Cat has nine lives." After all, I was glad to be a cat man. Now my friends could say *bas*[163] and I did not mind. As I was crippled for a month and watched my friends moiling, fasting approached very fast. Then I wanted to go back to my camp, but my friends encouraged me to stay put with them believing I would get better. They feared it was a shame for me to return to Arri-Addis camp in this manner and no shillings in the pocket. They convinced me to stay with them and I was afraid my end might be inside one of those ships. After I finished seven injections, they gave me another four from an insurance place I didn't know. My chest and leg pains still not improved at all. When a guy came from our refugee camp to work on the ship, he saw my leg and said, "I can fix it for you if not broken."

He made my heart smile, but his weird looking and lack of education scared me that he might rip off my legs and make it even worse than ever. After one day of refusal, my friends and people in the camp encouraged me to give him a chance. While fearing I agreed and he then stepped on my feet with one leg and twisted my ankle area. Severe pain made me squeal like fox and I thought he was wrecking my leg as I heard cracking and crunching of my bones. A few minutes later, I felt much better than before. I tried to put my feet on the ground and I was amazed that there was no more pain shooting my leg up to the waist like pregnant lady. I thanked him to be my leg mechanic and wished he could be a technician for my chest that would not let me breathe freely as my brain colligated and pretended to explode. My tongue was still intact after my teeth sank in it and just continued bleeding gore and popping out of my mouth like corns. My friends argue that bloody yogurt came from inside my body. I was glad to have my neck still in place and functioning well despite all that pressure of sacks on it. I was able to go to wash room leaping with walking cane like hundred ten year old man.

---

[163] Act of chasing cat.

When I got little better, I cooked rice for my friends like mom. After doing this for a while, I was almost healed and one of my friends found a construction job which he thought little easier for me and better paying than a ship work. I went with him to find out if I was indeed lucky and able do it. Then I found out that they were going to pay a maximum of only 250 shillings every day. I was very happy to hear this to be true. Even though I had still some pain, the pay motivated me to work with it. I made 1,250 shillings in five days. I was happy to hit this jackpot, but I got little sad when it ended in five days. Workers in the camp got jealous when they saw that I made good money in a short period of time while still in pain. "I could now buy a pant for Eid[164] of Ramadan," I slapped my behind. Luckily again I found another job of construction for 350 a day where I had to carry so many woods that wounded my shoulders. I pocketed another 1,200 shillings after my expenses which excited me. As this ended with a very good result, I again heard that there was a new cement factory in Barbara which paid 150 shillings a day. I went to work in this factory since it was better than ten shillings a day on a regular ship. I only worked two days, for the Somali workers kept calling me *abboy*. I tried to make them stop calling me this appellation by explaining to them that it was an insult toward me that I could not take it since it was given to us during war time by Ziad Barre, their president. I assured them that I was pure Oromo and *abbo* means *wariyya* in their language. I gave them another example to understand it: you might then call English speaking white man "Somali You," an Arab speaker "Somali Anta," or French speaker "Somali Twa," etc. you should be then "Somali Wariyya." Before the War of 1977, this Somali *abboy* did not exist and you still said this. When they didn't stop calling me *abboy*, I halted working in cement factory. I was shocked they kept forty shillings for tax and gave me only 260 shillings. I was able to buy a shirt eight hundred and a pant for 220 shillings. I was happy and lucky for Eid party. I realized that being rolled on the ship like ball gave me this opportunity to make this good money and to buy a couple of things.

---

[164] Celebration, holiday

Once I even got much better, I decided to work on the ship, but my dear friend Ibru got hurt a little bit on his leg. He left town for a while which disappointed me somewhat, but then came back quickly. After we encountered shortage of food, Ibru wanted to bring us some ration from the camp and we agreed. Then we heard my tent roommate who was collecting my ration had left camp. I was shocked and went with him to find out what happened to my ration. I was surprised that he had run with my wormy flours to Hargeisa and I was left empty-handed. After staying in the camp for two days, we again returned to Barbara to work on ships. Then my lips and eyelashes were trembling and dancing in a lunatic way than before. I have worried about something crazy about to happen which I couldn't lay my finger on it. I recalled similar experience when I was fourteen years old that I asked my mother why my eyes were shaking badly. She assured me that these were the warnings like seeing some new relatives I had never seen before. She also added some new things in life could happen. If it was from the eyes or lips, it would definitely be quarrel, or getting mad to something bad. Having two of them shaking at the same time concerned me so much that I was worried this was going to be different. When these things got very extreme for two days, I decided to tell my friends, but they commented that these were nothing to worry about, just part of body some times acting crazy. On the third day, I went to teahouse and saw a boy who was doing tally work on the ship. Since he knew that I could read and write, he advised me to get his work type. I liked his idea which I had never thought of before. He then surprised me to replace him for next day, for the reason he didn't explain. In the morning, I went to the ship, on his behalf to cover his spot. When I arrived at the gate of the ship, I lined up with tally markers, being very excited to do the job. Then Abdi Yared, the supervisor saw me and he shouted, "Who let this guy line up here? Who made him tally person?" I was shocked to say anything right away, but some workers replied, "He is replacing Abdu!"

Again Abdi cried, "I have already Abdu's replacement!" by pointing to a guy in the line up. Feeling so sad and shaken, I wanted him to be sorry for me, showing my leg that still not healed to do those heavy works of the ship. I begged him to leave me as tally boy, and he told me to go back to camp if I couldn't lift any sacks. He recommended me to find laborer jobs in town. I was very mad and went back to camp. I informed Abdu about this when I met him by chance in town. He told me he would discuss with port authority so that I got tally work. Again I was impressed by his thought, but felt that this might be a dream. Now I suspected that my eyes and lips shook had to do with this new chapter in my life. I wanted to go back to refugee camp at this point, but afraid that Arri-Addis must be almost vacant by now. Those remained were not nice refugees to deal with. Instead I encouraged myself resuming my labor on ship, or if lucky working other jobs in town. While brooding, what I should do next, the increasing of trembling also concerned me very much.

I sat in the camp for two days without work and on the third day as I was sitting, three strange people came to the door and asked me, "Where is that Hassan Oromo people talking about?" Unfortunately, Hassu was sitting with me after completing his morning teaching shift at Barbara Somalian secondary school which he had recently gotten because he spoke good Somalian language. He replied, "I am Hassan! What about Hassan?" They didn't say any word, but started searching inside his teaching materials for something they did not say. They began digging in them like chicken looking for grain in the haystack and all over the unit. They were unable to find what they were looking for at all. "Where is Oromo book?" they inquired. Hassu stated, "What Oromo book! I didn't see such things!" They ordered, "Come with us!" They moved him to a car waiting outside. I was terrified and followed them to see that they were going to kill him if they did not get this book, or this book must be a crime to have in Somalia. Then I recalled two people in town who had some issues with us for saying we were Oromo. They seemed to hate us and tried to make some troubles which I had forgotten about it. I was afraid somehow this might have to do with them. I returned to yard being shocked and sweated about Hassu, they might get him killed. Then my gut forced me to look for him and I decided to limp all the way to the Somalian soldier's house who happened to be from our country since he knew those troublemakers who hated us.

When I reached his house area, there I saw in a car those three security officers, or soldiers with one of the troublemakers who specially hated Hassu more than me. My guess was right; the trouble makers were behind this action. Hassu was talking to soldiers' wife standing at her door from a car and they were trying to move him. When I arrived, Hassu desperately said to me, "There I am caught! Try your best to call Hargeisa for help and tell them my news." Hearing what Hassu said in my language, the troublemaker interpreted to soldiers that I should be taken too, fearing that I would help Hassu from the situation. Then they ordered me to get in the car with him. When we reached at security office, they let me sit beside those two troublemakers while Hassu was taken for interrogation in a room. I now confirmed that the two were behind us and causing this problem to get rid of us from town. One of them named Dawud, from our country seemed to live in Barbara for a long time. He threatened, "You will see what we are going to do to Hassu!"

Once they got rid of Hassu, I had a feeling, he might try to push me in their political party same as those in Hargeisa when I was with Yusuf under hog tree. I suspected that Dawud was with Billisa's group, just a branch in Barbara to show us his power in Somalia. There was no doubt that they presented gifts that blinded security officials eyes accusing Hassan as Amhara and Ethiopian spy who carried forbidden Oromo's language books in Barbara which could prove why he had to be killed. Tafarri insisted I had to be taken with Hassu, too, for I was with him. Then Dawud said, "I know him. This boy is from my hometown. I know his dad. He was a little boy back then when I was there. He is not Amhara!" Then Tafarri who himself seemed to be true Amhara as his name testifies to me asked, "Did you see any Oromo books with Hassu?"

I answered, "No, I have never seen such books in glimpse with him." They didn't seem to be convinced with my answer. "Well, we will tie you like whole chicken to be roasted and hang you upside down and beat you unless you tell us where those books are. If you tell us we will not harm you." I again said, "I had never seen such thing with him." They then shouted to security, "Please take this boy, too," and said something in Somali which I didn't understand. I said to myself, "I am going to heaven with Hassu."

The securities began questioning me using Tafarri and Dawud as interpreter and I was afraid they would say things I didn't say at all. After they asked me my name and birthplace, they wanted to know what I was doing in town. I said that I was refugee from Arri-Addis and came to work on the ship so that I could buy clothes and meat, which I desperately needed to survive. They asked me if I was a student and I replied positive. They wanted to know my grade and I told them I was college graduate. Hearing about my education, Tafarri jaws were wide opened like hippo. "You look like poor farmer from the countryside that had never been to zero classes and probably never seen towns in Ethiopia at all. Your ugly farmer skirt was very deceiving and you probably wear this on purpose. I had never seen student acting like you before. I don't believe this in a million years." He was amazed as if I might be hiding under ugly skirts for some reason. Knowing this, his face was suddenly became inside slice of watermelon, ready to be served in Hilton hotel. I saw him biting his lips as if this was something made him on fire. Smokes began squirting from his nostrils and ears while saying how this person stayed in this town without us knowing him as student. As security wanted to know me more why I came to Somalia, I told them I was still registered political refugee in Somalia, settled in Arri-Addis camp by Somali government and UNHCR. There were shortage of daily necessities like food and clothing. Could you believe I had never eaten banana, orange, mango, any fruits almost one year since I left my country? Even I was not able to drink a cup of milk all this time and I came here just to work on the ship and buy one of these things one day. As you see me, I was hurt on the ship and unable to work for a while. They seemed not be sorry for me at all and continued asking "Do you know Hassu?"

I said, "Yes! I saw him in our refugee camp and as far as I know he came to work here long, long time ago. I just met him here again in this workers' camp. Now he is one of my best friends." "Is he Amhara, Oromo, or Somali?" I answered, "I didn't ask his ethnic group, but he speaks fluent Oromo and Somali. I doubted he is Oromo at all, but it is my policy never to ask anyone which race he or she belongs to especially from my country since there are over eighty-two languages and ethnic groups in the country. I had to be a computer to remember all these and especially after I arrived in Somalia my brain became worse lacking nutrients to remember everyone where they belong even I asked them."

They tried to verify with me what Hassu was saying, "He was claiming to be Somali, but what we hear was to be Amhara, we want you to bring those Oromo books now and we will be easy on you." I said, "I didn't see any of these books at all. If I had seen them, I will bring to you, or tell you so." They insisted, "You should bring the books that Hassu had and you saw and know where they were. If you don't bring them, know that we are going to kill you with him." I confirmed to them, "I didn't see those things with him." Then Tafarri whispered to them something I had a bad feeling about, to take me in prison with Hassu and get killed after.

They joined me with Hassu and ordered us to remove our shoes. They led us to a very smelly Barbara prison cells which urine streams flown like river and filled with very dangerous Somali criminals. I had never seen such stench and ugly place in my life that was killing me every second passing by as I was trying to gasp for fresh air. It seemed dying right away was much better than facing such disgusting place while alive. Even dead body would complain and cry to be removed from this place. They booked us to get shot at the beach of Indian Ocean, a familiar site we heard about. I saw Hassu's face shrank like two hundred years old man and the rest of his hair left on his bald, flattened as if tornado touched down on it. My heart started drumming and unexpectedly I felt I was ejaculating everything from my body without knowing where they came from. Now I confirmed what all those lips and eyelashes were talking about. I wished they had specified a little bit of this bad thing. I could have ran away the same way I did from my country. I was angry at my lips and eyes why they didn't clarify this and became so cruel to me. I said, "I just live one more day before my body would be hanging on a pole while covered face with white rag, and get riddled with bullets." I only might see myself like Jamaican say, "Ya see ya coffin alike!" My back facing Indian ocean and my face looking at Barbara town and toward west saying goodbye thousands miles away to my family who couldn't hear my cry and blood squirting from my heart and body. I was filming that king crabs were cutting my flesh with their forked arms and dip it in my blood as a sauce and give it to their children. At least, Hassu and I were glad to die together rather than separately as we discussed and promised each other before. Sometimes dreams and talk would come true like this waiting for us. We said, "Tomorrow morning, there will be no sun to rise for us." Anyway Hassu begged one soldier at prison at least to go and tell his wife his message that he was going to be killed tomorrow. A soldier somehow agreed to give his wife the message, not sure if he meant it, or not. Then after a while she came running and claiming to be a Somali clan that related to head of security leader in Barbara. She found him and told him that they were planning to kill my husband while she belongs to his clan. Then the leader came to our cell asked, "Where are Hassu and the Abboy boy?" Then Hassu spoke and the leader opened the door for us to get out.

I couldn't believe we were out just like that and walking in town freely with minor drumming heart and his wife. I thanked her for saving our muscles from being chopped by crabs that were sharpening scissors for their breakfast. I was filming their unhappiness with us by saying, "Hey, guys, were where you going, we need you right now, we were waiting for you all night long without sleep." I said, "Sorry, crabs, not today, at least! You could blame security leader and Hassus' wife."

"Well," they screamed, "We will cut Hassus' wife and security guy's legs when they come to swim at our residence. In the mean while, we have to settle with those not juicy, skinny, and very salty skins of Somali's criminals that were being thrown here whether they got shot, or drown for us." I was amazed by what crabs were saying and I couldn't thank enough Hassus' wife. When we arrived at the camp, two disabled friends told me bad news: Ibro, my other best friend had escaped fierce military beatings and rounding that occurred here while we were at the prison. I was dumbfounded by this news and left me helpless feeling that the earth intermingled with the sky. I did not know what to do and Hassu became shorter than before. When the workers came back from ships, they were surprised that we were still alive. They became happy we were not killed as our arresters spread the rumors we would be killed right away. Kadiro, ship supervisor was surprised to see us as he was informed about our death, too. He didn't say anything at all. He seemed to look for Ibro, but no one knew where he had gone.

In the morning, I heard from someone that they saw Ibro slept by beach and he was still somewhere in town. I was glad to hear this good news and went to look for him. Then I was happy to see him at tea place. He was very excited to see me get out of prison with Hassu. He said, "Abas! I was lucky to escape soldiers and I want you to sell my logs and belongings remained in the camp since you are kind of lame and safe from them. I must leave town as soon as you get me cash and things cool down a little bit." Anxiety began to prey on me as if I had already lost him. I had no options left, but to follow his footsteps to safety because this town endangered my life several times. While I was on a mission to sell his belongings, again the military showed up to the camp. They realized that I was crippled to be taken away even though I shaved the stinky hair I brought from prison. I was happy being crippled otherwise; I would have faced the same fate. As I heard it, today they were mostly searching for those who escaped from them. I was shocked to learn that the military was forcing refugees into their army regardless of their ethnic back ground, or any case they might have. I was extremely worried, for there was no place to run, or hide from them. I was crushed to pieces hearing that military did this round ups every six months, or so something I was unable to chew and swallow taking foreigners especially Ethiopians. Hearing a rumor that Kadiro was threatening ship workers to work hard and faster, or else he would call military to take them away had also appalled me because I would be on the menu. I heard he was once a soldier, too and he would like to support his country's military.

Two days later, as I stood on the gate area of the camp, I saw five youngsters running like antelope from tigers, jumping over the fence. I was shocked feeling that the second rounding up had began. One of the kids, ran and locked himself up in a room. He urged me to close and lock the door. Then I saw, they went after two boys on the other side. I stood frozen without running and kept watching them. In case they came toward me, I was ready to show them my leg and the letter to prove that I was incapable person to go with them. I was not making it up like some Somalis who were walking like lame person anytime they saw rounding up. They would hit this disable person to verify that he indeed a crippled person as I heard it. I was lucky they didn't hit and tested me to see that I was faking my disability. I was relieved when they went away. Now that military created shortages of workers in the camp, the supervisors pushed me to work on the two ships that came to load goats and camels. I decided to try it thinking that I might not be carrying them on my back just like those sacks. I felt it was an easy job to lead them as a shepherd did in a farm. When I arrived at the port, I learned that some workers were refusing to work on a ship came for camels for the reason I didn't know. Then we were led to camels' ship while I was feeling something might be wrong with this duty. Then the instruction came, to pick camel by tying a rope around its body and lift it in the sky by crane and lower it one by one to the deep cave of the ship. I was freaked to grab and tie rope on it, or untie it once it arrived in the ship predicting that a camel might be in a bad mood than it already was. My heart began choking my throat, being this job might be more dangerous than I thought. I was even more shocked when they ordered me to go in and untie them. I went in while shaking and determined that my life would come to end right there. Then two of them came swinging side to side with their legs waving to me while their loud cry deafening my ears. I saw ropes were cutting deep in their skin and they didn't seem to enjoy being lifted hundreds of meters in the air and hundreds more down in the ship where I was waiting. My heart was beaten and beaten, and I said this was going to be the end of my life. I ran to the corner in case they fell on me because I didn't trust those ropes to be snapped on top of my head. I dashed back to untie, hesitating this could be the end of my world. As I tried to untie one of them, it threw its legs to revenge on me and I jumped backward. Then a crane worker picked it up and let it down, might be to help cool it down. This had continued at the point a camel was frustrated. I ran back and forth to untie them. Once I managed to untie one, I had run to hide from it in the pile of hay at the corner. As a child back home, I used to keep myself away from them and sometimes I ran away when they approached me making grumbling noises. Now I couldn't believe becoming their unwanted roommates in the ship. Suddenly one extremely big camel arrived and every one scared for their lives. They yelled and pushed me to untie it because I was a new guy. I had no choice than to try my best and my heart dropped on the floor to approach it. All of the sudden it kicked me so hard on my left thigh and propelled me to sink in the pile of hay as a golf ball. I thought my chest was flattened to my spinal cord. I didn't see any blood spewing from my mouth either. I cried a little with fear, but not enough to teem down tears on my face. I found a minor bruise and swell on my leg, lucky to be slapped with its flat fluffy and spongy foot. Everyone ran toward me, thinking that I was hurt, or dead by its tough blow. They pulled me out of hay to check my condition and help me. I was still breathing after a few minutes and they didn't find any defects as they examined my body. I was glad I was not badly injured at all.

I rested about one hour being so shaken and at last got better wrestling with these creatures all night long. I repeated this duty for a couple of days having no other choice. Then Hassu pleaded about my problems with supervisors and helped me getting that tally work, which paid little better. I found that counting goats rushing in the vessel was not easy task either. It made my eyes and brain swell enough, besides I had to argue with another tally person who thought I made a mistake counting goats that went in the ship. I did this for several days. I expected to earn about five thousand shillings, but I got paid only six hundred shillings. I argued with the supervisor that I got paid less than fair. Other workers were also complaining about their pay. Some leaders backed us up with our argument and we went to complain to head officials of the ship. Then head officials supported supervisors that they were right and we got paid very fair. Since Hassu and I had not any permit to work as a tally person which required by their standard there, they banned us from ship yard indefinitely. Kadiro also threatened us; we were about to face something strange. This threat seemed more serious that we needed to run away before we regreted sitting there. We made our mind and ran to our refugee camp never to return again.

We continued to enjoy our wormy flour in the camp. When we became desperate for protein and crab meat, we tried to hunt for hare that was not easy to find around there. We were lucky to find just one rabbit after so many tries we had made. Then one day we found a huge tortoise and we decided to eat it, but it was not easy to take out its head to slaughter it. We sat with it and it took almost an entire day to get about half pound of meat from its ugly legs and shell. I was surprised to see so many pounds of grass it had eaten like a cow and it had no ample meat for all of us. When my friends cooked it, I tried to eat it, but I was unable to put in my mouth. I was surprised that they were fearless chewing this strange meat and swallowing it. I felt like throwing up as they were eating. I sat watching them being very jealous since they were getting protein. It reminded me of the Cuban army who boiled live turtles and hunted ducks in my country during Somalian war. I used to mock them being a white beasts that ate everything that moved on the ground and flew in the air. Now sitting with my friends, trying to eat such disgusting creatures amazed me that we became that beasty army from the west, which I even feared to walk by, they might eat me. I suffocated picturing how I tried to grab and pull its head and neck several times that was hiding in its shell to help my friends. I just realized that Cuban army had eaten these weird creatures in a desperate manner like us. I prayed day and night to the Almighty God to help me out of these problems so that one day I chewed real meat that donated by goat, chicken, and ox I used to eat back home. I managed to learn God's ninety nine names that attributed to him in the Quran by heart from the sheik in the refugee camp. Every morning, before dawn, I stood on a big rock next to our tent and shouted his ninety-nine names while crying to help me out of this situation so that I ate real meats someday.

While learning Quran and praying to God to help me out of this refugee life, suddenly Hassu and I had come across the information about a possibility of getting *Rohaniyyis*[165] that could be under our command at all times to get us whatever we needed: money, traditional medications to heal the sick, and whatever we wanted from this planet from coast to coast. We could not ask them to hurt anyone for any reason, or else they would disappear from our life for good once we let them hurt someone. We would be back to our miserable life again. Understanding this new opportunity and plenty of time we had in the refugee camp, we wanted to know how to get them and asked the sheik to help us. I thought that my first priority would be to ask them to bring me some meat, which I was desperately craving for just to satisfy myself. When we asked the sheik, he said that we must first learn how to call them by all their names from our heart. We must also read and master their book and its laws. Once all these encrypted in our heart, we must enter *Kalwa*[166] for forty days and nights without eating any food besides a popcorn that he would bring to us once in a while by himself without seeing us face-to-face, or saying any word that he was there. We must focus and keep calling Rohaniyyis names none stop by invoking Allah's names on them.

Once we kept calling and calling very vigorously, they would appear one by one becoming different scary creatures like anaconda that try to swallow us while wrapping around our body, a lion biting our face and legs, a tiger grapping us by neck to suck blood and suffocate us, an alligator ripping our heads and legs off, shark open mouth to shred us like cheese, etc. Besides trying to kill us, they would also make funny things like dance and jokes to see if we lost focus on them. They would verify that we were there seriously to get them. We must not run from these creatures, or stop calling their names because they threatened us, or done funny things. He warned us that if we ran, or laughed at any of their actions, we were going to lose our consciousness. We would act like category seven lunatic that ran naked like a baby who did not know any shame. Rohaniyyis would delete everything from our brains so that we did not say any-

---

[165] Hidden intelligent beings created by God that no one can see except us.
[166] Deep and dark hole found among huge rocks.

thing about them and what we saw. If we stuck to the rule and keep calling them as said, at last, the head master of Rohaniyyi's would appear truly face-to-face with us. Then he would call us by name, "Abas! Hassu! What do you want?" We would then say, "We want to meet you." He would finally say, "I am at your service!"

But if we scared, or stopped calling the names, we would immediately ran out of there becoming crazy people, never again able to act like normal human being, or recall anything that happened in our lives. Since we had no other choice and no life to live, we decided to take on the challenge as sheik said to us, on the promising not to fail ourselves. My friend, Hassu also agreed to do this rather than dying of malnutrition and other things that lurking on us at the camp. We began to study day and night very hard to master the way to bring Rohaniyyi to our life. After we finished and mastered the book, we had chosen the biggest rocks that looked perfect Kalwa for us, just sitting about a kilometer away from our tent. Those rocks were huge and they had a perfect hiding warren in the middle so that no one would come there except lizards and spiders that we did not invite at all.

By the time we were ready to go in, my other close friend called Mohammed asked me to help him set up a bakery at the main refugee camp which he got from someone. We rebuilt the bakery house while fetching firewood in the dangerous mountains. We had then learned and practiced how to bake bread to sale to the main refugee's camp. I didn't feel that there would be a success in this business with him so that I made good money to better my life. I helped him about three weeks while I was thinking to enter the rock with Hassan to change my life.

CHAPTER 11

Being a Cat Soldier

When the fourth week had begun, Mohammed and I slept in the bakery. At dawn, we were about to wake up to make breads dance in the camp and suddenly we heard giggling of guns. These unpleasant laughters felt like war times. My heart jumped and wiggled and it began hitting my ribs. I urged Mohammed, "We were doomed! Let's get up and run, there is war up on us in the Camp." Mohammed put his body in eighteenth gear just as I did to the door. As we put our hands on the door to exit, it exploded on our face like a real big bang of the universe I had never experienced before. While we were in such a panic state, guns were pointed to our face, and we were kicked with military boots. Gun bottoms pounded our buttocks, *wariyya so'oo!*[167] I suspected they were rounding us up for military since we had done no crime at all. Unless making bread in the refugee's camp was a crime, especially in Arri-Addis main refugee's camp. Pushing and shoving, they led us to their trucks like chicken going to slaughter place. There were hundreds of soldiers surrounded the camp and opening fire to put the refugee's camp under control so that no one dared to run away from the nest. They escalated rounding up and directed many of us to the green trucks that were waiting for us. My heart pounded very hard.

---

[167] You move.

"Is this really possible? From the refugee camp, taking Ethiopian refugees for Somali's military service? How they dare this? What right they have to force us? Where is the law of United Nations?" I was confused, having no help to answer these questions. "I am Oromo!" I screamed among many guys on the trucks. I was afraid they did not get it. I was shy even to say this. It was as if I was speaking alien words…bla bla. I shouldn't say I was Somali Abboy for they already knew it and what they liked to hear anyway.

They took us to a big yard where they told us to get down registering our names. I did not speak their language to fully explain my case, but all I could do was just show a colonel my refugee letters of recognition given to me by UNHCR. He looked at it for a minute and returned to me just like garbage paper ignoring what it said. Realizing that he didn't care at all, I spoke in English, "I am Oromo political refugee that came from Ethiopia here in Arri-Addis camp. I am not Somali origin and you can't take me." He didn't care and no one paid attention to me at all. Mohammed just dropped his ears like sick rabbit since he was usually very quiet human creature stable as a fat dung worm. After they booked our names and sorted us out, they loaded us to a place called Mandera, which I heard very far away from refugee camp. I wanted to jump off from moving trucks, but I was scared to die since there were no soft grasses to sacrifice my body on just to take a chance. After they ran us almost half day in the rugged roads and mountains, they dumped us in a big windowless hall of Mandera. There was no lights and it was as dark as a grave as if we were waiting for angels to question us what we did all our life. The cement floor kissed our buttocks without any lips and it was a very hard and bitter romance every minute past there. There was no room to move about and adjust body positions. We were frozen like iceberg because we were so jammed together as if bees were sucking on honeycomb. After we sat there until the afternoon without any word, they brought very ugly dark and tall pot. The steam came out of it like fog. Its vapour rising from it jammed the hall as if a cloud touched down on a mountain of winter season. We found out that volcanic rice that could cook the whole cow was behind all this smoke. Everyone was so hungry, they flew like bees to get their hands in the pot and a chance to feel the rice. Seeing the urgent actions and greed around me, I had no patience to wait, but went in action to be like everyone despite my dirty hands, which concerned me even to touch it. I said to myself there would be no time to worry about grubby hands anymore. There was only one pot for all these mucky palms of people and I knew waiting would be a bad choice. I tried very hard and squeezed my body and hand with those greedy impatient people and managed to touch it. It was so hot that it almost melted my fingers like butter. I screamed like wart hog bitten by lion and came with a few grains of rice that stuck on my fingers, which were still burning and toasting my skin. I was only able to lick my fingers while it was flaming my esophagus all the way to the stomach. Everyone was agonizing with pain, unable to carry magma rice to the hungry mouths, and dropped on each other. There were cursing and yelling escalated among us in the grave. There was no water to drink, and I was scared I could die right there. Then I tried to scoop it again, there the flame rice was gone in swift seconds. I only managed to caress an empty hot wall of a pot. I had kissed my fingers good night right there. I wondered if they did this on purpose, or there was a shortage of rice in Mandera's military camp. I feared that I wasn't going to survive if this continued at this pace. There was no mattress, carpet, or camel skin to lay the body on. We had to sleep on the rough concrete floor that made my skin cry in tears of blood the whole night.

When morning came, they woke us up for breakfast to rounded bread as small as twenty-five cents coin which hardly fit between my teeth. It was as if someone had thrown a racket ball in a football stadium. It hardly mixed with saliva and I swallowed it. Was this for real? How come military bakery made such small creature's of bread like ants? Even ants would complain about it to their cell administrator. There was no washing hands, brushing teeth, or washing face as if these were traditions of the ancient society. Having tea for breakfast, and water to wash hands and faces in the morning seemed things of luxury in the past. I could see many graves were opening at the same time, which one to swallow me first, became my only guesses. "Is this the way to treat a soldier? What kind of soldier they expect me to be when I have no energy to pick up even a single bullet?" I had no answer for these questions either. We sat there like rounded up monkeys being very hungry and filthy, crowded in a big ugly hall that even cattles would cry from. As the sun rose, they ordered us to go out of the hall and to form a line in the yard, it might be for registering. Then a huge tall guy as big as a killer whale that had so many shiny stars on his shoulder began checking our faces, what kind of animals they rounded up and brought to his camp. When he came closer to me, I pulled my letter to show him that I was registered political refugee in Hargeisa's province of Somalia and wanted to talk to him, but he told me to shut up and stand in line. After registration was over, I went to a few leaders with many stars on their shoulder to plead my case with my genuine document that written in English by United Nations and Somali-land security forces. I headed to a general who had more stars than the others on his nice hat and his uniform was very well written and groomed of all. I felt he was the one to free me from these troubles. I gave him my letter and told him in English, "I am Oromo refugee from Ethiopia. I was taken from Arri Addis refugee camp by force." I pleaded my case. He read the paper said to me, "I am an Oromo; too, my name is Colonel Abas!" He might be jerking me around, or he might be cloned from my body and telling me the truth. I was shocked by his words. He added, "You had to fight for Somalia just like me; you have to be responsible to defend the border." He threw back the papers to me. He assured, "I will never let you go." I cried, "This is not right…" He shut me down and refused to listen. I could see that he shut his face's door for good. I realized I had to become a cat soldier. I sadly left seeing his body language which told me that it was closed for me.

About midday, they took us to the field for training so hungry and filthy to march in lines. I tried to follow whatever those people ahead were doing even though I didn't understand what trainers were saying in Somalian. One of them so cruel began yelling so hard my ears was started to wine. Every time he hit someone in line while yelling so hard, my body shook and I hoped he did not reach me. Most of the yelling looked like bad words shooting at everyone in line while walking along the lines. My bare heels were hitting a ground several times per second; it began to hurt like someone hammering my feet with gravel shaving my skin like razor. I had no idea why shoes and uniforms were not given to us. Everyone was dancing with whatever we had: some swinging with dirty torn outfits and some with ugly skirts and pants. None of us had strong working muscles for marching back and forth as cruel coach wanted. He came close to me, *wariyya sidda guuska silka kabbahay waso'onesa!*[168] *Wham, wham,* hit my neck and a skinny boy ahead of me. My neck shrunk as a turtle saw a vulture in the sky when he smote me. I was about to fall to the side, unable to stand his pressure due to lack of energy and being very exhausted with my feet hurting in pain to stand. When he hit the skinny boy ahead of me saying the same insult and the boy fell down. I felt sad for him as image of weak penis went down on the ground which made me smile a bit. This gone all day long in the scorching sun, and I sweated, and dehydrated very badly, adding insult to injury. I realized hell was real thing while lived on the surface of mother earth. I cried and cried why this had to happen to me. It was as if I had to pay for the sins of my forefathers who refused to pay for their part and escaped to heavens.

After this torture was over, they took us like a camel to the small river by training camp which I didn't expect to see around there at all. I was so happy to drink it first regardless of its quality, and then splashed it on my body to cool it down. I then scooped river's sand on my palms and rubbed my body as soap to wash my dust down a little bit. I was so happy to cool myself and refresh the spirit at least for a couple hours. Being very tired about sun set, they brought us back to that hall. Then there the hot steaming rice was back again. This time, I decided to jump like kangaroo to fight through men to get to it before it was gone. I could otherwise die there regardless of its temperature, for it was the only way to survive. I managed to scoop and fill my palm with flaming rice that broiled my hand. I shoved it in my mouth and swallowed it quickly. It toasted my esophagus and stomach as if volcanic liquid poured down my throat from the mountain. While I was jumping up and down to recover

---

[168] You! You walk like a penis came out of vagina.

from this pain, there pot was emptied again and there was no chance to get even a single grain of rice. My stomach became as flat as a piece of paper and my ribs began to greet me.

Next morning an aggressive Somali young boy kept calling me *abboy, abboy....*" I told him to stop it. He didn't stop it and we fought with fist to fist. I had no energy to defend myself as if I was hundred ten-year-old man. He punched me in the nose and I was bleeding like slaughtered goat, blood ran down my chest. I continued fighting and there six soldiers came and beat me with the Somali boy because I couldn't explain to them that he was the aggressor. They beat me more for I was aggressive Abboy toward Somalian as the boy might have informed them. They didn't care about blood gushing from my nose and mouth they kept beat me until I became spineless worm flattened on the ground. Then they left me on the floor to die and I was afraid this was the end of my life since I lost so much blood. No one cared at all and later the blood started to dry on my cloth in the scorching sun. I was lucky those vultures from my country didn't see me there. I began to recover miraculously with serious pain from the beatings. I wished my refugee friends knew where I was and came to rescue me with United Nations officials. Many days passed and many more in this way without dying and no one came to rescue us. I kept counting month after month; I was hanging by thread at Mandera with my friend Mohammed. There was no doubt that now; I was becoming very filthy and skinny Somalian soldier like mosquito that not known to anyone before. They trained us how to walk like soldiers and how to disassemble and assemble guns, but there was no shooting practice. It was as if a donkey was going to be given a gun to hang on her hoof and fight for the country, which she didn't belong to. At last, six months had passed and they invited us to Hargiesa's best orchestra that came in the nearest bushes to entertain us like a soldiers who just graduated from Mandera. I enjoyed the band and music that didn't feel like my country. Songs might be to enforce our patriotism, but for me it was like water under the bridge. I understood that this music meant the refreshing of our brain and end of our training. Now they were ready to send us to war with happy face from Mandera.

Early next morning, they lined us up to a military trucks toward Hargeisa. We were taken to a highly secured military compound where we wouldn't be able to escape from them. We cried like sheep behind the heavy fortifications with hunger and at last they handed us only a few dates that made my intestines red. I wished the UNHCR officials knew that we arrived in town and came to get us out of there. I was worried where they were going to take us next. I was afraid that I could be dead soon fearing they were rushing us to the worst war place in Somalia. In the afternoon, without any guns and uniforms in our hands; we were loaded on the trucks like sacks of potatoes. I had no idea how we were going to defend ourselves if we were attacked on the way possessing only dry farts and shouting like mice. We were lucky if we found tree branches to swing at the enemy. They headed us out of Hargeisa as if we were going to border of Ethiopia. I couldn't believe this reality that we were facing. Were we going to face our own country men that sat across the border to defend their country? I was troubled as we were travelling in bumpy roads in the very mountainous part of Hargeisa. My dead brain GPS suggested and confirmed that we were indeed going toward Ethiopian border as the trucks swayed our body toward southwest part the country. I was dizzy and felt to throw up, but there was nothing to shoot out of my mouth except dried gut that stuck in my ribs. We went very far from Hargeisa the places I never heard, or imagined before. We suddenly heard that we were to be taken to Baley Shirre and its neighboring two camps. They were going to divide and drop us into three groups across the borders of Somalia and Ethiopia. I prayed to God to place my dear friend Mohammed with me.

After travelling whole day, they stopped us at a military camp and told us to get off. My heart cracked like watermelon that dropped from the cloud. I encouraged Mohammed to stand as close as possible to me so that we had a chance to stay together. They sorted one group and told them to stay there. The rest of us were being told to get on the trucks. Lucky Mohammed and I were stayed together for the next camp. While my heart beating we might be headed to the worst place and might be killed on the way as we went deeper and deeper west, I thanked God to keep Mohammed and I together. We jumped on the truck as it was getting dark and I hoped we knew where we were going. After approximately half an hour, we came to another heart cracking military camp that heavily guarded. Lucky, they didn't shoot at us. Again they told us to get down and I encouraged Mohammed to stand next to me while shaking that we might be separated. There another group sorted out and told them to remain there. Thank God! Mohammed left with me again to jump on the truck for Baley Shirre the last camp where they told us to get off in the total darkness. I was glad at least knowing that Mohammed and I were still side by side and we would be fading together since reaching our final destination.

There were so many tents full of soldiers and the camp seemed exceptional and very well guarded with a fence made of thorns. They warned us not to leave the tent area as the camp was infected with land mines. I was afraid my legs were going to be amputated and might die as these mines were placed to blow huge armoured tanks. Fearing the mines; I hesitated to run away, knowing that I was surely going to die. Mohammed and I thanked God to stay together in one camp and tent. We decided to die together, no matter what to happen. There we were given rice and dates to eat for the first time like a human being. We ate greedily, but our stomach was unable to take all rice and dates as if we had belly of a rodent. Then a sergeant came and warned us we shouldn't think to escape, or dare to run from the camp. If we tried to escape, we would face serious consequences like other people who were punished seriously, up to getting killed right there. He also showed us small potholes that they dug near the tents to shove those whom they caught in the action of getting away if they decided not to kill them. The holes were as small as just to hold two small rabbits and they said they were going to put us there alive with no food at all for several days.

We were so scared running was not an option specially being worthless Abboys that we knew anyway. We were given the tent to sleep in after dinner. Mohammed and I were decided to stick together for the night while fearing there might be war up on us while we were trying to sleep. I was so tired and fell as sleep while praying to God no shooting, or war to start because we were very close to Ethiopian border where there might be some fight happening from time to time. Luckily the sun smiled at us with peace next morning. We were very tired to get up and leave the tent. They ordered us to come out and soldier's uniforms were given to us with shoes. For the first time ever, we looked like soldiers with green commandos uniforms. I liked it being dressed like a real soldier, but I didn't think we could fight with guns which I was not trained for. I only became human cat, dressed in American military uniforms. They then showed us mounds of guns in the tent that we could pick, whatever we wanted. They explained what each gun did: how powerful they were, its scary bullets, how they kill, etc. I was impressed with a machine gun type called SKS 21 which they said could make the enemy facing you fart like donkey nonstop, and silenced them in your direction. I said to myself this was the one I needed if I wanted to save my life. The other popular gun impressed me was M-16, very light to carry around. They praised it how its poisonous bullet kills in seconds because it exploded inside enemy body right away. I was so scared of its bullets to hurt me and someone else and decided not to take it. My heart popped when they demonstrated how to pull a hand grenade and heard it could take my head and hands off if not thrown properly. I made my mind not to carry this thing no matter what happened, fearing that I would lose my special catty head that I brought all the way from Ethiopia. I was also scared when they showed us, the way out of camp, how to avoid stepping on the mines if we wanted to release gas and wastes in nearby bushes. Having no other choices, Mohammed and I studied where the mines were all around fortifications and at last became little confident to go for wee, wee duties. Like every soldier was doing, we needed to take a gun for protection with M-16 which scared me, but I had no choice and nothing was so light and comfortable to carry around. We pretended that we were veteran soldiers while being scared of mines and enemy that could kill us outside the camp.

As soon as we made alive, clearing the mines, we saw many fresh dead body of humans around the bushes where we wanted to sit down. Some bodies were only left with bare skeletons and skulls laughing at us while some where smouldering in fresh worms. My only guesses were these bodies belong to those soldiers who tried to run away from camp or bodies of *khulmis*[169] and Ethiopian Soldiers who got killed there during recent and past fighting. I also felt that the bodies were of those innocent people lived in the area killed as traitors and lesson to them, not to join the rebels that fought them. The area smelt so bad that I felt like throwing up my guts with the conditions I saw there. We had no choices and sat under small bushes bare butts, staring around in case someone like *Khulmis* shot at us. While being scared, I was disgusted seeing corpse that hadn't been buried and its cruelty. Mohammed and I had to go together at all times watching our backs from danger while we did our business. We tried to go little further every day with M-16, or A K E 45 with the intention to escape some day while pretending to collect firewoods for our cooking. The more we went further and further, little by little every day, we reached the area of shepherds whom we were able to communicate with broken Somali language. We asked which direction Arri-addis, our refugee camp was located so that we ran in that direction.

After a few days, we had been told to grab our guns and jump on the green Jeep. My heart watered, "This is it; I am going to die today in vain. I am not willing to put my finger on the trigger of this gun since I have no right to fire on someone, these trees, and bushes which lived here freely for hundreds of years. Besides, I had no training in shooting this beasty gun that terrorize everything dead and alive on this planet." I grabbed SKS 21 with long chains of heavy bullets winding on my shoulders to waist. I hopped on the jeep with this gun while my heart swung from one rib to the other. I imagined hundreds of enemy soldiers were rushing toward us with tanks. As our jeeps sped so fast, I was swallowed by its dust rising in the dense bushes and trees toward west as if we were going in the Ethiopian border. After dashing a few kilometers from our camp; they opened heavy fire without any orders to us. I found my heart dribbling in the dusty bushes and my ears went numb with guns' explosions. I couldn't believe I was in the middle of so many guns going off at

---

[169] Somalian rebel fighters.

one time. I saw trees were terrified and shook from bullets just like me. Then there, *wham! Wham!* And *Boom! Boom* had begun specially those explosions that restored my eyesight during war times was just happening from pipes mounted on the Jeep standing next to me. Its noises blew off my ears and brain silenced all fires right away. I faced worst day of my life and the first one in Baley Shire so far. I expected to be a bloody day and predicted that I might not go back to that tent alive again. Mohammed and I put our heads down not firing anything. I feared other side would respond to us sooner and I would be in serious hell than this. I was not sure why they opened fire because I did not see guns explosions coming from other side. I doubted that the Somalis wanted to instigate the war. They tried to scare and send messages to the Ethiopians and *SNM* that we were now very powerful army. However, they were trying to show us off to them, the new groups with no gun firing experience.

After half an hour of sweating in my bottom, firing ceased and we returned alive and safely to our camp. I could see Mohammed farted just as I did and he was happy to be alive one more day to eat rice and dates. We now seriously discussed about getting away as soon as possible rather than dying here and being tortured by many more explosions like today. We spent a few days in this panic state without going toward the border to fire. We began going further and further from the camp every day and coming back safe, planning to escape some day since no one questioned where we had gone. We didn't see any *SNM* that we feared lingering around that area besides Somali-land shepherds doing their duty. Once we went so far away, we felt we had to take our chance to get away, but came back fearing we might be caught. We were unable to make up our minds, but we started whispering every night about running away, having no other alternative even we get caught and killed while running. At last, after two weeks of nerve racking moments and planning, Mohammed and I agreed to run and die together.

One morning, after we ate our breakfast, we put on our ugly dress from training camp that we didn't throw away. I put on that half cut sandals and let it kissed my feet again so that it helped me to escape. We headed out without gun as my heart was kicking my chest like Kangaroo not to return at all. As my heart flamed like red beet, my pancreas showered my stomach with so much of its juice fearing we might be doomed soon. I advised Mohammed not to look back anymore, or swing his head backward in anyway so that no one could read and felt that we were trying to run away. If we got questioned by soldiers, I advised him to say we were going to fetch Wood for cooking. It was the most nerve gouging moment I had ever experienced in my life fearing they might catch us as running away chickens. We walked and walked slowly for half an hour without facing any trouble and seeing any soldiers who might be wondering around there. I prayed to God so hard like never before to shield their heart and shackle their feet from coming after us. I would do anything he expected me to do as a human being. When we didn't see any soldiers kilometers after kilometers, then we said this was it, no return and we must keep on increasing our strides. We walked and walked very fast to the east while wondering if we were on the right direction and what we might face, where we would end. I prayed more not to face, or step in any military camp. Now we dared to look behind from time to time feeling we had gone very far and make sure there was no Jeep rushing behind us. I was little glad that there was nothing behind us so far. I encouraged Mohammed to put his legs in higher gear than before, to give us extra chance to go further while we were worrying about the rebels or people live in the country side that might attack us if they suspected us to be Somali soldiers. Besides, we had no idea if we were going to step in the military camp, or gone where we supposed not to go. Rushing so blindly, we afraid that we might face something more dangerous, but we must go on, no matter what. We prepared to say that we were refugees from Arri-Addis camp searching for work in this rural area. My feet were hurting for the pricks were sinking in it from time to time and vigorous friction from walking on a rough ground. I could not believe that we had almost walked about five hours without any one chasing us. Then we saw an old man with his camels and dared to ask him which direction Arri-Addis camp was in very broken and ugly accent we had. He seemed to get what we said and kindly pointed to the direction we supposed to go. We thanked him and glad that we were still not out of bound too much and still going in the right direction.

As we kept going, we became so exhausted and thirsty. I suggested to Mohammed we should try to eat rare tiny leaves of thorny trees that camels were eating. He laughed with those weak lips I used to see on him, "How come we can eat like this big animal?" I tried to convince him "If camels didn't die, we should be fine too! We have to eat rather than die and besides it might taste like *Kat*." I had gripped a few leaves among thorns that were fighting me not to take their friends by pricking and blooding my fingers. Mohammed gazed me in a funny way, not thinking I was serious about it. I had no choice, I shoved it in my mouth because my throat was dried and cracked like crocodile legs while my lungs were stabbing my chest as air rushed in and out. I chewed and chewed the bitter juice of hard tiny leaves began to flood my mouth. I was scared it might kill me if I swallowed it, but I had no choice at this point. As people say, "Damned if you do it, damned if you don't." I closed my eyes and hardly swallowed it, believing it might help me like camel. As it bitters my esophagus all the way down, I expected it might run out of my anus right away and becoming a real camel. I saw its ears grew on my head and its tiny penis and tail stuck behind me. I feared to urinate behind me like them. I encouraged my friend to chew it so that he did not die on me and we both became camels together. He agreed and chewed it under my pressure and I saw his face shrank like million years old man. I couldn't believe he dared to chew and swallowed the bitterness leaves and he gave me little laughter where I supposed not to smile at all. I was surprised that we were members of camels in semi desert of Somalia. All that left was to be claimed by camel keepers. We collected a few more these skinny leaves while thorns were stabbing our hands not to take them away. We ate them for a few minutes and managed to wet the burning throat and stomach. I was afraid it might hurt our belly in some way, but we felt better to move on even though not feeling like we had real water and food. We continued our stride as much as we could even though air was rushing in the hollow stomach. We were so light like dry leaves; an ant could kick us on the ground like soccer balls if we stepped on them accidentally, or riled them up in anyway. I told Mohammed to pray for us not to be caught after walking all this distance. We jerked and jerked as much as we could to the direction an old man gave us.

After about eleven hours of walking, there the sun waved its red fingers from the west, trying to tell us that we might be free from being caught by them. I didn't trust it, but I said to Mohammed," Do you feel that we are free from being caught by Soldiers?" He replied, "Yes! It is possible we got away since they didn't come after us." He added, "God might have answered our prayer." I felt like him, but I doubted that the soldiers could reach us in split seconds once they realized that the two Abboys were missing from their tent, having a green Jeep and knew the area very well. At last, the sun dived in the ground behind us by leaving us with its friend darkness. We dreamed about being safe and delighted than before as if we got away, but the darkness began to worry me how we were going to survive in it. As darkness covered our dirty and tired body, we couldn't hide and run anymore. We decided to take a small break as reward and felt that we were getting away. After relaxing a bit, we were hardly able to get up and marched more to give ourselves more insurance of getting away. Adding insult to injury, thorny leaves and bushes, we didn't expect there began to slow us down by cutting and bleeding our skin. We refused to give up to them and kept pushing and pushing until it was dark enough we couldn't walk at all. Then we made unanimous decision to halt walking right there, definitely feeling that we got away. Now I worried my friend hyena might come to visit us with that stinky fur and sharp canine to moll us. I doubted that there might be tigers and lions which became another concern; I hoped none of them to wonder around there. I advised Mohammed to sleep for a while and I would guard him, and he would do the same for me after several hours of nap. We must use our military training and guarding style in case something came up. We didn't even have a small rock to defend ourselves, besides a small stick that lay on the ground. I did not believe it could harm even spineless worms. The only weapons I had left were throwing military style punches and kicks that I had learnt at Mandera's training camp.

As Mohammed agreed to sleep, my heart began drumming like I had never known before since I wasn't qualified with no licence to guard him. I kept my eyes moving in all directions, looking and listening for any creatures that might be lurking on us. Every time I looked in a direction, I could see the picture of an ugly hyenas coming from a bush. My heart was cracking what to do if he really showed up. I realized my being soldier and having commandos training in Somalia didn't erase my fear of hyena. I couldn't believe that Mohammed fell asleep in the middle of all these troubles when I checked on him. I was also scared that freedom fighters might get and slay us there. I managed to sit until past mid night in the freezing cold and woke him up for my turn. Then it was hard to close my eyes; unable to trust he could really defend me like I did. I imagined hyena dragging me from his side, besides my fear he could fall asleep while sitting. I had no choice than staring at the bush and listening for danger almost all night. About dawn, I was able to lose myself, but not long enough before morning freezing air pinched my body and opened my eyes. Mohammed managed to stay put as I did for him. We began our journey after the land was brightened by emerging sun. We began limping and bleeding from wounds that caused by thorns. We were glad to be alive second day and we were still not got caught by army. We were almost free to wonder around and blindly walk in that direction the old man pointed for us. After we danced for a while; we saw a very decent village ahead of us and decided to go in, having no other choices while we feared they might hurt us. We took a chance at a house and asked in Somali, *biyah nasiya*[170]. They kindly gave us water we asked for and some food to eat.

After we drank and ate, we had energy to march. Then we asked with broken Somali where about of Arri-Addis refugees camp. I couldn't believe that they showed us a milky mountain, which must be adjacent to a neighbor to our camp. We were excited as if we had returned. We thanked them so much, but one of them asked us if we were the Abboys working in a nearby farm villages, seeing that we were filthy foreigners. We were lucky that they didn't expect us to be

---

[170] Give us water.

soldiers on the run from army which they definitely did not like to see completely. We confirmed to them we were indeed those Abboys who were working in the farms they said to save our Life expecting there might be *SNM* there. We claimed that we wanted to go back to our camp, but somehow lost in this part of the country. I was excited knowing that there were some of our people came this far to work in the farms of Somali to make some shillings which shielded us from being a military goats. This new information gave us a good energy to go on and hope of survival in case we were questioned, just an ammunition to shoot from our mouth as we were passing through the unknown feared land toward our camp. We walked and walked until mid day to that marked creamy mountain which began to take a tall on us. Then we came to several mountains that swallowed our heads and confused us where we were heading to. We were concerned to be lost from there on. Then luckily we came to another village where we asked for direction and begged for food and people were nice to us again. We were able to eat, drink, and rested for a while. Then we resumed our journey with broken body until darkness smeared our body to the new direction they gave us. It seemed never ending story so we had to stop again for the second road's bed room, but this time with more experience of guarding each other. After one week of walking and suffering, we were able to reach our refugee camp at last. Everyone was surprised to see us escaped and came back alive. Then we learned that some of our friends we expected to see had gone places we didn't know and a few were already killed at the border of Ethiopia trying to leave Somalia. These rumors had blown our brain if it was really true. There were only a few students left in the camp with some seniors, women, and children.

Fearing other imminent round ups, we decided to leave the camp for Hargeisa since some offered to help us with a fare. Now that we had a big fire and a deep hole on both sides of the road or countries, we must go to Hargeisa to hide until we found a solution. Luckily, we made safe to Hargeisa without being caught at the check points. We managed to go to where some of our countrymen working as watchmen at those empty rich people's houses of Hargeisa. From here, we began brooding what to do, whether to run to the bushes to live like cave people or go back home to die with Oromo freedom fighters since we were on a rope of dying any way. We intended to communicate to United Nations if they could help us, but it didn't seem like a reality that they could do anything at all. Then God sent someone to United Nation officials for us and told us to go there to inform them about our remarkable escape from the army. Now we were in danger of being caught by security officials in the city who might put us out forever. After UNHCR confirmed our story and feared for us, they advised us to go toward Mogadishu first. Then we should make our way to Kenya if possible, or to Djibouti. These were the only two directions possible to go to if we wanted to breathe and walk to safety again. Otherwise, we had to run to that blue Indian Ocean to seek asylum at crabs and mermaids community. Then we realized that going to capital city of Mogadishu could be more dangerous than Hargeisa itself as if we ran from a tiger, then faced a lion. We turned our eyeballs toward Djibouti and there was no argument about it. I was glad that Mohammed would run with me to crunch those hot granites toward Agagub. We were given official letters to indicate that we were under refugees protection in Somalia office. Not only this, they would also fax a letter to officials in Djibouti city that we were on the way. These sounded very good if we could make it there alive. Then they dressed us with four thousand Somalian shillings each for our journey for fare and food. I could not believe that we hit a jack pot right there and I could see my heart dressed and smouldered up like rich man. We walked with smiling belly and happy feet to boys compound to spend the night so that we prepare to go on in the dawn.

When I advised him to leave early morning, he shot me with words, "I don't want to go...!" I counted on him as my dear friend and brother to march with me, but he turned around his eyes balls 360 degrees like black chameleon. I couldn't believe that this fat shillings given to him changed his heart and he might have another plan. I begged and begged him all night long, to try to convince him running was better rather than dying here. He seemed taking chances as if these shillings would defend him, or keep him alive for good. I reminded him that God still kept us together for a reason and for him not to ruin it. Besides we promised each other to die together. There was no doubt in my mind about his decision when I saw his eye balls glow red like sun setting over the mountain in the middle of the night. He insisted to stay in Hargeisa with that money as if it saved his life. He seemed he was paid for his suffering. I had wondered why he sold his life and future freedom for just shillings that only buy eight packs of cigarettes, or forty dishes of pasta. I told him good luck and respected his mind, but I felt sorry for him and for myself to be alone like divorced person. Now I had no one to call a friend who I could depend on as if I was left naked, swinging my black penile all alone toward Djibouti. God knew what would happen to me on the way and how long it would take me to go there. I worried how I could pass border guards pointing guns at each other. I was afraid to see my body being dragged in the middle of Somalia and Djibouti borders. I hardly slept all night long, thinking what would happen, then the sun rose gently and scraped away the night to encourage me to move on without him. I asked a boy with a watch man a favour to show me a truck station and he agreed. Mohammed, at least, came with me to say goodbye. When we arrived at the truck central station, waiting to board, I saw a girl speaking my language claiming to come from Djibouti. I was excited to get information about it and said to her, "Hi Girl! I am trying to go to Djibouti. Can you please tell me how I go there and what to expect?" she asked, "Where did you born?" I was glad to tell her Haramaya." She answered, "I am from there, too." We both shocked as if we were suddenly dropped from the same womb into our big blue lake full of cow fishes, swans, ducks, and frogs.

As we began to dive together, hardly breathing, at all, she informed me that she was the sister-in-law of one of my best friend I called him brother. Her sister was my sister too, whom we suffered together eating wormy flours at Arri-Addis camp and being born the same town and district. She had no idea how much we cared and loved each other at all. Then she said, "I came Hargeisa for a business and once I finished you go with me." I liked her offer because it would be the solution to my problems. I knew she wanted to help me, but when she said the business might take her about three weeks.

I was concerned that I might run out of this funds for transportation on food and smoke. There was a risk of getting caught by military or security forces since they declared that political refugees were no longer allowed in the city. Finding someone from my birth place was like winning a lottery for my trip, but I was so scared to wait for her for that long. I decided to throw away the luck I just won to move on and give myself a chance to get away. I assured her I could not wait because of my fear and she had gone her way.

I jumped on that Digolle truck with doubts if really this one to take me to Djibouti without passport. I waved to Mohammed my goodbyes while my tears rolled down my cheeks again as if I was leaving my family and second home country of Somalia to the unknown. There I had gone toward the bumpy road I had come before toward Borana once more feeling this might be for good, not to return at all if I made through all the heart stopping military posts. I felt I was like military thief, trying to steal Somalian military training out of the country and there was a chance I would be caught if they could read it on my face. I prayed to God, to seal their eyes and heart from figuring out what I was and where I was running. I concealed the letter written for me to the UNHCR office of Djibouti under my belt so that they did not see it in case they checked me. I tried to make some friends on the Digolle to help me on the way and lucky to find an Ethiopian Somali who was going to Djibouti. We were somehow able to communicate with each other with little Somali I spoke and some Ethiopian he knew. I had no idea why he was going there empty pocket, but I covered his expenses along bumpy road as much as I could. We had to make through tough military checkups with God's help all the way to Zeyla. When we reached town's entrance, we faced the toughest military camp ever seen that stopped us. They bombarded us with many questions like why we were entering it. We stressed the reason just to work in the salt farms as we heard that so many refugees were coming to dig it from beaches at east of this town. When they didn't seem to buy our idea to work there, but we begged and begged them hard for a long time. After several hours, they let us in town. Then I was shocked that digolle dumped us there without any explanation. I thought we had paid them to take us till border town which disappointed me. I found that Zeyla to be one of the hottest and busiest town I ever seen with people running back and forth doing many activities as if it was the central get away to Djibouti and working town specializing in production of salt. It had atmosphere and breathes just like Barbara's Indian ocean. Then we heard about the worst mother of all military checks in Somalian land's history at the road that exits this town which I might have to sell about one thousand camels just to pass it. We heard that trying to escape on foot was very deadly since there was no bush to run through. It was just plain flat beach ground that had very tiny bushes which couldn't hide a mouse where soldiers could easily snap anyone trying to go on foot. Once we found that it wasn't easy to get out, we were disappointed and went to teahouse to eat and relax since we were exhausted from trip anyway. I began to worry being trapped in Zeyla and going to Djibouti became harder than I thought. After several hours of worrying, my friend heard that we needed to find a soldier walking in town to let us pass, but we had to first pour butter in his dry and hungry pocket. Hearing this rumor, I believed that there was no chance at all unless I gave up the oils UN poured in my pocket. I was not sure if it was enough for me and the boy to get pass that check point. I feared I would be rounded up there, or got killed trying to run away on foot. While I was praying for miracles, someone gave a hint to my friend a soldier wondering around there to be one of the soldiers that mostly let people out of town and we needed to put our hand in his pocket to wet it. It seemed we needed thousands of shillings for both of us to just lubricate his pocket so that we passed easily.

Our chance of marinating soldiers' pocket looked very slim, knowing that we didn't have enough shillings required as he might demand. We decided to try our chance to walk out of town on foot pretending we were going to throw our faeces far out of town. We managed to walk about one kilometers and I thought we were getting away while my heart was dribbling. Not too long, they stormed us with guns pointed to shoot us. I passed gas several times expecting bullets run through my vain and falling in the sand. Then to their mercy, they brought us to check point and arrested us. We told them that we were simply going to wash room and after several hours they let us go back to town. We realized some of the guards roaming town to see people leaving and I was very scared at this point. We decided that the only way out was to give up on my shillings if it worked. My friend asked me for six hundred shilling to try that guy when we saw him and he told us we needed more and this wasn't enough. He begged and begged him to take it and helped us. At last, knowing that we had no more money to offer him, he took it and told us to drop by military check point next day. We spent the night sleepless in town and I was worried that he might deny us what we gave him and we were going to be stranded there. I was afraid my life would be at stake there. When the sun shined on the ocean, we headed to the check point fearing the worst. Suddenly a couple of soldiers yelled at us to go back toward town and that soldier came out of tent and saw us. He told them to let us pass and there we began walking on foot out of town toward the west to the unknown. My heart cracked with happiness, but I felt that I was a thief getting away. I tried to walk like civilian as if I had never been trained in the army while praying that they didn't find out that I was a Somalian soldier getting away. I mixed my hands and legs like porridge swinging in different directions so that they didn't look like soldier. I walked as if I was very weak and sick person. Who knew where we were going and what trouble awaited us, I was happy at least we passed the toughest place in Somalia. My heart was about to explode worrying and restricting my motions. I advised myself not to look back and just walk.

After we walked for miles and miles, we became very tired and decided to sit along the road. We decided to wait for the truck in case it came our way, knowing we were not to make it to the border like this. We didn't know how far the border was from there. Then lucky a Digolle came our way and we waved to stop for us. When my friend asked a driver to help us to the border, he wanted two hundred shillings. I was glad I had the shillings that left in my pocket rather than die on the road which we didn't know at all. No hesitation this time, I gave him the money if I could just make it to the border. We then took to the dust toward west and arrived at a small town said to be Loyadee smaller than Zeyla seeing no soldiers at all. Everyone got off as if this was the last town of Somalia and Digolles dumped us there. As we walked around there, we saw hundreds of people looking into the border of Djibouti like lion gazing at zebra. I was surprised at their actions being a wild animal and I started sharpening my claws, too. I could see they were waiting for the sun to hide as rumored. I confirmed from some people who spoke my language. I was surprised that all these people wanted to dash across the border once it got darker. I felt we might get caught unless Djibouti border guards were blind. They pointed for me to Djibouti's border guard's on tall post, being very close to us. They were able to see people walking around in town of Loyadee coast to coast.

I was afraid this escape was not possible from what I saw, being watched from only hundred meters away, staring at each other unless we did daring escape. I was not sure if they knew that we were waiting for the sun to go down. My heart began colliding with my ribs if I could really make it today. Once the sun was setting, everyone got prepared to run, but advised me we should only dash across border two by two to the escape route they showed me. I couldn't believe that we had to make our run just about hundred meters from the post guards. As we moved in position, then a huge couple of bright lights on top of guard post began scanning and running toward us from time to time. I bent my head down from those lights just like them. Two by two, they began to crawl like tiger on the ground from the lights and run toward that critical narrow get away road. I tried to run feeling it was my turn and some forced me to stay down and made me mad. I felt they were in panic state like me, but very selfish to push me behind. I began worrying and wondering when my turn would come. Then my heart badly waggled if this was really possible at all. After so many people run and run, at last, I forced myself to be as flat as a lizard and run on the ground to the gateway hole. There big light illuminated to my skeleton for the first time and I didn't know where I dropped my heart. All I saw was soldiers standing by me and saying the "stop" word and shooting at me. I ran and ran while expecting to be caught to the direction I thought people were running being very confused. I had never run like this before. I saw my guts were dropping on the ground pieces by pieces for the guards to get it. My body was socked wet with sweat and it begun braking on me from running at my potential. I had increased my speed as much as I could. I was able to catch up to those who already ran before me like crazy. Then they yelled at me to stay behind and not approach them. This time, I exchanged verbal quarrel with them to defend myself so that I kept running to give myself the chance not to get caught by border guards. No matter what being said, or done to me, I kept running like an ostrich. Suddenly I started to feel that even they came after me with a car, they wouldn't be able to catch me. With this urge to escape, I doubled the speed, and then stumbled and fell down. I felt so much pain losing skin from my palms and knees. I got up and ran, realizing it was no time to waste and babysit both pains. I kept running and running while diving to the ground every time those lights flashed toward me with feeling that they might have seen me.

After running a while, I saw a huge light in front of me in the horizon as big as Jupiter shinning to the sky. I wondered what it was, but kept running toward it as much as my legs could take me. I had never seen big city lights in the distance before, but I guessed that this huge planet light from heaven might be from Djibouti's capital city. My heart urged me to run to it even though I doubted it to be the city at all. The land was almost flat, but from time to time, my feet sank into the ground, holding me back from Jupiter lights. I kept dancing between border and Jupiter lights that had no ending to it at all. Once a while, I continued looking behind if cars from border guards were chasing me. After a while, I began to worry about running into military camp or fortification and kept running toward that visible light. In this state, I managed to reach a few people and asked them about the light if it was Djibouti city. They gave me affirmative response in a grumpy way. I completely felt that they didn't want to discuss with me anything and not friendly at all. About one-hour vigorous running of my life, I saw people running in a relaxing manner for the first time. They were yelling to each other to be cautious of forming large groups, which could be an invitation to problems and they must go far from each other. As these warning of them made me uncomfortable, they left me running alone. I felt better; at least,

I was still not caught, but not sure how long I had to run like this. I began to fear facing some kinds of beasts alone, besides the military until I touch that dream light ahead of me. I made my goal to reach it by end of the night. As I kept going far behind those nagging people, I came to pass through a cannel like ground, disappearing from the lights. I kept wondering if Jupiter was still alive and true to be seen again. The light seemed closer than before, but not close at all and it became even dimmer and dimmer the minute I shade my eyes on it. Then after a couple of hours of vigorous run and walking toward that dimmer lights, I managed to reach some more of my language speaking folks.

While fearing they might be mad at me, I inquired how long before we arrived to the city. One of them kindly said that we might arrive to the beautiful lights by midnight. They also confirmed to me that there were no military posts to face on the way for four hours more until we approached the city. Now I felt little better and began to relax my body like soft rubber and followed them, keeping my distance so they did not get upset to me. I was so exhausted, I had to walk for several hours trying to reach those lights. In five hours time, we came to land seemed like farm where there were people in it. They kept going, not stopping and I followed them. Almost at midnight, the huge light shined on my face. As I felt like it was caressing my body with its palms, I learnt that the city was gated by barbed wires and there were guards around it. I again learned from them that it was not easy to get in. Now I began to worry that I would be caught and a new nightmare kindled in my brain. As my heart dribbling, they advised me that from now on we needed to crawl on two by two so that the guards did not see us. We had to hide like rabbits behind bushes and objects and moved slowly so that guards did not notice anything. As we kept doing this, we came to a fence where we had to crawl under it one by one and then run for our lives from being caught. I watched everyone run like they said. I was left last with this one slow kid. I made it under wire and ran like chicken refused to get caught even for a kill. My heart was about to explode with fear I might be grabbed or, got shot at. I had no idea where I was and those running ahead of me were nowhere to be seen so that I could not follow them. The kid ran and got closer to me. I had no choice than to slow down a bit so that we ran together to the unknown. Then we reached a railway, we were not still caught. It was a very nerve wrecking to go along the railway, fearing the worst to happen. The feeling of being free shaded my brain, but braced for more problems.

After a while, we came to a road crossing the railway. Then a car showed up facing us and my heart dropped. We were going to be caught. We ran and hid on the side of the road to give ourselves a chance to be safe. After it had passed us, we felt better and kept going. Then we reached a farm that had a fence which I was surprised to see. There we found a couple of people working in it. We managed to talk to them and got a chance to rest there for a few minutes. We asked them where downtown was so that we went there first to lay our eyes on it and make sure we made it there alive. They gave us direction and said we might get caught by police, but relaxed us a little by saying during this time of Ramadan, the police had some mercy not to chase and harm us the way they usually would. I was relieved a bit and prayed for luck so that I saw the city and UNHCR office. We kept walking and walking while fearing to be caught in the unknown city in the direction given to us. After so many heart stopping moments, we stepped in the middle of Djibouti residents that sat and watched Arabic movies on television. It was a dead end road which had no way out. We had no choice than to sit down by their side while praying for them not to recognize us, or to harm us. I enjoyed the movie for free which I did not understand. It was my first time in front of a television screen in over five years. We were not asked where we came from and where we were going. I was relieved and enjoyed the moment that I even had a chance to sit and to watch television not being a real citizen.

After we relaxed a bit, we got up and walked out of there to the unknown. We managed to find a way out like super Mario out of dead ends and kept walking. Then we came to find exceptional roads and buildings that designed in sophisticated manner that reminded me my capital city of Addis Ababa. It was very quiet in the streets, rarely seeing a few cars, hoping not to be a police car. I prayed so hard that we safely reached city center. We walked and walked as downtown refused to get closer to us. After several hours of tiring walk, we came to mosque where people seemed ready to offer morning prayers. We entered as if we were praying and got a chance to sit down and took break. When the prayer started, we did like them, having no chance of sitting or sleeping there. After the prayer was over, anyone wanted could stay there, so we sat and took advantage to rest more. I was very drowsy, and wanted to nap right there. As my head dancing to fall, the sun showed up its face in the door of the mosque and we decided to move on. I prayed and dreamed to see anyone from my country so that I could get some help finding UN office. After about half an hour walking in the morning, I saw a group of young people talking in our language. I heard them calling each others' names as *abbo funyaan*[171], *abbo ilkee*[172], etc. very funny names I had never heard any one call each other before. It gave me a small laughter even though I was not in a position to crack louder in a stranger city. I was just so happy to see my country folks which I had never imagined to see again like that. I greeted and introduced myself as fresh legs just arrived from Somalia that needed assistance. They welcomed me without any troubles. I guessed they were city scavengers which had no home, or place to live from the way they dressed and appeared. They reminded me of the hog tree life I left in Hargeisa. It seemed inevitable to join them if I had no luck with UN office there as I had been told from Somalia. I asked them, just to confirm their situation, "Where do you sleep?" They answered, "Around building walls." When I said, "Where do you get food from?" They replied, "By begging!" There was no doubt in my mind, I could be one of them very soon, or later unless I got miracles I thought. They clarified that they had no regular places and sometimes slept under wall of any houses by moving around the city like nomads. They also declared that the police chased them around city to round them up and to deport them to Ethiopia. They ran and hid in Mosques where they slept at night after night. They appalled me and I was determined to find UN office right away. I asked, "Do you guys know where about of

---

[171]   You nose.

[172]   You teeth.

UNHCR? Are there any refugee camps?" They replied, "Yes, there is UNHCR office, but they would do nothing for you. There are still people stranded here more than 10 years, having no help from them, you could see these noses and mouths were your evidences. There were many deported to Ethiopia by police and there were some just keep coming back and live this life. You better choose to join us and don't waste your time going there. If you are lucky, better to find a job of foreigners or refugees in town." They added, "The cops were not very active and serious this month of Ramadan in arresting and deporting us, but soon you would face their music like us."

Understanding that my life was on the brink of ending soon, or about to be going through hell, I begged one of them to show me United Nations office, for I had the letter to show them, not to give in on their discouragement. I needed to find out the truth by myself so that I could rest my soul. After so much begging, at last one of them agreed to go with me. I managed to exchange my Somalian shillings to Djibouti franca as they called it and I bought some food to eat there for the first time. As we were walking toward UN office, someone who knew the boy greeted him from afar. The boy informed me that he was the police officer not on duty that dressed in a civilian way. When he walked toward us, my heart dropped on the concrete. We were going to be taken to jail. I was looking at my first police encounter at another country. After I was relieved he was not going to take us away due to fasting, and I picked my wobbling heart up and walked with the boy to the UN office while thanking Ramadan.

When we reached gate of UNHCR, a guard informed us that it was Tuesday and UN office was not open. I had to come back on Wednesday. I was sad the day to be Tuesday, but happy at a least I could come back the next day to find out my luck. We went back to city center where we left off and stayed there all day talking to all the scavengers who had different ideas about living in this city. They made me laugh, the way they talked to each other. I felt I would be living this kind of life, or deported to Ethiopia which meant dying for me. Then my first night arrived, we had to eat in the Mosque with people bring food there because of fasting. During Ramadan people ate together by bringing food to the Mosque which these scavenger already took advantage of whether you were ugly, poor, rich, or refugee. You could just go in and help yourself like buffet style which I first experienced there. I had a feeling these opportunities were also in my country's Mosque and Somalia too, but I had never chance like this before. Thanks to people there and Ramadan at least I was able to eat, pray, and sleep in the Mosque without worrying I would be caught. Next morning, I went to UN office and I showed my letter. They also confirmed to me that they had received a telegram from Hargeisa to help me. I was glad that they knew about and registered me as refugee. Then a social worker asked, "Where do you stay now?" I said, "Last night, I slept in the Mosque and I have no other place to stay." Then he advised, "You must come back next week on Wednesday to collect weekly allowance for survival." I was happy at least they recognized me as refugee and would give me some money that falsified what nose and mouth people said to me. Being little happy, I went back to Mosque area, but I worried how long I had to stay around Mosque and being safe.

On the third day, I saw a very large group of these noses and heads youths flocked to sleep in the Mosque where I was staying for the night. I didn't know the reason and where they came from, but very scary situation the way they landed in the Mosque. I didn't feel a bit good about it. After *teraweeh*[173], we slept there as usual very tightly with many street people. Suddenly the leaders of the Mosque were very upset, having many junky foreigners filling their Mosque. They told us to get out of it right away. I was kicked out with them to sleep on unsafe street for the first time in Djibouti. Rumors began to fly about in the group that a lady was murdered at one of a brothel nearby. I learned that these noses and teeth from Ethiopia were the primary suspects, the reason why we were kicked out of a Mosque. I sat all night long worrying and feeling to be unsafe on the street. I was unable to wait until the sun greeted me so that I ran to the UN office to help me find place to stay. I had no other choice than to go back to see if someone was there to help me even though the office was closed in the morning. I managed to reach there by myself while

---

[173] Long and special prayer of Ramadan.

my heart was getting toasted with fear and a guard ordered me to come on Wednesday. I refused to leave a compound area until they found me a place to stay. As I was standing there for hours, a *ferenji*[174] UN social worker with blonde hair saw me as he came out to relax and I waved to him in a desperate manner with tears full in my eyes. He kindly let me in and I told him I had no place to go for fear of things brewing in town. He understood my concerns and problem and told me to sit in their compound. I felt I was getting a help from Ferenji angel who had different skin than me. I requested to be taken to a safe place like refugee camp if there was one at all for I could not be safe anymore with those mouths and body parts in town. The day became one year and I kept praying so that I would find a place to be safe. The compound felt peaceful and I didn't mind sleeping there day and night on concrete or one of the tables in the yard forever if they didn't find me a safe place to lay my head down as long as they did not tell me to go out on those streets.

While I was brooding all day long what to happen to me, there this Ferenji officer asked me to hope in his nice car with him. His car was so clean and beautiful, I was embarrassed to push in my dirty and filthy body not to contaminate it. I couldn't believe his courage to allow me in his car like that. I felt this kind of body and mind did not belong in there and I had never sat in car like that before. I was little excited getting ride in car like that, but the feeling of ruining his car overshadowed my pleasure. While blessing and thanking him within my heart, I worried where he was about to take me. After a while, he drove me to the nicest and beautiful part of Djibouti which took my breath away. The buildings and gardens were smiling while many flags of the world on them waved their hands to me. I was reading every country's embassy names as we went along. I didn't believe this area was part of Djibouti at all. Then we entered a very nice marble and stone built villa that had a beautiful garden just across a couple of embassies. The social worker then introduced me to another Ferenji guy who must be his good friend. I was swallowed by compounds' beauty and stayed outside even though they invited

---

[174] Caucasian person.

me inside with them. I didn't feel good enough to enter with such smelly body again, besides, I had never been in marble house before which I didn't deserve and qualify to enter.

Just being safe in there made me very happy since no police would come there to massage my body. I asked, "Could I stay under car shade which enclosed by leafy coloured garden?" Since it looked deserted by car for a long time, it seemed made in heaven for my stinky body as if God had dropped it there from garden of paradise. Knowing I was safe from police, I didn't mind even if they planned for me to be like watchman living under it. I was extra happy feeling that there were no clouds and rain at all in the city, but its heat was a billion times worse than Barbara if not one of the body scorching city in the world. I felt that volcano and magma were bubbling around the city. My body began to simmer like red bean in the pot under the shade. After a few minutes of relaxing under shade, the owner of the house brought me fruits, bottled water, and bread, which I had never seen for a long time. He was also kind enough to say, "Come in the house from time to time to sit and chat with me." His kindness buttered my heart and began to heal some of my wounds of lung and stomach.

I decided not to enter his house and disturb his privacy as long as I could stay under the shade. After sitting an hour, or so, I looked around outside the gate and discovered that I was very close to ocean and its sandy beach. I guessed it to be Red sea since there was only one ocean between Djibouti, Arabian Peninsula, and my country which I studied on the globe map of my school. I was excited to see it if it was really red colour as its name implies. I also dreamed to swim in it to cool myself from burning if it's harmless to dip my body in it. I scanned the Embassy opposite my gate on the right, and suddenly saw a chubby watchman looked like an Ethiopian blood sparkling on his cheeks. I wondered if it was true and guessed that he might be brought there just like me. We saw face-to-face and he seemed to wonder about me, too. When he threw a word of Amharic toward me, I confirmed that he was an Ethiopian and I was happy to reply to him. Of course, he was different than my ethnic group and speaks different language and our family fight each other to control the country, but he felt special to me and I was to him, too. There was only love words we shot to each other and I was so happy to see him there trying to make him my true friend. As words flew between two fences, he informed me to be aware of cops ran around like ants just to get rid of scavengers like us that infecting the most respected part of town. He confirmed to me that we were at the area of Embassy of the world and Djibouti police were on the mission to remove foreign junkies out of here especially the Ethiopians. Fearing this, he would not dare to go out, but sometimes he must run like Ethiopian chicken to the shop close by to buy things he needed. I was glad to hear that there was a kind of small grocery shop around the corner where I might have to run to spend those franca given to me by UN office. I was glad to hear that UN office was close by, but I must do a daring run to get my weekly allowance, too.

It was still Ramadan time, but it meant nothing at this part of town since the police were on the mission to remove these smelly noses and mouths from Embassies' lands. Again I realized that I was in danger to go out and worried so much, but no choice than to run like my new friend in order to survive. It seemed I found a horse, but there was no land to ride on. I wished to have a coffee and smoke shop just in my compound for the money I had and got every week from UN office. I planned to run from time to time just to make it alive. After we chatted for a while with my friend, I needed to pee, but afraid to go in the house for it. After it hurt me for a while and my bladder was about to explode, I decided to pick hose up in the garden and turn on the water, poured on my chest down my pant, then felt hot urine burning down my thighs. When solid waste began to move my large intestine like baby, I tried to kick it back several times and able to control for couple of hours. Then I reached to the point I could not hold anymore and went to gate, gazed both sides of the street like lizard watching for eagle. When I did not see any police car, I dashed straight to the beach and lucky no one there. I sat down quickly made a hole in the sand like turtle burying an egg and pushed it out with the pressure of elephant ass while my heart was beating over two hundred times per minute, looking at all direction. There was no wood or leaf to wipe my bottom and I just scooped sand and rub it on around the ring of the anus couple of times, but the hot sand almost welded my bottom. I was concerned to have a big red bottom like monkey and hoped they didn't see me and laugh at me like I used to giggle at them. Then I quickly got up and run with sands dangling from my anus. It made my run very difficult, but I had no choice than to run like paralysed Iguana.

As soon as I made it halfway to my gate, I saw a little car marked as police coming, which I could kick it like soccer ball or pick it and throw it away like garbage. I couldn't believe this tiny car to be a police car, but it made my heart saggy like old huge two hundred kilogram breast. It made me run as much as I could toward my compound to escape it. They had run behind to catch me, and I ran like ostrich with no feather. By the time they came next to me, I managed to reach my friend's gate, and he quickly opened the gate, seeing me running by his fence and said, "Get in quickly." As I stepped my one leg in, one of them almost got my shirt and my friend slammed gate behind me and told me to push with him while he was crying madam, madam to the wife of the Embassy as if she came down and pushed door with us, or something else she could do for us. They pushed and we pushed. After few minutes struggle, he was able lock the gate. I was lucky to have strong friend there; otherwise I couldn't hold them away, for I was very weak lacking energy. I wished I had fart like skunk, or sharp pricks as porcupine to defend myself. Unable to grab us like two black fish that fallen from their hooks, they were angry and looked at us with evil eyes, and thrown bad words and left in anger to be back. They winterized my body and made me speechless. I was lucky to be saved by my friend.

Realizing how close I came to disaster, I decided to use my legs as Suez canal where I flooded and eroded with my urine. No doubt I smelled like lavatory. The owner of the villa had no family and he rarely came around and we saw each other. His maid also came to villa just to cook for him and there was no chance for me to ask when I was desperate, or needed emergency. The best solution was only using the canals I was already operating and kept crying to God to bring some solution. Once every two weeks, or so, I saw my social worker drop by his friend's house to chat. I tried to explain how I was suffering, but could not say much about peeing on myself and begged him to help me out of these problems. He seemed to understand and he didn't say very much at all. I didn't know how long until I became a human toilet and burn in the sun.

After one month, the owner of the house packed up and left without saying where he was going and for how long. I guessed he might be going to Italy for vacation, or business where he was originally from. I was afraid to be rotten in his compound, and might be taken by police. While I was pondering about this for a while, an older model relaxed and gentle ferenji moved in. He had a tasty Italian flavors and looks on his body, but very innocent and peaceful man. He began talking to me softly in Amharic as if I looked like an Ethiopian to him. I had never seen before a ferenji that speaking African language especially from my country. I was afraid he might be Ethiopian spy, or he must be working for Ethiopian government. I was excited to talk to him and he made me right away enter his heart. I was breathless wondering all about him and he told me he used to work for IGAD in Ethiopia and no wonder he could speak Ethiopian national language that I learned in school. I didn't care for not knowing my language and I loved him just for his friendliness and care for me. He sat with me where I had made my stench and listened to my story how I got there. Then he was even more sad which made me little guilty telling him all about it. He would bring apples and bananas and shared with me under that leafy hut. I had never imagined a ferenji would sit with me like that and made me his friend. He then broke my heart by saying that he came to stay in the villa for only one month to save money in rent until Ferdro came back. He supported me mentally and became like my father, which I would never forget. He even bought me pen and notebooks to write my story so that I did not forget and lose it. He kept me busy from wondering too much. I had never entered the house during his stay as I did with Ferdro to respect his privacy. I continued soaking and showering my thighs with urine which I didn't tell him either. Feeling very shy, I kept my suffering to myself. My ferenji social worker didn't show up all this time even though I wanted to complain of my suffering.

When the month ended, Sendro, the ferenji father, began packing and I was very sad just like I separated with my real father. We made our hard goodbyes, hoping to see each other someday. Then Ferdro came back to his house and the social worker also started visiting again. They seemed very dear to each other, but not as much to Sendro, my father. Out of frustration and so much suffering, I tied my stomach and dared to write a letter to the social worker. I explained my suffering as much as I could, and gave it to him as soon as he was passing by my hut. After reading it he said, "I was working on sending you some where safe, probably Egypt." I was happy hearing this promising word and thanked him about it, but it was not as fast as I wanted it. The light of hope at least flicked in my brain even if I didn't think it was going to happen at all. I kept guessing and became a patient skunk.

Three months gone by, by while I kept running back and forth from gate to ocean and ocean to shop and from shop to the gate in the scorching sun. I was lucky to escape police chase several times. I felt that my heart and soul had begun to depart to heaven where God was collecting them from people on earth. Then one morning there I was dreaming in hell it looked, hearing very loud car horn that blown my hair away and deafened my ears. My baby water broken with fear as if a car ran into my belly through the fence from the street, washing it away. There was no doubt in my mind this to be a police car which was waking me up, to take me away. I bounced from the ground up like soccer ball and hoped about two meters away as squirrel bitten by scorpion. My body had watered and salted faster than I did before. The honking went on and on, and I could not realize that it came in peace to put me in her mouth as lion picking its kitten. The shocks made me feel to take my baby and run away to the back of villa, but there was no place to hide. After all, this was not a dream at all and it was serious car call to me. As I was almost urinate on myself, a black man resembling a social worker at UN office who supports ferenji workers came out of a car. My heart felt little better, guessing that he had come to visit me at last and see my condition in the compound. It made me little excited while still my heart was pumping water rather than blood.

After confirming that it was the social worker who was encouraging me to come out, I slowly approached the gate where he was standing with caution and he ordered me to open door and come out to get in the car. I wondered why he told me to get into the car. As I get in, I saw the ferenji worker sitting in it. I greeted him and they informed, "We are going to city shopping center to do some shopping for you." They seemed to beautify me for a wedding, or a trip to see Ramses remains and nile river which I had never dreamed to see in my lifetime. While I doubted going to pharaoh's land to be true, I was scared that the police might snatched me from their side. "Really, am I going to Egypt? Is this the end of my stormy life in east Africa?" I questioned myself. I couldn't imagine myself flying to the land of pyramids which I saw in geography class and ancient ruins. I whispered, "Going there, will I erode my thighs with hot pee again, or free from it?" I doubted if I ever lived in peace. They might think it was better than Djibouti, the reason they said I had to go there. I was excited to get out of the compound and cruise in the city for the first time with little fear of being taken by police. I could see the light of freedom at the end of a tunnel as if I was in prison for the last hundred years.

I was glad to shop for clothe in a long time that I lost since I left my country. I couldn't believe they even grabbed a large bag to put my outfits in it for the first time which I had never had in my country before. Leaving Djibouti, a country so hot that was cooking me for its dinner and didn't let me pee peacefully in a long time and almost killed me was about to come to end. When shopping was over, I was still not caught by police, and I was happy to get full bag of new clothes. Then as we went back to their car with my bag, they hammered my head with the news, "You are flying to Egypt tomorrow morning, the safest country you can imagine for you. From there, you might get a chance to go to another country which might be your permanent home. UNHCR office in Cairo might help you with this process." I couldn't believe if this to be true at all. I was speechless, being excited, nothing to say, this seemed like impossible for what I went through so far. My brain had gone so wild that it had begun to spin like earth 200 km per second in space.

When they returned me at the compound, I laid down on my worn out rain bow rag and began wondering the whole night what would happen next and if all these things were really come to pass. I also wondered what I would face in Egypt, and how I would be treated there. My skin already seemed to cool down from suffering and the hope of shedding troubled one like a snake was getting reality. I realized I was still in Africa who knew if there was peace for me at all, or I must deal with another beast to chase me around, or if I had to stay with cobra in the desert refugee's camp, or fighting with vicious mummies that might come to hunt me down. As I was brooding and counting the stars all night, there the sun giggled at me. I got up and piddled on myself one more time as usual, hoping to be the last one.

I tried to prepare my body for the plane if it was true and I began to worry if I really dared to enter it. I tried to remove all the smell as much as I could so that a plane wouldn't eject me because of my stench of urine. When I put on my new dress, I felt fresh and brand new guy and believed that the plane would not kick me out. I began to be sad to leave behind my friend at the Embassy and my chewed up, torn sweaty mat. I gave my sad hard goodbyes to my friend and those who helped me there with my mat and hut. My heart cracked when another car arrived to pick me up and my leaving for a plane became true. I saw myself jumping in a car and leaving behind house after house, block by block while heat and problems were massaging my face and asking me not to leave them. I gave my salutations of goodbye to the police cars and every one I saw on the road for the last time.

At last, there I saw a small birds of planes sitting on the run away waiting for me. I was not sure if they allow me to go in and began to doubt it. Besides this was my first time ever heading to embark on a plane that was going to happen as I saw it. As I closed to the planes, it seemed true that I was about to embark on one of these things for the first time in my life. "Am I safe sitting in these torn out planes to Egypt? Is it possible that they were taking me to Ethiopia pretending that they sending me to Egypt? What my life will turn into Cairo? Where do I stay in city and how? What shall I eat?"

These things were bothering and scaring me while I was arriving to it. Then the social worker passed me the military checks and security clearances at the airport. Then he made me feel better by adding, "Someone will pick you up at the airport of Cairo and will help you. The officer at Cairo UNHCR was my friend and he was aware that you are coming." He encouraged me not to be afraid at all. I could not believe my eyes heading to one of those worn out, rusty small plane that was waving its wings to my face from coarse run ways as I was arriving to them. Beside happiness, another window of trouble and fear had opened in my mind.

366

CHAPTER 12

The Flight to Pharaoh Land

When I entered it, I felt as if I was in the belly of killer whale skeleton, not better than Digolle itself. Despite its scary conditions, the feeling of sitting in the plane for the first time, and going much better place than Djibouti, added spice to my adventure. Besides thrill, my heart was rattling very badly as UN officials at last waved their hands by window of a plane. I was lucky to sit by window and waved to them goodbye, too. Then it began rattling its tail and shaking on the ground like I had never imagined before. It was as if my nervous system were severed by sharp knife that cutting an Ox's neck as its noises from it deafened my ears, running on the ground as lunatic shark. When it lifted its nose in the sky, I was almost rolled back out of bottom as its waste. I couldn't imagine this crazy action that made my stomach dropped down to my waist. I desperately tried to hold on its seat harder and harder so that not to kick me out as it lifted me more and more. The city seemed to be scared of me, going way down and down, forming very deep hole that terrified me as I looked behind me. "Oh, God! Oh, God don't let me down from here! Please spare my life!" I began crying to him by calling his ninety nine names that attributed to him, thousand times per second as if my lips were piston of rocket engine. I hoped this time he would listen to me better than before since I was over the cloud and getting closer to the heavens where he lived. I also begged him to put me safely on the ground of pyramids where I hoped to land. I couldn't imagine going that high for the first time in my life and the big city began to shrink just like old man's forehead by the Red sea. I felt much better as it began to float straight rather than going nose up. I made my dying *shehada* several times seeing myself exploding like pumpkin on the ground at any moment if this crazy thing decided to go down.

Besides praying and terrifying by the plane, I observed carefully the direction it was going after liftoff. My heart began to bulge like tortoise hat seeing that it was flying in the direction of Ethiopia. I said, "There I go toward my country and these UN officials tricked me because the plane was not flying in the direction of Egypt as my brain compass indicated to me." My doubt of them what if they sent me back to Ethiopia rather than Egypt became reality. My stomach began to weep more with scary flight and the thought of going to a jaw of death. No wonder angel of death hovered on my head, ready to present my soul to God. Then after a few minutes of heart stopping flight moment toward my country, it changed direction toward north. This made me feel little better, hoping it did not change direction again toward my beasty country. I kept on praying to keep this plane toward north, but suddenly headed across Red sea. Again, I could not believe, it was going in the wrong direction since north east was the direction of Saudi Arabia, or Yemen as my school based compass of geography was telling me. This change of direction toward Arabian peninsula didn't sound good to me, but it made me little easy since this meant I was leaving African continent, Ethiopia, Somalia, and Djibouti that were burning and cooking me several years for their meals. I was little happy flying over the calm Red sea ocean knowing that I would have a chance to survive in case of the plane decided to french kiss it. While I was wondering why the plane wasn't flying in the direction of Egypt as I expected it, I began to be swallowed by the beauty of the ocean and Arabian land. I gazed everything way down from heaven floating like a vulture in the sky, forgetting all pee in Djibouti. I was mesmerized by nature's beauty, seeing amazing things I had never seen before from the ground and feeling of flying which overwhelmed my fear of crash. I started get-

ting better and better being swallowed by mother earth and its landscape in the bright day. I couldn't believe this was me sitting on the
plane with clean new cloth and a bag on the plane watching earth
from above like God.

After long hours of breathtaking flight, where there were no
trees and mountains at all, we reached Jeddah, Saudi Arabia where
we landed. I didn't know why, it took us there, but I enjoyed seeing
the city I was dreaming to visit for *hajj*[175] someday as our elders were
talking about it in my home land. After a while, I wasn't sure if it
took break, or unloaded something, it began to lift its nose again
and I wondered where it was going. This time I made my tiny *shehada*, trusting that God still helping me from crash and having some
flight experience of my life. I realised it started to fly backward as
if it was going back to Africa. I doubted it headed to Egypt since
Egypt was located in north Africa. My fear brewed some more, it
might return me to Djibouti or Ethiopia as we went back over Red
sea. Even though I was panicking going backward, seeing mountain
ranges that I had never seen before were giving me the hint that we
were in the middle eastern landscape type which might be leading to
Egypt. I drooled to see mount sinai where Moses talked with God as
I heard from religious scholars. I felt that one of these big mountains
to be where God appeared with his light to Moses and dropped the
commandments to Israelites if my brain maps didn't lie to me. I was
looking at the Mediterranean sea. I couldn't believe I had seen many
places which seemed exactly as I saw on the map of history and geography books. I was proud to learn these places in school, but I would
have never seen it if not for UN and Djibouti Digolle plane I was
scared of to crash me.

My heading to Egypt looked so real now and my skin began
shading its trouble to freedom and everything I learnt in school
becoming reality from history books. Then after long breathtaking
clear sky views of middle east and its hill ranges, I saw a very huge city
that blew my mind. It seemed had no begging and end, stretching far
and far. Then I saw a huge river that sliced it in half like pizza which

---

[175] Once in a lifetime visit to Holy Land

made me to believe it was Cairo. Again I screened my learning to verify that river abay of my country, Ethiopia flowing to Sudan then to Egypt becoming a nile river by cutting Cairo in half to flow to mediterranean sea which proved that I was arriving to Egypt. There was no denying the pile of evidence I was flipping like pages of a book in my mind that I should be happily arriving in Egypt. Then as I looked further, there I saw three huge milky triangular mountains seemed like pyramids of pharaoh hit my eyes. I first greeted the three pyramids, *asala mu-aley-kum, wa-ramatullahi, wa- barakatuhu*[176]: the father standing behind to the west, the mother standing toward the east of father, and the child standing further east. They all replied, *wa-aley-kumu salam wa-rahamatulahi, wa- barakatuhu*[177] that I gave them from the plane. I wondered of the miracles of pyramids how they guarded the city, knowing for sure I arrived in Egypt as UN officials said. I couldn't also believe that the Digolle plane landed me safely after long historical tiring flight trip of the sky that I had ever made in my life.

I was relieved and excited to reach Egypt even though I worried what to happen next, "Who will pick me up? Where do I stay? What do I eat? Am I safe here? Will I pee on myself? Do they have a safe refugee camp for me?" All questions began to bug me like a huge blue fly wanted to land on my feces. I was happy and excited for arriving in Cairo, but I left the rest with God while wondering about it. I stepped out of plane and wondered how I even get out of the airport which seemed more complicated than Djibouti. It was a big building that swallowed me alive and confused me way out of it. I just followed people blindly and began looking for someone who might be there from UN in case they recognized me. I was scared to be stranded there for a long time. I feared and began staring around looking for someone I did not know. My eye balls were almost popping out looking at everyone moving and standing there in case they were looking for someone coming from Djibouti. I scanned for any

---

[176] Peace and blessing of Allah be up on you!
[177] Peace and blessing of Allah be up on you, too!

ferenji looked like UN officer who might recognize me and ready to get me, but none of them caught my eyes at all.

While I was worrying about this, then I saw that airport officials were checking and screening people ahead of me. I began to be scared that they might arrest me, or returned me back to the plane. After they checked my document, they kindly let me go to grab my bag and began wondering where to go. There someone looked like me who had dark meat on his cheeks caught my eyes. I saw him staring at me like tiger and I paid back to him the same. He spoke broken English like *abyssinian*[178] accent and style, "I think you were the one I was looking for, coming from Djibouti." I was surprised that he was there to pick me up and little delighted that my country man was also there. I replied, "Yes! You are right." Then he threw my name, "Are you Abas sent from Djibouti by UN there?" I was happy to hear him say my name and confirmed, "Yes, I am." Some of my worrying began to peel off like boiled egg. I was glad someone was there looking for me and I felt that I would be in a good hand from there on. My heart began to dance rather than worrying how to get out of the airport. I started to take a shower of peace right away. My lungs began to sift fresh air of Cairo to my heart. He then led me to taxi standing outside airport and took me to a nice hotel after hair raising ride in the beautiful city of Cairo. I could not believe that I deserve to sleep in such nice hotel leaving behind my torn out plastic rag in Djibouti, just one day a go. I felt very shy and suddenly many fear and troubles were washed away like sin cleansed by God. My heart began buttering and swimming in peace like human being.

Many wounds had already begun to heal while breathing peaceful air. The hotel workers treated me like king of Egypt, Ramses the great and I couldn't believe that I would not see those Somalian tent and Djibouti tree hut. I could not believe this was the reality, but my seeing all these convinced me from the hotel room I was given to stay in. I had a nice bed to sleep in a long time, but did not know for how long it would be mine. Hotel employees respected me like multi-millionaire, but I didn't understand their language. They tried to

---

[178] Ethiopian

talk to me with very little English they could speak as black king and respected guest even though my pocket had not a single dollar in it. Then a person who brought me there left me in hotel saying, "I have brought you where I was told by UN and you have to stay here until they come and get you." I thanked him and he left me there in care of hotel who gave me some food and good treatment. I slept in peace for the first time in a long time without fear of anything. I would not seem to leave unless they dragged me out of that bed it looked.

In the morning, as I was arisen in peace in the city, there I was invaded and hammered by some men who spoke my birth language. I couldn't believe that there were many of them and came to visit and welcome me to Cairo. I was extra excited, but I had no idea what they did here. I feared they might have come from refugee camp to drag me there with them. I hoped they didn't push me to another tent and wormy flours. As I was wondering where they lived and what they did here, they asked me to go with them right away informing me that they were also refugees who lived in the city of Cairo. One of them seemed like head of them told by UN to come and bring me with them and realized that my nice bed at hotel was only for one night. They clarified that UN sent them to pick me up because I needed help. It was sad I left my nice bed in hotel, but excited at least I had some people to talk to in my own language and from same country. I was also glad that I wouldn't be stranded in Cairo anymore, knowing I had so many people here. Then one of them called Ibru asked me to stay with him and his wife for he was looking for room mate to help him with rent since he had two bedrooms he couldn't afford alone. I had accepted it since no other guys offered me this kind of opportunity.

Once I rested at Ibro's apartment where I was offered to stay, I couldn't believe I went with them to UN office without fearing any police in Cairo like loose rooster from cage. I saw no one cared where we went and what we did even though we were outsiders. There was no single thorn to prick my skin and no worries to damage my brain, just beautiful city and innocent people walking by road I had ever seen. I felt I was the heart of nubian people. They took me to UN office for my registration and they waited for me. I was excited to meet an officer who was looking forward to seeing me. He first welcomed me to Cairo and then chatted with me how he used to be a friend of the ferenji social worker who sent me to him. I found out he was very nice officer willing to help and I should not worry at all. I was extra excited to hear him say these good words as sweet as smooth mango flesh refreshing me head to toe. On top of this, I was given $110 Egyptian pounds that had no worms for my living expenses for one month. It was strange to me that I had to manage my own living expenses and to make these pounds last for one month for food, rent and entertainment, but glad that I had something to go on. Now I was lucky to have a wash room to take care of my business and the room to sleep in. Everyone was happy for me to have this money to survive on while they were not getting it like me for the reason I didn't understand. Ibru was happy to charge me $70 pounds for my unit. The rest of $40 pounds, I had to extend it to last for one months' food, clothing and entertainment. Some of the refugees here working in Egypt and some were getting help from family abroad. Everyone was trying to survive, but I was lucky enough, not to suffer and worry anymore like I used to in the past. All I left to worry was to stretch these forty pounds to last for one month. I still couldn't believe that I had a room of my own and free to walk around city without any restrictions as a Cat Man, swinging my tail freely side to side.

After a few months of leaving behind past troubles and my skin was healing some wounds, my mind began to worry how long I lived with these $110 pounds that I had to pull like rubber month after month. Then UN office surprised me with three applications to migrate from Egypt to other countries: one came from kangaroo's short front legs, other from beaver's round head and maple leaves, and last one from falcon's head and stars bangle banner lands. Hearing that I had a chance to go to these animals and plants land as a permanent resident and calling them my own country became a new dream that I could not imagine. I would not mind to call any of these animals my own family and shake my hand with them as long as I lived in peace. I wished to go to any of them very soon. I wanted to hatch my eggs that were dying inside of me which were almost rotten if I was killed in any of those countries I lived in the past including my own country. Life in Egypt was better as if I was promoted from sleeping on stone and dust to resting on a sofa, but I now began dreaming to sleep in comfortable bed for the rest of my life as I filled these three applications.

As I returned all the applications, I began praying to God very hard to free me more and to give me a chance to one of these countries as soon as possible. While I was scratching my head, these dreams to come true, the inevitable falcon invited me for an interview to see if it could allow me to go to its country. She began scratching my wounds and bleeding my veins in a tough manner for some reason I didn't understand. At last, she slapped me with her long strong wings out of her office. Once I fell down, she picked me to the sky and dropped me from the clouds and my brain exploded on top of the big pyramid. Somehow I was able to collect my brains together and waited for the other two animals to have some mercy and take me to their countries so that I planted and hatch my eggs in peace. Hearing this tragedy and bad news, the UN officials encouraged me that I still had two more chances and not worry so much. This made me feel better and tried to put myself together again with this sorrow.

After few months of this distress and fear, I got a letter from a beaver sitting under maple leaf for an interview. I was scared of this beaver to be like falcon, but he was very gentle from the beginning and sorry to hear my story which I could see on his face. He was one of the nicest animals I had ever encountered so far, gentle talk, soft claws and very thoughtful. At last, he told me that he would consider my application, shaking my hand, I felt he threw red maple leaves over my head, but it looked I must first pass all medical and security tests he required from me. Knowing that I would live with beaver for the rest of my life became good news, but I was afraid that my blood would not pass the test since I was afraid it became as black as a charcoal with several years of malnutrition and suffering in refugee's life. I was afraid even my legs were eroded by urine for several months at the horn of Africa wouldn't pass me my tests. This was why I couldn't imagine my blood's hemoglobin and plasma would be perfect after three years of refugee life, besides those sacks that dribbled over my head at ship of barbara town. Anyway, I did the medical exam and blood test where I was told to go by beaver's instruction and waited for result while praying to God to make my system all right so that beaver would be happy to let me go to his shelter.

In the mean while I was happy to be safe in Cairo, but my brain was conquered by many thoughts. What if I failed these tests? There was no chance for kangaroo to let me go to its country since kangaroo would also ask me to do the same medical examination even if it accepted me. I had no other chance left to be freed from my suffering and my eggs would be destroyed forever, not finding real home. God knew what then would happen to me. Passing my exams and tests also bothered me hearing how far beaver and kangaroo lands were, and there would be no chance to see my family again and Africa itself. I might specially die in the snow igloo I saw in the picture of these lands. Several months passed by and I didn't receive a letter from beaver and kangaroo which I was waiting for. It was as if I was chained with mummy in the coffin of Ramses worried what was happening. Then I received a letter from beaver saying that in about a week's time, I would depart to Vancouver which I never heard of it before. I wondered where it was and how far from Egypt, but very excited to go since it would be my new home country that everyone including UN officials were excited to hear it. I felt I finally got my permanent home. Everyone was happy for me to get this chance and unfortunately there was a city picture on our Cairo apartment which I was wishing to be my city. I thought it to be some European beautiful city which I would not get a chance to see it at all in a million years.

Knowing that I was going to maple leaf trees and beaver city, I kept dreaming and seeing myself on that picture of the wall. What Ibro and I did not know was that the picture we were mesmerized by was my future residence. One day as I was curious to know this beautiful dream city, I decided to know it and it happen to be beaver city of Vancouver where I was going. I could not believe it, it was sitting and saying hello to me all this time almost over thirteen months I was looking at it. Its down town buildings surrounded by ocean and land escapes on the south side could be seen on top of the hill. I could not believe that I was heading to it and call it my home at all if it was the same Vancouver the letter was talking about. My Lazuqli's apartment of Egypt was telling me something, but I doubted from time to time this to be true since no one could verify it for me. "It is a miracle if I go to this city," I said to myself and I fell in love with it. It had somewhat excited my nerves as if I was eating tasty chicken shewarama. I begged my God to make this city my destination and home for ever.

After one week of preparation, UN gave me a Red Cross's passport and there I picked my plane tickets from beavers' hand promising to pay it back with medical expenses in the future if I made it alive to its country after I got a job someday. When day of departure arrived, my friends gathered and threw a party and congratulated me. Leaving friends who became like my family and city that I loved was harder than I thought. Tears began to flow like river losing them just like that. There were some friends who had no family and no help at all just living on the soup of sugar and just begging friends who had some money. They took me to the airport and I embarked on plane tears running down my cheeks, and I was as if going to outer space never to see African air, Egypt, and friends anymore. I thanked all of them for their kindness and support, and I had no choice than to move forward to the unknown where I might have a chance to hatch my eggs and call home. The only things began to worry me was if I could make to Vancouver peacefully by plane and what would happen after I arrived there. I entered a plane looked nicer and bigger than Djibouti and prayed to be better and safer to fly on. This time with more experience under my claws, I made my second shehada and started praying as the plane lifted off. As I guessed, it looked quieter as it lifted me off and made some tilting and jerking around that scared me a little. I was happy having already a little confidence and experience of flying. As I looked down on the city and pyramids way below me from the sky, I continued calling on God's beautiful names that I knew since I was once again over the clouds and closer to his home. I waved my goodbye to Africa and pyramids, fearing that this was the last time I saw them. I felt much better flying north with very tiny fear that I might end up in Ethiopia again, or those countries threatened my life. Then I checked my documents one more time to verify that what beaver had given to me was real documents of permanent residence, plane tickets, and Red Cross passport. I attacked my fears from bothering me at all with these things as much as possible. I saw the beaver talking to me from my documents, too, not to doubt it anymore. Moreover, my brain compass and geography lessons came to my rescue again saying I was indeed flying toward Europe. I said, "A plane was flying in the right direction. I should feel strong and stop doubting it." I hoped it would fly toward west again after going north, first.

I continued praying to be safe and going in the right direction as the plane began passing over very scary dark clouds that I never imagined passing through. I was excited once more time to fly high above earth and clouds and began to pray from crashing. Passing many mountains, then I saw a big ocean that looked like Mediterranean sea. One more time my education was proven that this water had to be that same ocean I learnt in school. I said I might survive if plane dove in it since I learned how to swim in our Haro lake and Indian ocean of Barbara Somalia. While I was amazed by nature's beauty and started passing up and down in very scary darker clouds, I began to worry that the lightening might hit the plane. When I was a child, I heard that those devils would jump on top of each other to see where the rain came from and made God mad, why God then hit them with lighting bolt. I begged those satan to stay away from looking into heaven from this plane area. Then, there I saw heavy water accumulated on the wings of plane that scared me that we might sink down with it. I was surprised it was flying with all that water and weights it already was carrying. I admired who ever designed and created these things that fly in harsh conditions carrying all these burdens. I said these humans must be crazy to come up with such an idea that was useful, but very dangerous if something went wrong. I also wondered how big this planet to be that seemed never ending all these times I left my family.

After I counted thousands of mountains and clouds that made me tired, the plane landed in the airport of Athens where they told us to get out, staying in the hotel at the airport. I couldn't believe we were still in Europe and we had to sleep for the night. When I woke up in the morning, we had to take another nicer plane and kept going over Europe that made me do more of my shehadas and prayers. I stared as much as I could to learn where I was going over mother earth and then heard we had to land in Amsterdam airport. The land, lakes, rivers, cities, and surrounding scenes took my breath away. I began to shut down my doors of Africa and it seemed new world was taking over as I was dropping those suffering and pains one by one from the plane over Europe. After we landed in Amsterdam, they again told us we had to make another transfer to a new plane from there. I began to wonder if this trip of landing and getting up to the sky would be over soon. I was extremely tired and began to have super headache that wanted to below my brains like volcano. From Amsterdam airport, it seemed as if the plane was chasing the sun toward west where it was going sit down for the night as I thought from Ethiopian mountains. It would pass under earth to come up next day over our houses. There it seemed the day was not ending as we went west over what it seemed violent Atlantic ocean I believed to be.

I was afraid the Ocean was not ending and began getting tired of it while wondering how this plane was able to go far over ocean without taking any break. I again prayed not to crash since I might not able to swim back to Africa or Europe anymore. I wondered why the sun was still there and not able to reach it, or set at all. This trip from Europe over Atlantic seemed very different because the sun refused to go down as plane was rushing toward it. This was a mystery I didn't study about planet orbit around the sun which I couldn't prove in my head what was happening. I couldn't see the earth was turning and I was afraid they might have lied about this, for I had a chance to see from the top. I had slogan, "Seeing from the top could make it believing." I tried to remember where I was born and how I travelled so far and things didn't make sense since the sun was still there on the horizon of ocean.

While I was wondering of all these things, there at last, I saw some things looked like a white dress, or milk that thrown on the mountain ranges by ocean. It seemed that I was about to see those igloos made of ice like huts of my country. I was expected to see if it was the continent of North America. As the plane finished the ocean and began to fly over white lands and mountains covered with snow, I felt it to be land of the beaver, or falcons which I kept guessing it. Then the sun began to disappear and I was afraid I was closer to its home. As I was guessing it, there I saw a very huge city covered by snow as it looked sister of Cairo that also had no ending. I heard people saying it was Toronto, Canada. I couldn't believe I was about to land in canadian biggest city where yogurt covered all houses and trees. I couldn't believe we landed in that entire milky stuff that looked very cold. I began to taste it walking out of the plane being very chilly and smoke came from my nostrils. I was afraid to be Italian gelato I used to eat in my country of Ethiopia. Then I proceeded to checking officers at the airport and they checked my documents and welcomed me with open arms.

They then informed me that I had to catch another plane to Vancouver as the sun left me in darkness not knowing where it sank. I was tired so much as they showed me another plane sitting in the snow. I could see that my body began to shrink like old man, but no other choice must go on another five hours toward west from Toronto. Now I believed there might be another chance to see where the sun had gone down. I couldn't believe I had to go further and further west, knowing that there would be no chance of seeing anything look like Africa, or Ethiopia at all. I couldn't see where the plane was flying as if I was moving in the grave. My eye balls where tired to scan anything, and at last I gave up watching around. I felt this was never ending story. About midnight, there I landed in Vancouver airport. An immigration officer checked my documents and said, "Welcome me to Vancouver." Then an officer asked, "Where did you born?" I said, "I am from Ethiopia!" Then she replied, "You are lucky, this city is just like your country, not much snow here. The weather is as if you are in Africa." I couldn't believe this story to be true and my landing in Vancouver at all. I could see twenty five kilogram of trouble and worry just got off my body.

After about an hour stay in the airport, an officer walked me to a taxi outside. I was surprised there was no snow and there was a little cold chill I could live with. I was lucky not to stay in Toronto and I thanked my beaver for giving me this city as my home to be. Then I began looking around out of taxi and I couldn't believe I made it alive looking at my town to be without any guns on the road and never even seen any police. The shower of peace began to rain and wet my body while cleaning my heart that burnt for almost four years I left my country. I looked around from taxi in case it looked like the picture I saw on Cairo's wall, but I didn't see it the same and doubted it to be the same city that I saw. Then a taxi told me to get off after reaching welcome house that he was told by immigration officer to drop me off. I was tired, but excited to hear that I was finally reached a resting place in Vancouver where building workers welcomed me. Then I was led to a room they prepared for me to stay.

As I entered, I saw a little person who was swimming in my room like small fish, I doubted that nature eroded his body, or refugee life had taken tall on him, for he seemed to me a matured person. I was surprised that he also came from Africa just like me only about ten minutes ago as he began to swank his tiny british lips at me as if he was born in Britain. As he wowed me, I said in my heart, "He must have come from England rather than Sudan he mentioned to me." I was glad at least we could exchange our conversation in English and had someone to talk to even though we looked different ethnic back ground. We both had something in common like being black, same religion, and from east Africa to get along. It seemed beaver officers arranged this on purpose which I appreciated so much so that I couldn't be lonely, at least until the sun kicked out the darkness I faced for the first time in the city. I was excited and laid down in a soft furnished bed to remove some of my past pains and long trip I had made so far. After an hour resting and talking to my new room mate, I passed out not knowing what time it was in Vancouver at all as if I was in another planet.

When I was awaken, it looked as if I was in my grave, totally confused about what time it was, but I realized Ramses was not looking at me and neither inhaling African oxygen. It was very nice, cool air in the room that nicely furnished and things I had never seen before like fridge, kitchen and bathroom. After we explored our room, we decided to go out by taking the little map given to us so that we bought a few items and checked out the city, but we faced its darkness. We wondered where the sun had gone and not sure if we saw it at all, but we must go on to buy our food and cooked for ourselves as we were told on arrival since we were given $70 for a week for ration. The map showed where we could buy grocery from and we tried to follow it to see if the map was really true.

As we were walking the street, it was very calm and the city looked as if we were in the fridge. My nipples had shrunk like grain of mustard and my balls were frowned, but there was a very nice breathe in the beautiful city lights. I saw my little friend bald head crying like baby needed mother's milk. We walked and walked for almost fifteen minutes whining of cold a little bit to see super value store that indicated on the map from welcome house. Suddenly there we saw the store which said 'super value.' We believed the map was true to make us excited. The store had so many things that we had never seen before and we were amazed discovering many new things like Christopher Columbus. My friend disappeared looking for things while I was confused what to pick. After I reached Mamur, I saw him grabbed a lot of tuna cans, in the basket and I was surprised and picked one to read its' content. I found them it to be a cat and dog foods. I couldn't believe the store was selling animals food just as humans and Mamur made me laugh putting them in the basket for us to eat.

I couldn't believe he didn't use his British speaking lips to read the things written on the cans. He didn't believe what I said and when he read them very surprised by laughing with red face. I warned him to be careful form there on not to feed me wrong food since we had seen that every food in the store was not only for humans. We could be easily deceived by good things we were about to face moving forward in the new strange world where even animals had food with people in the isle of the stores. We bought some food and went back home while laughing how we had almost came close eating animals food that we discovered in the store. It was still dark as we headed back and went to bed after eating tuna and bread for the first time in Vancouver. We decided to walk in the city when the sun shined on us. When we woke up again, it was still dark. We asked when the sun would come, but they told us early morning. Most of the time the sun wouldn't come fast to see the city for it was winter season. We were excited to go out again and this time decided to walk around a Stanley Park shown on our map. As we headed toward Stanley, we saw many people were walking by breathtaking beach of pacific ocean which I couldn't imagine to see in my lifetime, or dreamed of at all.

As we walked and walked without being bothered by anyone, there we came up to so many birds and ducks walking along the road and side of us. We walked and passed in the middle of them. They did not seem to care or afraid of anyone. No one cared where they were going and they didn't care either. Where I came from, animals ran from people and people sometimes ran from animals. Especially birds did not take a chance as they detected you. I couldn't believe this was really a planet where animals and birds just walked by you without fear of being harmed. I couldn't believe this was part of our planet at all. I felt that God had dropped paradise from heaven by mistake. This was already the paradise where God was going to bring people after they died because I saw many people's races face-to-face I had never seen with my own eyes like Chinese, Indians, Brazilian, Native, different types of coloured people and whites like I had never seen before. They all walked by each other doing their walking and running. If my eyes were truly seeing what I saw, this proved to be a paradise promised by our God to those who did well, obeyed, and worshipped him. I was afraid I might be in after life. I might be dreaming to see this and the prayer I had done seemed to be answered as if I was once dead and now resurrected again to be in such heaven, walking with birds as God wanted me to live.

I couldn't believe, at last I came to the most peaceful place on earth. Suddenly as I passed the birds all suffering and sins were washed away in the pacific ocean. I came so clean from sins and past problems, seeing brand new hairs popping out of my body. Even my burnt nails shined like white gold. The trees were happily dancing with fresh air and while pacific ocean sat calm without spitting any saliva toward us like Barbara's Indian ocean which tried to jump and grab me as we walked by it. Even crabs and its creatures had never came out to scare me. We walked almost five kilometers around the Stanley park not getting tired and walked another five more around the downtown core where I was shocked to see that the picture I saw on my Cairo's apartment to be true Vancouver. Another prayer was answered indeed I came to the best city in the world so peaceful and breathtaking city anyone could dream of. The plates of cars even said Beautiful British Columbia which I proved that deserved its name given to it.

I couldn't believe I prayed in Arri-Addis camp tent for God to take me some where peaceful even I did not get any penny and stayed poor the rest of my life. After I saw police cars, my heart didn't crack very much as I was in Djibouti. I tried to remind myself I was in Vancouver, Canada. These were peaceful beavers' police that harmed no one. There was no reason to have shattering heart any more even though military and police naturally shivered people. After all, I decided to ignore the fears that sometimes came up in my heart if I saw a police and soldiers with guns. I wondered and surprised not seeing even a single soldier that roamed city with guns like Africa. This truly amazed me and I tried to put my soul to rest in peace as I saw some police were all harmless and peaceful. It was as if my heart suddenly dipped in butter, or margarine, no longer burning in fire like it used to do. Even my feet muscles relaxed, finding comfortable shoes from hot gravels used to cut it. My hair was not dry and fragile and my skull lubricated with agents I had never seen before. My body laid on soft bed where no longer termites took the bite out of my skins. I could no longer chase wart hogs and rabbit for meat seeing in store full shelves of variety meats. My eyes lubricated with green fruits and vegetables no longer worried what to eat. The beaver had given me jackets and blankets while I could make dress of maple leaves and its hat.

There I began dancing with beaver and its allies, the black bears who walked like humans. They told me to hatch my eggs with the respect to my queen and stand up and be responsible for my Canucks. Thanks to all the residents of British Columbia and Canada to make me taste and breathe this peace I dreamed off. My never ending thanks and appreciation also went to UN and its officers and countries that gave me help and asylum to reach my eternal life to be a happy Cat Man of Africa. At last, I reached where the sun set and made its last journey from Africa where I saw it ran all day and set next to me in Vancouver. From darkness to light, from misery to luxury, from poor to rich and from hot to cold, from crying to laughter, from grass mattress and cow skin carpet to wool mattress and oriental carpet, what could I say, the impossible now became possible. I had a house covered of maple tree as far as eyes could see and beaver danced around me.

About the Author

Abas Hasantu is an everyday man who works a full-time job and spends his leisure time with his family. His passion for writing and his need to share his path to Canada led him to the creation of this book, which is also his first publication. He currently lives in Beautiful British-Columbia.